How much of the growth of output can be accounted for by the growth of inputs and how much is due to the growth of productivity? This book is the most detailed attempt yet made to answer this question for Britain. Estimates of outputs and inputs for over 130 industries were constructed, following the methodology pioneered by Professor Dale Jorgenson of Harvard University and his collaborators. Apart from their intrinsic interest, these estimates can be employed to build up a picture of the performance of UK manufacturing as a whole. Contrary to the impression left by some previous authors, productivity growth is found to play a relatively minor role: growth of inputs, when properly measured, accounts for most of the growth of output.

The wealth of data which this book presents can also be used to shed light on a number of controversial views which have recently been put forward under the banner of the 'New Growth Theory'. According to the latter, externalities and increasing returns, often held to be associated with fixed investment, are the engine of economic growth. However, this book finds that the evidence does not support these claims.

THE NATIONAL INSTITUTE OF
ECONOMIC AND SOCIAL RESEARCH

Occasional Papers
XLVI

PRODUCTIVITY AND GROWTH
A study of British
industry, 1954–1986

PRODUCTIVITY AND GROWTH

A study of British industry,
1954–1986

NICHOLAS OULTON
AND
MARY O'MAHONY

CAMBRIDGE
UNIVERSITY PRESS

Published by the Press Syndicate of the University of Cambridge
The Pitt Building, Trumpington Street, Cambridge CB2 1RP
40 West 20th Street, New York, NY 10011-4211, USA
10 Stamford Road, Oakleigh, Melbourne 3166, Australia

First published 1994

Printed in Great Britain at the University Press, Cambridge

A catalogue record for this book is available from the British Library

Library of Congress cataloguing in publication data
Oulton, Nicholas.
Productivity and growth: a study of British industry, 1954–1986 /
Nicholas Oulton and Mary O'Mahony.
p.   cm. – (Occasional papers: 47)
Includes bibliographical references and index.
ISBN (invalid) 0–521–45848–8
1. Industrial productivity – Great Britain
2. Input–output analysis – Great Britain.
I. O'Mahony, Mary.   II. Title.
III. Series: Occasional papers (National Institute of Economic
and Social Research): 47.
HC280.I52O93   1994
338'.06'094109045–dc20   93–4798   CIP

ISBN 0 521 45345 3 hardback

CONTENTS

Contents

TABLES

CHARTS

ACKNOWLEDGEMENTS

This book is based on research carried out at the National Institute under a project directed by Nicholas Oulton. The Institute is grateful to the Leverhulme Trust for financial support for this work.

Parts of this book have already appeared in discussion paper form. Chapters 2, 3, 4, 5 and the Appendices are based on O'Mahony and Oulton (1990a and 1990b). Chapter 5 also draws on Oulton (1992b). Chapters 6 and 7 are based on Oulton (1991) and (1992a) respectively.

In the period during which this book has been prepared, some of the results have been presented at a number of conferences – including the 1989 European Production Study Group in Paris, the 1991 Royal Economic Society Conference at Warwick, and the 1992 European Economic Association Conference in Dublin – and also in various seminars, including EMRU, at the Centre for Economic Performance, at Lancaster University, and at the London Business School. We have benefited from the comments of participants.

We would like to thank Dick Allard and Tony Smith for providing us with data on investment and capital stocks. We are grateful to Darinka Martin for her excellent research assistance.

Thanks are also owed to Steve Broadberry, the late Edward Denison, Dale Jorgenson, David Mayes, Sig Prais, Tony Smith, Hilary Steedman and Bart Van Ark who commented on earlier versions or assisted and encouraged us in various ways. Finally, we are particularly grateful to the Director of the National Institute, Andrew Britton, to Robin Matthews, and to Angus Maddison for providing detailed comments on the book in draft form. Needless to say, none of these should be held responsible for the views expressed here nor for any errors which still remain.

AN OVERVIEW

This is a book about productivity. There are several possible concepts of productivity but the one on which we focus is multi-factor productivity (MFP), frequently also known as total factor productivity (TFP). Human beings will always be interested in *labour* productivity, whether measured as output per person or per person-hour. This is simply because in the long run the standard of living of everyone can only be raised if labour productivity increases. If robots ever take over the world, they will presumably be interested in robot productivity for similar reasons. But from the point of view of economic analysis, MFP, or more precisely the *growth* of MFP, is the more fundamental concept, at least if we are interested in understanding the causes of increasing labour productivity.

The interpretation of MFP

Theoretically, MFP growth is the rate at which output would have increased in some period, if all inputs had remained constant. In principle, MFP growth should be measured as the difference between the growth of output and the growth of total input. The growth of total input should in turn be measured as a weighted sum of the growth rates of individual inputs. In practice, it is customary to use the shares of the inputs in the value of output as the weights.[1] This procedure is adopted first because it is practical and secondly because it is hoped or believed that the resulting figure will be close to what MFP growth is meant to be in theory. If we calculate MFP growth over some time period and it turns out to be about zero, then we can at least say that any growth in labour productivity which occurred in this period must have been due to increased use of the other inputs. So we have at least a proximate explanation for rising labour productivity. If on the other hand MFP growth turns out to account for a substantial part of the rise in labour productivity, then we are clearly in need of some deeper explanation.

It might be thought that MFP growth would usually be zero, at least over the long term. Imagine that in a steel mill the quantities of all types of labour, of capital equipment, of energy, and of raw materials were held constant. Why should we expect to see any increase in output at all? It is true that it might be possible to raise output by some reorganisation of the flow of work or by the removal of restrictive practices (without changing labour effort of any sort) but such changes would be of a one-off nature. Alternatively, workers' skills might rise with experience (learning by doing). But in the absence of other changes, opportunities to learn would soon be exhausted (Arrow, 1962). It seems therefore that, aside from such temporary episodes, MFP growth should be generally zero. We cannot test this view directly since so far as we are aware MFP growth has not been measured at the level of an individual steel mill, but most usually at the level of the whole economy or of broad sectors within the economy. However at these levels, measures of MFP growth are almost invariably positive and of an economically significant size. To take the most striking example, Solow's pioneering calculation of MFP growth in the private non-farm sector of the US economy for 1909–49 found that 87.5 per cent of the growth of output per head over this period should be ascribed to MFP, and only 12.5 per cent to capital accumulation (Solow, 1957). Similar results were reported a little earlier by Abramovitz (1956), who commented: 'Since we know little about the causes of productivity increase, the indicated importance of this element [that is, MFP growth] may be taken to be some sort of measure of our ignorance about the causes of economic growth . . .'. When these findings first appeared, a debate started which has not so far been resolved.

One argument was that MFP growth should be interpreted as the effect of technical progress, but a difficulty with this argument, many people claimed, is that technical progress usually has to be incorporated into new capital goods and calculations of MFP growth already allowed for the effect of capital accumulation. It seemed implausible that the effects of scientific advances could be costlessly incorporated into production processes, thus effortlessly raising output and output per person over long periods of time. Another approach was to argue that the results of Solow and other pioneers were due to the crudity of the measurements: when measured properly, MFP growth would turn out to be negligible. In fact, the hidden agenda of much growth accounting (as the activity of measuring MFP growth came to be called) may be interpreted as an attempt to reduce the size of the measured residual. An early attempt along these lines was that of Jorgenson and Griliches (1967) who, by using more refined procedures (for example, Divisia index numbers) and better and more disaggregated data, reached a diametrically opposite conclusion to Solow's. They claimed that the residual was effectively zero for 1945–65: the growth of inputs accounted for 97 per cent of the growth of US private domestic product. However this claim has not withstood the test of time. In Jorgenson's later and still more refined calculations for a similar period, 1947–66, MFP growth now averages 1.28 per cent per annum and accounts for 32 per cent of the growth of output and for 42 per cent of the growth of output per person-hour.[2] Thus increasing refinement of measurement has indeed reduced the size of MFP but has far from eliminated it as an apparent cause of long-run growth.

Our approach

Numerous calculations of MFP growth have now been made for different countries and different time periods. Estimates are routinely produced by the US Bureau of Labour Statistics and by the OECD. There is a danger in fact of a blurring of the distinction between the theoretical concept of MFP growth, which as we shall see in chapter 2 can be given a rigorous foundation in the theory of production, and any particular empirical measure of MFP growth. It is one of the themes of this book that measurement matters: at every stage of an MFP calculation empirical and conceptual issues must be faced. Alternative decisions by the researcher can have profound effects on the resulting estimates. That is why it is important to follow a consistent methodology and this is what we have attempted to do.

A distinctive feature of our approach is that it starts from the level of individual industries. By contrast, most MFP estimates have been either at the level of the whole economy or of broad sectors such as manufacturing. We also provide estimates of MFP growth in manufacturing, but we do so by aggregating up from the industry-level estimates, a method which we will argue is superior: it also produces strikingly different results. A further advantage of industry-level estimates is that they constitute a wealth of data which can be put to use in testing hypotheses relating to, for example, increasing returns, a topic which has aroused much interest in recent years. Briefly, our estimates cover more than 130 industries, nearly all within UK manufacturing over a 32-year period, 1954–86. We believe that they are the most detailed that have so far been produced and also the most methodologically consistent. Our methodology is a neo-classical one (inspired in the main by Jorgenson *et al.*, 1987) so we are conscious that it will not command universal assent. But we hope that even those who are impatient with growth accounting will find something of value here. After all, to calculate MFP growth, one must first calculate outputs and inputs, so those who reject our methodology can put our estimates to their own preferred use.

Numerous studies of productivity have been conducted at the National Institute (see Matthews, 1988, for a review). Usually these have looked at labour productivity and often they have involved international comparisons, in an attempt both to measure and to explain the productivity gap between Britain and its competitors (for example, Prais, 1981; Smith *et al.*, 1982; Davies and Caves, 1987; O'Mahony, 1992a). Because our estimates of MFP growth are at a very disaggregated level, direct international comparisons would have been difficult because of differences in systems of industrial classification and we have not attempted any. Important insights into the reasons for Britain's comparatively low level of industrial productivity have also been derived from case studies of particular industries (for example, Steedman and Wagner, 1987 and 1989). By contrast the present study, in the tradition of Fabricant (1944) for the US and Salter (1966) and Wragg and Robertson (1978) for the UK, aims to be broader both in time span and coverage than earlier work, though at the price of being in consequence less deep.

A guide to the book

The remainder of this chapter will present an overview of the questions to be discussed and the main findings. Before launching into this, a brief guide to the chapters which are to follow is in order. Chapter 2 provides a detailed exposition of the theory of growth accounting, at the level of the industry. Issues to be discussed there include aggregation over types of inputs, the appropriate concept of output (gross output or value added), and returns to scale. This chapter also outlines the data sources and methods. Because of its complexity and interest, the part of the theory which relates to fixed capital is the subject of a separate chapter (chapter 3). Aggregation, this time over different vintages of the same type of capital, will again be an issue. Here will also be found a discussion of the perpetual inventory method of estimating capital stocks, a critique of the methods currently employed by the Central Statistical Office (CSO), and some sensitivity tests of the effect of different assumptions about asset life on capital stock estimates. Readers who are prepared to rely on the summary account of methodology and data which follows in the present chapter can skip chapters 2 and 3 and press on to chapter 4, which presents the estimates of MFP growth themselves at the industry level and discusses their main characteristics. The approach here is descriptive, seeing what the data can tell us; later, chapters 6 and 7 adopt a more analytical approach. In chapter 4 we look first at average behaviour and also at the extent of variability across industries. We also discuss the presence in our estimates of a number of empirical regularities which have been detected in other data sets by earlier workers, such as the positive relationship between output growth and productivity growth known as 'Fabricant's Law'. Chapter 5 is devoted to MFP estimates at a higher level of aggregation, UK manufacturing as a whole. A number of different methods are discussed, but the preferred method is a 'bottom-up' one, based on the industry-level estimates. Chapter 6 looks at the worldwide slowdown in productivity growth which occurred following the first oil shock of 1973. It asks whether the rise in energy prices, or in raw material prices generally, can account for the slowdown. In chapter

7, we revert to the industry-level estimates and ask whether the weight assigned to physical capital is too low – in other words, does investment in physical capital explain a great deal more of productivity growth than our method allows? We also ask, do the estimates of outputs and inputs reveal any sign of the presence of increasing returns to scale or the effects of externalities?

SUMMARY OF FINDINGS

The theoretical framework (chapter 2)

The estimation of MFP growth rates at the industry level in this book follows the methodology developed in Jorgenson, Gollop and Fraumeni (1987). Their approach ultimately rests on Solow (1957) who showed that, under certain conditions, the growth rate of MFP can be estimated as the growth rate of output minus the growth rate of total input, where the latter is equal to the sum of the value-share-weighted growth rates of individual inputs. The assumptions on which the approach rests are that producers are price takers in both output and input markets, so that output prices are equal to the marginal costs of production, and that the technology is characterised by constant returns to scale. These assumptions are very convenient, since they allow us to estimate MFP growth without having to estimate the parameters of the production function; the latter procedure would be difficult to implement since our data set has few time series observations.

In the light of the new growth theory (Romer, 1986; Lucas, 1988), which emphasises externalities and learning effects, this approach may seem at first old-fashioned. The new theory has rightly generated a great deal of intellectual excitement. But it is not yet clear that the factors which it emphasises are actually the crucial ones empirically.[3] In any case, it is important to realise that the calculation of inputs and outputs is not affected by the new theory, only the final stage, the calculation of MFP growth itself, may become problematical. Even if one of the new growth theories is true, it may affect the interpretation rather than the validity of MFP calculations: for example, in one of the models in Lucas (1988), MFP growth can be correctly interpreted as the rate at which an appropriately defined measure of human capital is accumulating. Finally, it is possible to use the estimates, derived on the assumptions of constant returns, absence of externalities, and so on, to *test* whether the patterns of productivity growth are indeed consistent with the assumptions (see particularly chapter 7).

Jorgenson *et al.* (1987) assume that for each industry there exists a production function relating output to inputs, and to time. For the *i*th industry,

$$Y_i = F^i(K_i, L_i, X_i, t), \qquad i = 1, \ldots, N, \tag{1.1}$$

where Y is real gross output, X is real intermediate input, K is real capital stock, L is labour input, t is time, and N is the number of industries. Capital, labour and intermediate input are, in turn, aggregates of their respective components; for example, capital is an aggregate of any number of different types of fixed capital and of inventories, the number being limited only by practical considerations. Under the given assumptions, the growth rate of MFP in the ith industry, denoted by μ_i, is in continuous time:

$$\mu_i = \mathrm{d}\ln Y_i/\mathrm{d}t - v^i_K(\mathrm{d}\ln K_i/\mathrm{d}t) - v^i_L(\mathrm{d}\ln L_i/\mathrm{d}t) - v^i_X(\mathrm{d}\ln X_i/\mathrm{d}t), \tag{1.2}$$

where v^i_K, v^i_L and v^i_X are the value shares of capital, labour and intermediate input respectively in the value of output. For example,

$$v^i_X \equiv p^i_X X_i / q_i Y_i$$

where p^i_X is the price of intermediate input to the ith industry and q_i is the price of the output of the ith industry, with analogous definitions for the other shares. The last three terms on the right-hand side of (1.2) are a Divisia index of total input growth. Instantaneous growth rates cannot be measured in practice, but the growth rate of MFP over the discrete time interval $t - u$ to t can be approximated as follows:

$$\Delta_u\ln(\mathrm{MFP}) = \Delta_u\ln Y_i - \bar{v}^i_K \Delta_u\ln K_i - \bar{v}^i_L \Delta_u\ln L_i - \bar{v}^i_X \Delta_u\ln X_i.$$

Here Δ_u is the difference between a variable at time t and time $t - u$, divided by the length of the time interval (u): for example, $\Delta_u\ln Z \equiv [\ln Z(t) - \ln Z(t - u)]/u$. $\bar{v}^i_K$, $\bar{v}^i_X$ and $\bar{v}^i_L$ are the value shares of capital, labour and intermediate input respectively, averaged over periods t and $t - u$. For example,

$$\bar{v}^i_X \equiv (1/2)[v^i_X(t) + v^i_X(t - y)]$$

and similarly for the other shares. Note that the shares are observable and add up to one. The expression for MFP growth contains a discrete, Törnqvist approximation to the ideal Divisia index of total input. The aggregates X_i, K_i and L_i are in turn estimated as Törnqvist indices of their components.

In this book, the measure of output is a gross one, which is preferred on theoretical grounds to a net measure such as value added. Gross output is also more intuitive: the output of a baker is bread, not value added in baking. No use is made of the concept of value added in estimating MFP growth at the industry level. However, at the aggregate level, one (though not the preferred) estimate of MFP growth is based on value added.

Sources for the measurement of output and inputs (chapter 2)

The primary, though far from the only, source for the estimates of MFP growth rates was the UK Census of Production. Our dependence on the Census was the main determinant of the period we chose to study, 1954–86. To achieve comparability over the chosen time span, the 1968 Standard Industrial Classification (SIC) was employed throughout, which allowed the estimation of MFP growth rates for more than 130 industries (nearly all in manufacturing) for at least some of this period and for 124 industries for the whole period.[4] The Census gives data on output, purchases of materials and services, stocks of inventories, and fixed investment (but not stocks of fixed capital), all in nominal terms. In addition, it gives numbers employed and average wages, but not hours worked. Data on prices and on hours worked were therefore obtained from alternative sources. Estimates were constructed for eight time periods within the overall span of 32 years: 1954–8, 1958–63, 1963–8, 1968–73, 1973–6, 1976–9, 1979–82 and 1982–6. With the exception of 1976 and 1982, these are all years of reasonably full capacity working.

The basis for the output estimates is the Census of Production concept of (nominal) gross output, adjusted to be consistent with national accounts definitions; the adjustments were to remove stock appreciation, and to avoid double-counting by excluding intra-industry purchases and sales, all of which are present in the original Census figures. The CSO's industry-level producer price indices, for home sales, were used to deflate nominal gross output.

We distinguish two types of intermediate input: first, purchases of materials and fuel and second non-industrial services (payments for transport, advertising and so on). Where available, the appropriate producer price indices were employed as deflators, otherwise deflators were constructed from other sources.

Labour input, for each type of worker, is measured by annual hours, which are computed as the product of numbers employed, weekly hours and weeks worked per year. Nine types of worker, five manual and four non-manual, are distinguished. The manual types are: full-time adult males; full-time adult females; part-time adult females; males aged under 21 and females aged under eighteen. The non-manual types are males; full-time females; part-time females and working proprietors.

We distinguish three kinds of fixed capital: plant & machinery; buildings & land; and vehicles – and two kinds of inventories: materials; and finished goods and work in progress. Stocks of fixed capital were estimated by the perpetual inventory method. For each stock, gross investment is cumulated over time, with allowance made for depreciation; the assumed rate of depreciation allows for both scrapping at the end of the assumed asset life and ageing or obsolescence in the period between installation and scrapping. That is, a 'net' capital stock concept is employed with depreciation assumed to be exponential.

Though it is convenient to speak of an industry-level capital aggregate, in the sense of an aggregate over different types of assets, strictly speaking such a concept is unnecessary: estimates of MFP growth can be constructed by considering each type of asset separately, though in practice the asset types distinguishable empirically may be more broadly defined than would be desirable (for example, 'plant & machinery'). However, aggregation becomes more of an issue when we recall that the stock of each type of asset is itself an aggregate of different vintages. The efficiency of an earlier vintage is lower than that of a later one both because of physical deterioration due to age and because of technical improvements embodied in later vintages. From the point of view of MFP measurement, it can be shown that different vintages of capital should be aggregated together by weighting each vintage by its relative marginal product. Under the assumptions followed elsewhere in this book, relative marginal products are measured by relative rental prices. If depreciation is exponential (or geometric), as the evidence suggests (at least for the US), then relative *rental* prices are equal to relative *asset* prices. In general, rental prices are not directly observable, but asset prices are much easier to measure.

The growth of fixed capital (chapter 3)

Estimates of the stocks of plant & machinery, of buildings and land, and of vehicles, were constructed for 140 industries (137 in manufacturing), using the Perpetual Inventory Method (PIM). Because there is much uncertainty about some crucial inputs required for the PIM, such as the length of the service life of assets or the rate at which assets depreciate due to ageing or obsolescence, a number of sensitivity analyses were performed. The most striking findings to emerge are as follows.

First, estimates of the levels of capital stocks are very sensitive to the assumptions required by the PIM. But estimates of the growth rates, which are what matter for MFP calculations, are *not* very sensitive. Second, the growth rates of the capital stocks have been slowing down steadily since the 1960s, particularly that of buildings. Third, the average age of the capital stock has risen since 1973 and, if no role is allowed for premature scrapping in the 1980s, was higher in 1985 than it had been in 1963. Fourth, the average age of plant in 1979 was some 11–15 years (depending on assumption) and about half of it was less than ten years old. The average age of buildings was some 23–29 years and on average about half of all buildings were less than twenty years old. Finally, it has frequently been argued that official PIM estimates overstate the size of

Table 1.1. *Growth rates of industry output and inputs: means and standard deviations (% p.a.)*

Period	N	MFP	Y	K	L	X
Means						
1954–73	124	0.88	3.32	3.81	− 0.77	3.59
1973–86	133	− 0.47	− 1.17	1.00	− 4.18	0.48
1954–86	124	0.35	1.50	2.64	− 2.16	2.31
Standard deviations						
1954–73	124	1.00	3.14	2.30	2.49	3.10
1973–86	133	1.56	3.07	1.89	2.66	3.17
1954–86	124	0.86	2.57	1.87	2.02	2.51

Source: Table 4.1.
Note: N: Number of industries.

the capital stock because they assume a fixed asset life and make no allowance for premature scrapping. Allegedly, much energy-intensive equipment was scrapped because of obsolescence following the 1973 oil price shock. Much more extensive scrapping occurred, it is often thought, as a result of the recession of the early 1980s. Though our estimates use different assumptions to those of the CSO, they are potentially vulnerable to the same criticism. Based on movements in the capital–output ratio in manufacturing as a whole in the period up to 1973, and relative to our PIM estimates, we find that premature scrapping may have reduced the stock of plant by 17 per cent and that of buildings by 7 per cent in 1986; in 1979 the corresponding figures were 9 per cent and 2 per cent. But other evidence suggests that scrapping in the 1973–9 period was *not* very significant. And an alternative calculation suggests that these estimates may be too high for 1986 as well: according to the latter, the upper limit for the reduction due to premature scrapping on the plant & machinery estimates in 1986 was about 10 per cent; the upper limit for buildings would be lower still because of the greater probability that buildings can be sold rather than scrapped when no longer needed.[5] However, all such estimates are extremely speculative and so, though there was undoubtedly *some* premature scrapping as a result of the 1980–81 recession, no adjustment was made to the PIM estimates.

The industry-level estimates (chapter 4)

As an average across all industries, MFP grew at 0.88 per cent per annum from 1954–73; thereafter it fell at 0.47 per cent per annum (table 1.1).[6] Closer examination shows that MFP actually fell from 1973–82, but grew again from 1982–6. Labour productivity by contrast grew on average in both halves of our period, by 4.09 per cent per annum in 1954–73 and by

Table 1.2. *Accounting for the growth of output per unit of labour (cross-industry averages)*

Period	Growth rates			Input contribution %	of which (total = 100%):	
	Y/L % p.a.	K/L % p.a.	X/L % p.a.		K/L %	X/L %
1954–73	4.09	4.58	4.36	78.5	23.4	76.6
1973–86	3.01	5.18	4.66	115.6	20.6	79.4
1954–86	3.66	4.80	4.47	90.4	22.0	78.0

Source: Table 4.7.

3.01 per cent in 1973–86 (table 1.2). For both kinds of productivity, there was considerable variation across industries, as evidenced by the standard deviations which are large in relation to the means. There was an even more striking contrast between the two halves of the period in the movements of output. Up to 1973, output grew rapidly, on average at 3.32 per cent per annum. Between 1973 and 1986, it fell at 1.17 per cent per annum (though growth resumed in the final sub-period, 1982–6). Labour input fell throughout the 32-year period and indeed in every sub-period, though much more rapidly after 1973; once again however there were large differences between industries. The growth rates of capital and of intermediate input also declined after 1973, but less sharply than that of labour. The result was that capital intensity (K/L) and intermediate input intensity (X/L), which both on average grew rapidly even before 1973, rose still more rapidly after that date.

Still considering cross-industry averages, we see from table 1.2 that the growth of inputs per unit of labour can account for much the greater part, some 79 per cent, of the growth of output per unit of labour up till 1973. For 1973–86, the contribution of total input to labour productivity growth exceeds 100 per cent, which simply reflects the fact that MFP growth is measured as negative over this period. Looking in more detail, it turns out that the major anomaly is the period 1973–82, and particularly 1973–6. For 1982–6, input growth explains 80 per cent of labour productivity growth. It turns out that even a generous allowance for accelerated scrapping of capital, much more generous than we have argued is reasonable, does not suffice to eliminate the puzzle of the 1973–82 period.

As was said above, the initial interest in MFP calculations arose because so little of output growth seemed to be due to input growth. So it is a little ironic that the UK seems to exhibit the opposite of this 'problem'. But it should be remembered that international comparisons of MFP growth seem to show that it is positively correlated with labour productivity growth (Denison 1967; Crafts, 1992); these two variables are also positively correlated across industries (see below). Now the UK has had a comparatively low rate of labour productivity growth over most of our period, but if it had had a higher one, perhaps we would have observed a higher rate of MFP growth.

Table 1.2 also decomposes the input contribution to labour productivity growth into the contribution of the growth of capital intensity and that of intermediate intensity. The latter accounts for about three quarters of the total 'explained': capital intensity only about one quarter. Suppose there had been no rise in capital intensity while intermediate intensity had risen at the actual recorded rate. Then it is tempting to interpret these figures as asserting that labour productivity growth would have been reduced by only one quarter of the input contribution, that is, by about 0.8 per cent per annum over 1954–86: so with no growth in capital intensity, labour productivity would still be predicted to rise at over 3 per cent per annum. However, this is an interpretation which should be resisted – the contributions of the different inputs can only be quantified when the hypothetical changes are small, not large as in the example just quoted. The reason that the contribution of intermediate input is three times that of capital is not because the former was growing much faster (we have already seen in table 1.1 that it was not), but because its value share is on average four times larger (58 per cent versus 15 per cent). This raises the issue, to which we return below, can the importance of capital in the growth process really be as low as this figure would suggest?

Do growth rates of MFP exhibit common factors? Such common factors might be specific to each industry over time or they might represent a shock of some sort which is common to all industries in a given time period. These possibilities can be represented by the following model:

$$\mu_{it} = \eta_i + \theta_t + \epsilon_{it}, \qquad E\epsilon_{it} = 0.$$

Here μ_{it} is MFP growth in the ith industry in period t, η_i is a fixed effect, specific to the ith industry, θ_t is a shock which is common to all industries during period t, and ϵ_{it} is an 'idiosyncratic' shock which varies both across industries and over time. This model was fitted as a panel regression. The 'period' effects (the θ_t) were found to be highly significant and to account for about 15 per cent of the variance of MFP growth rates. On the other hand, the industry fixed effects were not significant. It was found that the differences between sub-periods in the mean growth rates of MFP and output are significant: there appear to be common factors of varying size affecting MFP growth in any given period. Three of these factors, in

Table 1.3. *Cross-industry correlations between growth rates (124 industries)*

	MFP	Y	Y/L	q
1954–73				
MFP	1.00			
Y	0.51	1.00		
Y/L	0.67	0.62	1.00	
q	− 0.73	− 0.39	− 0.67	1.00
1973–86				
MFP	1.00			
Y	0.39	1.00		
Y/L	0.70	0.49	1.00	
q	− 0.76	− 0.31	− 0.67	1.00

Source: Table 4.11.
Note: q: output price.

1973–6, 1976–9 and 1979–82, were negative (relative to 1954–8). The same model was also fitted with output growth as the dependent variable. The fixed effects turned out to be significant here and together with the 'period' effects explain nearly half the variance of output growth.

Are productivity growth rates persistent over time? In other words, if an industry has high growth in one period, is it likely to have high growth in the subsequent one? Perhaps surprisingly, the answer is no. Whether we take MFP or labour productivity, persistence is low. This is the case both over short periods of 4–5 years as well as between the two halves of our 32-year period.

Some important empirical regularities, which were first detected by Fabricant (1942) for US industry in the early twentieth century and subsequently found to hold in the UK over 1924–50 by Salter (1966), were also discovered to hold in both halves of our period, 1954–73 and 1973–86. These regularities are: first, a significantly positive correlation between labour productivity growth and output growth; and second, a significantly negative correlation between output growth and price growth. Furthermore, similar relationships hold for MFP growth; that is, in both halves of our period, MFP growth is positively related to output growth and negatively to price growth. Though the relationships are not as strong as the corresponding ones for labour productivity, they are still statistically significant (table 1.3). It can be shown that these correlations are *not* due simply to a common measurement error affecting both productivity and output. The interpretation of these regularities is considered further below. Another of Salter's results, that wages rise no faster in industries where labour productivity is growing more rapidly, was found to hold too in our period.

Productivity growth in manufacturing as a whole (chapter 5)

How should MFP growth at the aggregate level, such as in the UK economy as a whole or, as in the present case, in aggregate UK manufacturing, be measured? It seems obvious that there should be *some* relationship between productivity growth in the industries of which an aggregate is composed and productivity growth in the aggregate itself, but it is not immediately obvious what that relationship should be. One might think that aggregate MFP growth should be some sort of weighted average of industry MFP growth rates, but this turns out not to be the case. The theoretical problem of how to measure aggregate MFP growth has in fact been solved, within certain limitations, by the contributions of Domar (1961) and of Hulten (1978), but the lessons of their work have not been widely appreciated. Instead many writers have favoured an approach based on aggregate value added, which is strictly only appropriate for a closed economy and can lead to seriously misleading conclusions. For instance, we find that for the aggregate considered here, namely total manufacturing, the value added method produces estimates of MFP growth which are twice those given by the preferred method.

Domar (1961) proposed that MFP growth at the aggregate level should be measured as a weighted *sum* of industry-level MFP growth rates (μ_i):

$$\mu^{DA} = \Sigma_i [(q_i Y_i)/\Sigma_i q_i Z_i]\mu_i.$$

Here the superscript 'DA' stands for 'Domar aggregation'. The weights are the ratios of nominal gross output in each industry to aggregate nominal final output (Z). Final output is that part of an industry's sales which is *not* destined to be used up in the current period by the industries included in the aggregate under study. So if the aggregate is the whole economy, aggregate final output is public and private consumption, investment and exports. If the aggregate is total UK manufacturing, aggregate final output is total sales of UK manufacturing firms *less* sales to other UK manufacturing firms of products which will be used up within the current period; alternatively, aggregate final output equals aggregate value added in manufacturing *plus* aggregate purchases by manufacturing from outside the manufacturing sector. Note that empirically the only extra information required to carry out Domar aggregation, over and above what is needed to calculate industry-level MFP growth rates, is aggregate nominal final output, that is, the denominator of the weights.

In Domar aggregation, the weights sum to more than one since aggregate gross output exceeds aggregate final output, because of the inclusion of sales made within the manufacturing sector in the former but not in the latter. The intuitive justification for the sum of the weights exceeding one is that an industry contributes not only directly to aggregate MFP growth but also indirectly, through helping to lower costs elsewhere in the economy when other industries buy its product. A deeper justification was provided by Hulten (1978), who showed that Domar aggregation is equal (under certain assumptions) to the rate at which the social production possibility frontier for the aggregate in question is shifting over time.

The more usual approach however has been to measure MFP growth at the aggregate level by the value added method, that is, as the growth of aggregate value added *less* the share weighted growth rates of aggregate labour and aggregate capital. In continuous time:

$$\mu^{AV} = (\dot{V}/V) - [p_K K/p_V V](\dot{K}/K) - [p_L L/p_V V](\dot{L}/L).$$

Here V is aggregate (real) value added and p_K, p_L and p_V are the prices of capital, labour and value added respectively; the superscript 'AV' stands for 'aggregate value added'. To implement this method, aggregate capital (K) and aggregate labour (L) can be built up from industry-level estimates. Aggregate real value added may be measured as a simple sum over industry-level value added:

$$V = \Sigma_i V_i.$$

In turn, industry-level value added may be derived by assuming that the industry-level production function (1.1) is separable in value added and intermediate input, from which, it is simple to show, we obtain

$$\dot{V}_i/V_i = [1/(1 - v_X^i)](\dot{Y}_i/Y_i) - [v_X^i/(1 - v_X^i)](\dot{X}_i/X_i).$$

Thus the aggregate value added method requires no extra information beyond industry-level data on output and the three inputs.[7]

Unfortunately, however, the aggregate value added method has no theoretical justification. It can be shown that it is only equivalent to the method of Domar aggregation in the case of a closed economy. In fact, it is likely to produce results similar to those that would result from calculating a weighted sum of industry-level MFP growth rates using as weights the ratios of industry gross output to aggregate *value added*, rather than (as with Domar aggregation) to aggregate *final output*. In the case of a closed economy, aggregate value added and aggregate final output coincide, but UK manufacturing is far from being a closed economy: in fact aggregate value added is only about half aggregate final output.

Despite these theoretical misgivings, the value added method has been implemented if only for comparison with Domar aggregation; table 1.4 summarises the results. In the first half of the period, value added grew at about the same rate as the cross-industry average of gross output, some 3.5 per cent per annum. But in the second half, it shows a precipitate

Table 1.4. *MFP growth in aggregate manufacturing: comparison of methods*
(% p.a.)

	Growth rates				
Period	V	K	L	μ^{AV}	μ^{DA}
1954–73	3.48	3.88	− 0.54	2.29	1.18
1973–86	− 2.84	1.26	− 3.83	− 0.88	− 0.54
1954–86	0.91	2.81	− 1.88	1.00	0.48

Source: Tables 5.1 and 5.2.

decline, falling at over 2.8 per cent per annum (though growth resumed after 1982). The growth rates of aggregate capital and labour are similar to the cross-industry averages.

The last two columns of table 1.4 show MFP growth according to the two methods. According to the preferred estimates, those made by Domar aggregation, over the nineteen-year period 1954–73, MFP growth averaged 1.18 per cent per annum. From 1973–82 MFP growth was negative: by 1982, the *level* of MFP had fallen by a total of 11 per cent since 1973. After 1982 MFP growth turned positive again, but not by enough to prevent the thirteen-year period 1973–86 from showing an overall decline (− 0.54 per cent per annum). For the whole period 1954–86 MFP growth has averaged about $\frac{1}{2}$ per cent per annum. Comparison of the last two columns of the table shows that the preferred estimates of MFP growth rates are about half those produced by the (misleading) aggregate value added method. The disparity is mostly due to the fact mentioned above that aggregate value added is only about one half aggregate final output.

What proportion of the growth in labour productivity in manufacturing as a whole is accounted for by the growth of inputs? The value added method can be applied to give one answer to this question (table 1.5). With this method, the only input whose contribution needs to be considered is capital. Growth of capital intensity (K/L) accounts for only 43 per cent of productivity growth in 1954–73, but it massively 'overaccounts' for growth in the second half of the period, since capital intensity accelerates while labour productivity slows down (μ^{AV} is negative). The picture presented by the aggregate value added method is quite different from the one previously obtained from the industry-level estimates. There we found that input growth could on average explain a much higher proportion of productivity growth (table 1.2).

The paradox can be resolved by employing a more appropriate concept of labour productivity, namely (real) final output per unit of

Table 1.5. *Accounting for labour productivity growth in aggregate manufacturing: comparison of methods*

	Growth of Z/L % p.a.	Growth of V/L % p.a.	Growth of K/L % p.a.	Growth of M/L % p.a.	Input contribution (final output) %	Input contribution (value added) %
1954–73	4.60	4.02	4.42	5.42	73.7	43.2
1973–86	2.23	0.98	5.08	3.68	126.7	191.2
1954–86	3.64	2.79	4.69	4.71	88.1	64.6

Source: Table 5.5.
Notes: Z: real final output. M: real external input into aggregate manufacturing.

labour. Though in principle measuring real final output is no more difficult than measuring real value added, in practice the necessary statistics are not available, so a somewhat indirect method has to be employed; the resulting estimates must therefore be treated with some caution. Table 1.5 compares the two measures of labour productivity. It will be seen that on the final output measure labour productivity shows a much less dramatic slowdown after 1973 than when value added is employed. With the final output measure, we have to consider the contribution of two sorts of input: firstly, capital as before, but now secondly also what is called here external input, that is, purchases by manufacturing of goods and services produced outside the manufacturing sector (either from abroad or from the non-manufacturing sector of the UK economy).[8] On this measure we now see that the two inputs together account for a much higher proportion of labour productivity growth. The results are now very similar to the cross-industry averages. Also, the apparent anomaly of 1973–86 is much less pronounced.

A comparison of the two measures of output casts a new light on the competitive strength of UK manufacturing. Final output grew more rapidly than did value added from 1954–73. And after 1973, final output fell to a lesser extent than did value added. The divergence between the two growth rates was in fact greater in the latter period. Thus some of the fall in value added after 1973 was due to substitution away from UK manufactured inputs, rather than to failure to maintain sales to buyers outside manufacturing. In other words, UK manufacturers managed to hang onto their markets to a greater extent than a consideration of value added alone would suggest, but they did so by using proportionately less of their own capital and labour and more bought-in inputs.

The role of energy and raw material prices in the post-1973 productivity slowdown (chapter 6)

After the first oil shock in 1973, labour productivity growth rates slowed down in all the advanced industrial countries. Where it has been possible to measure them, MFP growth rates appear to have fallen too: Jorgenson *et al.* (1987) found evidence for such a slowdown in the US and this study finds similar evidence for the UK (see table 1.1 and chapters 4 and 5). According to Maddison (1987), MFP growth decelerated in six countries (France, Germany, Netherlands, UK, Japan and the US) after 1973, even when various 'supplementary factors' are taken into account. Using a cruder methodology, Englander and Mittelstädt (1988) found that MFP growth slowed down in 21 OECD countries after 1973; neither in the business sector nor in manufacturing was there a single instance of a country with a higher MFP growth rate in 1979–86 than it had enjoyed in the pre-1973 period.

The connection between the oil and other commodity price rises and the slowdown has been much debated, but most of the debate has been concerned with labour productivity. Undoubtedly, many factors, including cyclical ones, played a role, particularly in the 1970s. However, the fact that no major industrial country has as yet recovered the growth rates of output and productivity which it enjoyed prior to 1973 certainly militates against a purely cyclical explanation (even one which relies on hysteresis effects on human and physical capital).

Here we concentrate on the slowdown in MFP rather than labour productivity growth and consider the role of one possible, purely micro effect, namely input substitution. In a nutshell, if technical progress is biased towards the use of particular commodities, and if the price of these commodities rises, then firms will use less of them and the growth rate of MFP will decline. Jorgenson (1984a, 1984b, 1988 and 1990) has argued that the slowdown in US productivity growth after 1973 is in fact due to precisely this cause, namely input substitution in response to the rising price of energy, since his econometric estimates show that in most industries productivity growth is energy-using. We assess this claim. We also ask whether a comparable claim can be made good for the UK in the same period.

In appraising the argument for the US, use is made of the estimates of Jorgenson *et al.* (1987) of the parameters of the translog production function, which they fitted to 21 US manufacturing sectors over the period 1948–79, together with their data on prices and quantities of inputs in 1973 and 1979. Employing their estimates, the method is to calculate what MFP growth would have been over 1973–9 in each sector had relative input prices remained at their 1973 level. MFP growth depends in general on input intensities, which depend in turn on relative input prices, but not in an entirely straightforward way: input intensities will in general be changing even if relative input prices are constant, because technical progress is usually biased.

For the translog production function, it can be shown that in the ith industry or sector

$$\mu_i = a_t^i + \beta_{Xt}^i \ln(X_i/L_i) + \beta_{Kt}^i \ln(K_i/L_i) + \beta_{tt}^i t, \qquad i = 1, \ldots, N.$$

where a_t^i, β_{Xt}^i, β_{Kt}^i, and β_{tt}^i are coefficients. Productivity growth is said to be intermediate-input-using if $\beta_{Xt} > 0$ and capital-using if $\beta_{Kt} > 0$. Jorgenson et al. (1987) found that in fifteen out of their 21 manufacturing sectors productivity growth was indeed intermediate-input-using. Having calculated input intensities on the assumption of constant relative input prices, we use this equation to estimate MFP growth on the same assumption. We then compare the predicted change in MFP with the actual change. The actual slowdown in US MFP growth was quite pronounced, comparing 1973–9 with 1969–73. In the earlier period MFP growth in the 21 sectors averaged 0.38 per cent per annum, in 1973–9 it averaged only − 0.74 per cent per annum, a decline of 1.12 percentage points. However, we find that changing input prices can only explain a small part of the slowdown. This is principally because, first, the rise in the price of intermediate input (relative to that of labour input) was fairly small − only 0.33 per cent per annum − and second, because in some sectors price changes were actually favourable to productivity growth. These negative conclusions relate to intermediate input prices, whereas Jorgenson has stressed the role of *energy* prices, which are only one component (and for many industries not a very important component) of intermediate input. However, consideration of alternative estimates for the US, in which energy prices were distinguished from other inputs, led to no change in the results.

Testing the argument for the UK required estimation of the parameters of the translog production function for UK manufacturing industries also. Because of a shortage of time series observations, it was not possible to estimate a separate production function for each industry; instead, production functions were estimated for groups of industries, employing a panel regression approach, but in other respects following a similar methodology to that of Jorgenson et al. (1987). In all thirteen industry groups, productivity growth was found to be intermediate-input-using. However, despite this, in the UK as in the US, input prices can explain only an insignificant part of the productivity slowdown. Specifically, changes in input prices are estimated to have led to a fall in MFP growth rates in 1973–9 in 50 industries but to a *rise* in 65 industries.

In no case did the predicted fall exceed about one half of a percentage point. On average across the 115 industries for which estimates were possible, the predicted effect of input price changes was a rise of 0.03 per cent per annum in MFP growth. A qualification is that the UK estimates were for a three input system (intermediate, capital and labour), so it was not possible to test whether it was specifically energy prices, rather than the broader category of intermediate input prices, which were the culprit in the UK productivity slowdown.

Investment, increasing returns, and the pattern of productivity growth (chapter 7)

Do conventional growth accounting calculations understate the role of capital formation? The small weight accorded to capital, typically some 14–15 per cent at the industry level and at the aggregate level only about 35–40 per cent even according to the value added method, has certainly made it seem so to many. If for example capital investment generates externalities because capital goods are the bearers of new knowledge, so that one firm's investment helps others to learn about new technology, then capital's true contribution is underestimated by capital's share of output (Romer, 1987). Also DeLong and Summers (1991) have claimed strong empirical support for the view that investment in plant and machinery (rather than investment in general) is a principal determinant of differences across countries in the growth rate of labour productivity. These and other related hypotheses were tested on our panel of 124 industries for which MFP growth has been estimated for all eight time periods. Two tests were conducted, each of which took the equality of capital's value share with the true social contribution of capital as the null hypothesis. First, MFP growth was regressed on the growth rates of the three inputs for each of the eight cross-sections. Under the null hypothesis, it can be shown that the coefficients of the growth rates should be insignificantly different from zero. This turned out to be generally the case. Second, the growth of labour productivity was regressed on the growth rates of capital-intensity, of intermediate-input-intensity and of the labour force. Under the null hypothesis, the coefficients on the growth rates of the intensities should be equal to the cross-industry average of the shares of these inputs, and the coefficient on labour force growth should be zero. When these expectations were tested in a panel regression, they were again found to be satisfied. The capital growth rate in these regressions is an aggregate of fixed capital and inventories. But when all elements of the aggregate, including plant & machinery, are entered separately in the regressions, the same sort of results emerge.

There is thus no support for the 'capital is special' view. In particular, Romer's claim that capital investment generates externalities is not supported by these data. The weight given to capital growth in the MFP calculations seems to have been correct on average. The Delong-Summers thesis, that investment in plant & machinery (rather than investment in general) is uniquely important for economic growth, also found no support using industry data. On these tests in fact, the assumptions on which the MFP calculations were based, namely constant returns to scale and prices equal to marginal costs, are not rejected by the data.

However, though capital investment does not seem to be a cause of externalities or to be associated with increasing returns, nevertheless there is other *prima facie* evidence for the importance of externalities and increasing returns. First of all, there is the fact that the average level of MFP growth is higher when manufacturing output as a whole is higher (though with only eight time periods no statistical significance can be claimed for this result). Secondly, there is Fabricant's Law, the positive cross-industry correlation between output growth and productivity growth (whether labour or MFP). One interpretation of the Law is that faster growth of demand for one industry leads, via externalities or increasing returns of some sort, to faster productivity growth. An alternative explanation reverses the causation. According to this view, for various accidental reasons technical progress is more rapid in some industries than in others; in the progressive industries, firms expand output and prices fall to absorb the increased supply. However the latter view turns out not to be supported by the evidence.

If increasing returns are of the dynamic kind, involving some kind of learning effects, then they should show up much more readily in those industries where growth is rapid than in those where it is slow or even negative (a common occurrence in our sample); the argument is that industries can learn but cannot forget, or at least that forgetting is a slower process than learning. In fact, no strong differences emerged between slow-growing and fast-growing industries. When the sample is split into fast-growing and slow-growing industries, the strength of the relationship between output growth and productivity growth is about the same in both groups. This test assumes that firms learn from their rivals in the same industry. Of course, learning might take many different forms, including learning from one particularly dynamic sector or learning from abroad.

What may seem to be the effect of increasing returns may in reality be due to quite different causes. For example, if there are fixed costs due to indivisibilities or if labour is hoarded during cyclical downturns, because of costs of adjustment, then an expansion of demand will raise productivity, mimicking the effect of increasing returns (Rotemberg and Summers, 1991). Labour hoarding seems to be the feature most likely to be common to a large number of industries. Since blue-collar workers are less likely to be hoarded than white-collar ones, the importance of labour hoarding should be greater the lower the share of blue-collar employment in the total. However, when the blue-collar share is included in regressions of MFP growth on output growth plus a battery of control variables, the results are somewhat mixed: no conclusive evidence of labour hoarding emerges.

The failure to find convincing evidence for externalities, taken together with the inconclusive results for labour hoarding, leaves the true explanation for Fabricant's Law still unclear. But here it is appropriate to recall an earlier conclusion: though the majority of the variation in MFP growth is industry-specific, strong evidence emerged of 'period' effects. It is possible therefore that Fabricant's Law and the 'period' effects on MFP have a common explanation, although the nature and mechanism of propagation of whatever economy-wide shocks lie behind the 'period' effects remain to be determined.

2

THEORY AND METHODS

The approach to the measurement of multi-factor productivity (MFP) employed in this book builds on the pioneering contributions of Solow (1957), Denison (1967) and Jorgenson and Griliches (1967).[1] The work of Jorgenson *et al.* (1987) on the US economy, which represents a considerable refinement of the earlier work, is the more immediate inspiration. The basis of these authors' approach is the production function: a relationship between output and inputs. The growth of MFP is the difference between the growth of output and that of total input and is identified with the rate at which the production frontier is shifting out over time. The different inputs are weighted together using market prices, a method which has the enormous practical advantage that only (in principle) observable quantities and values are required to estimate MFP growth. The justification for the use of market prices lies in the theory of marginal productivity, coupled with the assumptions of price-taking by firms and constant returns to scale.

This chapter will provide, in the next section, a detailed exposition of the theory of growth accounting; because of its complexity and interest, the part of the theory which relates to the fixed capital stock is the subject of a separate chapter (chapter 3). After the theory has been set out, it is followed by a description of the methods and sources employed to implement the theory empirically.

Because the assumptions on which growth accounting rests are controversial, and since there is a danger that the reader will be submerged in a flood of detail, some preliminary points are in order. First, nowhere in this book is the assumption of an economy-wide aggregate production function employed. Nor is the reader invited to believe in an economy-wide aggregate capital stock. Hence some (though not all) of the controversies which have bedevilled the discussion of the role of capital are irrelevant here. The production functions which form the basis of the analysis are industry-level ones, primarily within manufacturing, in which some 137 industries are distinguished. Even the concept of an industry-level aggregate capital stock is not essential. When productivity growth in aggregate manufacturing is analysed (chapter 5), the preferred estimate is built up from industry-level MFP growth rates. Though market prices play a crucial role in the analysis, the maintained hypothesis is simply that the firms within each industry are price-takers, not that all actors in the economy are atomistic. The reader is *not* asked to accept that trade unions have had no influence on wage rates, or that government purchases cannot influence prices.

Nevertheless, the assumptions of price-taking and constant returns to scale certainly require justification, especially in the light of new theories of economic growth (Lucas, 1988; Romer, 1986) which emphasise just those features, such as externalities and increasing returns, which seem to be ruled out here *a priori*. Part of the justification is pragmatic. The neo-classical approach to growth accounting is a discipline, which enforces consistent choices at every step along the way. Without this discipline, the researcher is liable to flounder in a swamp of 'adhocery'. Moreover no other approach has been so fully worked out.[2] That answer is of course not adequate by itself; a better one is that it is possible to use the estimates of outputs and inputs (derived on neo-classical assumptions) to *test* for the presence of externalities and increasing returns, as will be done in chapter 7.

According to the theory, MFP growth is the rate at which the production frontier is shifting out over time, due to advances in knowledge and improvements in organisation, which can be adopted costlessly and which do not have to be embodied in capital goods. However, to emphasise the different possible interpretations, this magnitude is often designated simply 'the residual' or even 'the measure of our ignorance'. What is called here 'MFP growth' *may* be in reality the effect of input growth in the presence of increasing returns; this possibility is discussed below. Another possibility is suggested by one of the models in Lucas (1988), in which growth in the average level of human capital (with or without externalities) can mimic the effect of MFP growth. From an empirical point of view, it would seem very difficult to decide whether calculated MFP growth is due to costless technical progress which is not embodied in capital goods, or to rising levels of human capital.[3] If the latter view were accepted, the results to be presented below would not be invalidated. But clearly the interpretation to be given to our figures would be affected.

A further possibility is simply errors in the data. This becomes especially plausible when we come to look at the actual results, which frequently show MFP growth as *negative*. It is difficult to believe that technical regress (an inward shift of the production frontier) is a common occurrence, though a deterioration of labour relations leading to poorer organisation of production is possible. Since this chapter is also concerned with describing the data employed, a little should be said about the likely sources of errors.

First, the 'industries' which are the subject of this study are statistical constructions: each consists of a changing collection of establishments classified (by the statisticians in charge of the Census of Production) to that industry. Since the Standard Industrial Classification (SIC) has gone through several revisions during the time span covered here, there is always the possibility that some establishments have been misclassified. This is particularly the case for the period after 1979, when there was a radical change in the SIC and reclassification of later data to achieve consistency with earlier figures had to be done by statistical means (see Appendix C).

Second, the price indices necessary to deflate the nominal values recorded in the Census of Production are not always available at the industry level, particularly for the earlier years. Even today, there are a number of industries for which an official producer price index is not published and the missing industries are often (not by accident) ones in which technical change is particularly rapid, for example, computers and office equipment. Even when indices are available, it is often suspected that they underestimate quality change and hence overestimate price rises; certainly this is the case for the United States (Gordon, 1990), where methods of constructing producer price indices are similar to those of the UK. An extreme form of upward bias can occur when a new good appears.[4] If price indices contain an upward bias, then both input and output will be underestimated, so the effect on MFP growth is uncertain.[5] A further difficulty with producer price indices is that they are only intended to cover sales on the home market, not exports (though sales which are ultimately for export but which are initially to a UK intermediary *are* covered). If, as is often alleged though without any firm evidence, export prices are lower than home market ones (because of greater competition) and if the proportion of exports in total sales is rising, then again there will be an upward bias in the producer price index.[6]

Third, the estimates of both labour input and capital input are not as refined as would be desirable. Though nine types of labour and five types of capital are distinguished, the components are still crude aggregates, for example, 'plant and machinery'. Further refinement would be very difficult at the industry level, since the capital stock estimates employ all the information on investment available in the Census of Production. The Census contains relatively crude data on labour input (numbers employed, broken down into three categories, with nothing on hours worked or whether full-time or part-time). Fortunately, other sources are available for labour. These have been exploited to some extent, but further research (beyond the scope of the present study) would be worthwhile.

Fourth, some of the inputs may be misclassified. For example, the present framework allows no role for intangible capital. Expenditures on R and D, product development, marketing, training, and so forth, are all in principle covered by the Census, but they will be counted as current expenses (labour, materials or purchased services). Hence they will be reckoned as contributing to current, not future output. Insofar as these expenses have an investment character, this is wrong: what is counted as expenditure on a current input should really be reckoned as gross investment in intangible capital. The correct approach would be to introduce one or more stocks of intangible capital, which accumulate as firms invest in them and which suffer from depreciation. Whether this would change the overall size of the residual by very much is doubtful, since the main effect would be to change the time pattern at which inputs are reckoned to make their contribution: in any one year, the contribution of current inputs would be lowered, but past expenditures on building up intangible capital would now be taken into account. In fact, if stocks of intangible capital had been rising at a constant rate for a long period the calculated rate of MFP growth would be correct, even though investment in intangible capital was misclassified as a current expense. This is because the contribution of any input is its growth rate times its value share and in a steady state gross investment grows at the same rate as the stock itself. Some types of intangible capital such as R and D may generate spillover effects (Griliches, 1991), in which case the value share may underestimate the contribution (see below), but this is of course a different point.[7]

These reservations about the quality of the estimates should be borne in mind when the results are eventually presented (chapter 4).

MFP GROWTH AT THE INDUSTRY LEVEL

The methodology of Jorgenson *et al.* (1987) provides a logically coherent framework for MFP measurement which has been followed here within the limits of the data available for the UK and the resources available for the study. The basis of their approach is as follows. They assume that at the industry level (or sector level in their case) there exists a production function relating output to capital, labour, intermediate input and time. Capital, labour and intermediate input are each aggregates which depend in turn on their components. Growth rates of output and inputs are measured in principle by Divisia indices; the latter, since growth rates cannot be observed continuously, are approximated by discrete, Törnqvist indices.

The following notation will be employed. Let

Y = Real gross output
X = Real intermediate input

K = Real capital stock
L = Labour input
N = Number of industries
t = Time
p = Input price (per unit flow of service)
q = Output price
v = Value share (a subscript indicates which share)
$\bar{v}$ = Average of v at two points in time, t and $t - u$.
$\varDelta_u$ = Difference between a variable at time t and time $t - u$, divided by the length of the interval, for example,

$$\varDelta_u \ln Z = [\ln Z(t) - \ln Z(t - u)]/u,$$

so that $\varDelta_u \ln Z$ is the average growth rate of Z per unit of time over the interval $t - u$ to t.

Subscript and superscript i refer to the ith industry. Subscript X, K and L refer to intermediate input, capital input and labour input respectively. Thus p^i_K is the rental price of one unit of capital input to industry i.

MFP growth

In each industry, the following accounting identity holds:

$$q_i Y_i = p^i_K K_i + p^i_L L_i + p^i_X X_i, \qquad i = 1, \ldots, N, \qquad (2.1)$$

that is, the value of output equals the value of the inputs. It is assumed that each industry's technology can be described by a constant-returns-to-scale production function

$$Y_i = F^i(K_i, L_i, X_i, t), \qquad i = 1, \ldots, N. \qquad (2.2)$$

The rate of growth of MFP, μ, is defined as the rate of growth of output with respect to time, holding all inputs constant:

$$
\begin{aligned}
\mu_i &\equiv \partial \ln Y_i / \partial t \\
&= d \ln Y_i / dt - (K_i / Y_i)(\partial Y_i / \partial K_i)(d \ln K_i / dt) \\
&\quad - (L_i / Y_i)(\partial Y_i / \partial L_i)(d \ln L_i / dt) \\
&\quad - (X_i / Y_i)(\partial Y_i / \partial X_i)(d \ln X_i / dt), \qquad (2.3)
\end{aligned}
$$

from (2.2). Now assuming that firms maximise profits and are price-takers in product and factor markets, then, as is well known, we can replace the elasticities in the last equation with value shares:

$$\mu_i = d \ln Y_i / dt - v^i_X(d \ln X_i / dt) - v^i_K(d \ln K_i / dt) - v^i_L(d \ln L_i / dt) \qquad (2.4)$$

where v^i_X, v^i_K and v^i_L are the value shares of intermediate input, capital and labour respectively and are given by:

$$v^i_X = p^i_X X_i / q_i Y_i$$
$$v^i_K = p^i_K K_i / q_i Y_i \qquad (2.5)$$
$$v^i_L = p^i_L L_i / q_i Y_i.$$

In other words, MFP growth in industry i is equal to the growth of output minus a value-share-weighted average of the growth of inputs.

The instantaneous growth rates of output and inputs in (2.4) cannot be directly observed. However, under the further assumption that the production function is translog, it can also be shown that the average growth of MFP over the discrete interval $t - u$ to t is measured exactly by the following Törnqvist index (Diewert, 1976):[8]

$$\Delta_u \ln(\mathrm{MFP}_i) = \Delta_u \ln Y_i - \bar{v}^i_X \Delta_u \ln X_i - \bar{v}^i_K \Delta_u \ln K_i - \bar{v}^i_L \Delta_u \ln L_i,$$
$$i = 1, \ldots, N, \qquad (2.6)$$

where

$$\bar{v}^i_X = (1/2)[v^i_X(t) + v^i_X(t - u)]$$
$$\bar{v}^i_K = (1/2)[v^i_K(t) + v^i_K(t - u)] \qquad (2.7)$$
$$\bar{v}^i_L = (1/2)[v^i_L(t) + v^i_L(t - u)].$$

Note that the shares are observable and add up to 1. However, X_i, K_i and L_i are not directly observable. To remedy this, we can define each of the inputs as a translog function of its components:

$$d \ln X_i / dt = \Sigma_j v^i_{Xj}(d \ln X_{ij}/dt)$$
$$d \ln K_i / dt = \Sigma_k v^i_{Kk}(d \ln K_{ik}/dt) \qquad (2.8)$$
$$d \ln L_i / dt = \Sigma_l v^i_{Ll}(d \ln L_{il}/dt) \qquad i = 1, \ldots, N.$$

where X_{ij} is i's purchases of materials of type j, K_{ik} is i's purchases of capital services of type k and L_{il} is i's purchases of labour services (annual hours worked) of type l. v^i_{Xj} is the share of purchases of intermediate input of type j in total purchases of intermediate input at times t and $t - u$, that is,

$$\bar{v}^i_{Xj} = p^i_{Xj} X_{ij} / \Sigma_j p^i_{Xj} X_{ij}, \qquad \Sigma_j v^i_{Xj} = 1,$$

The other shares, v^i_{Ll} and v^i_{Kk}, are similarly defined:

$$\bar{v}^i_{Ll} = p^i_{Ll} L_{il} / \Sigma_l p^i_{Ll} L_{il}, \qquad \Sigma_l v^i_{Ll} = 1,$$
$$\bar{v}^i_{Kk} = p^i_{Kk} K_{ik} / \Sigma_k p^i_{Kk} K_{ik}, \qquad \Sigma_k v^i_{Kk} = 1,$$

The corresponding Törnqvist approximations are:

$$\Delta_u \ln X_i = \Sigma_j \bar{v}^i_{Xj} \Delta_u \ln X_{ij}$$
$$\Delta_u \ln K_i = \Sigma_k \bar{v}^i_{Kk} \Delta_u \ln K_{ik} \qquad\qquad (2.8')$$
$$\Delta_u \ln L_i = \Sigma_l \bar{v}^i_{Ll} \Delta_u \ln L_{il} \qquad\qquad i = 1, \ldots, N.$$

where $\bar{v}^i_X$, $\bar{v}^i_K$, and $\bar{v}^i_L$ are the averages of the shares at times $t - u$ and t:

$$\bar{v}^i_{Xj} = (1/2)[v^i_{Xj}(t) + v^i_{Xj}(t - u)]$$
$$\bar{v}^i_{Kk} = (1/2)[v^i_{Kk}(t) + v^i_{Kk}(t - u)]$$
$$\bar{v}^i_{Ll} = (1/2)[v^i_{Ll}(t) + v^i_{Ll}(t - u)], \qquad\qquad i = 1, \ldots, N.$$

Capital stocks and rental prices

Each capital stock is assumed to evolve according (in discrete time) to:

$$K_{ik}(t) = I_{ik} + (1 - \delta_{ik})K_{ik}(t - 1), \qquad\qquad (2.9)$$

where I_{ik} is gross investment by industry i in capital of type k and δ_{ik} is the geometric rate of depreciation of capital of type k in industry i. Here it has been assumed that the services of each type of capital are proportionate to the corresponding stock and by choice of units we have set this constant of proportionality equal to one. As argued more fully in chapter 3, rates of depreciation can be estimated from the rates at which the prices of secondhand assets are observed to decline; the somewhat scanty empirical evidence supports the assumption that depreciation is indeed approximately geometric. Somewhat surprisingly, it makes no difference whether depreciation is caused by a decline in physical efficiency as a result of age or whether it is due to obsolescence; in either case depreciation can be estimated from secondhand asset prices.

Though the prices of the various types of intermediate input and of labour can be observed (at least in principle), the rental prices of different types of capital input (p^i_{Kk}) cannot usually be observed directly. But under the assumption of geometric depreciation, we can employ the formula, derived by Hall and Jorgenson (1967), relating asset prices and rental prices of each type of capital. In discrete time, this is

$$p^i_{Kk}(t) = \{r_i(t)P^i_{Kk}(t - 1) + \delta_{ik}P^i_{Kk}(t) - [P^i_{Kk}(t) - P^i_{Kk}(t - 1)]\}$$
$$\times [(1 - u(t)z_k(t))/(1 - u(t))] \qquad\qquad (2.10)$$

where r_i = Nominal, post-tax rate of return in industry i
         P^i_{Kk} = Purchase price of asset k to industry i
         u = Corporate tax rate, and
         z_k = Present value of depreciation allowances per £ spent on k.

The nominal post-tax rate of return r_i is not observed directly, but, following Jorgenson *et al.* (1987), it can be estimated by arguing that (under competitive conditions) it will be equalised across all assets and will be equated to whatever is the appropriate rate of discount for the industry. After multiplying the equation above by the stock of asset k, K_{ik}, and summing over asset types, the left-hand side becomes equal to gross profits. Hence, solving for r_i in this equation now yields

$$r_i = \{\text{Gross Profits} - \text{Corporation tax} - \text{Depreciation} \\ + \text{Capital gains}\} \div \text{Value of capital} \quad (2.11)$$

Therefore, the rate of return is the post-tax *realised* return on capital. Given r_i we can now calculate the rental prices of all types of capital. The use of actual profits, which obviously rise and fall with the business cycle, in estimating the rate of return is consistent with a theoretical result of Berndt and Fuss (1986). They found that changes in the degree of capacity utilisation should be dealt with for growth accounting purposes not by applying a capacity utilisation factor to the physical stock of capital, but by the use of actual profits to reflect the marginal product of capital; that is, adjustment for underutilisation of the capital stock should be done by adjusting the price of capital services, not the physical volume of capital.[9]

Prices of inputs

Now that we have measured the quantities K_i, L_i and X_i, and knowing the prices of the components of which each input is made up, we can (if desired) calculate the prices of capital, labour and intermediate input (p_K^i, p_L^i and p_X^i) as the ratios of the observable values to the corresponding quantities. This procedure ensures that the following accounting identities are preserved:

$$p_X^i X_i = \Sigma_j p_{Xj}^i X_{ij}$$
$$p_L^i L_i = \Sigma_l p_{Ll}^i L_{il} \quad (2.12)$$
$$p_K^i K_i = \Sigma_k p_{Kk}^i K_{ik}.$$

Quality of inputs

Following Jorgenson *et al.* (1987), we can develop an index of labour quality as the ratio of our measure of labour input divided by an index of total hours worked:

$$Q_L^i = L_i / \Sigma_l L_{il}$$

whence

$$\Delta_u \ln Q_L^i = \Delta_u \ln L_i - \Delta_u \ln[\Sigma_l L_{il}] \quad (2.13)$$

A similar index of capital quality can be developed as the ratio of our measure of capital input to the sum of capital inputs of all types which leads to:

$$\Delta_u \ln Q_K^i = \Delta_u \ln K_i - \Delta_u \ln[\Sigma_k K_{ik}] \qquad (2.14)$$

Jorgenson *et al.* (1987) also calculate a quality index for intermediate input since they disaggregate materials into a number of components. The unavailability of the requisite data forced us to distinguish only two types of materials input, one of which, non-industrial services, is a small fraction of the total. Therefore, it was not considered worthwhile to estimate an index of materials quality.

Aggregation and non-constant returns to scale

The methodology just outlined does not require the existence either of an economy-wide production function or of a sector-wide one. Nevertheless, even an industry-wide production function is not above criticism, especially given the fact that, though industries are defined by their 'principal product', there are some industries in which other products may constitute a significant proportion of total output. For example, in 1979 (the last year for which official data using the classification system employed in this study, namely the 1968 SIC, are available), the proportion of each industry's sales accounted for by the principal product ranged from a low of 57 per cent to a high of 100 per cent (*Summary Report on the Census of Production 1979*, table 4).[10] Moreover, the 'principal product' is not in practice a single homogeneous good but rather a range of products, whose composition is changing over time, no doubt more rapidly in some industries than in others. Having drawn attention to these facts, there is little more that can usefully be said.

The methodology may also seem to require the existence of capital, labour and intermediate aggregates. As the aggregation of capital above all is often thought to impose insuperable difficulties, something needs to be said on this head. Actually, however, the calculation of total input and hence MFP growth rates does *not* require the existence of either a capital or a labour or an intermediate aggregate, in the sense of an aggregate across different types. This is because the contribution to output growth of each component of (for example,) the labour force is the growth rate of that component weighted by its value share in total output; the contribution of labour as a whole is simply the sum of the contributions of the components. That is, using (2.6), (2.8) and (2.12), the contribution of labour as a whole to output growth is

$$v_L^i \, d\ln L_i/dt = v_L^i \Sigma_l v_{Ll}^i (d\ln L_{il}/dt) = (1/q_i Y_i) \Sigma_l p_{Ll}^i L_{il}(d\ln L_{il}/dt)$$

A similar point holds for capital and intermediate input. So even if a labour aggregate does not exist, we can still talk about the contribution of (say) chartered accountants to input growth. The existence of a labour aggregate only matters if we want to talk about the contribution of labour *as a whole* to input and output growth. Though with long usage this has become a very natural and intuitive way to discuss the contribution of the multifarious types of skilled and unskilled labour to economic growth, nothing very fundamental would be lost if it had to be given up. In what follows, it will be assumed that capital, labour and intermediate aggregates do exist, but anyone who objects to such an assumption should remember that the calculation of total input and MFP growth is not dependent on acceptance of this assumption.

A more serious problem is that in practice the components of which the aggregates are made up are themselves aggregates, for lack of any more detailed data. Thus we do not in fact have access to data on chartered accountants but only (as will be seen) to data on 'administrative, technical, and clerical employees'. Here we must hope that the prices of the goods and services included under the same heading do in fact move approximately together, but we have no way of testing whether this is in fact the case, nor of checking how far the results would be affected if it is not the case. In summary, aggregation across *types* of labour (or of capital or of intermediate input) is not a problem in principle, since the methodology does not require it to be done. However, in practice we are forced to aggregate to some extent, for lack of more disaggregated data. Note that in this respect capital is on all fours with labour and intermediate input.

There is however an additional problem with capital. Even if we had data on investment in, for example, turret lathes, estimation of the stock of turret lathes *via* equation (2.9) requires us to aggregate together different vintages of turret lathes. If depreciation were due solely to physical deterioration with age (for example, rusting), there would be no problem. However, arguably the bulk of depreciation is due to obsolescence: new turret lathes are better than old ones. As will be discussed further in chapter 3, aggregation across vintages of the same type of capital is possible but it requires that technical progress takes a purely capital-augmenting form. Aggregation across vintages would seem to be essential if it is to make any sense to attempt to measure the contribution of growth in the stock of turret lathes (or personal computers or warehouses) to the growth of output; without aggregation, each vintage of a turret lathe would have to be regarded as a different good.

Though at a pinch we can do without aggregates of different types of capital, labour and intermediate inputs, the existence of an aggregate of total input is required if MFP growth is to have any meaning. There are two general conditions under which aggregation is permissible. First, if the prices of the components of the proposed aggregate happen to grow at the same rate, then they can be treated as a Hicksian composite commo-

dity. This condition is not satisfied in the data studied here. Second, in
the absence of restrictions on the movements of prices, Leontief's aggregation theorem states that an aggregate exists if and only if the marginal
rate of substitution between any two components within the aggregate is
independent of the level of any component outside the aggregate. Also,
the Divisia index defining the growth of the aggregate will exhibit 'path
independence' if and only if this condition is satisfied.[11] In the present
context, this can be shown to be equivalent to requiring that the
production function (2.2) exhibits constant returns to scale (Hulten,
1973).

Suppose on the contrary that returns are in fact non-constant. Hulten
(1973) has shown that an index of total input can still be defined, but with
value shares replaced by the ratio of the value of marginal product to
value of output (for example, in the case of capital, $K_i(\partial Y_i/\partial K_i)/Y_i$).
Under increasing returns to scale, the value of marginal products exceeds
the value of output (by Euler's Theorem), so in this case the Hulten
weights will sum to more than one, unlike the value shares of the present
methodology. So with increasing returns to scale it might be thought that
our methodology will tend to underestimate total input and hence overestimate MFP growth, that is, we will be attributing to 'technical progress'
a part of productivity growth which is really a consequence of the growth
of inputs. However, this conclusion is not correct in general: it depends on
the nature of the increasing returns. Only if the increasing returns are
external to the firm but internal to the industry will the methodology
definitely overstate MFP growth. If increasing returns are internal to the
firm, then monopoly profit will accrue to some input, so the latter's value
share will be inflated above the competitive level; consequently, our
methodology could end up underestimating MFP growth, by giving an
excessive weight to this input.

An example will make this clear. Suppose that the production function
in the ith industry takes the simple form

$$Y_i = AK_i^\alpha L_i^{1-\alpha}, \qquad 0 < \alpha < 1,$$

where

$$A = K_i^\beta, \qquad \beta > 0,$$

that is, there is an externality associated with capital. Investment by any
one firm raises the productivity of all firms, perhaps through some
learning effect, and this is captured by the factor A. In this example, MFP
growth is zero, all growth in labour productivity coming from investment.
Suppose initially that this externality is external to firms but internal to
the industry (the Marshallian case), so that competitive conditions can
still prevail. Then the value shares of capital and labour will be α and

$(1 - \alpha)$ respectively and so our methodology will incorrectly estimate MFP growth as

$$\mathrm{d}\ln Y_i/\mathrm{d}t - \alpha\mathrm{d}\ln K_i/\mathrm{d}t - (1 - \alpha)\mathrm{d}\ln L_i/\mathrm{d}t = \beta\mathrm{d}\ln K_i/\mathrm{d}t.$$

But capital's true marginal product is higher than its rental price; the weight for labour is correct but the correct weight for capital should be $(\alpha + \beta)$ and the correct estimate of MFP growth should be

$$\mathrm{d}\ln Y_i/\mathrm{d}t - (\alpha + \beta)\mathrm{d}\ln K_i/\mathrm{d}t - (1 - \alpha)\mathrm{d}\ln L_i/\mathrm{d}t = 0.$$

Here the correct weights sum to $(1 + \beta)$, not 1. So in this case if capital growth is positive our methodology will clearly overestimate MFP growth.

Now suppose that increasing returns are internal to the firm, but continue to assume that the production function is given by

$$Y_i = K_i^{\alpha+\beta}L_i^{1-\alpha}.$$

Competitive conditions are no longer possible and inputs must be assumed to be paid their marginal revenue product, not the value of their marginal product. The value share of labour is

$$(\mathrm{MR}/q)(1 - \alpha),$$

where MR is marginal revenue, and if the monopoly profit is attributed to capital, the latter's value share is

$$1 - (\mathrm{MR}/q)(1 - \alpha).$$

If these value shares are used in a growth accounting calculation, the weight given to labour will now be too low (it should be $1 - \alpha$). However, the weight given to capital may be either lower or higher than the correct one $(\alpha + \beta)$. Consequently, the estimated MFP may be lower or higher than the true level. For example, if the growth rate of labour is zero, then the estimated growth of MFP will be *lower* than the true level (zero) if

$$\mathrm{MR}/q < (1 - \alpha - \beta)/(1 - \alpha),$$

which is quite possible if the elasticity of demand is low enough and β is not too large. For most of this book, the hypothesis of constant returns to scale will be maintained. However in chapter 7 the question of non-constant returns will be addressed directly.

Gross output versus value added

Value added is frequently used as the output measure despite the greater intuitive appeal of gross output. After all, under the latter concept, the output of a baker is loaves of bread, not value added in baking. Probably value added has been employed because it is thought that less data are required for its measurement, but as we shall see this is an illusion. Furthermore, the measure of MFP growth to which a value added concept of output leads turns out to be fatally flawed.

There is no problem in defining nominal value added as:

$$p_V^i V_i = q_i Y_i - p_X^i X_i, \tag{2.15}$$

where V is real value added and p_V is the price of nominal value added. But how should *real* value added itself (hereafter simply value added) be defined? Two methods have been commonly employed, single and double deflation. Single deflation means deflating nominal value added by the price of output (q). At first sight this approach is attractive, as data on intermediate input quantities and prices appear not to be needed. Single deflation however suffers from a fatal drawback. A fall in the relative price of intermediate input can cause a rise in real value added, which confuses a price effect with a quantity effect: with real output and real intermediate input held constant, a fall in intermediate price raises single deflated value added. Single deflation can only be defended if it so happens that the price of output and that of intermediate input rise at the same rate, an obviously unlikely occurrence and one which is certainly not the case for the industries which are the subject of this study.

Double deflation of value added is commonly defined as

$$V_i' = Y_i - X_i. \tag{2.16}$$

But this definition has no theoretical foundation, as can be seen by considering the conditions under which a real value added aggregate can exist. There are two possibilities (Bruno, 1978; Diewert, 1978). First, if the prices of output and intermediate input always rise at the same rate, then we can apply Hicks' composite commodity theorem to (2.15) and conclude that value added exists; but this has just been dismissed as empirically implausible. Second, the production function (2.2) may be separable in capital, labour and time:

$$Y_i = G^i(V_i, X_i), \tag{2.2'}$$

where

$$V_i = V_i(K_i, L_i, t). \tag{2.17}$$

If so, we can differentiate (2.2') to find

$$d \ln V_i / dt = (1/v_V^i)(d \ln Y_i / dt) - (v_X^i / v_V^i)(d \ln X_i / dt), \tag{2.18}$$

where v_V^i is the share of value added in the value of output and $v_V^i + v_X^i = 1$. Equation (2.18) provides a way of measuring value added, since the right-hand side consists only of observable quantities (output, intermediate input and the value shares), though for empirical purposes a discrete (Törnqvist) approximation would be employed. Comparing (2.16) and (2.18), it can readily be seen that the two methods of double deflation will only yield the same result if the prices of output and intermediate input are rising at the same rate (in which case *single* deflation would do just as well).

The upshot of the discussion is that measuring value added by single deflation is invalid, unless output and intermediate input prices happen to be rising at the same rate. Double deflation is superior, though the commonly employed method of double deflation is incorrect.[12] When double deflation is done correctly, the data requirements are just as great as for the gross output method.

To make sense, the value added method of measuring MFP growth requires that a value added aggregate exists. Even if this condition is satisfied, there is a further objection to the use of value added – it gives a distorted view of inter-industry differences in productivity growth rates. In fact, MFP growth as measured by the value added method will systematically exceed the measure based on gross output by a factor equal to the ratio of gross output to value added, as was first shown by Domar (1961), though the result has been periodically rediscovered. Since this ratio varies considerably across industries, not only will the average MFP growth rate be higher when measured by the value added method, but inter-industry comparisons will also be hopelessly distorted. This proposition can be proved as follows, using continuous time for simplicity.

According to the value added method, MFP growth (μ_i') is, from (2.17), given by

$$\mu_i' \equiv \partial \ln V_i / \partial t$$
$$= d \ln V_i / dt - (v_K^i / v_V^i)(d \ln K_i / dt) - (v_L^i / v_V^i)(d \ln L_i / dt), \qquad (2.19)$$

where as usual elasticities (in this case, of value added with respect to capital and labour) have been equated to market shares: thus v_K^i / v_V^i is the share of profits in value added. What is the relationship between μ_i' and MFP growth measured by the gross output method (μ_i)? Using (2.4) and (2.18), we find

$$\mu_i' = (1/v_V^i)\mu_i, \qquad (2.20)$$

as asserted. In other words, two industries could have the same rate of MFP growth measured on a gross output basis, but different rates measured on a value added basis, if the proportion of materials in total costs differed. Since the production function (2.2), of which the value added form (2.2′) is just a special case, underlies both measures, this seems counter-intuitive. For these reasons therefore, the value added method has not been employed at the industry level in this study. However, when we come to consider aggregate manufacturing in chapter

5, the value added method will be considered further and estimates using value added will be presented, though again other methods will turn out to be preferable.

ISSUES IN THE MEASUREMENT OF OUTPUT AND INPUTS

Having outlined the theory, it is now time to consider the data sources employed to put the theory into practice. Before doing so, it should be stressed that what follows is only an outline. The interested reader can find further details in the Appendices.[13] Also, because of the interest which attaches to capital, the next chapter is devoted to a fuller justification of both the approach to the measurement of capital input adopted here and the sensitivity of the estimates to variation in the assumptions.

The primary source for the estimates of MFP growth rates is the Census of Production, from which data on the nominal values of output and inputs by industry were obtained. These data had to be supplemented by additional sources to convert from nominal to real quantities and to estimate stocks and returns to capital. In addition, it was considered necessary to adjust some of the nominal values to be consistent with the theoretical framework outlined above.

The Census of Production was published for the years 1954, 1958, 1963, 1968 and annually from 1970; the latest year for which data were available at the time the estimation stage of the study was completed was 1986. The starting date for the study is 1954, since before that date producer price indices were constructed on a quite different and less detailed basis. Were it not for this, 1948 would have been chosen as the starting date, since prior to then the Census ceases to be at all comparable with later years. Growth rates of output, inputs and MFP were estimated for the periods between the data years in the 1950s and 1960s (1954–8, 1958–63 and 1963–8) and for the periods 1968–73, 1973–6, 1976–9, 1979–82 and 1982–6. Both 1973 and 1979 are cyclical peaks so that estimates were required for those years and for 1986. The years 1976 and 1982 were also included in the data set since they provide some information on the cyclical pattern of the variables. There are thus estimated growth rates for eight time periods within the overall span of 32 years, 1954–86.

The Census of Production covers (in addition to manufacturing) mining and quarrying, energy and water, and construction. The 'industries' of this study are in most cases the Minimum List Headings (MLH) of the 1968 Standard Industrial Classification (SIC), though in some cases, where the census gives data at a more detailed level, sub-headings of an MLH have been employed. A full list of the industries included in the study, together with their titles, is in Appendix A. The number of industries which it is possible to distinguish is constrained by (amongst other things) the number covered by the Census, which has tended to increase over time, since some headings were sub-divided during the lifetime of this version of the SIC. The criterion was to select the maximum number of industries for which data consistent over time can be constructed. This proved to provide 137 industries in manufacturing, with a further eight in mining, energy and water. Construction, a single MLH under the 1968 SIC, was excluded, on the grounds that the employment figures were too dubious. In practice the estimates are nearly all for manufacturing, due to various difficulties in obtaining the requisite data for the non-manufacturing industries. The maximum number of industries for which MFP growth rates could be obtained was 133 (for the periods after 1973). It proved possible to make MFP growth estimates for 124 manufacturing industries for all of the eight periods.

A major problem in producing estimates over such a long span of time is changes in the SIC. The Census of 1954 was originally produced under the 1948 SIC and those of 1958 and 1963 under the 1958 SIC; the Censuses of 1968 and 1970–79 were produced under the 1968 SIC. Fortunately, the Business Statistics Office subsequently published a volume in which the earlier Censuses were reclassified to the 1968 SIC (BSO, 1978). Reasonably consistent data are thus available from 1954 to 1979. The principle difficulty is posed by the changeover from the 1968 to the 1980 SIC. From 1980 onwards Census data have been published exclusively in accordance with the 1980 SIC which is more detailed than the 1968 one; for example, within manufacturing, there are some 206 activity headings (AH) in the former compared with about 137 MLH in the latter. The greater detail in the 1980 SIC implied that it was more sensible to reclassify from AH to MLH rather than the other way round. Fortunately, the Central Statistics Office (CSO) has published a 'reconciliation' between the two classifications (CSO, 1980a) which shows for each AH the one or more MLH to which it corresponds. This, together with the fact that the 1979 Census was published separately in accordance with each SIC, enabled reclassification from AH to MLH; details of the reclassification algorithm and the computer programs used can be found in Appendix C.

Output

The output definitions in the Census are as follows:

GROSS OUTPUT = value of sales *plus* the change in stocks of work in progress and of goods on hand for sale

NET OUTPUT   = GROSS OUTPUT *minus* purchases of
                          materials and fuel and of industrial ser-
                          vices *plus* the changes in stocks of mater-
                          ials and fuel
GROSS VALUE ADDED = NET OUTPUT *minus* the cost of non-
                          industrial services.

The basis of the calculations is GROSS OUTPUT. But there are a
number of problems with Census definitions of output. Firstly, they are
not consistent with those used in either the national accounts or the
input–output tables in that they are gross of stock appreciation. Secondly,
gross output includes intra-industry purchases within total purchases and
intra-industry sales within total sales, thus leading to a double counting
problem. Thirdly, Census figures add the value of excise taxes on sales to,
and subtract the value of subsidies from, the value of output (note
however that the Census excludes VAT from the value of both sales and
purchases); this is inconsistent with a factor cost definition of output. In
the production function framework outlined above, the quantity of
output produced should be attributable to quantities of inputs. Real
output, as measured by nominal output deflated by a price index, should
not be inflated by nominal factors such as stock appreciation or by double
counting and should be measured at factor cost. Accordingly, three
adjustments have been made to the Census figures of nominal gross
output to allow for (i) stock appreciation; (ii) excise payments and subsidies; and (iii) intra-industry purchases. These adjustments will be outlined in turn; a more detailed account is in Appendix D.

(i) Stock appreciation
The Census gives the book value, at (for most though not all establishments) the end of the Census year, of three sorts of stocks or inventories: 'Materials, Stores and Fuel', 'Work in Progress', and 'Goods on
Hand for Sale', the latter two usually being aggregated together. It also
records the increase over the course of the year in the value of these stocks.
Both gross and net output as defined in the Census are gross of stock
appreciation, that is, part of the nominal value of output is represented by
the 'increase in the value of stocks' rather than the 'value of the physical
increase in stocks', the latter being the concept employed in the national
accounts. The adjustment for stock appreciation is conceptually similar to
the one used in the national accounts, and involves multiplying the value
of the three types of stocks listed above at the beginning of a period by the
proportional change in an appropriate price index during the course of
that period. The resulting estimates of stock appreciation in 'Goods on
Hand for Sale' and 'Work in Progress' are subtracted from gross output.

When developing the estimates of value added, appreciation in stocks of 'Materials, Stores and Fuel' is also subtracted.

(ii) Excise payments and subsidies

The industries most affected by excise payments are naturally the tobacoo and alcoholic drink industries. Also a number of the food industries were affected by both excise payments and subsidies, for example, bacon curing, meat and fish products, sugar, bread and flour confectionery and cocoa and chocolate confectionery. Data on the nominal values of excise payments and subsidies are available in the Census of Production volumes. The producer price indices for the above products also include duties; to be consistent with the adjustment to nominal output, it is necessary to exclude these taxes from the price indices (and to include subsidies). This is the approach adopted by Jorgenson *et al.* (1987) where they adjust the deflators by dividing by one plus the indirect tax rate. The deflators were adjusted by multiplying the producer price indices by one minus the ratio of the excise payments to gross output (one plus the ratio for subsidies), rather than by attempting to estimate excise tax rates.

(iii) Intra-industry purchases

The most important and most difficult adjustment to gross ouptut is to exclude purchases by one establishment from another in the same industry. The statistical unit in the Census is the establishment, that is, all productive activities carried out at a single address. If the output of one establishment is used as an input by another establishment classified to the same industry then this is included both in the value of final sales and in purchases of materials. The classic example is the motor vehicles industry, MLH 381, which includes both establishments producing finished cars and establishments producing components used in their construction.

It is obvious that inclusion of intra-industry purchases means that the Census gross output figures will be sensitive to changes in the degree of vertical integration of an MLH in a way which has nothing to do with changes in the production capabilities of the industry. This dependence of the measure of output on the structure of the industry is unsatisfactory. However, even if the structure of the industry is not changing, the inclusion of intra-industry purchases will bias the MFP growth rate calculations since the share of materials is overestimated at the expense of the shares of both capital and labour. The cost of the final goods producer of the components bought within the industry is included in both the capital and labour used in the components section and in its purchases of these components, under the Census definitions of both gross output and materials.

In view of the above objections, it was considered necessary to attempt to estimate the importance of own purchases within each MLH. Fortunately, table D of the input–output tables, which shows purchases by each industry group from itself, can form the basis of such an estimate, at least for selected years, that is, 1968, 1974, 1979 and 1984 when such tables were published. For a large number of MLH the adjustment to gross output was estimated as one minus the ratio of own purchases to gross output (including own purchases), this ratio being taken from the input–output tables. For other industries, which were not separately distinguished in the input–output tables, recourse was had to the regular 'Purchases Inquiries' (conducted as part of the Census), supplemented by information on imported inputs from table C of the input–output tables. In this way, estimates of the ratio of intra-industry purchases to gross output were produced for the years 1968, 1974, 1979 and 1984. Estimates for 1973 and 1976 were produced by interpolation, and for 1986 by extrapolating from 1984. The 1968 ratios were used for 1954, 1958 and 1963. A fuller account will be found in Appendix D.

Output prices

The producer price indices for home sales, formerly wholesale price indices, published in various issues of *The Annual Abstract of Statistics* and *British Business*, were used to deflate nominal gross output; the CSO also supplied some unpublished price indices for the earlier years, though sadly, some of the data once available has now apparently been destroyed. Unfortunately the CSO did not publish deflators for a significant number of industries which included shipbuilding, aerospace, motor cycles, some of the chemicals industries and some MLH in electrical engineering, including computers. Wherever an MLH output price index was lacking, the general approach was to use the Order price, which, except for Order X (Shipbuilding and marine engineering), is available throughout the period studied up till 1979. After 1979, any missing prices were supplied from the (SIC80) 2-digit price indices. Of course, where an Order price has to be used, the quality of our estimates must be lower.[14]

In some cases it proved possible to use other sources to estimate an MLH level price index. Official producer price indices are only available for the food industries (MLH 211–229/2) from 1974. Estimates for 1973 and 1968 were produced by making use of retail prices. The procedure used was to regress each producer price on the corresponding retail price(s) and the index for all food industries for the years from 1974 to 1986. The resulting equations were then used to extrapolate back to 1968.

Producer price indices on an AH basis for the years 1979–86 were reclassified to an MLH basis, using 1979 gross output as weights (see

Appendix C), and then spliced onto the MLH series in 1979. Further details on the price indices will be found in Appendix E.

Intermediate input

The Census allows two types of intermediate input to be distinguished: (1) materials and fuel purchased from production industries, agriculture and utilities and from abroad; and (2) non-industrial services. The former was calculated as the difference between gross output (adjusted for stock appreciation, excise payments and intra-industry purchases), and net output (similarly adjusted). Therefore, the estimates of purchases of materials and fuel exclude intra-industry purchases. Non-industrial services include the cost of professional services, payments for transport, communications and royalties. They equal the Census definition of non-industrial services, except that payments for the hire of plant and equipment, rent of buildings, bank charges and commercial insurance premiums are excluded. The excluded items were considered to form part of profits (the return to capital).

Prices of intermediate input

(1) Materials and fuel

Disaggregated price indices for materials and fuel were published by the CSO back to 1974; these were on an AH basis. After reclassification to an MLH basis using purchases as weights, these were used for the years after 1974. Unfortunately very little detailed information on such prices exists prior to 1974. It was considered inappropriate to use prices for Orders of the 1968 SIC for the MLH within each Order, as the CSO nets out all intra-industry transactions in calculating these price indices; hence official materials and fuel price indices at the Order level cover only items purchased from industries outside the Order.

Instead the information on industry purchases from the input–output tables was used to construct alternative price indices. The procedure used was in two stages. The first constructed a price index for materials and fuel purchased from *domestic* sources by weighting the prices of each input–output group's purchases by the shares of each item in the total value of that group's domestic purchases. The producer price indices for home sales were used to measure the prices of items purchased and the 1974 domestic purchases matrix (from the 1974 input–output tables) was used to measure the shares.

In view of the very large rise in the prices of imports of intermediate commodities in the early 1970s, it was considered essential to make a separate calculation for imports of materials and fuel. In the single year between 1973 and 1974, the producer price index for the output of manufacturing as a whole rose by 24 per cent whereas the corresponding index for materials and fuel purchased (a large part of which is made up of imports) increased by 50 per cent. The import component of the price index was calculated as a weighted average of individual import prices, with the weights being taken from the commodity × commodity import matrix of the 1974 input–output tables. Prices of imports, where available, were taken either from the 'Price indices of commodities wholly or mainly imported into the UK' in the *Annual Abstract of Statistics* or were calculated from unit values of imports using data in *Overseas Trade Statistics of the United Kingdom*. To maintain consistency of the shares, the producer price index (home sales) was used if no import price information was available, which occurred mainly in the clothing and engineering industries.

Finally, the materials and fuel price index was calculated as a weighted average of the domestic and the import components, the weights being the shares of each component in total purchases, the latter taken again from the 1974 input–output tables. The price indices so derived were for the groups distinguished in the input–output tables; the group price index was assumed to apply to all MLH within a group.[15] The prices were then spliced on to the published indices in 1974.

As a check, our price indices were aggregated up to the Order level (using value added weights) in order to compare them with the Order-level indices which the CSO publishes. The latter, as stated above, give no weight to prices of goods purchased by one industry from another within the same order. For the period 1973–6, when prices of imported materials were rising much faster than those of home-produced goods, it was found, as we would expect, that our indices rose less rapidly than the CSO's, usually by about 2–3 percentage points per annum. However, in some cases the difference between the two sets of estimates was rather larger than could plausibly be assigned to this cause. Hence for this period (1973–6) the estimated growth rates of intermediate input (and consequently the derived estimates of MFP growth) are probably subject to a greater than normal margin of error.

(2) Non-industrial services

No producer price indices exist to cover non-industrial services. A price index for this item was constructed by weighting implicit deflators for financial services, transport and communication (derived from the Blue Book) by their shares in aggregate manufacturing purchases of these inputs; the weights were taken from the 1979 input–output tables.

Labour input

Labour input, for each type of worker, is measured by annual hours, which are computed as the product of numbers employed, weekly hours and weeks worked per year. The share of each type of worker is the wage bill of that type (hourly earnings times annual hours) divided by the total wage bill of all types of workers. Nine types of worker have been distinguished, five manual and four non-manual. The five manual types are: (1) full-time males, aged 21 and over; (2) full-time females, aged eighteen and over; (3) part-time females, aged eighteen and over; (4) males aged less than 21 and (5) females aged under 18. The four non-manual types are (1) males; (2) full-time females; (3) part-time females and (4) working proprietors. The overall split between manual and non-manual workers for each industry comes from the Census of Production, which gives us the wage bill and the employment level of 'operatives' and 'administrative, technical and clerical' (ATC) workers. 'Working proprietors' are a small, residual category. The Census of Production figures for wage bills and employment served as control totals.

Manual workers were split into their five groups using information from the 'Annual inquiry into earnings and hours of manual workers', carried out by the Department of Employment; earnings and hours of each group were derived from the same source. Unfortunately, much less information is available for non-manuals. These were split into types using proportions derived from the Census of Employment. To achieve comparability with the earlier years, it was necessary to use a single hourly earnings series and a single weekly hours series for each type of non-manual worker; that is, no variation across industries was possible. These series, which are averages over all index of production industries, were taken from the New Earnings Survey from 1973 onwards and extrapolated backwards using *manual* earnings and hours, except that working proprietors were assumed to earn the average wage of ATC workers (taken from the Census of Production). A single series for annual weeks worked, which draws on the work of Matthews *et al.* (1982), was used. It allows for time lost due to strikes, sickness and holidays and shows a steady decline in weeks worked per year from 46.3 in 1954 to 42.3 in 1986.

It would have been desirable to break each of the labour types down further by educational level. In principle it would be possible to do something along these lines making use of the Labour Force Survey and the Census of Population, but the resources available for the study did not permit this. Any effect on productivity arising from a change in the average educational level within each of the labour types will therefore be subsumed within the estimate of the growth of multi-factor productivity. In gauging the importance of this omission, it should be noted that only a minority of the UK population has any post-compulsory qualification whatsoever. The main difference between individuals arises from age, older individuals having left school earlier when the minimum school-leaving age was lower – the school-leaving age was raised from fourteen to fifteen in 1947 and from fifteen to sixteen in 1973.[16] There is also the vexed question of the quality of schooling received by those who leave full-time education at the earliest opportunity. If, as some suspect, the quality has fallen in recent years, this should be offset against the increase in quantity (years of schooling).[17]

Further details of the methodology for calculating labour input are in Appendix F.

Capital input

Capital input growth is estimated as a Törnqvist index of five types of asset. Three kinds of fixed capital are distinguished – plant & machinery; buildings & land; and vehicles – and two kinds of inventories – materials, stores & fuel; and work in progress and goods on hand for sale.

Fixed capital

As chapter 3 is devoted to the issue of capital stock measurement, only a brief account will be given here. The Census of Production presents data on the nominal value of investment in three types of fixed asset: plant and machinery, buildings[18] and vehicles. These data form the basis of the estimates of capital stocks disaggregated to the MLH level. To convert investment flows into stocks a variant of the perpetual inventory method (PIM), also used by the CSO in their capital stock estimates which are at a higher level of aggregation, is employed. Nominal values of investment were deflated using the same deflators as used by the CSO (see Appendix B for details). The estimates of the rental prices of fixed capital services are dual to the PIM estimates of the stocks, as they should be for logical consistency (Jorgenson, 1989).

The PIM calculates the so-called 'gross' capital stock as the sum of past investments minus the sum of past retirements, which in turn depends on the life of the asset. For the 'net' capital stock, depreciation is also subtracted from surviving assets. In practice there is little information on the service lives of assets. Until recently the CSO assumptions on asset lives were based on the work of Dean (1964); then in 1983 the CSO revised its estimates downwards referring to (unpublished) 'discussions with manufacturers' as its basis for doing so (CSO, 1985, p. 201). These new, lower estimates have been employed throughout. Thus buildings are assumed to have an average life of 60 years and vehicles of ten years; for plant and machinery, the average life varies from 23–30 years, depending on the industry. Note that the investment series are for acquisitions net of disposals, so that where (as would usually be the case for example for vehicles) an asset is sold before the end of its economic life, the estimates will reflect this fact. But 'disposals', which are recorded separately in the

Census of Production, do not include scrapping, as the introductory notes to the Summary Report of each Census make clear, hence the necessity to make assumptions about asset life.

The MFP calculations employ a 'net' capital stock concept, as theory would suggest is preferable. Depreciation is assumed to be exponential (or geometric). The annual depreciation factor is e^{-d} where d is the sum of two components. The first component is to take account of retirement or scrapping, and is equal to the inverse of average asset life, where (as stated above) the latter is set equal to the revised (lower) CSO assumptions for each asset type. It is thus being assumed that retirements (or scrapping) are distributed around the mean retirement age in accordance with an exponential distribution. The second component is to take account of ageing or obsolescence and is derived from the work of Hulten and Wykoff (1981a and 1981b). Hulten and Wykoff's studies of the prices of secondhand capital assets in the US support exponential decay as a good approximation to the actual pattern of decline in the prices of surviving secondhand assets; exponential decay is also a good approximation when retired assets are included as well. Unfortunately there have been no comparable studies for the UK along the lines of Hulten and Wykoff's work, so in the absence of any direct evidence on depreciation for the UK, the latter's US estimates were used. The combination of Hulten and Wykoff's ageing (or obsolescence) estimates and the CSO's asset life assumptions produces rates of total economic depreciation which are quite high: the geometric rate is 2.91 per cent per annum for buildings, 28.1 per cent per annum for vehicles and varies between 4.46 per cent and 39.2 per cent for plant and machinery (see chapter 3, table 3.4).

Inventories

The Census allows two types of inventory to be distinguished: it gives the nominal, end-period book value of, first, the sum of Work in Progress and Goods on hand for Sale, and, second, Materials, Stores and Fuel. To convert to real stocks of inventories, we again follow, with a slight modification, the methodology in Jorgenson *et al.* (1987) which was based in turn on earlier work by the US Bureau of Economic Analysis (BEA) as outlined in the December 1972 issue of *Survey of Current Business*.

The estimation procedure was to calculate the nominal investment in inventories in each year as the difference between the book value of stocks at the beginning and end of each year. These were then deflated by the appropriate price index (wholesale prices for goods and materials prices for materials) and cumulated from some initial year. An adjustment for stock appreciation is necessary since the end-year value of inventory includes items acquired at different prices over the course of the year. If we let S_t denote the nominal values of inventories (adjusted for stock appreciation) and P_t denote the price index then at period t the real value of stocks of inventories is given by:

$$S_T = (S_0/P_0) + \Sigma_{t=1}^{t=T} (\Delta S_t/P_t).$$

This formula was used to calculate the real stocks of inventories in the years after 1970, using the real value of stocks in 1970 as the base value. This calculation requires annual data on changes in the nominal values of inventories which are not available prior to 1970. Instead we have to make do with data for the years for which the Census of Production was available, that is, 1954, 1958, 1963 and 1968. For those years the real stocks of inventories were calculated as the end-year nominal value of stocks deflated by that year's price index. The difference between this calculation and that given by the equation above is negligible if price changes are small or if there is not much variation in the real value of inventories from year to year. Fortunately, we have annual data on inventories in the period after 1970 when price changes were very large.

Rental prices of capital assets

The rental prices of all five capital assets were estimated in accordance with equation (2.10). The sources were the same as for the corresponding stocks. In practice, the main difficulty arose in estimating the nominal return r_i from equation (2.11), since using *actual* capital gains frequently produced negative estimates. Experiments with a number of specifications for capital gains, details of which are given in Appendix G, suggested that use of a three-year moving average of asset prices was most likely to produce reasonable results.

In the formula for the rate of return, gross profits are equal to Net Output *minus* wages and salaries *minus* employers' National Insurance contributions *minus* non-industrial services, where each component is net of any of the adjustments to output described above. The present value of tax allowances and grants on a unit of investment in asset type k was calculated using the methodology in Melliss and Richardson (1975) and Kelly and Owen (1985) and data from Inland Revenue Statistics.

The return to each type of asset is the product of its rental price and the quantity of the asset. The share of each asset type is the return as a proportion of gross profit. An advantage of this approach is that it is consistent with control totals like gross profits. It preserves the accounting relationship that the total value of capital services (sum over all assets of rental price times asset quantity) should equal total profits.

The asset shares just described were used to construct the Törnqvist index of capital stock growth (equation (2.8′)). A more detailed account of the estimation of rental prices is in Appendix G.

Shares of the inputs

The shares of the inputs – intermediate, labour and capital – were calculated using, respectively, nominal expenditure on materials, fuel and non-industrial services; the wage bill plus employers' National Insurance contributions; and gross profits, each taken as a fraction of nominal gross output, the latter adjusted as described above. By construction, the shares sum to one.

3

ESTIMATING THE STOCK OF FIXED CAPITAL

INTRODUCTION

The purpose of this chapter is to discuss the method of estimating fixed capital stocks in manufacturing at the industry level. Estimates will be presented for three types of assets – plant & machinery, buildings, and vehicles. The method is based on, though not identical to, that employed by the CSO, namely the Perpetual Inventory Method (PIM).[1] It proved possible to develop estimates for 140 industries (MLH) classified by the 1968 SIC.[2] The present estimates assume that assets are subject to depreciation at a geometric (or exponential) rate. The service life and the rate of depreciation differ between asset types. As will be made clear below, geometric decay is supported by the rather sparse empirical evidence available in this area. It also has great theoretical advantages, which accounts for its choice in the numerous productivity studies of Jorgenson and his collaborators (for example, Jorgenson *et al.*, 1986 and 1987). First, it allows one to estimate the dual, rental price of capital in a particularly simple form; second, it allows the aggregation of investment of different vintages, again in a simple way, as will be explained below.

The CSO presents its own capital stock estimates on two different bases, 'gross stock' and 'net stock'. Under the former, retirement of assets at the end of their assumed service lives is allowed for but otherwise depreciation is ignored; under the latter, assets are assumed to depreciate in a straight line manner over their service lives.[3] The 'net stock' estimates are the closest in concept to the ones developed here, but the straight line depreciation assumption is different. The CSO publishes capital stock estimates for sixteen groups in manufacturing on both a gross and a net stock basis; they publish no industry-level estimates. Other estimates of the capital stock in manufacturing have been made by Armstrong (1979) and Allard (1982). Armstrong's estimates were for 23 groups within manufacturing over the period 1947–76. Allard's were for 133 industries in manufacturing over the period 1947–79. His study is therefore the closest to the present one. However, Allard's study differs from the present one in his assumptions about service lives (his are the same as those of, at the time of his study, the CSO), and in his assumptions about depreciation; also, his estimates stop in 1979.

As will be argued below, the most satisfactory concept of the capital stock for growth accounting purposes is a net one, provided that depreciation is properly measured. The estimates of net stocks use US findings on depreciation rates, coupled with UK assumptions about the service lives of assets. The estimates are tested for sensitivity by means of different assumptions about depreciation and by studying perturbations in a steady state growth model.

The plan of this chapter is as follows. The following section considers the issue of aggregation over different vintages of capital. It is demonstrated that a theoretically consistent capital aggregate weights each vintage in accordance with its rental price. If depreciation is geometric, this is equvalent to weighting by new and secondhand *asset* prices. In the third section, the assumptions required by the PIM are considered, in particular the length of service lives and the pattern of depreciation. The fourth section examines issues in the measurement of investment; in particular, methods used to interpolate and extrapolate investment from the Census of Production for years prior to 1970 (when annual series were not available), are discussed, together with the treatment of financial leasing. The fifth section assesses the sensitivity of the estimates to differences in the assumptions about service lives and ageing. The sixth section looks at the estimates for the controversial period of the 1980s and considers whether the PIM needs modification in view of the widespread belief that the early 1980s saw large-scale premature scrapping. The final section summarises the conclusions.

AGGREGATION OVER VINTAGES, DEPRECIATION AND OBSOLESCENCE

If all capital were homogenous, and if capital assets were subject only to physical deterioration at a constant, geometric (or exponential) rate, a rate moreover which was independent of usage, then the measurement of the capital stock would present no theoretical difficulties. Controversies over how to measure capital are, of course, of long standing and there is no space to review the whole field.[4] But something must be said by way of theoretical justification of the procedures followed here, before getting on to the no less real empirical difficulties faced by workers in this field. As was shown in chapter 2, aggregation over different types of capital is not a problem (at least, not in principle), but the issue of aggregating over different vintages of the same type of capital needs more discussion.

The evolution of each type of capital is represented by equation (2.9), which requires us to estimate the rate of depreciation. Now although assets depreciate in value over their economic life, this may not represent physical deterioration, that is, a loss of productive capacity due solely to ageing. Certainly one reason for the prices of secondhand assets to decline is obsolescence. Some might claim (for example, Scott, 1989 and 1992; see also the exchange between Denison, 1991 and Scott, 1991) that obsolescence is the *principal* reason for depreciation. If so, is it right to deduct depreciation from the constant price estimates of the capital stock? After all, obsolescence just means that the profitability of earlier vintages of a certain type of asset is lowered by the appearance of newer, improved versions. But the productive capacity of the earlier vintages is unchanged, unlike if assets deteriorate with age. So depreciation due to physical deterioration would seem to merit different treatment from depreciation due to obsolescence. Perhaps surprisingly, this is not the case, as the following argument shows.

Consideration of equation (2.9) shows that the stock of asset type k is to be measured as a weighted sum of past investments:

$$K_{ik}(t) = \Sigma_{v=0}^{v=m} (1 - \delta_{ik})^v I_{ik}(t - v), \tag{3.1}$$

where m is the age of the oldest vintage still in use in industry i. In other words, all vintages in use must be aggregated together. The fundamental result on the conditions under which different vintages of capital can be aggregated together is due to Fisher (1965). In discrete time, suppose that there is a constant-returns-to-scale production function for each vintage v of capital, $h^v(\cdot)$, relating output at time t produced from vintage v capital, $Y(t,v)$, to vintage v capital, $I(v)$, and to labour employed at t on vintage v capital, $L(t,v)$:[5]

$$Y(t,v) = L(t,v)h^v(I(v)/L(t,v)). \qquad v = t, \ldots, t - m$$

The capital aggregation problem is as follows: assuming that labour is allocated optimally across vintages (which implies that the marginal product of labour is the same across vintages), does there exist a function relating total output to total labour and aggregate capital? Such a function would have the form

$$Y(t) = \Sigma_v Y(t,v) = F(L(t), K(I(t), \ldots, I(t - m))), \tag{3.2}$$

where $L(t) = \Sigma_v L(t,v)$. Fisher (1965) showed that necessary and sufficient conditions for the existence of such a function are that the vintage production functions can be written

$$h^v(I(v)/L(t,v)) = h(b_{t-v}I(v)/L(t,v)), \qquad b_{t-v} > 0, \text{ all } v$$

in which case the capital aggregate is (from Hulten, 1990, equations (1) and (8), and using the fact that the marginal product of labour is the same across vintages):

$$K(t) = K(I(t), \ldots, I(t - m))$$
$$= I(t) + (b_1/b_0) I(t - 1) + \ldots + (b_{t-m}/b_0) I(t - m). \tag{3.3}$$

Cost minimisation implies that capital of each vintage will be rented up to the point that the value of its marginal product is equal to the rental price. Let $p_K(t,v)$ be the rental price at time t of an asset of vintage v. Partially differentiating (3.2) and using (3.3),

$$p_K(t,v)/p_K(t,t) = b_{t-v}/b_0, \qquad \text{all } v. \qquad (3.4)$$

If the b_{t-v} decline in a geometric fashion, then a similar relationship holds for the asset prices, $P_K(t,v)$:[6]

$$P_K(t,v)/P_K(t,t) = b_{t-v}/b_0, \qquad \text{all } v.$$

In other words, if secondhand asset prices are observed to decline geometrically with age (due to a combination of obsolescence and physical deterioration), then we can use these rates of price decline to estimate the ratios b_{t-v}/b_0 and so to construct the capital aggregate (3.3).

As a result of these formal arguments, we can now see why the intuitive argument, that depreciation due to obsolescence should be treated differently from depreciation due to physical deterioration, is incorrect. Older capital only becomes obsolete when better capital becomes available, better either because it produces more output for the same sacrifice of consumption, or because it requires less of other inputs. In either case, it is right to give less weight to older capital in measuring the capital stock. Under certain assumptions, the correct weights are given by market prices.[7]

In addition to the stock of asset k, we need also to describe how the share of asset k in total profits (the $\bar{v}_{Kk}$ of equation (2.8$'$)) is to be calculated, in order to complete the description of how the contribution of each type of capital to output growth is to be measured. The profits generated by any asset type are (reverting to the notation of chapter 2 by adding subscript k to denote asset type k and subscript or superscript i to denote industry i):

$$\Sigma_v p^i_{Kk}(t,v) I_{ik}(v) = p^i_{Kk}(t,t) \Sigma_v [p^i_{Kk}(t,v)/p^i_{Kk}(t,t)] I_{ik}(v)$$
$$= p^i_{Kk}(t,t) K_{ik}(t),$$

from (3.3) and (3.4). Thus the share of asset type k in total profits is the rental price of a new asset of type k times the quantity of asset k, divided by total profits. In turn, the rental price of a new asset of type k can be estimated from the corresponding asset price using the Jorgenson-Hall formula (equation (2.10)), on the assumption that depreciation is geometric. Since in practice rental prices are usually not observed but the prices of new assets are, this relationship is useful.[8]

CAPITAL STOCK METHODOLOGY

The Perpetual Inventory Method

The Perpetual Inventory Method (PIM) of estimating the capital stock can be concisely described in the following formula:

$$K_{ik}(t) = \Sigma_{v=t_0}^{v=t} S_{ik}(t,v)\, \phi_{ik}(t,v)\, I_{ik}(v), \qquad t \geq t_0 \qquad (3.5)$$

which is a generalisation of (3.1). Here $S_{ik}(t,v)$ is the proportion of investment in asset type k made at time v which survives to time t, and $\phi_{ik}(t,v)$ is the 'efficiency' at time t of an asset installed at time v which has survived to t, as a fraction of its 'efficiency' when new. The term 'efficiency' is meant, following the argument of the previous section, to cover both a loss of physical efficiency with age and also obsolescence. t_0 is the starting date for the PIM calculation. The choice of t_0 is a practical matter, determined by the availability of investment data – following the CSO, t_0 is 1852 for buildings, 1888 for plant & machinery and 1936 for vehicles. The form of the 'survival' function $S_{ik}(t,v)$ depends on the assumptions made about the average service life of an asset type, and the pattern of retirement around the average service life. The form of the efficiency function $\phi_{ik}(t,v)$ depends on what is assumed about depreciation: does it cover only physical ageing or does it include obsolescence also? Each of these factors will be considered in turn.

Service lives

As far as investment in plant & machinery is concerned, the CSO's approach, followed here, is to divide it into 'classes', each class having a different assumed life. The proportion of investment assumed to go into each class, given in table 3.1, is based on the work of Redfern (1955) and Dean (1964), who in turn derived their estimates from information on depreciation allowances for tax purposes from Inland Revenue (1953), and flows of purchases by industries from the mechanical engineering sector, derived from the 1958 Census of Production. No attempt is made to distinguish different types of buildings; at any moment, the same service life is assumed for buildings in all industries. A similar assumption is made for vehicles.

How plausible are the CSO assumptions of fixed proportions of investment in each class of plant and machinery? As stated above, these proportions were derived from rather crude data from the 1950s. Table 3.2 summarises information on the shares of investment in plant and machinery from the input–output tables. The shares of each asset type do show considerable variation across time in each industry but it is the increasing share of office machinery, whose service life is likely to be

Table 3.1. *Proportion of gross investment in plant & machinery devoted to each class of asset, by sector (%)*

Sector	A	B	Class C	D	E
1. Food, drink & tobacco (MLH 211–240)	2.0	0.0	22.0	68.0	8.0
2. Coal & petroleum (MLH 261–263)	3.4	2.7	6.8	56.9	30.2
3. Chemicals (MLH 271–279)	3.4	2.7	6.8	56.9	30.2
4. Iron & steel (MLH 311–313)	0.0	13.8	3.7	77.9	4.6
5. Engineering & metals (MLH 109, 321–370, 390–399)	1.4	10.0	20.0	56.5	12.1
6. Vehicles[a] (MLH 380–385)	3.0	0.0	13.0	69.0	15.0
7. Textiles (MLH 411–429)	0.0	0.0	2.6	89.7	7.7
8. Leather, clothing & fur (MLH 431–433, 441–450, 491–499)	0.0	0.0	73.0	4.0	23.0
9. Bricks, pottery & glass (MLH 461–469)	5.0	24.0	19.0	14.0	38.0
10. Timber & furniture (MLH 471–479)	0.0	0.0	76.0	5.0	19.0
11. Paper, printing & publishing (MLH 481–489)	0.0	0.0	4.5	54.5	41.0
12. Stone & slate quarrying (MLH 102/103)	3.0	15.0	31.0	28.0	23.0

Source: Griffin (1976); CSO (unpublished) for MLH 102/103 (assigned to class 23 of SIC 1980).
Note: Class A: Machine tools and instruments
                B: Plant and construction equipment
                C: Office machinery
                D: Shorter-lived industrial machinery
                E: Longer-lived industrial machinery
[a]MLH 380 and 381 are also assumed to invest in 'special tools' with a life of five years.

shorter than other assets, which is more disturbing. However, office machinery represents a relatively small proportion of investment in plant and machinery in most industries.

The service lives assumed for the PIM are given in table 3.3. The 'long' lives correspond to what the CSO used to assume (in their estimates made prior to 1983); the 'short' lives correspond to what they currently assume about newly purchased assets. The central assumption of the present study is that the 'short' lives apply throughout the period: that is, the 'short' lives are used to generate the starting capital stock in 1947 and also the capital stock in all subsequent years up to the last year, 1986. The central assumption is chosen in part because of the doubts expressed by

Table 3.2. *Proportion of gross investment in plant & machinery devoted to types of asset, by sector (%)*

	1968	1974	1979	1984
A. Machine tools & instruments				
1. Food, drink & tobacco	1.9	2.9	0.6	3.6
2. Coal & petroleum & Chemicals	5.1	6.6	2.7	20.8
3. Iron & steel	4.9	14.7	10.0	10.5
4. Engineering & metals	60.6	56.2	49.3	26.5
5. Vehicles	51.1	61.3	51.8	30.2
6. Textiles	1.0	7.5	5.2	8.9
7. Bricks, pottery & glass	NA	11.5	2.5	4.4
8. Timber & furniture	NA	7.5	1.3	1.6
9. Paper, printing & publishing	1.5	3.0	6.1	1.1
10. Clothing, leather and other	NA	11.1	7.3	3.1
Total Manufacturing	21.7	24.4	20.2	15.4
B. Plant & construction equipment				
1. Food, drink & tobacco	23.1	41.5	30.8	3.2
2. Coal & petroleum & Chemicals	70.9	65.3	49.7	41.0
3. Iron & steel	37.7	57.1	19.0	11.9
4. Engineering & metals	18.5	24.9	10.1	8.0
5. Vehicles	37.5	17.0	13.7	2.3
6. Textiles	12.4	14.5	14.4	2.9
7. Bricks, pottery & glass	NA	49.0	63.0	73.2
8. Timber & furniture	NA	20.0	18.2	6.2
9. Paper, printing & publishing	27.3	6.0	13.2	0.6
10. Clothing, leather and other	NA	11.1	17.6	2.6
Total Manufacturing	36.8	34.5	25.7	14.8
C. Office machinery				
1. Food, drink & tobacco	5.8	1.8	10.9	10.4
2. Coal & petroleum & Chemicals	2.5	2.3	11.6	6.9
3. Iron & steel	4.9	2.9	12.2	8.5
4. Engineering & metals	10.2	7.9	13.4	25.1
5. Vehicles	6.8	7.2	10.8	12.1
6. Textiles	3.8	3.8	2.9	0.0
7. Bricks, pottery & glass	NA	1.9	4.2	8.7
8. Timber & furniture	NA	5.0	7.8	6.7
9. Paper, printing & publishing	9.1	3.7	7.3	5.1
10. Clothing, leather and other	NA	3.4	5.3	7.5
Total Manufacturing	6.4	4.4	10.3	12.4
D & E. Industrial machinery				
1. Food, drink & tobacco	69.2	53.8	57.7	82.9
2. Coal & petroleum & Chemicals	20.3	25.7	36.0	31.3
3. Iron & steel	52.5	25.3	58.8	69.1
4. Engineering & metals	10.6	11.0	27.2	40.4
5. Vehicles	4.5	14.4	23.7	55.4
6. Textiles	82.9	74.2	77.6	88.3
7. Bricks, pottery & glass	NA	37.5	30.3	13.6
8. Timber & furniture	NA	67.5	72.7	85.5
9. Paper, printing & publishing	62.1	87.3	73.4	93.2
10. Clothing, leather and other	NA	74.4	69.8	86.8
Total Manufacturing	35.2	36.7	43.7	57.5

Source: Input–output tables.

Table 3.3. *Assumed average service lives, by type of asset (years)*

	'Long'	'Short'
Plant & machinery		
Class A	16	12
B	19	14
C	25	19
D	34	26
E	50	37
Buildings	80	60
Vehicles	10	10

Source: Own assumptions, based on Griffin (1976) and CSO (1985).
Note: In addition to the above assets, the vehicle industries (MLH 380 and 381) are also assumed to invest in 'special tools' whose life is always five years.

Prais (1986) as to whether service lives really have declined after 1970, as the CSO now assumes. In addition, the short life assumption addresses the concern expressed by Smith (1987), who found that the PIM with long lives systematically overestimated the capital stock in comparison with estimates based on the current cost accounts of companies. However, in order to test for sensitivity, estimates were also made using a variety of assumptions about ageing and asset lives (see below and also O'Mahony and Oulton, 1990a).

The CSO's current assumptions about service lives are somewhat different. Up to 1983, their assumptions corresponded to what is called the 'long' assumption here. In their work from 1983 onwards, they have assumed that service lives decline steadily from the 'long' towards the 'short' ones of table 3.3. Theirs might be called a 'vintage wine' assumption. Thus a building constructed in 1889 is assumed to last (on average) for 80 years, so will still appear in the capital stock up till 1969, whereas one built in 1890 is assumed to last for only 76 years on average and will therefore be expected to disappear from the stock after 1966. This approach might be appropriate if physical durability were the crucial factor: just as some vintages of wine keep better than others, the same might be true of plant or buildings. Perhaps in 1889 buildings were built to last but this has been less and less the case thereafter. However, a much more plausible cause of shorter service lives, and the one which is usually cited in this context, is the allegedly increasing pace of change which tends to make all assets become obsolete more rapidly. But if more rapid obsolescence is the cause of shorter service lives, it should affect assets of *all* vintages, not just the more recent ones.[9] Hence the CSO's declining life assumption does not seem a very good way of capturing the possibility that obsolescence has become more rapid in recent years.[10]

In practice, great uncertainty attaches to the assumptions required by the PIM. In particular, information about the service lives of assets is not based on any thorough and up-to-date surveys. For example, until recently the official estimates of service lives were based on the work of Dean (1964); then in 1983 the CSO revised its estimates downwards referring to (unpublished) 'discussions with manufacturers' as its basis for doing so (CSO, 1985, p. 201). Nor is information readily available for other countries which might be used as a check on the British figures; for example, service lives assumed in the US are based on what the Internal Revenue Service thought reasonable in the 1940s. Only Japan apparently does a comprehensive survey of service lives and these are far lower than any suggested for the UK (Blades, 1983).

Even the 'short' life assumptions however may seem at first implausibly long. By contrast we may note that in the US the Bureau of Economic Analysis (BEA), the body responsible for capital stock estimates, assume much shorter lives: typically a 10–20 year life for plant and machinery, with some categories such as office machinery having even shorter lives (eight years), a 27-year life for industrial buildings and a 36-year life for office buildings (Young and Musgrave, 1980, table 1). In defence of our (and the CSO's) assumptions, we can argue that it is perfectly possible for UK lives to be longer than US ones. In any case, the American life assumptions rest on weak foundations, being based on what the Internal Revenue Service allowed for tax purposes in 1942, the so-called 'Bulletin F' lives, somewhat arbitrarily reduced (in most cases) by 15 per cent. Also, in the only case where direct evidence has been gathered, the surveys of the stocks of machine tools done on a similar basis in both countries, the service lives were found to be similar in both countries and closer to the CSO's than to the BEA's assumptions.[11] Finally, we should note that the length of an asset's life is an economic decision, dependent on the input prices and the stage of the business cycle, as has been emphasised by Baily (1981); however, in the absence of solid evidence on asset lives, we are driven back on rather crude assumptions such as those of table 3.3.

Retirement

This study assumes that asset 'mortality' follows an exponential (or geometric) pattern: so that the proportion of a year's investment in a given class of assets surviving after t years is $e^{-t/T}$ where T is the assumed average life.[12] By contrast, the CSO assumes (for their gross stock concept) that assets are scrapped at a uniform rate throughout the interval of plus or minus 20 per cent around the average service life. Thus the investment of a given year in an asset with a service life of, say, twenty years will be scrapped at an even rate between sixteen and 24 years later.

In other words, a uniform distribution of service lives is assumed, the endpoints being the mean life plus or minus 20 per cent. In fact, very little is known about the actual pattern of retirement, so one is forced back on what is 'reasonable'. The CSO's assumption is not based on any survey evidence, nor do there appear to be any non-official studies for the UK, with the exception of Barna (1961), who, basing himself on survey evidence from the 1950s, found a linear pattern of retirement, at least after the first few years. The only American study is very out of date now and was in any case confined to a narrow class of assets (Winfrey, 1935; his main findings are summarised in Marston et al., 1953, chapter 7 and Appendix B).

An item of capital is not necessarily retained till the end of its service life by the firm or even the industry which purchased it. From the point of view of the industry, 'retirement' of an asset may be when the asset is sold, not when it is scrapped. In the case of plant & machinery and vehicles, this is allowed for since the concept of investment is a net one – acquisitions (of old or new assets) less disposals, which is what the Census records. In practice, disposals of plant & machinery as a percentage of acquisitions have been fairly low; they were 4.1 per cent in 1979 for total manufacturing rising to 7.5 per cent in 1981 and falling back to 4.8 per cent in 1985. Prior to 1979 they varied between 3 and 5 per cent.[13] It should be noted that 'disposals' are only recorded for assets which are sold for continued use; disposals for scrap are *not* recorded.[14]

As far as vehicles are concerned, following the CSO a ten-year life is assumed (table 3.3). At first sight this seems excessive given that most of these vehicles are probably passenger cars and trucks. Though the *physical* life of these assets may well be as long as ten years, it seems very unlikely that they are retained for their whole life by the industries which purchased them; cars for example may well be sold after 3–4 years to the personal sector. But once again this is not a problem, since the investment concept used is a net one (acquisition less disposals). In fact, given the very high level of disposals of vehicles it is unlikely that the estimates are sensitive to the service life assumed.

A similar point applies in principle to buildings. However, though the Census has always recorded investment in *new* buildings, it is only since 1963 that it has also recorded separately acquisitions and disposals of land and *existing* buildings. The CSO's own estimates for the stock of buildings only include *new* buildings; in this study, land and existing buildings are included in the stock when the sources allow (that is, after 1970),[15] since a second-hand building is just as much part of the capital stock as a new one. For buildings, disposals as a percentage of total acquisitions (new building work plus acquisitions of land and existing buildings) have been a good bit higher than in the case of the corresponding ratio for plant &

machinery, which no doubt reflects the more active second-hand market available for buildings.[16] From a low of 10 per cent in 1979 the ratio rose to 25.7 per cent in 1983 before falling somewhat to 19.7 per cent in 1985; a similar range of variation can be observed prior to 1979.

Obsolescence and ageing

In their extensive studies of second-hand asset prices, Hulten and Wykoff (1981a and 1981b) found that, for both buildings and plant, prices of surviving assets declined with an asset's age in a manner which could be closely approximated by geometric (or exponential) decay. For industrial buildings they found a pure ageing effect of 1.28 per cent per annum, that is, this is the rate at which the prices of *surviving* buildings were found to decline with age (Hulten and Wykoff, 1981a, table 1). One interpretation of their findings is that the physical efficiency of assets declines with age. This is plausible for assets like cars, where for example rusting may occur irrespective of use, but arguably less so for plant, where the 'light bulb' pattern – unchanged efficiency up till the moment of failure – might seem more likely. However, an alternative, and in many cases more plausible, interpretation of decline in second-hand asset prices is rising efficiency of new assets or, its mirror image, increasing obsolescence of older ones; as Hulten and Wykoff (1981a) remark, this effect is observationally indistinguishable in their data from the effect of physical decay.[17] It should be noted that the exponential pattern of decline which Hulten and Wykoff found cannot be explained simply as the consequence of assets approaching the end of a fixed life (so that the present value of expected future profits from the asset falls with age); if this were the only reason for second-hand asset prices to decline, they would fall at an increasing, not a constant, rate.[18]

Hulten and Wykoff also found that geometric decay was a good approximation to the pattern of *total* depreciation, taking account of both ageing (as revealed by their price studies) and retirement (where they used an assumed pattern similar to that employed in official estimates of US capital stocks). Unfortunately, there have been no recent studies of UK asset prices to parallel those of Hulten and Wykoff for the US.[19] It was therefore decided to adopt the latter's estimates of price decline due to ageing, while retaining the CSO's current assumptions about service lives.[20] Using the CSO's 'short' life assumptions (see table 3.3) and Hulten and Wykoff's estimates of ageing applied to the corresponding asset types in the UK, we obtain the rates of total economic depreciation given in table 3.4; these rates will be used for our preferred estimates of 'net' stocks. In summary, (one minus) the rates in this table correspond to the product $S_{ik}(t,v)\,\phi_{ik}(t,v)$ in equation (3.5) describing the PIM. Note that, though they differ between asset types, they are assumed to be

Table 3.4. *Geometric rates of total economic depreciation (%, p.a.)*

Asset type	Rate
Plant	
'Special tools'[a]	39.20
Class A	18.17
Class B	15.57
Class C	10.32
Class D	6.35
Class E	4.46
Buildings	2.91
Vehicles	28.10

Source: estimated as DBR/T, where DBR, the 'declining balance rate', is derived from Hulten and Wykoff (1981b) and T, the service life, is the 'short' life from table 3.3. Rates include both retirement and ageing (obsolescence). See text for further explanation.
[a]MLH 380 and 381 only.

otherwise the same for all industries and to be constant over time. Though lower than the US ones, the depreciation rates of table 3.4 are nevertheless quite high. For example, using the shares in table 3.1, the annual rate of depreciation of plant and equipment as a whole varies between 7 per cent and 9 per cent across the twelve manufacturing sectors. By way of illustration, a 9 per cent rate of depreciation means that an asset has lost 38 per cent of its original value after five years and 61 per cent after ten years.

ESTIMATION OF ANNUAL REAL INVESTMENT SERIES BY INDUSTRY

In this section the main problems encountered in assembling consistent, annual, investment series in constant prices by industry are discussed. Further details on the sources of the data will be found in Appendix B.

Constructing annual investment series at the industry level

In order to derive estimates of the capital stock by MLH the PIM requires complete series on investment at constant prices. Investment data from the Census of Production are available on a consistent basis only for selected years prior to 1970. For most MLH, data are available for the years 1948, 1949, 1951, 1954, 1958, 1963 and 1968. However, in a significant number of industries no investment information is available prior to 1954 and in a small number of cases investment data is not available before 1958 or 1963. Although annual series on investment are available from 1970 to 1986 for most MLH, for reasons of confidentiality there are missing observations for some MLH and asset types for the years 1978–83.

The methodology used to complete the series differed between the pre-1970 and post-1970 data. In the former case interpolations between actual observations, employing regression techniques, were used to complete the series. Annual investment data from 1948–79 (produced by the CSO) are available for 25 industry 'groups' which in most cases comprise data at the industry Order level but in some cases are at the individual MLH level. The interpolation procedure was similar to that employed by Allard (1982) and involved regressing the share of investment by each MLH in their group total on two explanatory variables; the regression parameter estimates were then used to interpolate between Census years. The explanatory variables were time, designed to capture long-term trends in an industry's share of investment, and labour force proportions, which were included to capture cyclical effects. In practice, since capital stocks cumulate past investment, experiment showed that the choice of interpolation method did not have a very significant effect; after allowing for differences in other assumptions, the present estimates were very similar to those produced by Allard whose sole explanatory variable was time. From 1978 to 1983 the additional information provided by Order totals and aggregate investment over asset types allows the use of the RAS method, developed by Stone (Stone and Brown, 1962) to fill in the missing values.

This procedure yielded annual investment series by MLH from 1948–86. Prior to 1948 investment data at the industry level we are concerned with here do not exist. However, because of the long lives assumed for many assets, the PIM requires us to construct such data. The basis for the extrapolation was unpublished annual series for the three types of assets on eleven industry groups in manufacturing which have been constructed by the CSO; these were apportioned among the industries in the study using the average share of an industry in its group over the period 1948–54. The number of years available between 1948 and 1954 varied between industries; many industries had four years available – 1948, 1949, 1951 and 1954 – but some had only one. Applying these shares an investment series in each asset was constructed for each industry. The plant & machinery series go back to 1888, the buildings series to 1852 and the vehicles one to 1936. For 1920–38, it was possible to improve on the CSO's series by employing the estimates of Feinstein (1965, table 8.01), which are for a larger number of groups.[21]

The group investment data are themselves somewhat speculative and become more so the further we move back in time. So we cannot expect the industry-level figures to represent much more than a reasonable guess at investment prior to 1948. This means that we cannot take our estimates of the capital stock in 1947 by industry very seriously. But the further we move towards the present the less the influence of the pre-1948 data becomes.

Investment deflators

The investment series from the Census are in current prices. Unfortunately, deflators are nothing like as plentiful as would be desirable and this must be regarded as a serious (though unquantifiable) limitation on the accuracy of the estimates. The best situation is with plant & machinery. Here, from 1956 onwards, separate deflators are available for a number of industries or industry groups, the number varying over time. But prior to 1956, only a single deflator is available. For buildings and vehicles, only a single deflator covering all industries is available throughout the period studied. After 1980 (1984 for vehicles) the deflators are taken from the BSO's *Price Index Numbers for Current Cost Accounting*; earlier years use unpublished CSO estimates. For further details, see Appendix B.

Reclassification from the 1980 SIC to the 1968 SIC

From 1948–79 the Census of Production investment series are available under the 1968 SIC. From 1980 on, Census data has been published according to the 1980 SIC. In order to continue the capital stock estimates beyond 1979, it is necessary to reclassify the investment series from the 1980 SIC to the 1968 one. Using the method described in Appendix C, the investment data for 1980–86, which were originally classified by Activity Heading, were reclassified to the same basis as the earlier data, that is, by Minimum List Heading.

Financial leasing

Since the early 1970s financial leasing has become increasingly important. For most economic purposes it is the capital in use in, rather than the capital owned by, an industry which matters. Hence the capital stock estimates include assets leased from financial institutions.[22] The basis for the adjustment for financial leasing is two unpublished CSO series giving gross investment (separately for plant & machinery and vehicles) by financial institutions for the purpose of leasing, in 1980 prices, for the years 1967–86.[23] It was assumed that one half of the investment in plant and one quarter of that in vehicles was for leasing to manufacturing, a 'guesstimate' derived from table 1 of Penneck and Woods (1982). The same source also suggested that financial leasing of buildings was negligible for manufacturing. The total amount was then apportioned among the industries using the share of each industry in 'Hire of plant, machinery and vehicles' recorded in the 1979 Census (SIC 1980 version). As these payments were recorded by AH they were first reclassified to an MLH basis by the method described in Appendix C.

Table 3.5. *Growth rates of capital stocks in manufacturing:*[a] *descriptive statistics (%, p.a.)*

	MSF	WG	PM	BL	V
			Mean		
1954–58	0.99	5.12	3.75	4.37	2.29
1958–63	2.32	3.65	3.96	4.09	6.19
1963–68	3.86	3.74	4.72	3.67	6.45
1968–73	4.92	3.15	4.19	2.10	4.88
1973–76	0.80	3.93	2.96	0.67	1.13
1976–79	0.60	2.77	3.12	1.00	6.22
1979–82	− 9.89	− 7.04	1.48	− 0.66	− 6.55
1982–86	− 0.54	− 0.53	2.07	− 0.34	− 1.91
			S.D.		
1954–58	6.50	7.16	3.28	4.84	8.58
1958–63	5.12	6.19	3.14	6.51	6.40
1963–68	5.92	7.46	3.31	4.05	6.46
1968–73	5.78	5.07	3.11	3.08	6.37
1973–76	6.77	6.27	2.79	2.04	6.19
1976–79	6.06	5.39	2.76	2.27	5.75
1979–82	10.51	6.31	3.19	2.40	5.71
1982–86	9.19	6.19	3.31	2.70	4.48

Source: Fixed capital: PIM estimates, using depreciation rates from table 3.4. Inventories (MSF and WG): see Appendix B.
Notes: MSF: Materials, stores and fuel
          WG: Work in progress and goods on hand for sale
          PM: Plant & machinery
          BL: Buildings and land
          V: Vehicles
[a] 1968 SIC definition (MLH 211–499), 137 industries.

THE CAPITAL STOCK ESTIMATES

The results

To recapitulate, the preferred estimates use the depreciation rates of table 3.4, which cover both ageing (or obsolescence) and retirement, and they also allow for financial leasing. The estimates for buildings are inclusive of net acquisition of land and existing buildings from 1970 onwards.[24] Table 3.5 shows summary statistics of the growth rates of the stocks in each of the eight time periods; for completeness, this table also includes the growth rates of the two stocks of inventories, which (together with the three stocks of fixed capital) comprise total capital.[25] Here the sample comprises the 137 industries which make up manufacturing (on the SIC 1968 definition). Aggregating over all 137 industries, plant & machinery accounted for 63.8 per cent by value of total fixed capital, buildings for 34.4 per cent and vehicles for only 1.8 per cent. Hence in what follows vehicles will receive less attention than the other two assets. The general message of this table is that the growth rates of both plant & machinery and buildings decelerated after 1968. The deceleration was particularly sharp for buildings with declining growth rates continuing into the 1980s. For the much smaller category of vehicles, the 1970s saw a see-saw pattern and the 1980s a collapse. It is noteworthy that, though the growth rate of plant & machinery is shown as falling in 1979–82, it still remains positive and indeed recovers still further in 1982–6. It must be recalled that these estimates apply the same depreciation rates throughout, making no allowance for the possibility of premature scrapping in the 1980s; later we shall consider whether the relatively modest impact of the 1980–81 recession on plant & machinery is consistent with the larger impact on buildings and the still larger effect on vehicles.

The cross-industry pattern of variation in growth rates (measured by the standard deviation) seems to have changed very little for plant & machinery; it has fallen somewhat for buildings and (after 1976) for vehicles. The standard deviation is important as one check on the accuracy of the initial capital stocks. Since (as explained above) there are no proper investment series at the industry level prior to 1948, the PIM is clearly dependent on what is assumed about capital stocks in that year. So if the 1947 stocks assigned to each industry were seriously in error, we would expect that the standard deviation of growth rates would be initially high, but falling over time as the influence of the 1947 stocks dies away. However, only for vehicles is the standard deviation particularly high in the earliest period, 1954–8.

Sensitivity tests

The preferred estimates assume a constant asset life throughout the period studied. Many people believe, though there is very little direct evidence, that asset lives are in reality much shorter or at any rate that they have become much shorter in recent years.[26] In addition, as we have seen, considerable uncertainty attaches to the assumed rates of ageing, which are based on US, not UK, data. For either of these reasons the true rate of economic depreciation could be very different from what we have assumed. It is important therefore to test the estimates for sensitivity to the assumptions underlying them. The stocks have therefore also been calculated under widely separated depreciation assumptions, which bracket the preferred estimates. For plant, the low estimate is 4 per cent and the high one is 14.27 per cent; for buildings, the low estimate is 1.67 per cent, the high one 3.68 per cent.[27] The low depreciation rates correspond approximately to assuming the same rates of retirement as for the preferred estimates, but making no allowance for ageing or obsolescence (that is a 'gross' capital stock concept). The high rates are similar

Table 3.6. *Mean and SD of growth rates of fixed capital stocks (%, p.a.): low versus high assumed depreciation rate*

	Mean Depreciation rate:		SD Depreciation rate:	
	4%	14.27%	4%	14.27%
Plant and machinery				
1954–58	3.90	4.10	2.52	4.34
1958–63	4.10	4.37	2.45	4.00
1963–68	4.66	5.09	2.80	4.16
1968–73	4.24	4.00	2.71	3.71
1973–79	3.27	2.56	2.13	3.10
1979–85	2.27	0.97	2.65	4.22

	Mean Depreciation rate:		SD Depreciation rate:	
	1.67%	3.68%	1.67%	3.68%
Buildings				
1954–58	4.13	4.94	4.30	5.05
1958–63	4.00	4.50	5.73	6.52
1963–68	3.58	3.80	3.80	4.11
1968–73	2.48	2.28	2.51	2.98
1973–79	0.78	0.07	1.48	1.77
1979–85	− 0.00	− 1.06	1.59	2.06

Source: PIM estimates. Sample size is 139 industries.

to the ones used for the US by Jorgenson and his collaborators, who assume much shorter service lives.[28]

A comparison between estimates on the high and low assumptions will be found in tables 3.6 and 3.7, for all 139 industries. Table 3.6 shows that, for both plant & machinery and buildings, the deceleration of growth (which is apparent under both assumptions after 1968) is nevertheless greater under high depreciation. The difference between the two assumptions reaches a maximum in 1979–85,[29] when there is a bit more than a 1 percentage point difference in the estimated mean growth rates. The dispersion of growth rates across industries, as measured by the standard deviation, is also higher under high depreciation. Nevertheless, the cross industry pattern of growth rates is still very similar under the two assumptions, as evidenced by the very high correlation coefficients between the two sets of estimated growth rates (table 3.7). As far as growth rates are concerned therefore, the estimates seem relatively insensitive to the (widely-separated) assumptions about depreciation.

Further sensitivity tests will be found in O'Mahony and Oulton (1990b), who looked at the effect of assuming different service lives and

Table 3.7. *Correlation coefficients between estimates of fixed capital stocks: low versus high depreciation rates*

	Plant and machinery	Buildings
Correlation coefficients between levels		
1954	0.989	0.992
1958	0.988	0.995
1963	0.993	0.997
1968	0.991	0.997
1973	0.993	0.997
1979	0.996	0.997
1985	0.982	0.995
Correlation coefficients between growth rates		
1954–58	0.941	0.963
1958–63	0.934	0.995
1963–68	0.947	0.986
1968–73	0.939	0.983
1973–79	0.880	0.979
1979–85	0.961	0.992

Source: PIM estimates. Sample size is 139 industries. 'Low' and 'high' depreciation rates as in table 3.6.

different patterns of retirement. They found, for example, that for plant & machinery in 1979, estimates assuming 'short' lives were on average some 13–14 per cent lower than those assuming 'long' lives (depending on the retirement assumption). Although the short lives are 25 per cent less than the long ones, investment has grown steadily so more recently acquired assets have a bigger weight in the total. The same goes for buildings, where making the 'short' life assumption reduces the stock by 10–13 per cent. The exponential retirement assumption lowers the stock of plant by 17–19 per cent on average, compared with the CSO's uniform distribution assumption, and the stock of buildings by 22–25 per cent (depending on the life assumption). These are substantial differences but for many purposes it is the cross-industry pattern which is important. Changes in the assumptions were found to make very little difference here: for both 1963 and 1979, the pattern is virtually identical – the correlation coefficients between estimates made under the different assumptions all exceed 0.99 – for both plant and buildings. Turning from levels to growth rates, it was found that the mean and standard deviation of growth rates across industries appeared similar under all assumptions. Though shorter lives and exponential retirement both tend to reduce growth rates somewhat, the effect is far smaller than it is on the levels. The cross-industry pattern of growth rates was also found to be fairly insensitive to changes in assumptions, with correlation coefficients between estimates of growth rates made under different assumptions always exceeding 0.93.

Sensitivity of estimates: a theoretical approach

The question of sensitivity can also be illuminated by means of some theory. In what follows we assume a continuous time model with exponential depreciation. The capital stock K then evolves according to:

$$\dot{K}(t) = I(t) - \delta K(t) \tag{3.6}$$

where I is investment and δ is the depreciation rate. We assume further that investment grows at a constant rate μ so that

$$I(t) = I_0 e^{\mu t}, \qquad I_0 \text{ given} \tag{3.7}$$

This assumption is not too far from the truth for the UK over selected periods, for example, 1948–73. The general solution to the differential equation (3.6) is:

$$K(t) = e^{-\delta t}[K_0 - I_0 \theta] + e^{\mu t} I_0 \theta \tag{3.8}$$

where $\theta = 1/(\mu + \delta)$.

In a steady state, which the system approaches over time,

$$K(t) = e^{\mu t} I_0 \theta \tag{3.9}$$

and

$$K(t)/I(t) = \theta \tag{3.10}$$

In steady state, the growth rate of K is μ, that is, it is independent of the depreciation rate. So it is only insofar as the investment rate does *not* show a pattern of stable growth that the depreciation rate matters for estimating the capital stock.

Now suppose that at some date R the capital stock is in a steady state; in our case R might be interpreted as 1973. After R, the growth rate of investment changes, while remaining constant at its new level.[30] Let μ_1 be the growth rate of investment up till R and μ_2 be the growth rate after R; define δ_1 and δ_2 analogously. Let

$$\theta_i = 1/(\mu_i + \delta_i), \qquad i = 1, 2 \tag{3.11}$$

Now consider the capital stock at some date S after R. From (3.8),

$$K(S) = e^{-\delta_2(S-R)}[K(R) - I(R)\theta_2] + e^{\mu_2(S-R)} I(R) \theta_2. \tag{3.12}$$

By the assumption of a steady state at R, and using (3.10),

$$K(R)/I(R) = \theta_1. \tag{3.13}$$

From (3.6), the growth rate of the capital stock at S is

Table 3.8. *Growth rate of capital stock six years and twelve years after reduction in investment growth rate (%, p.a.): Case A*

	S − R = 6		S − R = 12	
	$\delta = 4\%$	$\delta = 14.27\%$	$\delta = 4\%$	$\delta = 14.27\%$
$\mu_1 = 2\%$				
$\mu_2 = 0\%$	1.42	0.79	1.04	0.32
$\mu_1 = 4\%$				
$\mu_2 = 0\%$	2.59	1.46	1.79	0.59
$= 2\%$	3.27	2.70	2.83	2.26
$\mu_1 = 6\%$				
$\mu_2 = 0\%$	3.58	2.05	2.36	0.81
$= 2\%$	4.32	3.31	3.45	2.47
$= 4\%$	5.13	4.62	4.66	4.20

Note: Calculated from equation (3.14), assuming depreciation rate constant at either 4 per cent or 14.27 per cent. For further explanation, see text.

$$\dot{K}(S)/K(S) = (I(S)/K(S)) - \delta_2.$$

Plugging (3.9) and (3.10) into this last equation, we obtain

$$\dot{K}(S)/K(S) = -\delta_2 + 1/[(\theta_1 - \theta_2)\,\mathrm{e}^{-(S-R)/\theta_2} + \theta_2] \qquad (3.14)$$

(Note that $\dot{K}(S)/K(S) \to \mu_2$ as $(R - S) \to \infty$.) We can use this last equation to evaluate the effect of different assumptions about depreciation rates on capital stock growth, that is, we fix μ_1, μ_2 and $(S - R)$ and vary the δ_i. In what follows we consider two cases, A and B. In case A, the same depreciation rate is assumed to prevail throughout the period, that is, $\delta_1 = \delta_2 = \delta$, but we test the sensitivity of the growth rate to different values of δ. In case B, the depreciation rate is assumed to increase at time R and we test the effect of this on the growth rate, compared with the situation where the depreciation rate remains unchanged.

Case A: $\delta_1 = \delta_2 = \delta$

Before considering the calculations, notice first of all that, as we can see from equation (3.14), a change in δ will have *no* effect unless the investment growth rates before and after R differ ($\mu_2 \neq \mu_1$); if the growth rates do *not* differ ($\mu_1 = \mu_2 = \mu$), then the RHS of (3.14) reduces to $-\delta + \theta_2 = \mu$, the steady state solution.

Table 3.8 contains some calculations based on equation (3.14). If we think of R as 1973 then S could be taken to be 1979 or 1985, so that $S - R$ equals either six or twelve. The two depreciation rates are 4 per cent and 14.27 per cent, corresponding to the low and high assumptions of table

Table 3.9. *Growth rate of capital stock six years and twelve years after rise in depreciation rate and fall in investment growth rate (%, p.a.): Case B*

	$(\delta_1 = 4\%)$			
	$S - R = 6$		$S - R = 12$	
	$\delta_2 = 4\%$	$\delta_2 = 14.27\%$	$\delta_2 = 4\%$	$\delta_2 = 14.27\%$
$\mu_1 = 2\%$				
$\quad \mu_2 = 0\%$	1.42	− 5.27	1.04	− 2.84
$\quad \mu_2 = 2\%$	2.00	− 4.38	2.00	− 1.18
$\mu_1 = 4\%$				
$\quad \mu_2 = 0\%$	2.59	− 3.56	1.79	− 1.77
$\quad \mu_2 = 2\%$	3.27	− 2.56	2.83	− 0.08
$\quad \mu_2 = 4\%$	4.00	− 1.48	4.00	1.71
$\mu_1 = 6\%$				
$\quad \mu_2 = 0\%$	3.58	− 2.19	2.36	− 1.02
$\quad \mu_2 = 2\%$	4.32	− 1.11	3.45	0.67
$\quad \mu_2 = 4\%$	5.13	0.04	4.66	2.46
$\quad \mu_2 = 6\%$	6.00	1.27	6.00	4.32

Note: Calculated from equation (3.14). For further explanation, see text.

3.6. If we take the most extreme case, a reduction in investment growth from 6 per cent to 0 per cent, then the difference between the estimated capital stock growth rates under the two depreciation assumptions can be as much as 1.5 percentage points, whether after six years or twelve years. For more moderate reductions in investment growth, for example, 2 percentage points, naturally the difference in capital stock growth estimates is less, about $\frac{1}{2}$ of a percentage point. The results in table 3.8, derived from steady state theory, therefore agree quite well with the results of table 3.6, which were derived from *actual* investment data.

Are these differences large or small? That depends on the use to which the capital stock estimates are to be put. As a proportion of the growth rate, the depreciation assumption has a potentially large effect. But if we were interested in calculating multi-factor productivity (MFP) growth, we would be multiplying the growth rate by capital's share, which averages about 15 per cent of gross output,[31] so that the effect of a reduction of even 1.5 percentage points in capital's growth would only increase MFP growth by (0.15 × 1.5 =) 0.23 percentage points. This point of course applies generally to any suggested change in the assumptions underlying the estimates. However, it must be recalled that the low weight accorded to capital by growth accounting is itself controversial – implausibly low in the view of some – so caution must be exercised before dismissing any revisions to the estimated growth rates as insignificant.

Case B:$\delta_1 \neq \delta_2$

In this calculation we illustrate the effect of a drastic increase in the depreciation rate at time R, accompanied by a slowdown in the growth rate of investment (table 3.9). The effect on the calculated growth rate of tripling the depreciation rate at time R, compared with leaving it unchanged at 4 per cent, is very marked. Even if the growth rate of investment is assumed unchanged, after twelve years the growth rate of the capital stock is still a long way away from its steady state value: for example, if investment growth is set at 6 per cent throughout, growth of the capital stock has only reached 4.32 per cent twelve years after the depreciation rate is assumed to have risen. *A fortiori*, if the investment rate is assumed to fall at the same time as the depreciation rate rises, the resulting reduction in the growth rate of the stock is even more marked and long lasting. The conclusion must be that if depreciation were to increase by anything like this amount, then the capital stock estimates would be seriously affected. However, the increase considered here is fortunately far greater than it is plausible to assume.

Age structure of the capital stock

Considerable interest attaches to the age structure of the capital stock. One reason is that price indices of capital goods may not fully capture improvements in quality; the CSO's Producer Price Indices for example are only designed to reflect those quality improvements which increase the cost of manufacture (CSO, 1980b). The work of Gordon (1990) for the US suggests that price indices for durable goods substantially under-state quality change. So a younger capital stock may be more productive than an older one with the same measured value.

The average age of the capital stock has been calculated under a number of different assumptions about service lives and the pattern of retirement. Service lives can be either 'long' (L) or 'short' (S); see table 3.3. Retirement can either follow the CSO's assumption (C), under which scrapping is uniformly distributed in an interval of $\pm$ 20 per cent around the mean service life, or it can be exponential (E), whereby a fraction of the stock equal to $e^{-1/T}$ retires each year (T is the mean service life). This gives four possible combinations, labelled mnemonically LC, LE, SC and SE.[32] The average ages are calculated under what amounts to a 'gross stock' or 'one-hoss shay' assumption; that is, no allowance is made for physical deterioration due to age, so that an asset's contribution is constant from installation to retirement:

$$\text{Average age at } t = \Sigma_{v=t_0}^{v=t}(t-v)\,S_{ik}(t,v)\,I_{ik}(v) \div \Sigma_{v=t_0}^{v=t}S_{ik}(t,v)\,I_{ik}(v).$$

It turns out that there is considerable variation across industries; under assumption LC for example, the maximum across industries of average

Table 3.10. *Summary statistics of average age of capital stock under different assumptions (years)*

Statistic	Assumption	1963	1968	1973	1979	1985
Plant & machinery						
Mean	LC	12.6	12.3	12.4	12.8	13.8
	SC	10.0	9.8	9.9	10.5	11.2
	LE	15.3	14.8	14.7	15.0	15.9
	SE	13.3	12.8	12.7	13.1	14.1
SD	LC	1.9	2.2	2.5	2.4	2.6
	SC	1.6	1.7	1.8	1.7	1.9
	LE	3.2	3.5	3.7	3.8	4.4
	SE	2.7	2.9	3.2	3.3	3.8
Buildings						
Mean	LC	27.2	26.4	26.6	28.5	31.3
	SC	22.0	21.4	21.5	23.1	25.6
	LE	24.8	24.0	24.2	26.1	29.2
	SE	22.8	22.0	22.4	24.3	27.5
SD	LC	7.4	7.4	7.3	7.3	7.4
	SC	5.6	5.5	5.4	5.2	5.3
	LE	7.5	7.5	7.5	7.4	7.8
	SE	7.0	6.9	6.9	6.9	7.4

Note: Each assumption is identified by a 2-letter code. The first letter denotes the average asset life (see table 3): L Long life; S Short life. The second letter denotes the asset mortality assumption: C CSO; that is, retirement is uniformly distributed in intervals of ± 20 per cent around the average service life. E Exponential; that is, depreciation factor is $e^{-1/T}$, where T is the average service life. See text for further details. Sample is all manufacturing (SIC 1968, 137 industries).

age of plant is three times the minimum and the disparity is even wider for buildings.

The results are summarised for these four assumptions in table 3.10. The mean average age of plant (that is, the unweighted mean of each industry's average age) was 11–15 years in 1979, depending on the assumptions, and of buildings was 23–29 years. All the assumptions have the mean average age of both plant and buildings falling in the 1960s but rising after 1973. The fact that the mean average age is estimated to rise after 1979 as well is particularly noteworthy. Indeed, the mean average age is higher for both types of asset in 1985 than in 1963. This result must call into question the assumption of 'no premature scrapping in the 1980s' on which the calculations are based. Nevertheless, a rise in the average age is not a universal finding; for example, 24 (out of 139) industries experienced a *fall* in their average age after 1979 on the LC assumption. As table 3.10 shows, the dispersion in average age across industries is quite wide on any assumption, particularly in buildings. However, for buildings dispersion has remained fairly constant for the last 25 years while for plant it has steadily increased.

Table 3.11. *Summary statistics of the proportions of the 1979 capital stock in different age groups under different assumptions (%)*

Statistic	Assumption	Age group (years)					
		0–9	10–19	20–29	30–39	40–49	50+
Plant & machinery							
Mean	LC	44.7	32.1	16.8	4.8	1.3	0.3
	SC	51.5	34.8	12.0	1.6	0.1	0.0
	LE	48.0	25.8	12.4	5.9	3.2	4.6
	SE	52.4	25.8	11.4	5.0	2.5	3.0
SD	LC	9.8	4.7	6.5	4.1	1.3	0.4
	SC	9.2	5.4	5.8	1.7	0.1	0.0
	LE	10.6	4.4	4.5	5.4	1.9	3.5
	SE	10.3	4.5	4.4	4.8	1.6	2.4

		Age group (years)				
		0–19	20–39	40–59	60–79	80+
Buildings						
Mean	LC	45.3	26.2	17.1	9.9	1.5
	SC	51.1	30.1	16.5	2.2	0.0
	LE	52.1	24.8	12.6	7.3	3.2
	SE	55.2	24.6	11.6	6.2	2.5
SD	LC	16.0	9.5	7.9	7.0	1.1
	SC	15.2	10.2	8.6	1.9	0.0
	LE	15.7	9.3	6.5	5.4	2.5
	SE	15.4	9.2	6.3	4.8	2.0

Note: For explanation see note to table 3.10. Sample is all manufacturing (SIC 1968, 137 industries).

The age distribution of the capital stock in 1979 is summarised in table 3.11. Under exponential retirement, the length of asset lives assumed makes virtually no difference to the age distribution; under the CSO's scrapping assumption, as might be expected, the effect is rather greater. Though there is substantial variation across industries, it appears that on average around half the plant & machinery in manufacturing is less than ten years old and around half the buildings are less than twenty years old.[33]

ASSESSING THE EVIDENCE FOR PREMATURE SCRAPPING IN THE 1970S AND 1980S

The assumption of fixed service lives of assets underlying the perpetual inventory method of estimating capital stocks has been criticised by a number of authors, for example, Baily (1981) and Mendis and Muellbauer (1984), who argue that service lives should reflect changing economic conditions such as variations in output and input prices and the state of demand. In particular it is argued that the worldwide large rise in the relative prices of fuel and raw materials after 1973 probably led to firms scrapping some of their capital assets prematurely, that is, before the expiration of the time period during which the asset was physically viable. This occurred because the capital stock became inefficient in the changed economic circumstances. Also in the specific British context, Mendis and Muellbauer suggest that the collapse of British manufacturing industry in 1980–81 probably also led to wholesale scrapping. The large number of plant closures during this period (Oulton, 1987) and the retrenchment by surviving plants probably resulted in machinery being sold abroad or simply thrown away.

These considerations naturally led to a number of papers aimed at attempting to estimate the extent of premature scrapping since 1973, or to derive alternative estimates of the capital stock. These include Robinson (1985) and Robinson and Wade (1985), Wadhwani and Wall (1986), Smith (1987) and Minford, Wall and Wren-Lewis (1988) as well as an estimate in the Mendis and Muellbauer (1984) paper; in addition, there are estimates of plant closures after 1979 in Oulton (1987).[34]

The starting point for most of these papers was the estimate of cumulative scrapping of 35 per cent of the capital stock by 1983 cited in Mendis and Muellbauer (1984). This estimate was derived by allowing shifts in time trends for a number of periods in an aggregate production function and then calculating the cumulative impact of the two trends for the period in which premature scrapping was thought to be a problem. Robinson (1985) and Robinson and Wade (1985) estimate the trend in the capital–labour ratio in manufacturing since 1950 and then calculate the difference between the capital stock as measured by the CSO, and its level implied by assuming the capital–labour ratio was at its trend value. They concluded that the official measure over-estimated by about 15 per cent in 1983.

Wadhwani and Wall (1986) and Smith (1987) examined company accounts directly to see if they could shed any light on the extent of premature scrapping. Wadhwani and Wall base their estimates on company accounts from a sample of 333 manufacturing companies from the FT 500 index. Since the accounts were on an historic cost basis, they first inflation adjust them to give estimates of the change in the capital stock in each year. They then present a wide range of estimates of the growth rate of the capital stock which depend on various assumptions on the average age of capital assets. If it is assumed that the CSO estimates were correct for 1972, the capital stock value for that year can be used as a base to gross up the Wadhwani and Wall estimates. A comparison with the CSO published estimates of gross capital stock in 1982 shows that the implied over-estimation using the PIM method ranged between 1 per cent and 38.5 per cent with the authors' preferred estimate implying a 7 per cent overstatement. However, their preferred estimate relies on a preferred assumption about asset lives, so there is an element of circularity in the argument.

Smith (1987) derived data on gross capital stock directly from companies' current cost accounts. This restricted his sample to companies who used the CCA method and who reported information on gross capital stock. He estimated a per worker equipment estimate from his sample and then used total employment in manufacturing to gross up his estimates. This yielded a PIM overestimate of 36 per cent in 1983. It is important to note that Smith's estimates are for plant and machinery and do not include buildings and land. The other estimates discussed above are for gross capital stock for all assets.

Minford, Wall and Wren-Lewis (1988), using a series for capacity utilisation which they derived from the CBI's *Industrial Trends Survey*, estimate a 'capacity' series which they interpret as a series on the services of the capital stock. In the period 1974–82 the Minford *et al.* series declined by 9.1 per cent. In the same period, the gross capital stock as measured by the CSO increased by 16.6 per cent. Suppose again that both estimates were identical in 1974; then this paper suggests that the PIM method overstated the capital stock by about 28 per cent. However, this latter figure is not strictly comparable with the previous results since the services of a given physical stock could grow at a slower rate if there is increased non-utilisation or 'mothballing' of existing machinery.

On a quite different basis, it may be deduced from figures in Oulton (1987, tables 2 and 6) that, on an employment weighted basis, about 18 per cent of manufacturing plants closed between 1979 and 1986; on a capital stock weighted basis, the result would probably be similar. This figure is net of any new plants opened during this period. It does not however include the effects of any scrapping of capital by plants which remained in existence throughout the period.

All these estimates rely on a 'gross stock' approach to measuring capital. So they are all likely to be overestimates from a 'net stock' point of view, if premature scrapping was concentrated on older, less efficient assets, and hence ones with the lowest value in a 'net stock' concept of capital. However, contrary to the popular view, it is by no means clear that scrapping as a result of the 1980–81 recession (or the 1974–5 one) *was* concentrated on the least efficient assets.[35] Nevertheless, there is some reason to expect that premature scrapping will have less effect on a 'net stock' estimate than it will on a 'gross stock' one, as the following back-of-the-envelope calculation illustrates. Output in manufacturing fell by 17.4 per cent between 1979Q2 and 1981Q1 – respectively, the previous peak quarter and the trough of the recession (*Economic Trends Annual Supplement 1992*, table 15). It seems unlikely that premature scrapping can have reduced the capital stock by *more* than this percentage, since manufacturers must have been expecting some recovery in demand after 1981. Suppose in fact that a quantity of plant & machinery equal to 17.4 per cent of the 1979 stock was prematurely scrapped in 1981. Obviously, compared to an estimate which assumes *no* premature scrapping, the effect on the stock in (say) 1982 will be dramatic. But the effect on the estimated stock four years later in 1986 is much less so. Assuming an average rate of depreciation for plant & machinery of 8 per cent per annum and given that (without premature scrapping) the 1986 stock is estimated to have been 11.9 per cent larger than in 1979, allowing for premature scrapping can be calculated to reduce the 1986 stock by $(0.92^5 \times 17.4 \div 1.119 =)$ 10.2 per cent below what it otherwise would have been; consequently the estimated growth rate over 1979–86 will be reduced by about 1.5 percentage points per annum.[36] This just illustrates the point that all assets eventually depreciate to nothing and that premature scrapping simply speeds up the process, but less so than might at first be thought, because the depreciation rates assumed here are quite rapid. The effect on estimates of the stock of buildings of a similar amount of premature scrapping will of course be larger, because of the lower depreciation rate for buildings. But on the other hand it is very unlikely that unrecorded disposals of buildings were as large as those of plant, because of the greater chance of sales on the second-hand market, including to firms outside UK manufacturing; such sales will be recorded in the Census and will therefore already be reflected in the present estimates.

The plausibility of the PIM estimates

Clearly, there is a wide divergence of view about the likely extent of premature scrapping. This is hardly surprising given the differences in methodologies, time periods considered and data used by the different authors. However, as we have already seen, there is *prima facie* evidence in the present estimates for the presence of premature scrapping, at least in the 1980s. First, there is the fact alluded to above that the growth rate of the stock of vehicles (arguably the best measure because of the extensive second-hand market) is recorded as falling after 1979 by much more than did the growth rate of plant & machinery (see table 3.5). Second, there is the fact that, as measured, the average age of capital appears to be rising after 1973 (table 3.10).

The plausibility of the estimates produced by the PIM will now be assessed further by examining trends in the estimated capital–output ratio, to see if this will shed more light on the capital scrapping issue.

Table 3.12. *Annual average changes in capital/output ratios: total manufacturing (%, p.a.)*

		1979–85	1973–9	1964–73	1955–64
NK	All Assets	1.9	2.7	0.5	1.2
	Plant & Machinery	2.7	3.5	1.2	1.6
	Buildings	0.8	1.4	− 0.6	0.6
GKCSO	All Assets	1.7	3.0	0.6	0.8
GKLC	All Assets	2.9	3.3	0.6	0.7
GKSE	All Assets	2.4	3.0	0.6	0.9

Notes: NK: Net stocks, own preferred estimates; GKCSO: Gross stocks, CSO estimates; GKLC: Gross stocks, assuming 'long' asset lives and uniform retirements; GKSE: Gross stocks, assuming 'short' lives and exponential retirement. See table 3.3 for 'short' and 'long' lives.

Annual percentage changes in the capital–output ratios for various time periods were estimated as a first test of the plausibility of the capital stock estimates. In forming these ratios, real output is measured by the 'Index of industrial production at constant factor cost' from various issues of the *Blue Book* (see Appendix B for details). Table 3.12 shows the average annual percentage increases in the capital–output ratios for total manufacturing using various capital stock measures. Whatever the capital stock measure, there is a pronounced rise in the capital–output ratio after 1973, with the LC measure showing the greatest change. Using the CSO's estimates, the stocks also show substantial rises despite the use of a declining life assumption. Increases in the capital–output ratios for plant & equipment have in general been higher than those for buildings. In all cases the rise is greater in the period 1973–9 than in the period 1979–85.

These pronounced increases in the capital–output ratio may well be thought implausible. They strongly suggest that the PIM overestimates the capital stock by 1985. But does it overestimate during the earlier period 1973–9 also? The answer would seem to be yes. A possible objection is that the rising real wages characteristic of the period might lead firms to adopt more capital intensive techniques (synonymous with a higher capital–output ratio under constant returns to scale), but this should also lead to rising labour productivity. However, it is notorious that labour productivity stagnated or even fell in the 1973–9 period (see Oulton, 1988, table 4, for some estimates at the MLH level).

Table 3.13 shows the trend in capital–output ratios disaggregated by industry order. We see that there was considerable variation across industries in the extent of increase. Some industries, for example, food, drink and tobacco and electrical engineering, show no apparent upward

Table 3.13. *Annual average changes in capital/output ratios, by sector (%, p.a.)*

		1968–85	1973–9	1964–73	1955–64
All Assets					
III	Food, Drink & Tobacco	1.6	2.0	1.5	2.6
IV	Coal etc. Products	3.7	1.5	− 0.5	− 2.2
V	Chemicals	0.6	0.8	− 1.6	− 0.2
VI	Metal Manufacture	− 0.1	5.1	1.9	3.8
VII	Mechanical Engineering	3.5	3.7	− 0.3	0.4
VIII	Instrument Engineering	0.9	1.7	1.2	− 1.8
IX	Electrical Engineering	− 1.5	1.3	− 1.2	− 0.8
XI	Vehicles & Ships	4.2	4.5	0.8	0.4
XII	Other Metal Goods nes.	3.0	4.1	2.6	1.7
XIII	Textiles	1.6	2.9	− 0.2	1.5
XV	Clothing, Leather & Footwear	2.6	0.5	0.4	1.1
XVI	Bricks, Pottery, Glass etc.	3.8	3.8	1.9	2.4
XVII	Timber & Furniture	2.1	5.9	1.6	− 0.5
XVIII	Printing & Publishing	4.1	2.6	0.5	2.1
XIX	Other Manufacturing	1.2	0.4	1.3	− 1.2
Plant and Machinery					
III	Food, Drink & Tobacco	2.9	3.6	2.6	2.8
IV	Coal etc. Products	4.4	1.6	0.6	− 1.9
V	Chemicals	0.6	1.2	− 0.6	0.5
VI	Metal Manufacture	− 0.2	5.7	2.0	4.8
VII	Mechanical Engineering	5.0	4.8	0.4	0.3
VIII	Instrument Engineering	1.2	2.1	2.3	− 1.9
IX	Electrical Engineering	− 0.5	2.5	− 0.2	− 0.5
XI	Vehicles & Ships	6.1	5.5	1.3	− 0.1
XII	Other Metal Goods nes.	4.1	5.2	3.1	2.1
XIII	Textiles	1.7	3.0	0.4	1.7
XV	Clothing, Leather & Footwear	5.1	2.0	1.9	1.9
XVI	Bricks, Pottery, Glass etc.	5.1	4.9	2.7	2.6
XVII	Timber & Furniture	4.7	8.7	3.4	− 1.4
XVIII	Printing & Publishing	5.3	3.8	1.3	2.5
XIX	Other Manufacturing	2.3	1.0	2.7	1.2
Buildings					
III	Food, Drink & Tobacco	0.4	0.5	0.6	2.4
IV	Coal etc. Products	1.3	0.8	− 3.5	− 3.0
V	Chemicals	0.7	− 0.2	− 3.7	− 1.4
VI	Metal Manufacture	0.2	3.7	1.7	2.2
VII	Mechanical Engineering	1.9	2.3	− 1.3	0.5
VIII	Instrument Engineering	1.0	0.3	− 1.0	− 1.6
IX	Electrical Engineering	− 3.1	− 0.7	− 2.5	− 1.1
XI	Vehicles & Ships	2.1	3.1	0.3	0.8
XII	Other Metal Goods nes.	1.5	2.4	1.8	1.2
XIII	Textiles	1.6	2.6	− 1.3	1.1
XV	Clothing, Leather & Footwear	0.7	− 0.8	− 0.7	0.6
XVI	Bricks, Pottery, Glass etc.	2.2	2.4	1.0	1.9
XVII	Timber & Furniture	0.9	4.4	0.6	− 0.4
XVIII	Printing & Publishing	1.9	0.3	− 0.8	1.6
XIX	Other Manufacturing	− 0.5	− 0.6	− 0.6	− 3.2

Source: Capital stocks: own estimates. Output: *Blue Book* (see Appendix B).

trend in their capital–output ratios whereas others, such as mechanical engineering and vehicles and ships, show very large rises. On the whole, however, the disaggregated figures confirm the impression derived from the aggregate ones that estimated capital–output ratios rose more rapidly in the 1973–9 period.

An alternative estimate of premature scrapping

The above results suggest the importance of deriving estimates of the rates of premature scrapping, particularly for the 1980–81 recession. One possibility is to attempt to estimate the trend in the capital–output ratio over a period after which it is believed that scrapping became important. This trend can then be used to project forward the capital–output ratio and hence the implied capital stock. The difference between this and the measured capital stock, at the point in the business cycle when it is believed that the capital–output ratio should be on trend, could then serve as an estimate of the proportion of the capital stock which has been scrapped. This methodology is similar to the one employed by Robinson and Wade (1985) but is based on trends in the capital–output rather than the capital–labour ratio. The former is used because annual data, on a consistent basis, are available only for output.

In the long run the capital–output ratio will depend on trends in the relative prices of capital to labour and on the trend rate of technological progress, whether biased or neutral. Suppose this relationship is given by

$$\ln[K_t / Y_t] = \alpha + \beta t \tag{3.15}$$

where t is time and α and β are parameters. In the short run the capital–output ratio will behave procyclically since in recessions capital is typically underutilised, that is, there are long lags in the adjustment of capital stocks to their desired long-run levels. In order to use (3.15) to estimate scrapping rates we need to examine the difference between the measured and forecast capital stocks in a year when it is thought that the capital–output ratio should have been on trend.

Equation (3.15) implies that the growth rates of capital and output, in the long run, differ by a constant amount, β. However, if the difference in growth rates accelerates or decelerates over time then estimation by OLS is inappropriate. Therefore, before estimating (3.15) it is necessary to first check if the capital–output ratio is trend-stationary.

Following Nelson and Plosser (1982) and Nelson and Kang (1984), if the capital–output ratio is trend stationary, and the trend is linear, then it can be represented by the model:

$$\ln[K_t / Y_t] = a + \beta t + \epsilon_t \tag{3.16}$$

where ϵ_t is a stationary series with zero mean and constant variance, σ_ϵ^2.

An alternative model of the time path of the capital–output ratio is that it is 'difference-stationary', that is, it can be represented by the model:

$$\ln[K_t/Y_t] = \alpha + \ln[K_{t-1}/Y_{t-1}] + \epsilon_t. \tag{3.17}$$

The simplest version of (3.14) is the random walk where the ϵ_t are assumed to be uncorrelated. Equation (3.14) can then be rewritten as:

$$\ln[K_t/Y_t] = \alpha t + \ln[K_0/Y_0] + \Sigma \epsilon_t \tag{3.18}$$

This equation differs from (3.16) in that the disturbances are non-stationary – in the random walk case the variance is $t\sigma_\epsilon^2$ which increases without bound as time progresses. Also the intercept is not a constant but rather depends on the initial value of the capital–output ratio and hence on past history. If a series is difference- rather than trend-stationary, then the detrended series does not have a fixed mean and the series will have a tendency to move further away from its initial state as time progresses. Therefore, OLS regressions of the form of equation (3.16) will not be appropriate and the forecasts from such regressions will be biased.

As discussed by Granger (1986), one reason why a series may be observed to be non-trend-stationary is that the series are measured with error. If the measurement errors are themselves stationary then they will not affect the stationarity of the calculated series. However, the premature scrapping argument is one of non-stationary or cumulative errors of measurement. The PIM methodology cumulates past investments minus past retirements – if retirements are too low for a number of years then the measured capital stock will move further and further away from the true stock, at least up to the point when the previously scrapped stocks would have been retired anyway. Therefore if premature scrapping is important after 1973, we should subsequently observe that the capital–output ratio becomes non-stationary.

It is important, therefore, to be able to distinguish if a series is trend- or difference-stationary. To test for non-stationarity we use the Dickey-Fuller test for unit roots. Following Nelson and Plosser (1982) we estimate equations of the form:

$$\ln[K_t/Y_t] = \alpha + \beta t + \rho \ln[K_{t-1}/Y_{t-1}] + \rho_1 \{\ln[K_{t-1}/Y_{t-1}] \\ - \ln[K_{t-2}/Y_{t-2}]\} + \epsilon_t. \tag{3.19}$$

Ignoring the term with parameter ρ_1, if the joint hypothesis, $\beta = 0$ and $\rho = 1$, is correct then (3.19) reduces to the difference-stationary model (3.17). The term involving the difference in lagged values of the capital–output ratio is included to ensure that the error process is white noise; the inclusion of this term was necessary in all the regressions reported below. The Dickey-Fuller test of the hypothesis that $\rho = 1$ involves calculating

Table 3.14. *Testing for trend-stationarity, total manufacturing*

		ρ	β	ρ_1	d.w.
1952–73					
NK	All Assets	− 0.095	0.008	0.672	1.96
		(− 4.71)	(3.78)	(3.41)	
	Plant	− 0.078	0.014	0.681	2.00
		(− 4.87)	(4.39)	(3.48)	
	Buildings	0.054	− 0.0004	0.626	1.71
		(− 3.72)	(− 0.34)	(2.85)	
GKCSO	All Assets	− 0.249	0.008	0.633	2.39
		(− 5.36)	(4.52)	(3.34)	
1952–86					
NK	All Assets	0.619	0.005	0.390	1.71
		(− 3.14)	(2.98)	(2.41)	
	Plant	0.662	0.007	0.365	1.70
		(− 2.92)	(2.98)	(2.23)	
	Buildings	0.510	0.002	0.454	1.74
		(− 3.69)	(2.07)	(2.90)	
GKCSO	All Assets	0.689	0.004	0.335	1.77
		(− 2.79)	(2.68)	(2.05)	

Note: Regression equation is (3.16). *t* ratios in parentheses. Regressions included a constant (not reported). NK: Net stocks, own preferred estimates. GKCSO: Gross stocks, CSO estimates.

the *t*-ratio for ρ as $(\rho - 1)/\mathrm{se}(\rho)$, where $\mathrm{se}(\rho)$ is the estimated standard error of ρ in (3.19). The critical *t*-values at significance levels of 5 per cent and 1 per cent and with 25-observations are given as − 3.60 and − 4.38 respectively by Dickey (1976). The regression results are given in table 3.14.

The most striking feature of table 3.14 is that the tests accept trend-stationarity for all series for the period 1952–73 but in almost all cases rejects trend-stationarity when the post-1973 years are included in the sample. This provides further evidence that premature scrapping may have been a problem in the post-oil-shock era. The one exception to this pattern is that trend stationarity is not rejected in the period 1952–86 for buildings. Since there is a much more active second-hand market for buildings, it may then be the case that any premature scrapping of buildings is better reflected in our estimates (which, to repeat, are based on acquisitions less disposals), than is premature scrapping of plant.

Given that the capital–output ratios appear to be trend-stationary over the period 1952–73, it was decided to estimate equation (3.15) over these years and then calculate the proportion of the capital stock which was likely to have been scrapped using forecasts from the trend regressions. Table 3.15 presents the implied scrapping rates, defined by:

Table 3.15. *Premature scrapping rates: total manufacturing (%)*[a]

		1979	1986
NK	All Assets	7.1	13.3
	Plant	9.2	16.6
	Buildings	2.2	6.7
GKCSO	All Assets	10.7	16.4

Note: NK: Net stocks, own preferred estimates. GKCSO: Gross stocks, CSO estimates.
[a]Estimated percentage by which stocks should be reduced to allow for premature scrapping, based on estimates of equation (3.13).

$$S_{it} = \frac{[K_i - \hat{K_i}]}{K_i}$$

where K is the capital stock of industry i, derived using the PIM methodology, and $\hat{K}$ is the forecast capital stock. The rates are shown for the two years 1979 and 1986. It seems that, relative to the net stock estimates presented earlier, premature scrapping may have reduced the stock of plant in manufacturing as a whole by 17 per cent and that of buildings by 7 per cent in 1986; in 1979 the corresponding figures were 9 per cent and 2 per cent.[37] These figures are at the low end of the range of estimates produced by the authors whose work has been discussed above. It is noteworthy that premature scrapping of plant is estimated to have been proportionately larger in the 1970s than in the 1980s; for example, on the net stock estimates, 9.2 per cent of plant was prematurely scrapped over 1973–9, but only $(16.6 - 9.2 =)$ 7.4 per cent over 1979–86.

This exercise suffers from a number of deficiencies. The forecast period was chosen so that scrapping in the post-1973 recession could be estimated, but this involves projecting forward the capital–output ratio for thirteen years. During this period there could have been changes in the trend rate of growth of the capital–output ratio for other reasons, for example, variations in the relative costs of capital to other inputs, in the degree of bias in technical change or in the shares of industries with different capital intensities within manufacturing.

It is fairly easy to see if the rise in the post-1973 capital–output ratio is due to the last of the above list, that is, to changes in the composition of manufacturing. To do so we fix the capital–output ratio in each industry at its 1973 level and multiply by its share in total value added from 1973 to 1986, that is, we estimate:

$$\frac{K_t}{Y_t} = \Sigma s_{it} \frac{K_{73}}{Y_{73}}$$

where s_{it} is the share of industry i in total manufacturing value added. Using data at the level of the industry order of the 1968 SIC we find that the above calculation leads to a small *reduction* in the capital–output ratio, by 1.9 per cent in 1979 and 0.3 per cent in 1986. Therefore, the rise in the capital–output ratio cannot be explained by a move towards more capital-intensive industries within manufacturing.

However, another potential source of bias is harder to eliminate. If part of the explanation for the faster rate of growth of labour productivity in the 1980s is the removal of restrictive practices and increased flexibility in the use of labour, then this could have led to a fall in the capital–output ratio, as the effective utilisation of capital rose.[39] After all, we know that the inventories–output ratio fell substantially in the 1980s, and probably for similar reasons. More speculatively, the capital–output ratio may actually have *risen* in the 1973–9 period in response to rising labour conflicts. In addition, the capital–output ratio may have been allowed to rise in this period because of over-optimistic expectations of demand (Darby and Wren-Lewis, 1991). These factors may account for the fact noted above that our estimates show more scrapping in the 1970s than in the 1980s.

The finding that premature scrapping was apparently higher in 1973–9 than after 1979 is hard to square with other evidence. Though it is often argued that the rise in energy prices in the early 1970s led to large-scale obsolescence and scrapping of energy-intensive equipment, evidence to the contrary has been presented by Hulten *et al.* (1989): the prices of second-hand, energy-intensive equipment should have declined in relative terms on this hypothesis, but Hulten *et al.* found no evidence for this effect. For the UK, further evidence of the difference between the 1974–5 and the 1980–81 recessions comes from redundancy statistics. So-called 'confirmed redundancies' in manufacturing in Great Britain were 102,000 in 1974 and 216,000 in 1975; thereafter they fell, before rising sharply to 400,000 in 1980 and 398,000 in 1981. They were still 281,000 in 1982 (McCormick, 1988, Data Appendix, citing unpublished Department of Employment figures). These figures confirm the exceptional scale of the 1980–81 recession, both absolutely and in comparison with the 1974–5 one. Since scrapping of capital is likely to go hand-in-hand with scrapping of labour, they also suggest that premature scrapping of capital was heavier in the 1980s than in the 1970s.

To sum up the discussion: there is considerable evidence for premature scrapping in the early 1980s. This evidence is partly anecdotal, partly statistical, and partly based on some implausibilities in the estimates which assume that it did *not* occur. There is much less evidence for premature scrapping in the 1973–9 period. Estimates based on trends in the capital–output ratio suggest that premature scrapping might lead one to reduce the estimate of the 1986 stock of plant & machinery in manufacturing as a whole by about 17 per cent and that of buildings by about 7 per cent (table 3.15). The back-of-the-envelope estimate suggests substantially lower figures: for plant & machinery, an upper limit on the reduction of about 10 per cent. However, the degree of confidence which can be attached to these estimates is such that it was not felt justifiable to abandon the assumptions of the PIM. With misgivings, therefore, it was decided to make *no* adjustment in the capital stock estimates for premature scrapping, since any such adjustment would have to be essentially *ad hoc*.

CONCLUSIONS

Estimates of the stocks of plant & machinery, of buildings and land, and of vehicles have been presented and discussed for 140 industries (137 in manufacturing). These estimates are based on the PIM and employ geometric rates of depreciation (table 3.3) which allow for both retirement and ageing (or obsolescence). From a growth accounting point of view, it was argued that this concept of capital is the most appropriate one. The most striking findings to emerge are as follows: first, estimates of the levels of the capital stocks are very sensitive to the assumptions required for the PIM. But estimates of the growth rates, which are what matter for MFP calculations, are *not* very sensitive. Second, the growth rates of the capital stock have been slowing down steadily, since the 1960s, particularly that of buildings (table 3.5). Third, the average age of the capital stock has risen since 1973 and, if no role is allowed for premature scrapping in the 1980s, was higher in 1985 than it had been in 1963 (table 3.10). Fourth, the average age of plant in 1979 was some 11–15 years (depending on assumption) and about half of it was less than ten years old. The average age of buildings was some 23–29 years and on average about half of all buildings were less than twenty years old (tables 3.10 and 3.11). Fifth, based on movements in the capital–output ratio in manufacturing as a whole in the period up to 1973, and relative to the estimates presented above, premature scrapping may have reduced the stock of plant by 17 per cent and that of buildings by 7 per cent in 1986; in 1979 the corresponding figures were 9 per cent and 2 per cent (table 3.15). But an alternative, back-of-the-envelope calculation suggests these estimates may be too high. For the reasons discussed above, all such estimates are extremely speculative and so, though there was undoubtedly *some* premature scrapping as a result of the 1980–81 recession, no adjustment has been made to the PIM estimates.

Finally, the figures reveal a considerable diversity of experience across industries. The growth rates and average ages of the capital stock differ widely. Hence many exceptions can be found to the findings just described, which relate only to the average experience of British manufacturing.

4

OUTPUT, INPUT AND PRODUCTIVITY GROWTH AT THE INDUSTRY LEVEL

INTRODUCTION

In this chapter the main characteristics of the estimates at the industry level are discussed. The approach here is descriptive, seeing what the data can tell us; chapters 6 and 7 adopt a more analytical, hypothesis-testing, perspective. We look first at average behaviour, and also at the extent of variability across industries. Then we address a traditional concern of growth accounting, by asking how much of the growth of output and of output per unit of labour is accounted for by input growth. Next we ask, are there common factors – specific to each industry or to each time period – lying behind the growth rates of output and MFP? Also, do these growth rates display persistence over time? Finally, this chapter takes a first look at the relationships which appear to exist between the growth rates of output, inputs and prices.

The estimates themselves – output, inputs and the corresponding prices – will be found in Appendix H. To assist the reader in assimilating the results, histograms of the growth rates of MFP, output, inputs and prices over two long periods, 1954–73 and 1973–86, appear in Charts 4.1–4.12. Summary statistics (means and standard deviations) of the growth rates of MFP and its components over both short and long periods appear in table 4.1, and similar statistics for the shares of capital, labour and intermediate input in gross output will be found in table 4.2.

MAIN FEATURES OF THE ESTIMATES

Average growth rates

We shall consider first average experience, looking at mean growth rates of MFP, output and inputs, which will be found in table 4.1. Output grew steadily up till 1973 as did capital and intermediate input. After 1973 output has been generally stagnant or falling (an exceptionally sharp fall occurred in 1979–82). In fact in 1986 output was on average lower by some 14 per cent than it had been in 1973. Up to 1973 capital growth followed a similar course to output growth, though the former was somewhat faster: 3.81 per cent per annum up to 1973, compared with 3.32 per cent. The growth rate of capital slackened considerably after

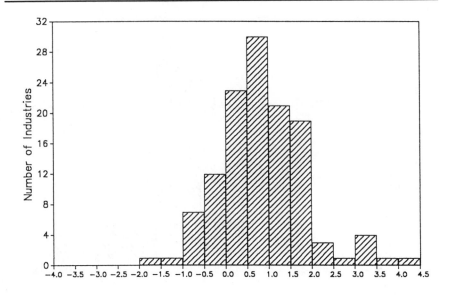

Chart 4.1 Distribution of growth of MFP, 1954–73 (124 industries, % p.a.)

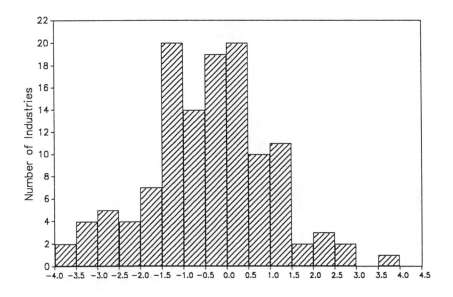

Chart 4.2 Distribution of growth of MFP, 1973–86 (124 industries, % p.a.)

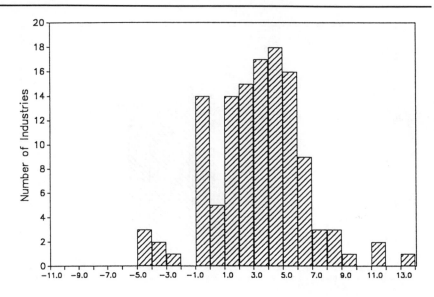

Chart 4.3   Distribution of growth of Y, 1954–73 (124 industries, % p.a.)

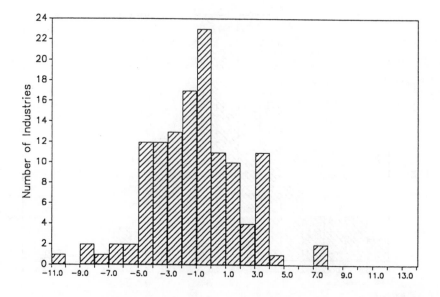

Chart 4.4   Distribution of growth of Y, 1973–86 (124 industries, % p.a.)

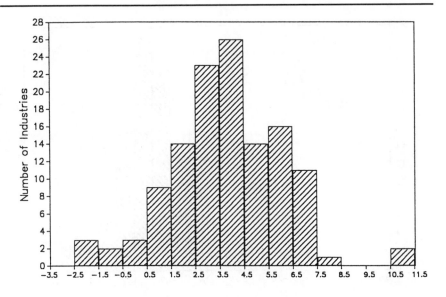

Chart 4.5   Distribution of growth of K, 1954–73 (124 industries, % p.a.)

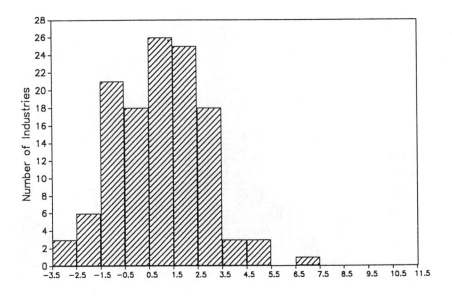

Chart 4.6   Distribution of growth of K, 1973–86 (124 industries, % p.a.)

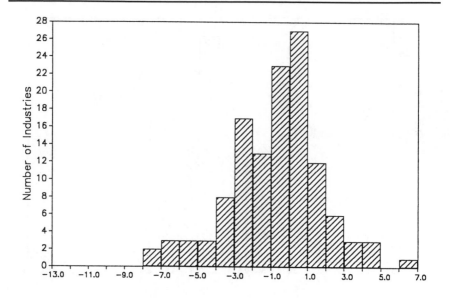

Chart 4.7   Distribution of growth of *L*, 1954–73 (124 industries, % p.a.)

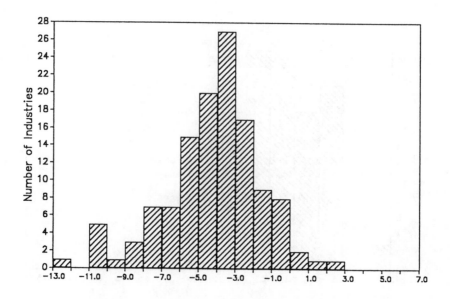

Chart 4.8   Distribution of growth of *L*, 1973–86 (124 industries, % p.a.)

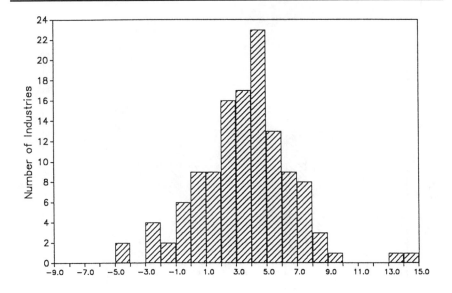

Chart 4.9   Distribution of growth of X, 1954–73 (124 industries, % p.a.)

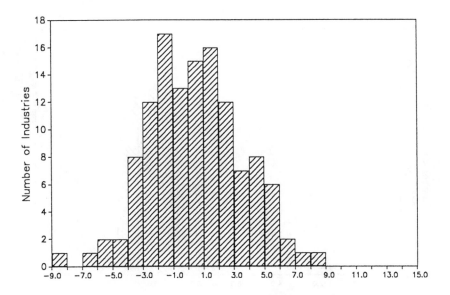

Chart 4.10   Distribution of growth of X, 1973–86 (124 industries, % p.a.)

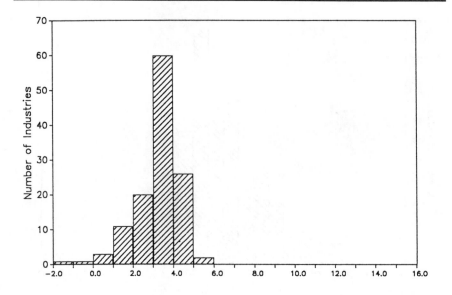

Chart 4.11   Distribution of growth of q, 1954–73 (124 industries, % p.a.)

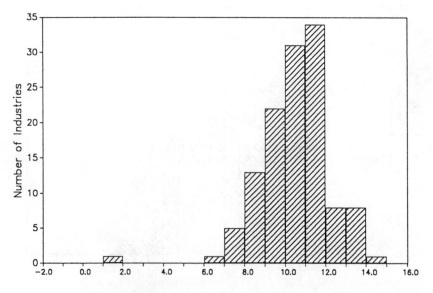

Chart 4.12   Distribution of growth of q, 1973–86 (124 industries, % p.a.)

Table 4.1. *Growth rate of MFP and constituents: summary statistics (%, p.a.)*

Period	N	MFP Mean	SD	Y Mean	SD	K Mean	SD	L Mean	SD	X Mean	SD
Quantities (outputs and inputs)											
Short periods											
1954–58	124	− 0.15	2.04	1.94	4.63	3.34	3.18	− 0.27	3.67	2.86	5.05
1958–63	124	1.24	1.60	3.74	4.67	3.97	2.95	− 0.24	3.66	3.27	5.11
1963–68	130	1.03	1.63	4.20	5.04	4.38	3.61	− 0.84	3.82	4.86	5.50
1968–73	130	1.22	2.26	3.40	3.89	3.60	2.84	− 1.49	2.64	3.57	4.44
1973–76	133	− 1.61	4.19	− 1.04	5.60	1.99	2.08	− 2.30	3.82	1.49	5.91
1976–79	133	− 0.88	2.38	0.66	4.47	2.45	2.17	− 2.03	3.45	3.01	5.18
1979–82	133	− 0.67	2.89	− 6.14	5.85	− 0.92	2.53	− 9.59	5.10	− 4.56	6.21
1982–86	133	0.85	2.08	1.08	5.30	0.62	2.81	− 3.16	4.62	1.61	5.69
1973–79	133	− 1.25	2.59	− 0.19	3.88	2.22	1.81	− 2.16	2.93	2.25	4.13
1979–86	133	0.20	1.81	− 2.01	4.12	− 0.04	2.34	− 5.92	3.67	− 1.03	4.25
Long periods											
1954–73	124	0.88	1.00	3.32	3.14	3.81	2.30	− 0.77	2.49	3.59	3.10
1973–86	133	− 0.47	1.56	− 1.17	3.07	1.00	1.89	− 4.18	2.66	0.48	3.17
1954–86	124	0.35	0.86	1.50	2.57	2.64	1.87	− 2.16	2.02	2.31	2.51

Period	N	q Mean	SD	p_X Mean	SD	p_L Mean	SD	p_K Mean	SD
Prices									
Short periods									
1954–58	124	3.10	2.87	2.56	2.07	6.51	1.95	− 0.47	6.52
1958–63	124	1.09	1.21	0.63	0.53	5.64	0.86	3.66	6.12
1963–68	130	2.11	1.47	1.65	0.70	8.61	0.79	− 0.39	4.53
1968–73	130	6.61	2.02	6.62	1.90	10.00	1.03	8.25	5.99
1973–76	133	18.61	3.91	18.36	3.41	20.52	1.58	6.31	13.06
1976–79	133	12.41	1.95	10.57	1.78	14.73	1.48	8.35	13.25
1979–82	133	8.44	3.18	6.56	2.47	13.51	2.35	0.09	22.00
1982–86	133	4.90	1.65	4.04	1.26	7.09	1.63	12.84	16.48
1973–79	133	15.51	2.45	14.47	2.08	17.63	0.97	7.33	8.89
1979–86	133	6.41	1.87	5.12	1.35	9.84	1.03	7.38	8.56
Long periods									
1954–73	124	3.24	1.11	2.89	0.86	7.74	0.56	2.94	1.87
1973–86	133	10.61	1.79	9.43	1.23	13.43	0.67	7.35	4.19
1954–86	124	6.22	1.04	5.53	0.80	10.05	0.46	4.80	1.70

Source: Appendix H.
Note: N: Number of industries.

1973, becoming particularly low in the 1980s. Recall that these estimates do *not* make any allowance for accelerated scrapping (see chapter 3), but do include the effect of the sharp reduction in inventories, both of materials and of finished goods, which is common to virtually all industries after 1979. The latter initially occurred as a response to the 1980–81

Table 4.2. *Shares of inputs in gross output: summary statistics (%)*

Period	N	Capital Mean	SD	Labour Mean	SD	Intermediate Mean	SD
1954–58	124	16.4	5.9	24.9	9.7	58.7	12.2
1958–63	124	16.7	5.6	25.7	9.6	57.6	11.6
1963–68	130	17.0	5.6	26.9	9.5	56.2	11.3
1968–73	130	16.7	5.4	26.7	9.2	56.6	10.5
1973–76	133	15.7	5.4	26.0	8.9	58.3	9.9
1976–79	133	13.4	5.1	26.0	8.8	60.6	9.5
1979–82	133	12.9	5.5	26.4	8.6	60.8	9.2
1982–86	133	14.1	5.5	25.9	8.2	60.0	8.5

Source: Appendix H.
Note: Shares are calculated from equations (2.5) and (2.7). N: Number of industries.

recession, but although output has recovered the earlier inventory-output ratios have in fact never been restored.

Labour input has been generally falling throughout, with a particularly dramatic decline in 1979–82. Labour input fell by a total of 14 per cent between 1954 and 1973 and by 42 per cent between 1973 and 1986. A small part of this decline is due to falling average hours per week; a larger part is due to a reduction in weeks worked per year (which accounts for about a 9 per cent fall in input over the whole 32-year period), but of course there has also been a big reduction in numbers employed. In addition, labour input may change because of changes in the composition of the labour force, discussed in chapter 2 under the heading of changes in labour force 'quality', measures of which are discussed below.

Intermediate input growth was on average positive, though somewhat slower than that of capital: 3.59 per cent for 1954–73 and 0.48 per cent for 1973–86. Its pattern over time is similar to that of output and capital, peaking in the period 1963–8. It has generally been faster than that of output and this disparity was particularly marked in the 1970s.

As may be calculated from table 4.1, capital intensity (capital per unit of labour, K/L) has been rising strongly throughout our period – on average at 4.58 per cent for 1954–73 and at 5.18 per cent per annum for 1973–86. The same is true for intermediate input intensity (intermediate input per unit of labour, X/L), which rose at 4.36 per cent per annum for 1954–73 and at 4.66 per cent per annum for 1973–86. These findings, particularly that for intermediate intensity, may seem a little surprising. However, it is worth noting that they are not inconsistent with the pattern of movement in relative input prices (see the lower panel of table 4.1). Thus, relative to wages, the prices of both capital and of intermedi-

ate input have been falling, and this is true in every sub-period. Even in
1973–6, when intermediate prices were rising most rapidly, they declined
relative to labour by 2.16 per cent per annum.

The growth of MFP depends on the value shares as well as on the
growth of output and inputs. But as table 4.2 shows, there has not been
much change in the cross-industry average level of these shares. Hence
changes in average MFP growth must be explained by changes in growth
rates of output or inputs. Nevertheless the broad movements of these
shares are of some interest. The share of intermediate has varied from 56.2
per cent to 60.8 per cent, that of labour from 24.9 per cent to 26.9 per
cent. The most obvious feature is the fall in capital's share from a high of
17.0 per cent in 1963–8 to a low of 12.9 per cent in 1979–82, since when it
has recovered to 14.1 per cent. Labour's share rose in the 1950s and 1960s
at the expense of intermediate and thereafter has remained virtually
constant. So the fall in capital's share in the 1970s was due (arithmetically) to a rise in intermediate's, not labour's, share.

The average pattern of MFP growth depends then, in an arithmetic
sense, largely on the pattern of growth of output and the three inputs. In
fact, the growth of MFP shows a similar pattern to that of output. It
appears to rise in the 1950s and 1960s, to fall and turn negative over
1973–9 and to recover somewhat in the 1980s. However it is still negative
in 1979–82 and over the whole period 1979–86 it averages only 0.20 per
cent per annum. Over 1954–73, MFP growth averaged 0.88 per cent per
annum and over 1973–86, − 0.47 per cent per annum; for the whole 32
year span, the figure is 0.35 per cent per annum.

Quality of inputs

Table 4.3 summarises our results for capital 'quality', which rose
throughout most of the period. This rise is due primarily to the slower
growth rate of building stocks relative to that of plant and machinery. In
general buildings have smaller rental prices, which in turn is due to both
lower depreciation rates and higher inflation in buildings prices, particularly in the 1970s. The very large rise in capital 'quality' between
1979 and 1982 is due also to the decline in stocks of inventories whose
rental prices tend to be lower than those for fixed assets.

For labour, 'quality' change is usually positive (table 4.3). Recall that
the growth of labour 'quality' is the difference between the growth of our
measure of labour input and the growth of a crude index of hours worked
in which each type of worker's hours are weighted equally. The increase
in 'quality' is a result of two partially off-setting forces. The first is the rise
in white-collar at the expense of blue-collar employment; since the former
are paid more, this raises labour force quality. The second is the rise in
female employment; since women are paid less than men, even on a per

Productivity and Growth

Table 4.3. *Growth rates of input 'quality': summary statistics (%, p.a.)*

	1954–8	1958–63	1963–8	1968–73	1973–6	1976–9	1979–82	1982–6
Capital								
Mean	− 0.14	0.14	0.10	0.27	0.13	0.42	1.05	0.03
SD	0.77	0.58	0.68	0.47	0.70	1.00	1.39	0.61
Minimum	− 4.16	− 2.04	− 3.38	− 1.55	− 1.82	− 3.26	− 1.63	− 3.88
Maximum	4.12	1.78	2.69	2.66	2.96	4.79	10.64	1.51
Labour								
Mean	0.32	− 0.08	0.37	0.26	0.16	0.25	0.45	0.03
SD	0.36	0.49	0.42	0.40	0.45	0.57	1.08	0.71
Minimum	− 0.77	− 1.67	− 1.02	− 1.63	− 2.06	− 0.87	− 7.74	− 1.74
Maximum	1.46	1.02	1.42	1.38	1.48	3.26	1.94	6.10

Note: 'Quality' is calculated using equations (2.13) and (2.14).

hour basis, this lowers labour force 'quality'. There is of course no evidence to suggest that women are inherently less productive than men. Nevertheless, although paying women less money than men *for the same work* has been illegal in the UK for many years (though not in the 1950s and 1960s), there is substantial impressionistic evidence that the sexes are segregated occupationally so that changes in the sex ratio may well be picking up changes in the occupational mix.

Variability across industries

So far we have been concerned with average growth rates. But as table 4.1 also shows, there is considerable variation across industries. The standard deviation of the growth rates is similar for output and the three inputs. Comparing the period after 1973 with the period before, the variability of output fell slightly, as did that of capital, but the variability of labour rose (also that of intermediate, but by a trivial amount). The variability of MFP growth is markedly less than that of any of its components; 1 per cent in 1954–73, it increased to 1.56 per cent in the second half of the period.

Focusing on the 124 industries whose performance can be tracked throughout 1954–86, we find that in the first half of the period, 1954–73, 21 industries had negative MFP growth, while in 29 MFP grew at more than 1.5 per cent. During the second half of the period, 1973–86, 75 industries experienced negative MFP growth, while only eight grew faster than 1.5 per cent per annum. Over the whole period (1954–86) MFP declined in 39 industries, while its growth exceeded 1.5 per cent in 11.

For output and labour even more striking differences between industries appear. From the same group of 124 industries, we find that output fell in twenty industries in 1954–73 (while mean growth was 3.32 per cent); in 1973–86, it fell in 85 industries, and over the whole period in 36 industries. On the other hand, in the first half of the period output growth exceeded 4 per cent in 53 industries, in the second half in only three. Over 1954–86, sixteen industries grew faster than 4 per cent per annum.

As we have seen, the overall trend of labour input was downwards, even before 1973. Nevertheless, labour input grew in 52 industries up to 1973, in four industries even in 1973–86 and in fifteen industries over the whole period.

It is also worth considering the variability in output prices, in part because the calculation of real gross output depends on them. It will be seen that there is some tendency for the variability of output price rises across industries to increase as the average level of inflation increases, a phenomenon which has been noted elsewhere (Vining and Elwertowski, 1976, but see Driffill *et al.*, 1990, for a sceptical view). As for input prices, intermediate input prices are less variable than output prices, not surprisingly given that they are calculated as a sort of average of the latter. Capital prices are twice as variable as output prices, while labour prices are only half as variable.

A striking feature revealed by table 4.1 is that variability falls as the time period lengthens, for both quantities and prices of output and inputs. Thus the standard deviation of output growth is 4–5 per cent in the short sub-periods of 3–5 years in length, but is only 2.57 per cent for the whole span 1954–86. Similarly, the variability of MFP growth over the whole period is roughly half what it is in the sub-periods. Thus some sort of 'regression towards the mean' seems to be in operation. That this is in fact the case is revealed by the low correlations between growth rates over the first half of the period (1954–73) and growth rates over the second half (1973–86), which were as follows:

1954–73 growth rates versus 1973–86 growth rates
(124 industries)

Variable	Correlation Coefficient
MFP	0.08
Y	0.36
K	0.53
L	0.23
X	0.30
q	0.21

Though some of these coefficients are significant in a statistical sense, they are all low (except that for capital), particularly the coefficient for MFP growth.[1]

Looking at variability in more detail, we can ask which industries show particularly slow or particularly fast MFP growth? Taking two standard deviations below the mean as the criterion for exceptionally slow growth, the following industries stand out as slow growers:

MLH	Industry	Growth (% p.a.)
	1954–73	
216	Sugar	− 1.20
240	Tobacco	− 1.76
	1973–86	
102/103	Stone & slate quarrying	− 5.09
215	Milk & milk products	− 3.89
418	Lace	− 3.96
	1954–86	
216	Sugar	− 1.49
240	Tobacco	− 2.34
392	Cutlery, etc.	− 1.49

Thus MLH 392 shows up as a slow grower overall, though not as such in either of the two half-periods.

Defining exceptionally fast growth as two standard deviations above the mean, the following show up as fast growers:

MLH	Industry	Growth (% p.a.)
	1954–73	
272	Pharmaceuticals	3.25
276	Synthetic resins & plastics	4.44
368	Domestic electric appliances	3.06
395	Cans & metal boxes	3.08
411	Man-made fibres	3.74
499	Miscellaneous manufacturing	3.43
	1973–86	
221	Oils & fats	3.98
365	Broadcast receiving & sound reproducing equipment	4.60
414	Woollen & worsted	2.94
	1954–86	
276	Synthetic resins & plastics	2.20
368	Domestic electric appliances	2.24
411	Man-made fibres	2.82

Table 4.4. *MFP growth rates by SIC Order: summary statistics*

Order	N	1954–86 Mean	SD	1954–73 Mean	SD	1973–86 Mean	SD
Food, Drink & Tobacco	15	− 0.17	1.00	0.25	0.98	− 0.80	1.83
Chemicals	15	0.61	0.82	1.54	1.20	− 0.74	0.98
Metals	6	− 0.36	0.67	0.06	0.70	− 0.97	1.34
Mechanical Eng.	15	0.41	0.52	0.70	0.59	− 0.06	1.04
Instrument Eng.	4	0.87	0.49	1.25	0.57	0.32	0.57
Electrical Eng.	8	0.95	1.13	1.39	1.08	0.66	1.91
Ships	1	− 0.01	0.00	0.67	0.00	− 0.99	0.00
Vehicles	5	0.44	0.79	1.38	0.85	− 1.32	1.37
Other metal goods	9	− 0.08	0.96	0.75	1.15	− 1.30	1.10
Textiles	14	0.47	1.08	0.72	1.21	0.12	1.82
Leather and Fur	3	0.49	0.04	0.03	0.72	1.16	1.05
Clothing & Footwear	9	1.05	0.52	1.27	0.70	0.73	0.73
Bricks, etc.	6	0.08	0.84	1.01	0.88	− 1.27	1.62
Timber & Furniture	6	0.34	0.34	0.94	0.46	− 0.54	0.68
Paper & Printing	7	− 0.09	0.54	0.73	0.52	− 1.28	1.54
Other Manufacturing	8	0.76	0.95	1.41	1.29	− 0.53	0.92
All manufacturing	133	0.35	0.86	0.88	1.00	− 0.47	1.56

Source: Appendix H.
Note: N: the number of industries in each order for which data were available in the period 1973–86. In earlier periods there was one less observation in mechanical engineering and vehicles, two less in other manufacturing and three less in electrical engineering. Figures for total manufacturing are taken from table 4.1. Since no observations were available for Order 2, Mining and quarrying, prior to 1973 it was decided to exclude this from the table.

Six of the industries which show up as fast growers in one of the half-periods fail to do so overall. However, the three industries which were fast growers overall (MLH 276, 368 and 411) were also fast growers in 1954–73. On the whole then, these results confirm the tendency towards regression to the mean which has already been noted.

It also seems worthwhile to present some descriptive statistics on MFP growth rates by industry groups. This information is summarised in table 4.4 where the industry groups correspond to Orders of the 1968 SIC. The table confirms that there is considerable variation across industry groups. Over the entire period 1954–86 the groups with mean MFP growth rates above the average for all manufacturing include Chemicals, Instrument engineering, Electrical engineering, Vehicles, Bricks, pottery & glass and Other manufacturing. The poor performers include Food, Metals, Shipbuilding, Other metal goods and Paper and printing. Some industries such as Instrument and Electrical engineering experienced consistently high growth rates up to 1973. Metal manufacture, Shipbuilding and Paper and printing are consistently low performers. On the other hand Chemicals and Vehicles experienced above average growth rates

Table 4.5. *Accounting for the growth of output (cross-industry averages)*

Period	Output growth (% p.a.)	Total input growth (% p.a.)	Input growth as % of output growth
Short periods			
1954–58	1.94	2.09	107.7
1958–63	3.74	2.50	66.8
1963–68	4.20	3.17	75.5
1968–73	3.40	2.18	64.1
1973–76	− 1.04	0.57	− 54.8
1976–79	0.66	1.54	233.3
1979–82	− 6.14	− 5.47	89.1
1982–86	1.08	0.23	21.3
1973–79	− 0.19	1.06	− 555.3
1979–86	− 2.01	− 2.21	106.6
Long periods			
1954–73	3.32	2.44	73.5
1973–86	− 1.17	− 0.70	59.8
1954–86	1.50	1.15	76.7
Allowing for accelerated scrapping:			
1973–79	− 0.19	0.73	− 384.2
1979–86	− 2.01	− 2.54	122.5

Source: Table 4.1.
Note: Total input growth is output growth minus MFP growth. See text for details of accelerated scrapping calculation.

pre-1973 but performed worse than average subsequently; the reverse is true for Textiles and Mechanical engineering.

ACCOUNTING FOR THE GROWTH OF OUTPUT AND OF OUTPUT PER UNIT OF LABOUR

What proportion of the growth of output can on average be accounted for by the growth of total input? Table 4.5 gives the answer. Up till 1968, most of output growth could be accounted for by input growth. Then after 1973 input growth continues but output growth becomes stagnant or negative (hence the negative numbers in 1973–6). If we compress the four periods since 1973 into two, 1973–9 and 1979–86, then the experience of the 1980s is almost exactly acounted for by input growth, while that of 1973–9 remains a puzzle.

To what extent would these results be altered if we allowed for accelerated scrapping of capital after 1973? In view of the discussion in the previous chapter, an extremely generous allowance would be to reduce the capital stock by 15 per cent in 1979 and by 30 per cent in 1986

– recall that on one calculation the upper limit for the effect of premature scrapping on plant & machinery in 1986 is 10 per cent, that a lower allowance should be made for buildings, and that in any case inventories, for which no adjustment is necessary, are also part of the capital stock. However that may be, this allowance would lower the average growth rate of capital by 2.71 percentage points per annum over 1973–9 and by 2.77 percentage points over 1979–86. Because of the relatively small share of capital in total input (about 14–15 per cent on average) the growth rate of total input would be reduced by only about 0.325 percentage points per annum over 1973–9 and by about 0.33 percentage points per annum over 1979–86. The last two lines of table 4.5 give the result of making this adjustment. It will be seen that the 1973–9 result is made to look more normal, though not much so, at the price of making the 1980s performance look more extraordinary. Note that figures greater than 100 indicate that though both input and output fell in 1979–86, input fell faster.

The results in table 4.5 suggest that, with the possible exception of 1982–6, MFP growth is not, on average, the primary source of output growth. For the US, Jorgenson *et al.* (1987) found that MFP was an important source of growth in only a small number of industries. Table 4.6 is designed to see if the same is true for British industries by showing the number of industries where MFP growth was a 'significant' contributor to output growth. MFP growth was defined to be a significant source of growth in an industry if (i) it was positive and if (ii) *either* aggregate input growth accounted for less than 50 per cent of a rise in output in an industry *or* the fall in aggregate input was more than 50 per cent greater than the fall in output.[2] In the table we confine our attention to those industries for which data are available for all time periods so that the number of industries in each time period is 124.

For the entire period 1954–86, MFP growth is a significant contributor to output growth in only a minority of industries; this is consistent with the findings of Jorgenson *et al.* However, MFP growth becomes more important in the period since 1979 and particularly since 1982. Against this the number of industries experiencing positive MFP growth was lower in the period 1979–86 than in the 1960s. Only five MLH showed 'significant' MFP growth in both the period 1954–73 and 1973–86; this is increased to only seven MLH if we compare 1954–73 with 1979–86. The five industries were explosives (MLH 279/3), woollen and worsted (MLH 414), textile finishing (MLH 423), women's outerwear (MLH 443), and footwear (MLH 450). The additional two industries were weatherproof outerwear (MLH 441), and wooden containers and baskets (MLH 475). Therefore, the industries with significant MFP growth are not confined to a few with high performance in

Table 4.6. *Number of industries with 'significant'[a] MFP growth*

Period	Number of industries: with significant MFP growth	with positive MFP growth
Short periods		
1954–58	19	89
1958–63	21	101
1963–68	10	34
1968–73	31	69
1973–76	43	83
1976–79	12	43
1979–82	18	49
1982–86	43	83
1973–79	13	34
1979–86	31	69
Long periods		
1954–73	19	102
1973–86	19	45
1954–86	20	82

Source: Appendix H.

[a] 'Significant' means MFP growth was positive; and total input growth was *either* less than 50 per cent of rise in output *or* more than 50 per cent of fall in output.

all periods. The question of persistence of MFP growth rates is considered further below.

Just as one can ask what proportion of the rise in output can (on average) be accounted for by the rise in inputs, so one can ask a similar question about the rise in output per unit of labour. From equation (2.6) we can easily derive that

$$\Delta_u \ln(Y_i/L_i) = \Delta_u \ln(\text{MFP}) + \bar{v}_X^i \Delta_u \ln(X_i/L_i) + \bar{v}_K^i \Delta_u \ln(K_i/L_i). \quad (4.1)$$

Using this equation as the basis for the decomposition, we obtain the results reported in table 4.7.

On average over the industries in our sample, output per unit of labour grew at 4.09 per cent over 1954–73 and at 3.01 per cent over 1973–86. Growth slowed down sharply after 1973, recovered a bit in the later 1970s, and then accelerated sharply in the 1980s. As mentioned earlier, both capital intensity and intermediate intensity have also (on average) risen strongly throughout our period. By contrast with output per unit of labour, the capital and intermediate intensities slowed down only a little after 1973 and have continued to grow rapidly in the 1980s. The result is

Table 4.7. *Accounting for the growth of output per unit of labour (cross-industry averages)*

Period	Growth rates % p.a.			Input contribution %	of which:	
	Y/L	K/L	X/L		K/L %	X/L %
Short periods						
1954–58	2.21	3.61	3.13	106.8	24.4	75.6
1958–63	3.98	4.21	3.51	68.8	25.8	74.2
1963–68	5.04	5.22	5.70	79.6	21.7	78.3
1968–73	4.89	5.09	5.06	75.1	22.9	77.1
1973–76	1.26	4.29	3.79	227.8	23.4	76.6
1976–79	2.69	4.48	5.04	132.7	16.4	83.6
1979–82	3.45	8.67	5.03	119.4	26.8	73.2
1982–86	4.24	3.78	4.77	80.0	15.7	84.3
1973–79	1.97	4.38	4.41	163.5	19.6	80.4
1979–86	3.91	5.88	4.89	94.9	21.2	78.8
Long periods						
1954–73	4.09	4.58	4.36	78.5	23.4	76.6
1973–86	3.01	5.18	4.66	115.6	20.6	79.4
1954–86	3.66	4.80	4.47	90.4	22.0	78.0

Source: Growth rates are from table 4.1. Inputs are weighted together using shares from table 4.2. Number of industries varies – see table 4.1.

that we are able to account for a high proportion of the growth of output per unit of labour by the growth of total input per unit of labour – in fact, when MFP growth is negative (as in 1973–82), the proportion exceeds 100 per cent. In sub-periods when MFP growth is positive and in the whole first half of our period (1954–73), the proportion accounted for is between about three quarters and four fifths. Of the proportion accounted for, between 76 and 84 per cent (the share is increasing over time) is due to rising intermediate intensity.

It may seem strange that only a quarter or less is due to rising capital intensity; arithmetically, this follows from the fact that the share of intermediate input is four times that of capital. We shall return to the issue of whether the weight accorded to capital is too low in chapter 7. It must also be remembered that our output measure is gross and cannot be aggregated across industries; the purpose of taking averages across industries is to enable judgements to be made about typical behaviour, and not necessarily to evaluate aggregate performance, which is the task of chapter 5.

The results which are most directly comparable with the present ones are those of Wragg and Robertson (1978), who give MFP growth rates for 82 industries in manufacturing (classified by the 1958 SIC) for the period 1963–73. Nevertheless, there are considerable differences in methodology. Wragg and Robertson used gross output, as here (though not adjusted in the ways detailed in chapter 2), but in other respects they followed the 'value added' methodology: their other inputs are labour and capital only, weighted together by shares in value added, the latter derived from the 1968 input–output tables (*op. cit.*, p. 40). Their capital stocks are based on estimates at the order level, disaggregated to the MLH level using the depreciation/sales ratio from company accounts. No allowance was made for depreciation. They do not give the composition of their stocks, so it is not clear how many asset types are included. Their labour input is numbers employed, with no allowance for hours worked or for different types of worker. Despite their use of gross output, it seems likely that their estimates are similar to what would have been produced by a full-blown 'value added' approach; as discussed in section 2, MFP growth rates calculated using value added are systematically greater than those using gross output, by a factor approximately equal to the ratio of gross output to value added.

It was possible to match the present estimates with Wragg and Robertson's for 68 industries; the unweighted mean growth rate for their estimates was 2.9 per cent per annum and for ours was 1 per cent per annum. Given an average 60 per cent share of materials in gross output, we would expect the 'value added' approach to produce estimates about 2.5 times estimates based on gross output, which is confirmed by the above numbers. The cross-section correlation between the two sets of estimates of MFP growth rates was 0.35; again, we would not expect this correlation to be very high since the share of intermediate input varies considerably across industries.

COMMON FACTORS AND PERSISTENCE IN GROWTH RATES

Common factors

Do growth rates of MFP exhibit common factors? Such common factors might be specific to each industry over time or they might represent a shock of some sort which is common to all industries in a given time period. The following equation gives a framework for testing these possibilities.

$$\mu_{it} = \eta_i + \theta_t + \epsilon_{it}. \tag{4.2}$$

Here η_i is a fixed effect, which is specific to industry i and constant over time, θ_t is a shock which is common to all industries during period t, and ϵ_{it} is an 'idiosyncratic' shock which varies both across industries and over time; without loss of generality we can assume that ϵ_{it} has zero mean. The dependent variable here is MFP growth (μ_{it}) but the same model will also be applied to output growth and to labour productivity growth.

This equation subsumes a number of factors which have been emphasised in quite different literatures. For example, Salter (1966), in seeking to explain the cross-industry correlation he and others observed between output growth and labour productivity growth,[3] emphasised the shocks which are specific to each industry, though without discussing whether they are persistent (the η_i) or time-varying (the ϵ_{it}). Real business cycle theorists (for example, Prescott 1986), seeking to explain the time series correlation between aggregate output and aggregate labour productivity (often called, or miscalled, Verdoorn's Law) emphasise the 'technology' shocks which are common to all industries, but which vary over time, the θ_t: on this view, a favourable shock raises labour productivity and hence wages, leading to increased labour supply and higher output.

Various versions of equation (4.2) were fitted to the sample of 124 industries for which MFP growth rates are available for all eight time periods. The common shocks (θ_t) are represented by eight time-period dummies. Omitting the first of these, the included ones are:

D5863 = 1 in 1958–63, 0 otherwise
D6368 = 1 ,, 1963–68, 0 .   ,,
D6873 = 1 ,, 1968–73, 0   ,,
D7376 = 1 ,, 1973–76, 0   ,,
D7679 = 1 ,, 1976–79, 0   ,,
D7982 = 1 ,, 1979–82, 0   ,,
D8286 = 1 ,, 1982–86, 0   ,,

The results are in table 4.8. Taking output growth first, the inclusion of both fixed effects and time-period dummies is supported statistically. With time-period dummies alone, R^2 is 0.2919. The inclusion of fixed effects raises R^2 to 0.4847 and is strongly supported by the F test. So about half of the variation in output growth can be accounted for by period and industry-specific effects. The fact that inclusion of the time-period dummies is so strongly supported statistically shows that the differences in mean growth rates between periods, which are visible in table 4.11, are indeed not due to chance.

A rather different picture emerges with MFP growth. Here we find that

Table 4.8. *Panel regressions for output, MFP and labour productivity growth*

| | Dependent variable | | | | | |
| | Output growth | | MFP growth | | Y/L growth | |
Variable	Coefficient	t ratio	Coefficient	t ratio	Coefficient	t ratio
D5863	2.97	6.42**	1.38	4.41**	1.77	3.98**
D6368	3.53	8.56**	1.14	3.63**	2.76	6.20**
D6873	2.62	6.34**	1.37	4.37**	2.58	5.79**
D7376	− 1.61	3.91**	− 1.37	4.38**	− 0.76	1.70
D7679	0.09	0.21	− 0.70	2.22*	0.42	0.94
D7982	− 6.80	16.47**	− 0.56	1.78	1.08	2.43*
D8286	0.62	1.51	1.11	3.53**	2.13	4.79**
R^2	0.4847		0.1463		0.1047	
NOBS	992		992		992	
NVARS	131		8		8	
F *test for inclusion of fixed effects:*						
$F (123, 861)$	2.37**		1.13		1.08	

Notes: NOBS: number of observations (8 time periods, 124 industries). NVARS: number of right hand side variables (including constant and, where applicable, fixed effects). The regression for output growth includes fixed effects; the ones for MFP and labour productivity growth do not, though they do include a constant which is not reported.
*indicates significant at the 5 per cent level or better.
**indicates significant at the 1 per cent level or better.

with time-period dummies but no fixed effects, R^2 is 0.1463; the dummies are highly significant on an F test. With both time-period dummies and fixed effects included, R^2 rises to 0.2646. So the macro shocks (the time-period dummies) explain more than the industry-specific shocks (the fixed effects). And indeed the fixed effects are not significant (the calculated value of F for inclusion of fixed effects is 1.13 with a p-value of 0.18, hence their inclusion is rejected). The coefficients on the time-period dummies can be interpreted as follows: relative to 1954–8, there were common, favourable shocks to MFP growth in the subsequent three periods; there then followed three periods (1973–82) in which the shocks were negative; in the last period there was once again a positive shock, of similar size to the ones in 1958–73.

The inclusion of fixed effects is equivalent to adding 123 variables to the regression. A more parsimonious way of adding some industry-specific information is to see whether there is any evidence for 'Order' effects on MFP growth. In other words, does an industry's membership of a particular Order of the SIC have a significant effect on productivity? To test for this, Order dummies (taking the value 1 if an industry belongs to the Order in question, 0 otherwise) were included in the panel model; this is equivalent to adding fifteen variables to the regression.[4] However, adding these variables to the MFP equation without fixed effects only raises R^2 to 0.1563 and their inclusion is rejected by the F test. Order effects also proved to be insignificant in the output growth equation. Some experiments were also made with the inclusion of a battery of variables describing the characteristics of the industries in the sample; these industry characteristic (IC) variables are described in more detail in chapter 7 and in Appendix B. Again the results were negative. For example, with MFP growth as the dependent variable a panel regression with time-period dummies, 34 IC variables (including the fifteen Order dummies), but no fixed effects, yielded an R^2 of 0.1781; an F test rejects the IC variables at the 5 per cent level. Though with more effort it is possible to find a more restricted set of IC variables which is statistically significant, the point emphasised here is that such variables do not add much explanatory power.

The bulk of the variation in MFP growth is thus found to be in the component which varies both over time and across industries, but with a zero expected value. One obvious candidate for explaining part, but surely not the whole, of this latter component is simply measurement error. Nevertheless, the presence of common, time-varying shocks *is* supported by these data, which is in accordance with the real business cycle view. However, it does not necessarily follow that the mechanism proposed by real business cycle theorists (intertemporal substitution of labour) is the true one.[5]

Another conclusion is that the slowdown in MFP growth after 1973 and the subsequent recovery, apparent already from the average growth rates of table 4.1, were real phenomena. The changes in the values of the time-period dummies in table 4.10 are both economically significant and far too large to be explained by chance alone, as the t statistics demonstrate. The time-period dummy for MFP growth falls by nearly 3 percentage points in 1973–6 and thereafter slowly recovers. A similar conclusion holds for labour productivity.[6]

Persistence

We have already seen that the correlation between MFP growth (and to a lesser extent output growth) in the first and second halves of the 32-year period under study is low. Nevertheless although MFP growth does not display persistence over long time periods, it may do so over short periods. Again, it may be that there is persistence in labour productivity but not in MFP. Therefore it seems worthwhile to consider cross-section correlations over shorter time periods. The results are presented in table 4.9 and show that, using either measure of productivity, the correlations are generally low and frequently negative. Correlations between adjacent time periods may be artificially lowered by a measurement error in the common year:

Table 4.9. *Persistence of productivity growth rates: correlation coefficients between periods*

	MFP	Labour productivity
Correlations between consecutive time periods		
1954–58 & 1958–63	− 0.15	− 0.02
1958–63 & 1963–68	0.29	− 0.05
1963–68 & 1968–73	− 0.09	0.26
1968–73 & 1973–76	− 0.04	0.02
1973–76 & 1976–79	− 0.18	− 0.05
1976–79 & 1979–82	− 0.05	− 0.18
1979–82 & 1982–86	0.12	0.03
1954–73 & 1973–86	0.10	0.21
1973–79 & 1979–86	− 0.09	− 0.07
Correlations between non-consecutive time periods		
1954–58 & 1963–68	0.11	− 0.06
1958–63 & 1968–73	0.20	− 0.02
1963–68 & 1973–76	− 0.21	− 0.17
1968–73 & 1976–79	− 0.07	− 0.01
1973–76 & 1979–82	0.00	0.08
1976–79 & 1982–86	− 0.04	− 0.03

Note: The growth rate of labour productivity is the growth rate of output minus the growth rate of the Törnqvist index of labour input.

if for example there is a positive error in the output measure for a particular industry in 1958, then productivity growth in that industry will be overestimated for 1954–8 and underestimated for 1958–63. To guard against this, table 4.9 also shows correlations between productivity growth rates in non-consecutive periods (the correlation between the growth rate and its own value lagged twice). These turn out to be no higher than the correlations between consecutive periods, suggesting that measurement error is not the cause of low measured persistence.

An additional test for persistence was to add lagged MFP growth to the panel model of equation (4.2). With fixed effects excluded, the lagged term is not significant in the MFP equation ($t = 0.32$). Nor is lagged growth significant in the output equation with fixed effects included ($t = 1.27$). These results are not surprising, given that a fixed effect is itself a special kind of persistence.

Although in general persistence seems low, it might still be the case that some industries experienced sustained high or low MFP growth for extended lengths of time. Table 4.10 shows the number of MLH with very high or low MFP growth cross-classified by the number of time periods (maximum of eight) for which this occurs. This helps to identify the persistently high or low performers. The number of industries with very

Table 4.10. *Number of MLH with high or low MFP growth classified by the number of time periods when this occurred*

Number of time periods	Number with MFP growth > 2% p.a.	Number with MFP growth < − 2% p.a.
1	42	47
2	31	36
3	23	13
4	5	8
5	5	0
6	1	0

high or low MFP growth for four or more of the eight time periods are very small. The five industries with greater than 2 per cent MFP growth for four time periods were Pharmaceuticals (MLH 272), Man-made fibres (MLH 411), Woollen and worsted (MLH 414), Hosiery and knitted goods (MLH 417), and Men's outerwear (MLH 442). The industries with MFP growth greater than 2 per cent per annum for five time periods include Synthetic resins (MLH 276), Telecommunications equipment (MLH 363), Domestic electric appliances (MLH 368), Aerospace (MLH 383), and Miscellaneous manufacturing industries (MLH 499). Broadcast receiving and sound reproducing equipment (MLH 365) experienced more than 2 per cent MFP growth for six of the eight time periods.[7] The industries which performed poorly for four time periods were Stone quarrying, clay, etc. (MLH 102/103), Sugar (MLH 216), Brewing (MLH 231), Tobacco (MLH 240), Toilet preparations (MLH 273), Adhesives (MLH 279/2), Other base metals (MLH 323), and Motor cycles (MLH 382).

THE PATTERN OF THE RESULTS: A MORE DETAILED ANALYSIS

In this section we shall look in more detail at the pattern of our results. We shall be particularly interested in whether they display any marked empirical regularities, either across industries or over time. Previous writers (Fabricant, 1942; Salter, 1963, and Wragg and Robertson, 1978) have described a number of such regularities, connecting labour productivity, output and employment, but little has been written about regularities involving MFP (neither Fabricant nor Salter calculated MFP growth). As a starting point, a matrix of correlation coefficients between the long-period growth rates of (multi- and single-factor) productivity, output, inputs, input intensities and prices is presented in table 4.11. The various significant[8] relationships revealed here will be discussed one by one.

Table 4.11. *Correlation coefficients between growth rates, by period (124 industries)*

	MFP	Y	K	L	X	q	Y/K	Y/L	Y/X	K/L	X/L
1954–73											
MFP											
Y	0.51										
K	0.22	0.86									
L	0.21	0.86	0.80								
X	0.26	0.94	0.85	0.83							
q	−0.73	−0.39	−0.19	−0.05	−0.17						
Y/K	0.66	0.71	0.25	0.52	0.61	−0.47					
Y/L	0.67	0.62	0.44	0.13	0.54	−0.67	0.56				
Y/X	0.71	0.21	0.07	0.10	−0.15	−0.63	0.29	0.24			
K/L	−0.01	−0.10	0.20	−0.43	−0.08	−0.20	−0.48	0.46	−0.06		
X/L	0.17	0.45	0.37	0.05	0.60	−0.23	0.34	0.78	−0.41	0.47	
1973–86											
MFP											
Y	0.39										
K	0.02	0.73									
L	−0.06	0.79	0.77								
X	−0.08	0.85	0.72	0.78							
q	−0.76	−0.31	0.10	0.12	0.09						
Y/K	0.54	0.80	0.17	0.45	0.60	−0.53					
Y/L	0.70	0.49	0.09	−0.15	0.26	−0.67	0.64				
Y/X	0.86	0.24	0.00	−0.02	−0.30	−0.72	0.34	0.41			
K/L	0.11	−0.43	−0.11	−0.72	−0.44	−0.09	−0.52	0.33	0.04		
X/L	−0.05	0.28	0.08	−0.13	0.52	−0.04	0.33	0.63	−0.45	0.29	
1954–86											
MFP											
Y	0.45										
K	0.15	0.86									
L	0.09	0.85	0.85								
X	0.22	0.94	0.86	0.86							
q	−0.70	−0.33	−0.05	0.02	−0.10						
Y/K	0.66	0.71	0.25	0.45	0.60	−0.56					
Y/L	0.73	0.63	0.37	0.13	0.51	−0.67	0.68				
Y/X	0.70	0.23	0.05	0.05	−0.11	−0.70	0.36	0.37			
K/L	0.08	−0.10	0.15	−0.40	−0.11	−0.14	−0.40	0.40	0.01		
X/L	0.29	0.49	0.35	0.10	0.60	−0.23	0.46	0.79	−0.28	0.41	

The relationship between multi- and single-factor productivity growth

The first question to which we turn is the relationship between multi-factor and single-factor productivity growth. With three inputs, there are three single-factor productivity growth rates to consider – labour, capital and intermediate. Cross-industry average rates of growth of these quantities (from table 4.1) have been as follows over long periods:

Period	MFP	Y/L	Y/K	Y/X
1954–73	0.88	4.09	− 0.49	− 0.27
1973–86	− 0.47	3.01	− 2.17	− 1.65
1954–86	0.35	3.66	− 1.14	− 0.81

Two conclusions stand out from these figures. First, capital and inter-mediate productivity growth have been negative throughout, while labour productivity growth has of course been positive. Second, all productivity growth rates, both multi- and single, were lower in the second half of the period, that is, multi- and single-factor productivity growth rates have tended to move together. The second point is reinforced by consideration of the correlations between the various productivity concepts (table 4.11). MFP is quite highly correlated with all three single-factor measures, in both halves of the period. In other words, industries with high MFP growth rates tend also to have high (or less negative) single-factor productivity growth rates.[9] The correlation with intermediate productivity is particularly high in 1973–86 (0.86). Labour productivity tends to be moderately well correlated with capital productivity, but neither is particularly strongly related to intermediate productivity.

Fabricant's 'Law'

Fabricant (1942), in his study of US industrial growth between 1899 and 1939, was apparently the first to draw attention to a number of empirical regularities, which have subsequently been confirmed for different coun-tries and time periods by other writers. The particular regularities with which we shall be concerned here are the following: first, a positive correlation across industries between the growth of output and the growth of labour productivity. Following Scott (1989), this regularity will be called Fabricant's Law.[10] Second, a negative correlation between the growth of output and the growth of output prices. Third, a negative correlation between the growth of unit labour costs and the growth of prices.

Fabricant's Law has been observed by subsequent authors to hold for a number of other time periods and countries, for example, by Caves and Barton (1991) for the US after World War II, by Salter (1966) for 28 UK industries over 1924–50, and by Wragg and Robertson (1978) for the UK over 1954–73. Fabricant's Law shows up strongly in the present sample too. The growth of labour productivity is indeed highly correlated with the growth of output, though the relationship weakens after 1973 – the values are 0.62 in 1954–73, 0.49 in 1973–86 and 0.63 for the whole span (table 4.11). For 1924–50, Salter reports a value of 0.81 (*op cit*, table 16).[11] The same relationship also holds over shorter periods (table 4.14,

Table 4.12. *Correlation coefficients between MFP growth and growth of:*

Period	N	Y	K	L	X	q
1954–58	124	0.42	0.02	0.04	− 0.04	− 0.80
1958–63	124	0.45	0.05	0.17	0.16	− 0.76
1963–68	130	0.34	− 0.03	0.09	0.08	− 0.80
1968–73	130	0.51	0.13	0.20	− 0.15	− 0.71
1973–76	133	0.63	0.16	0.11	− 0.22	− 0.75
1976–79	133	0.48	0.01	− 0.04	− 0.04	− 0.47
1979–82	133	0.49	− 0.17	− 0.19	0.09	− 0.64
1982–86	133	0.42	0.02	0.07	0.03	− 0.45

Note: N = Number of industries.

column 1), though interestingly we can see that its strength declines steadily in each sub-period after 1973. Nevertheless, the elasticity of labour productivity with respect to output is virtually the same in the two halves of our period: in regressions of the growth of Y/L on the growth of Y, the coefficients on the growth of Y were as follows (124 industries):[12]

	1954–73	*1973–86*
Coefficient	0.320	0.308
(*t* ratio)	(8.69)	(6.28)

The second empirical regularity noted by Fabricant also shows up as highly significant statistically, but less strong economically. Growth of output (Y) is negatively correlated with growth of prices (q), but the coefficient of − 0.33 (table 4.11), is much less in absolute value than the one Salter reports (− 0.84). On the other hand, the correlation between the growth of labour productivity (Y/L) and that of prices is considerably higher in absolute value, at − 0.67, though once again lower absolutely than the corresponding figure of Salter's (− 0.88).

Do similar relationships hold for MFP as for labour productivity? The answer is yes. In every sub-period there is a significantly positive correlation between MFP growth and output growth and a significantly negative one with price growth (table 4.12), though there is some sign of both relationships weakening after 1973. These two relationships are also found to hold over long periods, both before and after 1973, and are of the same strength as in shorter periods (table 4.11 and Charts 4.13–4.16). The elasticities of MFP with respect to output, from regressions of MFP growth on output growth, were as follows (124 industries, constant included):

	1954–73	*1973–86*
Coefficient	0.163	0.184
(*t* ratio)	(6.56)	(4.65)

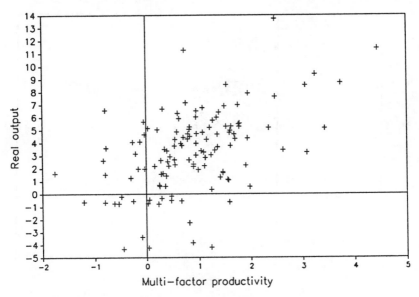

Chart 4.13   MFP and output (growth rates, per cent p.a., 1954–73)

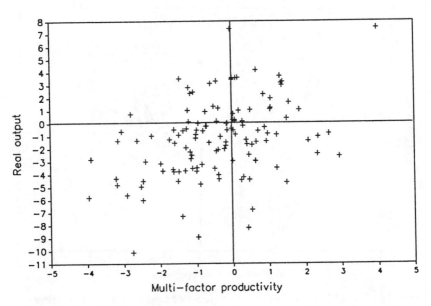

Chart 4.14   MFP and output (growth rates, per cent p.a., 1973–86)

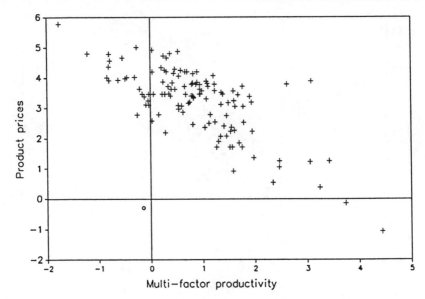

Chart 4.15 MFP and product prices (growth rates, per cent p.a.,
1954–73)

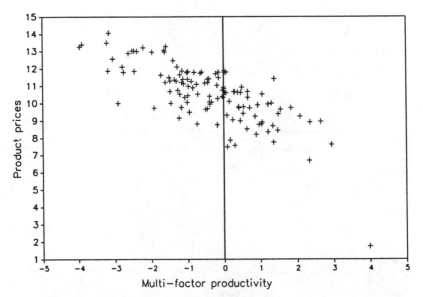

Chart 4.16 MFP and product prices (growth rates, per cent p.a.,
1973–86)

The elasticity is somewhat higher in the second half of the period, even though the regression 'explains' rather less of the variance of MFP growth.

Though Fabricant's Law appears to hold for both labour productivity and MFP, there is an important possible qualification to consider. The statistically significant correlation coefficients might be entirely due to a common measurement error affecting both output growth and productivity growth. After all, productivity growth (whether MFP or labour) is actually calculated as output growth *minus* input growth. So an error in the estimation of output growth might explain these statistically significant results. To see whether this is so or not, consider the correlation coefficient between measured output growth and measured MFP growth, on the asumption that the true correlation is zero but that a common measurement error affects both variables. Assume that measured output growth, $\hat{Y}'$, where a 'hat' denotes a growth rate, and measured MFP growth, μ', are related to the true values ($\hat{Y}$ and μ) as follows:

$$\hat{Y}' = \hat{Y} + u$$

$$\mu' = \mu + u, \qquad \mathrm{E}(u) = \mathrm{E}(\hat{Y}u) = \mathrm{E}(\mu u) = 0,$$

where u is the measurement error. The correlation coefficient (ρ) between measured output growth and measured MFP growth is

$$\rho(\hat{Y}',\mu') = \mathrm{Cov}(\hat{Y}',\mu')/[\sigma(\hat{Y}')\,\sigma(\mu')]$$
$$= [\mathrm{Cov}(\hat{Y},\mu) + \sigma^2(u)]/[\sigma(\hat{Y}')\,\sigma(\mu')]$$
$$= \sigma^2(u)/[\sigma(\hat{Y}')\,\sigma(\mu')],$$

since by hypothesis $\mathrm{Cov}(\hat{Y},\mu) = 0$. Obviously we have no direct knowledge of the size of the measurement error u. But the most likely source of serious error is in the producer prices, where as discussed in chapter 2 the quality of the data deteriorates the further back in time we go. A reasonable upper bound for the standard deviation of the measurement error is one half the standard deviation of measured price growth ($\Delta \ln q$): the latter was 1.11 in 1954–73 and 1.79 in 1973–86 (table 4.1). The upper bound for the size of the spurious correlation coefficient is then, applying the relevant numbers from table 4.1 to the formula just derived, 0.10 for 1954–73 and 0.17 for 1973–86. Adding two standard errors yields 0.28 and 0.35 respectively.[13] The correlation coefficients between output and MFP growth in table 4.11 clearly exceed these figures, so we can reject the hypothesis that the true correlation is zero. A similar calculation yields the same conclusion for shorter periods (table 4.12). *A fortiori*, what holds for MFP is also true for labour productivity: the correlations cannot be explained simply as the consequence of measurement error. A further point to consider is that any measurement error in the *inputs*, which are also partly dependent on producer prices, will tend to reduce the observed correlations *below* their true value.

Finally, is there any relationship between the growth of MFP and the growth of inputs? The sign of the correlation between MFP growth and the employment of inputs will depend on the extent of scale economies, the bias of technical change and the elasticity of demand for the industry's output. The general idea is that technical change lowers costs and hence induces firms to produce more output. But technical change allows the production of more output with the same inputs so that even under constant returns and unbiased technical change, there are contradictory pressures at work. Therefore, there is no *a priori* reason to expect a significant positive or negative correlation between MFP growth and input growth. It turns out that this expectation is confirmed: the correlations between MFP growth and the growth rates of our three inputs (tables 4.11 and 4.12) vary in sign for different time periods, are always small and are usually insignificant.

Wages and labour productivity

The third of Fabricant's empirical regularities, a negative correlation between unit labour costs (in our notation, $p_L L/Y$) and price (q), follows from the first and second, provided that the growth of wages (p_L) is not too highly correlated with the growth of labour productivity ($y \equiv Y/L$): if $\hat{y}$ is positively correlated with $\hat{Y}$, and $\hat{Y}$ is negatively correlated with $\hat{q}$, then the growth of unit labour costs ($p_L - \hat{y}$) will be negatively correlated with $\hat{q}$, provided that the correlation between p_L and $\hat{y}$ is not too strongly positive.[14] In other words, if nominal wages tend to go up at the same rate in all industries, then industries in which labour productivity rises fastest will (*ceteris paribus*) be the ones in which costs and prices are falling fastest and hence the ones in which output is rising most rapidly. On the other hand, it is possible that some of the benefits of technical change may be appropriated by labour in terms of higher wages (or by firms in increased profits), rather than going to the consumer in the form of lower product prices.

Salter rejected the latter possibility, arguing that (1966, p. 115), 'the market for labour is common to all industries and, over the long run, the movement of wages in each industry is primarily determined by the movements of wages in the economy as a whole'. In this connection he cited the relatively low dispersion of wage growth compared to that of productivity growth, found also in the present sample.[15] Salter and, following him, Wragg and Robertson (1978) found no significant correlation between the growth of wages and labour productivity. His conclusion has recently been disputed by Carruth and Oswald (1989, p. 91),

Table 4.13. *Correlation coefficients between the growth rates of MFP and the growth rates of:*

Period	Y/L	p_L	p_K	p_X
Short periods				
1954–58	0.70	− 0.09	0.18	− 0.39
1958–63	0.48	− 0.12	0.39	0.01
1963–68	0.45	− 0.05	0.36	0.01
1968–73	0.43	0.17	0.35	0.34
1973–76	0.71	− 0.11	0.27	0.30
1976–79	0.68	0.19	0.44	0.29
1979–82	0.79	0.05	0.22	0.03
1982–86	0.59	0.23	0.45	0.13
1973–79	0.72	− 0.13	0.19	0.31
1979–86	0.69	− 0.07	0.42	0.09
Long periods				
1954–73	0.69	0.01	0.20	− 0.02
1973–86	0.73	− 0.05	0.13	0.01
1954–86	0.74	− 0.07	0.09	− 0.04

Note: Number of industries varies – see table 4.1.

and hence some care is needed in distinguishing between the various concepts of real and nominal productivity and wages.

We might ask, first of all, does the real *consumption* wage rise faster in industries in which *physical* productivity is rising faster? That is, do workers benefit in terms of spending power over consumption goods, when their physical productivity is rising rapidly? (An analogous question could be asked about capitalists.) If the answer to this question were yes, it would mean that increased physical productivity was *not* being translated into lower prices for consumers. Since the prices of consumption goods rise at the same rate for all workers, we can answer this question by correlating the growth of *nominal* wages (p_L) with the growth of either MFP or of labour productivity (Y/L). The results are in tables 4.13 and 4.14. It is clear that for MFP growth the correlation is virtually zero in long periods, though it is just barely significant in three out of eight sub-periods. Though the correlation is a little higher for labour productivity, and does become significant in five out of eight sub-periods, it is never very large and over long periods it is insignificant. This is a similar relationship to the one considered by Salter (he actually correlated nominal earnings per operative with output per operative) and for which he reported a coefficient of 0.09 (his figure 14, p. 115); his conclusion is thus confirmed.

There is rather more evidence that capital gets higher rewards when

Productivity and Growth

Table 4.14. *Growth rates of real and nominal labour productivity: correlations with other variables*

Period	Y	Real labour productivity (Y/L) and: q	p_L	Nominal labour productivity (qY/L) and p_L
Short periods				
1954–58	0.61	− 0.60	0.07	0.34
1958–63	0.62	− 0.38	0.37	0.46
1963–68	0.65	− 0.32	0.27	0.28
1968–73	0.74	− 0.52	0.16	0.24
1973–76	0.73	− 0.65	− 0.09	0.14
1976–79	0.65	− 0.34	0.33	0.32
1979–82	0.56	− 0.58	0.17	0.33
1982–86	0.50	− 0.33	0.39	0.41
1973–79	0.65	− 0.70	− 0.04	0.13
1979–86	0.49	− 0.57	0.15	0.26
Long periods				
1954–73	0.62	− 0.67	0.13	0.26
1973–86	0.51	− 0.69	0.15	0.35
1954–86	0.63	− 0.67	0.19	0.43

Note: Number of industries varies – see table 4.1. 1973–86 uses 133 industries, which accounts for slight difference with figures for this period in table 4.11.

physical productivity is rising more rapidly: the correlation between MFP growth and the growth of the price of capital services is quite high in sub-periods (0.35–0.45) and invariably positive, though in long periods it is considerably lower: 0.20 for 1954–73 and 0.13 for 1973–86 (table 4.13).

An alternative question is, when the available pie is rising rapidly, do workers get higher rewards? This question can be answered by correlating the growth of wages (p_L) with the growth of *nominal* productivity (qY/L) – see the last column of table 4.14. Here the coefficients are rather higher and generally significant; interestingly, the correlation is just as high or higher over long periods as over short (for example, 0.43 for 1954–86, compared with 0.26 for 1954–73 and 0.35 for 1973–86).[16]

An objection commonly made to the possibility of persistently high correlations between the growth of MFP or of labour productivity and wages is that we would then observe a widening dispersion of wages, which is not the case. On the contrary, in the long run migration of labour across industries should tend to equalise earnings. The results above support this objection. A similar point should apply to the return on capital: high profits should induce entry of new firms, but the correlations above between MFP growth and profitability (p_K) are invariably positive. However, as we have already seen, there is little persistence in MFP growth rates, so the long-run adjustment mechanism is not required to operate: the industries with high (low) MFP growth in one period are by and large not the same as those with high (low) growth in the subsequent one.

CONCLUSIONS

Estimates have been presented of the growth of MFP for the period 1954–86, divided up into eight sub-periods. For the whole period, estimates for 124 industries are available; the maximum number for any sub-period was 133. To develop these estimates, it was also necessary to estimate the growth rates of output, capital, labour and intermediate input, together with the shares of each input in the value of gross output. The main empirical findings were as follows.

Up till 1973, the growth of inputs can account for the greater part of the growth of output; the same is largely true of the period since 1982. The major anomaly is the period 1973–82; even a generous allowance for accelerated scrapping of capital does not suffice to eliminate the puzzle.

There appear to be common factors affecting MFP growth in any given period; three of these factors, in 1973–6, 1976–9 and 1979–82, were negative (relative to 1954–8).

The slowdown in both MFP growth and in labour productivity growth in the 1970s and the subsequent recovery in the 1980s were substantial changes from an economic point of view. Moreover, they were also statistically significant changes.

There is little persistence in the growth rates of output, inputs and productivity, even over long periods.

The empirical regularities, which were first detected by Fabricant (1942) for the US and subsequently confirmed for the UK by Salter (1966), continued to hold in both halves of our period, 1954–73 and 1973–86. These regularities are: firstly, a positive correlation between labour productivity growth and output growth; and secondly, a negative correlation between output growth and price growth. It was also found that similar relationships hold for MFP growth; that is, in both halves of our period, MFP growth is positively related to output growth and negatively to price growth, though the relationship is not as strong as the one for labour productivity.

Another of Salter's results, that wages rise no faster in industries where labour productivity is growing more rapidly, was found to hold in our period too.

5

OUTPUT AND PRODUCTIVITY GROWTH IN AGGREGATE MANUFACTURING

INTRODUCTION

In chapter 2 the theory of productivity measurement at the industry level was discussed. Nothing was said however about MFP growth at higher levels of aggregation, for instance manufacturing as a whole. It seems obvious that there should be *some* relationship between productivity growth in the industries of which an aggregate is composed and productivity growth in the aggregate itself, but it is not immediately obvious what that relationship should be. One might think that MFP growth at the aggregate level should be some sort of weighted average of industry MFP growth rates, but this turns out not to be the case. In this chapter we first review the theory of MFP measurement at the aggregate level, before going on to present estimates, using a variety of methods, for total manufacturing. It will be argued that the theoretical problem of how to measure MFP growth at the aggregate level has in fact been solved, within certain limitations, by the contributions of Domar (1961) and of Hulten (1978), but that the lessons of their work have not been widely appreciated. Instead many writers have favoured an approach based on aggregate value added, which, it will be argued, is seriously flawed. For instance, it will be shown that for the aggregate of concern here, namely total manufacturing, the value added method produces estimates of MFP growth which are twice those given by the preferred method. As a by-product of the critique of the value added approach, an alternative measure of total manufacturing output, namely final output, is proposed and estimates using this concept are presented and discussed.

ALTERNATIVE MEASURES OF AGGREGATE MFP GROWTH

Initially, three methods of measuring MFP growth at the aggregate level which have attracted theoretical attention will be considered; later a fourth will also be discussed. In summary form, the three methods are: first, Hulten's method, defined as growth of a Divisia index of final outputs *minus* growth of a Divisia index of primary inputs, where primary inputs include, but are not necessarily confined to, capital and labour (Hulten, 1978); second, Domar's method, defined as 'Domar aggregation' over industry (or sectoral) MFP growth rates (Domar, 1961); and third, the aggregate value added method, defined as growth of aggregate value added *minus* growth of Divisia indices of aggregate capital and labour (Jorgenson and Griliches, 1967; Gollop, 1985; Jorgenson *et al.*, 1987). We shall refer to the three different concepts of MFP growth as μ^H, μ^{DA} and μ^{AV} respectively, where the superscripts are to remind us that the first method is based on the work of Hulten (H), the second on Domar aggregation (DA) over industries and the third on aggregate value added (AV).

Hulten's method

The first method of calculating aggregate MFP growth can be written as:

$$\mu^H = \Sigma_i[q_i Z_i/\Sigma_i q_i Z_i][\dot{Z}_i/Z_i] - \Sigma_k[w_k J_k/\Sigma_k w_k J_k][\dot{J}_k/J_k] \qquad (5.1)$$

where Z_i is final output of the product of the ith industry ($i = 1, \ldots, n$), q_i is its price, J_k is the kth primary input ($k = 1, \ldots, m$) and w_k its price (assumed common to all industries).[1] By 'final output' is meant that part of industry sales which is *not* destined to be used up in the current period by the industries included in the aggregate under study. So if the aggregate under study is the whole economy, final output is public and private consumption, investment and exports. If the aggregate is total UK manufacturing, final output is total sales of UK manufacturing firms *less* sales to other UK manufacturing firms of products which will be used up within the current period;[2] alternatively, final output equals aggregate value added in manufacturing *plus* aggregate purchases from outside the manufacturing sector. The seminal contribution of Hulten (1978) was to derive the aggregate MFP growth rate as the solution to a maximisation problem. He showed that if (1) the economy is competitive; (2) for all j, the jth primary factor is paid the same in all industries; and (3) the underlying industry-level production functions are homogeneous of degree one, then μ^H measures the outward shift of the social production possibility frontier. In symbols, if the social production possibility frontier is given by

$$F(Z_1, \ldots, Z_n; \ J_1, \ldots, J_m; \ T) = 0,$$

then

$$\mu^H = \dot{F}/\Sigma_i(\partial F/\partial Z_i) Z_i,$$

where the denominator of the right-hand side can be interpreted as the value of output. Note that the social production possibility frontier is a much more general concept than the aggregate production function – we are not required, as we are in the case of the latter, to aggregate either outputs or inputs.

Domar aggregation

The second method, Domar aggregation, can be defined as:

$$\mu^{DA} = \Sigma_i[(q_i Y_i)/\Sigma_i q_i Z_i]\mu_i, \tag{5.2}$$

where μ_i is the growth rate of MFP in the ith industry, which for empirical purposes can be calculated by equation (2.6). Note that μ^{DA} is a weighted sum (*not* a weighted average) of the industry MFP growth rates, where the weights are the ratios of nominal gross output of each industry to total nominal final output. The weights will clearly sum to more than one, since aggregate gross output exceeds aggregate final output (because of the inclusion of sales made within the manufacturing sector in gross output but not in final output). Domar (1961) derived his weighting scheme by asking, what system of weights would produce an aggregate MFP growth rate which is invariant to the degree of integration or aggregation of the economy? His scheme satisfies this requirement, while earlier alternatives, such as that proposed by Leontief (1953) do not.[3] The intuition behind Domar aggregation is that an industry which sells a great deal to others receives a higher weight, because MFP growth in this industry contributes not only directly to aggregate MFP growth but also indirectly, through lowering costs elsewhere in the economy.

Hulten (1978) showed that under his assumptions his method and Domar's are equivalent, that is, $\mu^H = \mu^{DA}$. This is an important result: the Hulten method has a strong theoretical rationale, but the Domar method is, as we shall see, much easier to implement, so that the fact that the two methods are equivalent (at least under certain assumptions) is very useful.

In calculating μ^H, an important point of interpretation revolves around the issue of what are to be counted as primary inputs. For a totally closed economy, the answer (within the framework of the industry production function (2.2)) is labour and capital only; a corollary is that total final output is equal to aggregate value added. In an open economy, or when aggregating to the level of a sector within a closed economy (for example, total manufacturing), it is necessary to count also as primary inputs those goods or services which are purchased outside the aggregate and which are used up in the production process. Intuitively, this can be seen by considering a one-industry economy, in which the single output is produced by means of domestic labour and capital and an imported raw material. Clearly the imported raw material should be considered as a primary input from the point of view of the domestic economy. Clearly too, aggregate and industry MFP growth are in this case identical, but equation (5.2) must still hold; this will only be the case if $Z_1 = Y_1$, that is, if final output is measured inclusive of the value of imports.[4]

The assumptions necessary to establish the equivalence of the Hulten and Domar methods, and therefore to establish that the Domar method can be interpreted as measuring the outward shift of the social production possibility frontier, are clearly restrictive. However, most of them are necessary anyway in order to be able to interpret our empirical measures of industry-level MFP as corresponding to the theoretical concept (see chapter 2): they amount to assuming that market prices measure social marginal products. The only additional assumption is that an input is paid the same wage in all industries. A test of this last assumption would be to calculate aggregate MFP growth by both Hulten's and Domar's method and check whether there was a 'significant' difference between them. Unfortunately, however, as we shall see, Hulten's method cannot be implemented in practice, at least not for the UK.

Aggregate value added method
The third method of calculating MFP growth is based on calculating aggregate value added, aggregate capital and aggregate labour, and is the one used most often in practice. Following Jorgenson *et al.* (1987), it can be formalised as follows:

$$\mu^{AV} = (\dot{V}/V) - [p_K K/p_V V](\dot{K}/K) - [p_L L/p_V V](\dot{L}/L), \qquad (5.3)$$

where V is aggregate (real) value added, K is aggregate capital, L is aggregate labour and p_V, p_K and p_L are the corresponding prices.

The accounting identity relating output and inputs is

$$p_V V = p_K K + p_L L.$$

How aggregate value added, capital and labour should be calculated will now be discussed. First of all, aggregate value added is constructed from industry-level value added (V_i), in fact as a simple sum of the latter:

$$V = \Sigma_i V_i. \qquad (5.4)$$

This equation assumes that the industry-level prices of value added, p_V^i, are all equal and so can be normalised to one in the base year. The justification for this assumption will be discussed below. The growth rate of aggregate value added is derived as follows. Differentiating equation (5.4) logarithmically with respect to time and using the assumption that the price of value added is the same in all industries we find:

$$\dot{V}/V = \Sigma_i(\dot{V}_i/V_i)(p_V^i V_i/p_V V). \qquad (5.6)$$

In other words, the growth of aggregate value added is a weighted average of the growth rates of industry value added, where the weights are the shares of each industry in aggregate nominal value added, these shares being of course observable. In order to calculate the V_i, a special-ised form of the industry production function (2.1) is now assumed:

$$Y_i = Y_i(V_i, X_i), \qquad i = 1, \ldots, n, \qquad (5.7)$$

where

$$V_i = V_i(K_i, L_i, t), \qquad (5.8)$$

the value added function. Note that a value added function will only exist if *either* the prices of intermediate input and output happen to rise at the same rate (which is certainly not the case for the present data set) *or* if intermediate input is (weakly) separable from the other inputs and from time, that is, if the marginal rate of substitution between capital and labour is independent of the level of intermediate input and of time. The latter condition is of course.restrictive: for example, the existence of a value added function is inconsistent with the frequently asserted claim, that energy and capital are complements while energy and labour are substitutes.[5]

If the production function (5.7) has the translog form, and assuming as usual that elasticities can be replaced by value shares, differentiation of (5.7) gives

$$\Delta_u \ln V_i = (1/\bar{v}_V^i) \Delta_u \ln Y_i - (\bar{v}_X^i/\bar{v}_V^i) \Delta_u \ln X_i, \qquad (5.9)$$

where $\bar{v}_V^i$ and $\bar{v}_X^i$ are the average shares of nominal value added and intermediate input in nominal gross output, that is,

$$\bar{v}_V^i = (1/2)[v_V^i(T) + v_V^i(T - u)]$$

and

$$\bar{v}_X^i = (1/2)[v_X^i(T) + v_X^i(T - u)],$$

and the shares are given by

$$v_V^i = p_V^i V_i / q_i Y_i$$

$$v_X^i = p_X^i X_i / q_i Y_i, \qquad v_V^i + v_X^i = 1.$$

Since the shares are observable, (5.7) can be implemented to calculate the growth rate of each V_i. Also, if desired, we can calculate the price of value added in each industry, p_V^i, as the ratio of nominal value added to real value added (V_i). Given the growth of value added in each industry, the growth of aggregate value added can now be derived from (5.6). Finally, if required, the price of aggregate value added can be calculated as the ratio of aggregate nominal value added to aggregate real value added.[6]

When the value added method is applied in practice, frequently single rather than (as here) double deflation is employed and this is often justified by reference to Hill (1971). The latter argued that the error in measuring the growth rate of value added in (5.9) exceeds the error in measuring the growth rate of output and therefore single deflation, though biased, might be preferable in practice.[7] This point is valid for a single industry or sector, but here value added in manufacturing is being measured by aggregating over individual industries as in (5.6), so unless there are errors which are common across industries, the errors in individual industries will tend to cancel out.

Aggregate capital is assumed to be a translog function of the different types of capital:

$$\Delta_u \ln K = \Sigma_k \bar{v}_{Kk} \Delta_u \ln K_k, \qquad (5.10)$$

where

$$K_k = \Sigma_i K_{ik}$$

and $\bar{v}_{Kk}$ is the average share of capital of type k in total payments to capital, that is

$$\bar{v}_{Kk} = (1/2)[v_{Kk}(t) + v_{Kk}(t-u)]$$

and $\qquad v_{Kk} = p_{Kk} K_k / \Sigma_k p_{Kk} K_k.$

In exactly the same way, aggregate labour input can be measured as

$$\Delta_u \ln L = \Sigma_l \bar{v}_{Ll} \Delta_u \ln L_l \qquad (5.11)$$

where

$$L_l = \Sigma_i L_{il},$$

$$\bar{v}_{Ll} = (1/2)[v_{Ll}(t) + v_{Ll}(t-u)]$$

and $\qquad v_{Ll} = p_{Ll} L_l / \Sigma_l p_{Ll} L_l.$

Since the labour and capital shares are observable, the labour and capital aggregates are computable from (5.10) and (5.11). Consequently, μ^{AV} in equation (5.3) is now also computable.

The methods compared

Clearly, the aggregate value added method will not in general give the same results as Hulten's, so it is worth asking under what conditions the two methods are in fact equivalent. Jorgenson *et al.* (1987) show that, in a closed economy,[8] if each industry production function takes the specialised form of (5.7), and furthermore if all the value added functions are the same except for an (inessential) scalar multiple, then there exists an aggregate value added function, or simply an aggregate production function:

$$V = V(K, L, t).$$

The scalar multiple can be normalised to unity in each industry, so that if this assumption holds, the price of value added in each industy will be everywhere the same, that is,

$$p_V^i = p_V, \quad \text{all } i.$$

It is then permissible to aggregate value added as a simple sum of value added in each industry, as is done in (5.4). Finally, if competitive conditions prevail in product and factor markets, so that each input receives a common market price, then μ^{AV} as given in equation (5.3) is the correct measure of aggregate MFP growth.

Just as Hulten's and Domar's methods can be shown to be equal under certain assumptions, an analogous relationship holds for the aggregate value added method. Jorgenson *et al.* (1987, chapter 2) show that if all the above assumptions hold, then[9]

$$\mu^{AV} = \Sigma_i [q_i Y_i / \Sigma_i p_V^i V_i] \mu_i. \tag{5.12}$$

The right-hand side of (5.12) might be termed the 'bottom-up' version of the aggregate value added method, while (5.3) might be termed the 'top-down' version. If the same input is paid at different rates in different industries, then (5.12) is no longer true. Jorgenson *et al.* show that in this case terms reflecting the reallocation of value added and of labour and capital inputs across industries must be included (see also Gollop, 1985):

$$\mu^{AV} = \Sigma_i [q_i Y_i / \Sigma_i p_V^i V_i] \mu_i + \Sigma_i [(p_K^i - p_K) \dot{K}_i + (p_L^i - p_L) \dot{L}_i \\ - (p_V^i - p_V) \dot{V}][\Sigma_i p_V^i V_i]^{-1} \tag{5.13}$$

How should this equation be interpreted? Jorgenson *et al.* state (1987, p. 314): 'We can interpret the contributions of reallocations of value added and the primary-factor inputs as measures of departures from the assumptions that underlie our model of aggregate production.' In other words, the size of the reallocation terms is a test of the consistency of the assumptions. However, they go on to say, *à propos* of their empirical results: 'The departures from these very stringent assumptions have a sizeable impact on the aggregate productivity rate.' In other words, they are claiming (along with Gollop, 1985) that μ^{AV} (equation (5.3)) is the correct measure of productivity growth, even when the assumptions are not satisfied, and that the reallocation terms measure the effect on aggregate MFP growth of shifts of value added and of primary inputs between industries. This interpretation of the equation is quite different from the first one and is hard to justify. If the two sides of equation (5.12) differ by a 'significant' amount, then the assumptions on which the value added method relies must be rejected, so the left-hand side of (5.12) cannot be relied on. In that case, it is difficult to see what conclusions can be drawn from aggregating over industry MFP growth rates (the right-hand side of (5.12)), since the theoretical meaning of this calculation is now unclear.

The final output method

If we compare Domar's method, equation (5.2), with the 'bottom-up' version of the aggregate value added method, equation (5.12), we see that the only difference between them is in the denominator of the weights. Domar aggregation employs total nominal final output, while the other method employs total nominal value added. In the case of a closed economy, value added and final output are equal. In some cases, use of the value added method may be justified because the aggregate being studied is approximately closed. For instance, the aggregate MFP growth esti-mates of Jorgenson *et al.* (1987) were for the whole US economy. In their case therefore, the only difference between aggregate value added and aggregate final output is imported raw materials, a small proportion of GDP in the US. In the present case, however, the aggregate studied is a single sector, manufacturing, of a much more open economy, the UK, hence we cannot afford to ignore the issue (it turns out for example, as we shall see, that in 1984 value added was less than half of final output of manufacturing).

This suggests a fourth method of measuring aggregate MFP growth, in which final output would play the role of value added. For this method, final output is assumed to be a function of labour, capital and external input (M), where the latter is goods and services for intermediate use pur-chased outside the sector under consideration. At the industry level, inter-mediate input (X) is now split up into goods and services purchased from within the sector being aggregated (say, X'), and external input. Aggre-gate external input is assumed to be a translog function of its components, in just the same way as aggregate labour and capital (see equations (5.10) and (5.11)). In parallel with equations (5.7), (5.4) and (5.8), we assume

$$Y_i = Y_i(Z_i, X_i'), \tag{5.14}$$

$$Z_i = Z_i(K_i, L_i, M_i, t) \tag{5.15}$$

and

$$Z = \Sigma_i Z_i. \tag{5.16}$$

The accounting identity becomes:

$$p_Z Z = p_K K + p_L L + p_M M, \tag{5.17}$$

where p_Z and p_M are the prices of aggregate final output and of aggregate external input respectively. Of course, the production function (5.14) embodies a restrictive assumption, but less so than the analogous assump-tion required for the value added method (equation (5.7)).

Aggregate MFP growth under the final output method, μ^{FO}, can now be defined analogously with μ^{AV} (cf equation (5.3)) as[10]

$$\mu^{FO} = \dot{Z}/Z - [p_K K/p_Z Z](\dot{K}/K) - [p_L L/p_Z Z](\dot{L}/L)$$
$$- [p_M M/p_Z Z](\dot{M}/M). \tag{5.18}$$

By analogy with the result established by Jorgenson *et al.* (1987, chapter 2) and reproduced here as equation (5.12), we can show under similar assumptions that

$$\mu^{FO} = \Sigma_i[q_i Y_i/\Sigma_i p_Z^i Z_i]\mu_i. \tag{5.19}$$

That is, Domar aggregation and the final output method are equivalent.

Let us now sum up the advantages and disadvantages of the different methods. The Hulten method (equation (5.1)) has the clearest theoretical rationale. Empirically, however, it is hard to implement, since it requires us to know the final output of each industry; in the UK case, the data are inadequate for this task.[11] Fortunately, however, where its assumptions are satisfied, Hulten's method is equivalent to Domar aggregation (equation (5.2)). To implement Domar aggregation, the only additional information necessary, beyond what is required anyway to calculate industry MFP growth, is the nominal value of aggregate final output (for manufacturing, in our case). The aggregate value added method (equation (5.3)), as we have seen, is conceptually incorrect for an open economy. However, because it has frequently been used by other researchers, and in order to facilitate comparison with their work, results will be presented later on this basis also. Lastly, the final output method (equation (5.18)), is superior to the value added method, but suffers from some of the same practical drawbacks as Hulten's method. Hence no attempt has been made to implement it.

However, though an independent estimate of MFP growth cannot be derived by the final output method, the method can be put to a different use. Equations (5.18) and (5.19) can be combined and rearranged, to derive an estimate of the growth of aggregate final output of UK manufacturing:

$$\dot{Z}/Z = [p_K K/p_Z Z](\dot{K}/K) + [p_L L/p_Z Z](\dot{L}/L) + [p_M M/p_Z Z](\dot{M}/M)$$
$$+ \Sigma_i[q_i Y_i/\Sigma_i p_Z^i Z_i]\mu_i. \tag{5.20}$$

In addition to the data required to implement Donar aggregation, we only need data on the growth of external input into manufacturing (M) in order to calculate the growth of final output. It turns out (see below) that (somewhat rough) estimates can be made of these. The interest of this calculation is that final output is an alternative and arguably superior measure of output to value added.

As an interpretive tool, final output has a number of advantages over value added. Suppose that value added in UK manufacturing is observed to fall. This could be either because UK manufacturers are becoming less successful in selling their products to final buyers, or it could be because UK manufacturers are choosing to purchase more of the inputs they require from outside the UK manufacturing sector. These two explanations clearly have quite different implications, but observation of value added alone can never tell us which is nearer the truth. However, measurement of final output and external input yields the required information.

METHODS OF CALCULATION

MFP growth at the level of total manufacturing has been calculated by the method of Domar aggregation and by the aggregate value added method. To recapitulate, Domar aggregation employs a weighted sum of industry MFP growth rates, where the weights are the ratios of nominal industry gross output to nominal total final output in manufacturing (equation (5.2)). Two versions of the value added approach have been implemented, 'top-down' and 'bottom-up'. The 'top-down' version calculates aggregate MFP growth as the growth rate of aggregate value added minus the share-weighted growth rates of aggregate capital and aggregate labour and is based on equation (5.3). In the 'bottom-up' version aggregate MFP growth is calculated by aggregating over industry MFP growth rates, using the ratios of nominal industry gross output to nominal total value added as weights, following equation (5.12).

We shall consider the value added approach first. In more detail, the estimates of the 'top-down' version are derived from a Törnqvist approximation to equation (5.3):

$$\Delta_u \ln \text{MFP} = \Delta_u \ln V - \bar{w}_K \Delta_u \ln K - \bar{w}_L \Delta_u \ln L, \qquad (5.21)$$

where

$$\bar{w}_K = [w_K(t) + w_K(t-u)]/2$$
$$\bar{w}_L = [w_L(t) + w_L(t-u)]/2,$$

and

$$w_K = p_K K / p_V V$$
$$w_L = p_L L / p_V V,$$

the shares of capital and labour in value added. The growth rates of capital and labour are calculated from equations (5.10) and (5.11). The growth rate of aggregate value added, in continuous time, was given in equation (5.6). The actual calculation employed a Törnqvist approximation to this equation:

$$\Delta_u \ln V = \Sigma_i \bar{w}_V^i \Delta_u \ln V_i, \tag{5.22}$$

where

$$\bar{w}_V^i = [w_V^i(t) + w_V^i(t - u)]/2$$
$$\bar{w}_V^i = p_V^i V_i / p_V V.$$

For the 'bottom-up' version of the value added approach a Törnqvist approximation to equation (5.12) was employed:

$$\Delta_u \ln(\text{MFP}) = (1/2) \Sigma_i [(q_i(t)\, Y_i(t)/p_V(t)\, V(t))$$
$$+ (q_i(t - u)\, Y_i(t - u)/p_V(t - u)\, V(t - u))] \Delta_u \ln(\text{MFP}_i) \tag{5.23}$$

Turning now to the preferred Domar method, the calculations are based on equation (5.2), whose empirical counterpart was again a Törnqvist index:

$$\Delta_u \ln(\text{MFP}) = (1/2) \Sigma_i [(q_i(t)\, Y_i(t)/FO(t))$$
$$+ (q_i(t - u)\, Y_i(t - u)/FO(t - u)] \Delta_u \ln(\text{MFP}_i), \tag{5.24}$$

where $FO = \Sigma_i q_i Z_i$ is total nominal final output.

Final output of manufacturing, which is equal to total value added in manufacturing *plus* imports from abroad purchased by the manufacturing sector *plus* purchases by manufacturing from domestic non-manufacturing, can be derived from the input–output tables, but not from the Census of Production. Because the input–output tables are deliberately made consistent with the *Blue Book*, and not with the Census of Production (the latter not being used in compiling national income statistics), final output was calculated as follows: first of all, the ratio of final output to value added in total manufacturing was derived from the input–output tables and then this ratio was used to gross up the Census of Production figure for total value added, to obtain an estimate of final output. Input–output tables are available for 1954, 1963, 1968, 1973, 1979 and 1984. They are not available for 1958, 1976 or 1986. 1984 was used for 1986 and the other missing years were filled in by simple interpolation. The ratios derived from the input–output tables were as follows:

Final output ÷ Value added

1954	1.86
1963	1.72
1968	1.83
1973	1.99
1979	2.24
1984	2.03

Recalling that aggregate MFP growth is a weighted *sum*, not a weighted average, of industry MFP growth rates, it is clear that the rise in the ratio after 1968 will tend to reduce the aggregate growth rate of MFP.

The same calculation also yields (from the accounting identity (5.17)) the nominal value of external input into UK manufacturing. To calculate the growth of final output, we need an appropriate deflator for external input. Unfortunately, only a rough and ready one can be found. Three different price indices were combined together: the official 'price index of materials and fuel purchased by manufacturing industry';[12] the price index of non-industrial services constructed for this study (see Appendix B); and a price index of imported manufactured goods of an intermediate nature.[13] The weights used to combine the three indices were purchases by manufacturing of agriculture and other domestic raw materials, non-manufactured imports, energy and water; services; and manufactured imports. These purchases were estimated from the input–output tables (those of 1968, 1974 and 1984).[14] The first of these categories of expenditure corresponds roughly to what the official price index covers: note that the official index excludes services and all domestic manufactured goods, though it does include some imported semi-manufactures.[15] The other categories are self-explanatory. In 1984, these weights were 23.6 per cent, 39.1 per cent and 37.3 per cent respectively; there has been some tendency for the weight given to manufactured imports to rise – in 1974, it was only 25.0 per cent.

THE ESTIMATES

Aggregate value added method

Estimates made by the aggregate value added method appear in table 5.1. From 1954 to 1973, value added grew quite rapidly at an average rate of 3.5 per cent. Capital grew at 3.9 per cent, while labour declined moderately at 0.5 per cent. Because labour is accorded a much larger weight than capital, the result was that MFP growth was also high, at 2.3 per cent per annum. From 1973 to 1982 value added fell, by an astonishing total of 35 per cent. Since 1982, growth has recovered to a modest level. The growth of capital also slowed after 1973, but to nothing like the same extent; only in 1979–82 was growth actually negative. However the decline of the labour input accelerated sharply; on average since 1973 labour has been falling at 3.8 per cent per annum. MFP growth since 1973 has also been negative, averaging − 0.9 per cent per annum (though it has turned positive since 1982). It is noteworthy that capital's share fell sharply by about a tenth after 1973; since 1979 it has recovered to nearly its former level.

Matthews *et al.* (1982) have produced estimates for manufacturing by

Table 5.1. *Sources of growth in aggregate manufacturing: aggregate value added method*

Period	Growth rates (% p.a.)			Shares (%)		μ^{AV} (% p.a.)
	V	K	L	K	L	
Short periods						
1954–58	0.86	4.18	0.14	39.63	60.37	− 0.88
1958–63	4.85	3.79	− 0.23	39.72	60.29	3.48
1963–68	4.19	4.24	− 0.68	39.13	60.87	2.94
1968–73	3.51	3.35	− 1.25	38.92	61.08	2.97
1973–76	− 4.55	2.25	− 2.18	37.82	62.18	− 4.04
1976–79	− 2.39	2.44	− 2.01	35.77	64.23	− 1.97
1979–82	− 7.42	− 0.45	− 8.83	35.62	64.38	− 1.57
1982–86	1.53	0.91	− 2.67	38.45	61.55	2.83
1973–79	− 3.47	2.35	− 2.10	–	–	− 3.01
1979–86	− 2.30	0.33	− 5.31	–	–	0.94
Long periods						
1954–73	3.48	3.88	− 0.54	–	–	2.29
1973–86	− 2.84	1.26	− 3.83	–	–	− 0.88
1954–86	0.91	2.81	− 1.88	–	–	1.00

Notes: $\dot{K}/K$: calculated from equation (5.10). $\dot{L}/L$: calculated from equation (5.11). $\dot{V}/V$: calculated from equation (5.22). μ^{AV}: calculated from equation (5.21).

the aggregate value added method which may be compared with these. They find that, over the period 1955–73, output grew at an exponential rate of 2.9 per cent per annum, capital at 3.2 per cent per annum, labour at − 1.0 per cent per annum and MFP at 2.6 per cent per annum (calculated from their table K.1 – note that they use compound annual growth rates, not exponential ones). The last figure is fairly close to this study's estimate of 2.29 per cent for 1954–73 (table 17). This agreement is however something of a coincidence, since there are larger, though off-setting, differences between our and their estimates of the components of MFP growth. Taking these in turn, their capital estimates are gross (that is, not allowing for depreciation), and so may be expected to be a bit lower than ours. Their estimate of labour input is person-hours and does not reflect the shift towards white-collar work, hence produces a larger decline than ours. Surprisingly, the biggest difference is between the estimates of output growth. Theirs, which derive from the *Blue Book*, amount to single deflation of a nominal aggregate; ours are built up from industry-level nominal gross output and nominal intermediate input and use (in effect) double deflation. The nominal aggregate they used was a gross one (see their Appendix I, p. 594). It so happens that over this period the growth rates of manufacturing output prices and of manufacturing input prices were almost identical – according to CSO (1980b,

Appendix G), the former grew at 3.36 per cent per annum and the latter at 3.39 per cent per annum over 1954–73. Hence double or single deflation should not affect the results much over this period (though it would over the subsequent one). However, as the Census of Production shows, nominal gross output and nominal net output (adjusted for definition change) grew at very different rates, with the result that, deflating by the output price index for aggregate manufacturing, we may calculate that 'real' net output in manufacturing as a whole grew at 4.1 per cent per annum over 1954–73, while 'real' gross output grew at only 3.4 per cent per annum.[16] The difference between these two growth rates is similar to the difference between our estimate of the growth of manufacturing value added and the corresponding estimate of Matthews *et al.*, which suggests that their use of gross output is the cause of the divergence between us.

The work of Mendis and Muellbauer (1984) can also be used to derive MFP estimates by the aggregate value added method. From an econometric equation (essentially a Cobb-Douglas production function with additional variables to allow for biases in the measurement of manufacturing output and for varying cyclical utilisation of labour) estimated on quarterly data for total manufacturing, they conclude that the underlying growth rate of *labour* productivity was 3.4 per cent from 1955Q1 to 1973Q1 and 1.4 per cent from 1973Q1 to 1979Q3. Since they define the underlying growth rate of labour productivity as the growth of output minus the share-weighted growth of labour, we may subtract from their estimate the share-weighted growth of capital, to obtain an estimate of MFP growth. Using their figures for capital stock growth (3.7 per cent p.a. for 1955Q1–1973Q1 and 2.5 per cent per annum for 1973Q1–1979Q3, which derive from the CSO's 'gross' stock estimates), we obtain MFP growth rates of 2.2 per cent for the first period and 0.6 per cent for the second. The first of these is very close to our estimate in table 5.1; the second is very different, the reason probably being Mendis and Muellbauer's adjustment for labour utilisation, which obviously affected this period more than the other.[17]

As far as accounting for the sources of growth is concerned, the main message of table 5.1 seems to be that the growth of inputs accounts for only a minor proportion of the growth of output, about one third over 1954–73. The corollary is that MFP growth is the principal source of output growth, at least according to the value added method. However, as we have already seen, such an impression is contradicted by the industry level results. As table 4.5 (discussed in chapter 4 above) shows, on average input growth accounts for most of the growth of output, except in the 1973–9 period. Here then is one case where the choice of method is absolutely crucial to the qualitative conclusion reached. The

Table 5.2. *Growth rate of MFP in aggregate manufacturing: comparison of aggregate value added and Domar aggregation methods (%, p.a.)*

Period	μ^{AV} top-down	μ^{AV} bottom-up	μ^{DA}
Short periods			
1954–58	− 0.88	− 0.91	− 0.50
1958–63	3.48	3.25	1.85
1963–68	2.94	2.76	1.55
1968–73	2.97	2.81	1.48
1973–76	− 4.04	− 4.18	− 2.04
1976–79	− 1.97	− 2.23	− 1.03
1979–82	− 1.57	− 2.07	− 0.95
1982–86	2.83	2.58	1.24
1973–79	− 3.01	− 3.21	− 1.53
1979–86	0.94	0.59	0.30
Long periods			
1954–73	2.29	2.13	1.18
1973–86	− 0.88	− 1.17	− 0.54
1954–86	1.00	0.79	0.48

Note: Column 1: see note to table (5.1). Column 2: calculated from equation (5.23). Column 3: calculated from equation (5.24).

industry level results give us one picture, the aggregate value added method another. However, as we have argued all along, the aggregate value added method is likely to systematically overestimate MFP growth.

Aggregate value added versus Domar aggregation: a comparison of estimates

Table 5.2 compares three different ways of estimating MFP growth in total manufacturing. Column 1 repeats the 'top-down', aggregate value added estimates just discussed; the estimates in column 2 are by the 'bottom-up' version of the same method, produced by aggregating over industry MFP growth rates, using ratios of gross output to value added. If all the assumptions of the aggregate value added method were satisfied, then these two columns should be identical (see equation (5.12)). As can be seen, they are very similar but the second column's figures are smaller in every period, albeit by a small amount. It is reassuring that the difference is not large, since it suggests that the difference between the Hulten and Domar aggregation methods would also be small, if it were possible to make the comparison.

The preferred estimates, those made by Domar aggregation, appear in the last column of table 5.2. Over the 19-year period 1954–73, MFP growth averaged 1.18 per cent per annum. From 1973–82 MFP growth was negative: by 1982, MFP had fallen by a total of 11 per cent since

1973. After 1982 growth has turned positive again, but not by enough to prevent the 13-year period 1973–86 from showing an overall decline. For the whole period 1954–86 MFP growth has averaged about $\frac{1}{2}$ per cent per annum. The preferred estimates of MFP growth rates are thus about half those produced by the aggregate value added method.

The sensitivity of MFP growth rates to errors in the measurement of durable goods prices

It has long been suspected that price indices may in general underestimate quality change and so overestimate inflation. It seems to be generally believed, though without any systematic evidence either way, that quality change is particularly important for durable goods. If the rise in the prices of durable goods is overstated then obviously the growth rate of the capital stock will be underestimated, by an amount equal to the growth rate of the error in the price index. In turn, aggregate input will be underestimated by this error times the share of capital in total input. Consequently, other things being equal, MFP growth will be *over*estimated by an identical amount. There is however an offsetting effect since the output of the durable goods industries will be *under*estimated by the amount of the error in prices. The net effect on estimates of MFP growth at the aggregate level depends on the importance of durable goods industries as outputs relative to their importance as suppliers of capital inputs. Jorgenson (1966) analysed the closed economy case. He showed that, if durable goods prices are overstated, then in a steady state MFP growth will be overestimated if the value share of capital in total input exceeds the value share of investment in total output. The present case is a little different, since we are dealing with UK manufacturing, in which output of investment goods does not equal investment because of exports out of and imports into the manufacturing sector. So even in a steady state the growth rate of the manufacturing capital stock does not necessarily equal the growth rate of UK investment goods output. But it is fairly straightforward to simulate numerically the effect of a different rate of inflation of durable goods prices, as will be seen in a moment.

The issue of whether the prices of investment goods are generally overestimated is relevant for the embodiment hypothesis, which holds that for productivity to rise, new technology, embodied in new capital goods, must be introduced (Solow, 1960). On this view, much (or even all) of productivity growth attributed to disembodied technical change and included under MFP growth should in reality be ascribed to investment in new equipment; sizeable measured MFP growth rates simply reflect a failure to calculate the contribution of capital correctly.[18]

The results of Gordon (1990) make it highly likely that the growth of US durable goods prices has indeed been substantially overestimated by

Table 5.3. *The effect on estimates of MFP growth rates of possible errors in durable goods prices (%, p.a.)*

	Original estimates	Alternative estimates	Difference (alternative − original)
Short periods			
1954–58	− 0.50	− 0.18	0.32
1958–63	1.85	2.21	0.36
1963–68	1.55	2.05	0.49
1968–73	1.48	1.95	0.47
1973–76	− 2.04	− 1.58	0.46
1976–79	− 1.03	− 0.53	0.50
1979–82	− 0.95	− 0.46	0.49
1982–86	1.24	1.73	0.49
1973–79	− 1.53	− 1.05	0.48
1979–86	0.30	0.79	0.49
Long periods			
1954–73	1.18	1.60	0.42
1973–86	− 0.54	− 0.06	0.48
1954–86	0.48	0.92	0.44

Note: Alternative estimates assume prices of producer and consumer durable goods rose 3 per cent per annum slower than in original estimates. Original estimates are from last column of table 5.2.

official price indices, due to insufficient allowance for quality change. Gordon found that official US indices overestimated the rate of inflation of durable goods (both consumer and producer) by some 3 per cent per annum over 1947–83. Since US and UK methods of developing producer price indices are similar, it is quite possible, though unproven, that UK prices are overestimated too. To get an idea of the possible error in MFP growth attributable to overestimation of durable goods prices, industry level MFP growth rates have been recalculated assuming that the stock of plant and equipment in fact grew 3 per cent faster than in the original estimates; simultaneously, output of producer and consumer durable goods was assumed to grow 3 per cent faster.[19] The resulting estimates were weighted together by the preferred method (Domar aggregation, using the ratio of industry gross output to total final demand as the weights). The alternative estimated growth rates of MFP in aggregate manufacturing appear in table 5.3, together with the original estimates for comparison.

The effect of the assumed lower rate of growth of durable goods prices is to *raise* the estimates of MFP growth by about a half of a percentage point; if the prices of vehicles are left unchanged on both the input and the output side, then the effect on MFP growth rates of correcting for the presumed error in the prices of other durable goods is to raise them by about one quarter of a percentage point. In other words, the effect of the assumed error on output has outweighed the effect on input. By contrast, Gordon (1990, table 1.3) found that his new estimates *lowered* MFP growth for the whole US economy by 0.17 per cent per annum over 1947–83.[20] A qualification to both Gordon's and these results is that if Gordon's methods were applied to non-durable goods, it is possible that they would suggest equally large revisions to those prices too. So the eventual effect of improved price indices on estimates of MFP growth is unclear.

Composition effects

To what extent is the aggregate MFP growth rate influenced by changes in the composition of output? A number of American studies have addressed this issue, motivated particularly by a desire to explain the productivity slowdown of the 1970s. These have been reviewed by Wolff (1985). Composition effects have been found to be both very large and very small, depending on the pattern of weighting adopted by different writers. Indeed, Baumol and Wolff (1984) show that under competitive conditions a current-weighted average of MFP growth rates will tend to show a zero effect of composition changes; the mechanism at work is the invisible hand, which tends to drive down the prices of expanding industries and drive up the prices of their inputs, thus equalising, in value terms, the *level* of MFP across industries.

One possible approach is that of Jorgenson, Gollop and Fraumeni (1987) and Gollop (1985). This has already been discussed above (equation (5.13)) and rejected. Instead, we take as our starting point Domar aggregation: repeating equation (5.2),

$$\mu^{DA} = \Sigma_i [(q_i Y_i)/\Sigma_i q_i Z_i]\mu_i.$$

Changes in the weights can occur over time for two reasons. First, because of changes in the pattern of final output: individual weights can change, but with the sum of the weights remaining the same. Second, the weights can also change because of changes in the extent of 'import' penetration (where 'imports' include in our case purchases from domestic non-manufacturing): the sum of the weights can rise or fall, even if the relative pattern of the weights is unchanged. We can certainly ask, supposing that (hypothetically) the weights had remained those of a particular year, what would have been the effect on μ^{DA}? This question is answered in table (5.4), which gives MFP growth calculated using in turn the weights of each of the nine reference years. For comparison, the last column shows again the preferred estimates (μ^{DA}) made using the Törnqvist approximation to equation (5.2), equation (5.24), under which the weights shift over time.

Table 5.4. *Aggregate MFP growth in manufacturing: effect of different weights (%, p.a.)*

| Period | MFP growth calculated using weights of: | | | | | | | | | μ^{DA} |
	1954	1958	1963	1968	1973	1976	1979	1982	1986	
Short periods										
1954–58	−0.40	−0.59	−0.56	−0.52	−0.41	−0.44	−0.41	−0.38	−0.21	−0.50
1958–63	1.72	1.81	1.89	1.86	1.72	1.86	1.77	1.85	1.97	1.85
1963–68	1.53	1.63	1.60	1.51	1.39	1.48	1.36	1.45	1.55	1.55
1968–73	1.01	1.27	1.28	1.51	1.45	1.55	1.54	1.75	1.84	1.48
1973–76	−2.24	−2.52	−2.27	−2.30	−1.96	−2.12	−1.99	−2.13	−2.11	−2.04
1976–79	−1.25	−1.42	−1.24	−1.31	−1.12	−1.12	−0.94	−0.89	−1.03	−1.03
1979–82	−0.39	−0.46	−0.59	−0.60	−0.59	−0.86	−0.92	−0.98	−0.72	−0.95
1982–86	1.66	1.69	1.57	1.42	1.31	1.43	1.26	1.22	1.26	1.24
1973–79	−1.74	−1.97	−1.76	−1.81	−1.54	−1.62	−1.47	−1.51	−1.57	−1.53
1979–86	0.78	0.77	0.64	0.55	0.50	0.45	0.33	0.28	0.41	0.30
Long periods										
1954–73	1.03	1.11	1.14	1.17	1.11	1.19	1.14	1.25	1.37	1.18
1973–86	−0.39	−0.49	−0.46	−0.54	−0.44	−0.51	−0.50	−0.55	−0.50	−0.54
1954–86	0.46	0.46	0.49	0.48	0.48	0.50	0.48	0.52	0.61	0.48

Note: The weights are ratios of industry gross output to total final output in manufacturing. In columns 1–9 the weights are the same throughout, namely those of the indicated year. Column 10 is from the last column of table 5.2, that is, the weights change over time, in accordance with equation (5.21).

Composition effects turn out to be quite important. If the composition of the manufacturing sector in 1973 had continued unchanged down to 1986 then the MFP growth rate would have been 0.11 percentage points higher over this period. This is due to the unfavourable shift in the final output–value added ratio mentioned above. On the other hand, there appears to have been a favourable shift in the structure of demand for different industries' products, since if the 1986 structure of demand had prevailed throughout the whole 32-year period then the growth rate would have been 0.61 per cent per annum instead of 0.48 per cent. However, if we are concerned just with performance in the most recent period 1982–6, then we must conclude that the composition is now less favourable; if the composition of the 1950s or 1960s still prevailed the post-1982 recovery would have been even more striking.

Accounting for productivity growth: final output versus aggregate value added

Estimates of the growth of output and labour productivity in manufacturing as a whole appear in table 5.5, using two different concepts of output, value added and final output.[21] Because of the rather rough nature of the final output estimates, it is best to concentrate on the results for longer periods.[22] Final output (column 1) grew at a similar rate to value added (column 8) from 1954–73, but afterwards a large gap opens up. From 1973–9, final output per unit of labour continued to grow (at 1.66 per cent per annum), while value added per unit of labour fell (at − 1.37 per cent per annum). Whichever measure is employed, output itself grew in the first half of the period and fell in the second half. The difference between the two measures is larger in the second half – final output grew more than 1 percentage point faster than did value added. However the largest difference occurs in the sub-period 1973–9; here final output fell by 0.44 per cent per annum, while value added fell by a massive 3.47 per cent per annum.[23] The difference between the final output and the value added estimates of output after 1973 suggests that a substantial proportion of the fall in value added is due to increased use of inputs from outside UK manufacturing, rather than to a decline in the demand for UK manufactures on the part of final buyers.

Surprisingly, capital per unit of labour (column 3) grew faster (by about half a percentage point) over 1973–86 than it had in the first half of the period. This reflects of course the particularly rapid decline in employment rather than any unusually rapid increase in the capital stock (recall also the discussion of the premature scrapping issue in chapter 3). But the opposite was the case for external input per unit of labour, which grew more slowly in the second half.

When a value added measure of labour productivity is used, paradoxical results often appear. Thus value added per unit of labour fell by 1.37

Table 5.5. *Accounting for labour productivity growth in aggregate manufacturing, 1954–86*

	(1)	(2)	(3)	(4)	(5)	(6)	(7)	(8)	(9)	(10)
			A. Final output method					B. Value added method		
						Contributions to $\Delta\ln(Z/L)$ of:				Contribution to $\Delta\ln(V/L)$
Period	$\Delta\ln(Z/L)$ % p.a.	$\Delta\ln L$ % p.a.	$\Delta\ln(K/L)$ % p.a.	$\Delta\ln(M/L)$ % p.a.	μ^{DA} % p.a.	$\Delta\ln(K/L)$ %	$\Delta\ln(M)$ %	$\Delta\ln(V/L)$ % p.a.	μ^{AV} % p.a.	of $\Delta\ln(K/L)$ %
Short periods										
1954–58	1.80	0.14	4.05	3.13	− 0.50	48.7	78.9	0.72	− 0.88	222.2
1958–63	3.93	− 0.23	4.02	2.71	1.85	23.1	29.8	5.08	3.48	31.5
1963–68	5.62	− 0.68	4.92	6.84	1.55	19.3	53.1	4.86	2.94	39.6
1968–73	6.48	− 1.25	4.61	8.54	1.48	14.5	62.7	4.76	2.97	37.6
1973–76	3.80	− 2.18	4.44	9.78	− 2.04	21.5	132.1	− 2.37	− 4.04	− 70.9
1976–79	− 0.47	− 2.01	4.45	− 0.32	− 1.03	− 154.2	37.0	− 0.38	− 1.97	− 420.2
1979–82	1.36	− 8.83	8.39	1.74	− 0.95	100.9	68.7	1.41	− 1.57	211.4
1982–86	3.75	− 2.67	3.57	3.57	1.24	17.7	49.2	4.20	2.83	32.7
1973–79	1.66	− 2.10	4.44	4.73	− 1.53	46.6	149.9	− 1.37	− 3.01	− 119.0
1979–86	2.73	− 5.31	5.64	2.78	0.30	36.5	53.8	3.01	0.94	69.8
Long periods										
1954–73	4.60	− 0.54	4.42	5.42	1.18	20.8	52.9	4.02	2.29	43.2
1973–86	2.23	− 3.83	5.08	3.68	− 0.54	39.9	86.8	0.98	− 0.88	191.2
1954–86	3.64	− 1.88	4.69	4.71	0.48	25.8	62.3	2.79	1.00	64.6

Source: Columns (2), (3), (8) and (9): Table (5.1). Column (4): nominal value of external input (from input–output table), deflated by price index which is weighted average of materials and fuels price index, price of non-industrial services and price of manufactured imports (see text for details). Column (5): Table (5.2). Column (1): $\dot{Z}/Z$ calculated from Törnqvist approximation to equation (5.19).
Note: Contribution of capital is measured as capital share x growth rate of K/L, divided by growth rate of labour productivity (Z/L or V/L); contribution of external input (M) is measured as external input share x growth rate of M/L, divided by growth rate of labour productivity (Z/L).

per cent per annum from 1973–9. Since 1973 and 1979 were both years in which capacity utilisation was high, it seems puzzling that labour productivity could actually decline over this period, especially as capital per unit of labour is shown as rising at 4.44 per cent per annum over the same period. On the alternative, final output, measure the paradox disappears: labour productivity continues to rise over 1973–9, albeit at a slower rate than in earlier decades. Both capital and external input per unit of labour rose at roughly equal rates, so a rise in labour productivity should not be surprising: the only puzzle is that the growth in labour productivity was not higher (MFP growth is negative in this period).

It is frequently argued that manufacturing firms became more efficient in the 1980s by sub-contracting many of their activities to non-manufacturing firms. No doubt this was the case for certain kinds of service (for example, contract cleaning). The estimates in table 5.5 allow this thesis to be assessed from a more general point of view. External inputs per unit of labour did indeed continue to grow in the 1980s. But we can see from these figures that the most rapid growth actually occurred between 1963 and 1976. This probably reflects a different kind of sub-contracting, namely the increasing use in the 1960s and 1970s of foreign manufacturing firms to supply components (a conspicuous example of this occurring in car assembly).[24]

To what extent can the measured inputs explain the growth of labour productivity? Let us consider first the picture presented by the value added approach (panel B of table 5.5). In interpreting the contribution of capital, it should be noted that capital's share in value added varied from 36 to 40 per cent over the period studied. For 1954–73, the growth of capital can account for only 43 per cent of labour productivity growth (last column of table 5.5); the rest is due to MFP growth. For the second half of the time span, 1973–86, capital appears to over-account for growth, but this is because MFP growth is apparently negative. Because of the exceptional nature of the 1973–9 sub-period, which was soon to be followed by the extremely severe recession of 1980–81, it may be more sensible to focus attention on the sub-period 1979–86, in which capital accounted for 70 per cent of labour productivity growth.

However, as argued above, MFP measured by the value added method is systematically too high, by a factor of about two. A rather different picture emerges if we look at the final output method (last two columns of Panel A in table 5.5). Here it should be noted that external input has much the largest share in final output (rising from 44 per cent in 1963–8 to 52 per cent after 1973); the share of capital fell from about 22 to about 18 per cent, that of labour from about 34 to 30 per cent between the two halves of the study period. For 1954–73, capital accounts for 21 per cent but external input for 53 per cent of productivity growth; overall nearly three quarters of productivity growth is accounted for. In the second half, 1973–86, the contribution of the inputs exceeds 100 per cent, because MFP growth is once again measured as negative (though to a lesser extent than under the value added method). For 1979–86, the contributions of capital and external inputs are 37 per cent and 54 per cent respectively and together account for 90 per cent of growth.

Thus the preferred final output method can account for much the greater part of labour productivity growth, leaving only a minor role to MFP growth. But one qualification to this conclusion should be noted. Cross-country studies show that labour productivity growth and MFP growth are correlated and also that the higher these rates, the higher also is the proportion of growth accounted for by MFP.[25] Judging by this evidence, if labour productivity had grown faster in the UK, then we might have observed a faster rate of MFP growth and also that MFP growth accounted for a larger proportion of labour productivity growth.

In summary, both methods have difficulty accounting for 1973–9. Ignoring this sub-period, the preferred final output method can account for a larger proportion of its measure of labour productivity: 73 per cent of output growth in 1954–73 and 91 per cent in 1973–86. Both methods seem to be in agreement that the importance of capital has increased, if we compare 1979–86 with the previous period of 'normalcy' (1954–73). However, according to what has been argued to be the superior method, in all periods (except for the wholly exceptional one of 1976–9), capital is substantially less important than external input as a source of productivity growth. A qualification to this is that the increasing use of external inputs by manufacturing firms may reflect technical progress in the industries supplying these inputs, progress which is itself dependent on capital investment. But whatever the importance of capital elsewhere in the economy or abroad, this does not alter the fact that investment in *manufacturing* is measured as having only a relatively minor role. Can the role of capital really be as small as these figures suggest? Perhaps this conclusion arises simply from the untested assumptions of the growth accounting approach, which weights the contribution of each input in accordance with its value share. After all, as noted above, the share of capital in final output has varied from only about 18–22 per cent, while that of external input is much larger, varying from about 44 to 52 per cent.[26] We shall return to these questions in chapter 7, when these and other arguments designed to show that capital is 'special' in some sense will be considered in depth.

CONCLUSIONS

The principal conclusions for total manufacturing are as follows. First, according to the preferred estimates, those made by Domar aggregation, over the 19-year period 1954–73, MFP growth averaged 1.18 per cent per annum. From 1973 to 1982 MFP growth was negative: by 1982, the *level* of MFP had fallen by a total of 11 per cent since 1973. After 1982 MFP growth has turned positive again, but not by enough to prevent the 13-year period 1973–86 from showing an overall decline. For the whole period 1954–86 MFP growth has averaged about $\frac{1}{2}$ per cent per annum. The preferred estimates of MFP growth rates turn out to be about half those produced by the (misleading) aggregate value added method. Second, the growth of measured inputs can account for the greater part of the growth of both output and of output per unit of labour. Finally, final output grew more rapidly than did value added from 1954–73, and after 1973, final output fell to a lesser extent than did value added. Thus some of the fall in value added after 1973 was due to substitution away from UK manufactured inputs, rather than to failure to maintain sales to buyers outside manufacturing.

6

RAW MATERIAL PRICES AND THE POST-1973 PRODUCTIVITY SLOWDOWN

INTRODUCTION

After the first oil shock in 1973, labour productivity growth rates slowed down in all the advanced industrial countries. Where it has been possible to measure them, multi-factor productivity (MFP) growth rates appear to have fallen too: Jorgenson, Gollop and Fraumeni (1987), hereafter JGF, found evidence for such a slowdown in the US and similar evidence has already been presented for the UK (see chapters 3 and 4). According to Maddison (1987), MFP growth decelerated in six countries (France, Germany, the Netherlands, the UK, Japan and the US) after 1973, even when various 'supplementary factors' are taken into account. Using a cruder methodology, Englander and Mittelstädt (1988) found that MFP growth slowed down in 21 OECD countries after 1973; neither in the business sector nor in manufacturing was there a single instance of a country with a higher MFP growth rate in 1979–86 than it had enjoyed in the pre-1973 period.[1]

The connection between the oil and other commodity price rises and the slowdown has been much debated, but most of the debate has been concerned with labour productivity. Undoubtedly, many factors, including cyclical ones,[2] played a role, particularly in the 1970s (Bruno and Sachs, 1985; Lindbeck, 1983; Maddison, 1987; Berndt and Wood, 1986b). However, the fact that no major industrial country has as yet recovered the growth rates of output and productivity which it enjoyed prior to 1973 certainly militates against a purely cyclical explanation (even one which relies on hysteresis effects on human and physical capital).

This chapter concentrates on the slowdown in MFP rather than labour productivity growth and considers the role of one possible, purely micro effect, namely input substitution. In a nutshell, if technical progress is biased towards the use of particular commodities, and if the price of these commodities rises, then firms will use less of them and the growth rate of MFP will decline.

Jorgenson (1984a, 1984b, 1988 and 1990) has argued that the slowdown in US productivity growth after 1973 is in fact due to precisely this cause, namely input substitution in response to the rising price of energy, since his econometric estimates show that in most industries productivity growth is energy-using. In this chapter, this claim will be assessed; we shall also ask whether a comparable claim can be made good for the UK in the same period. In the UK case, it will not be possible to test for the effect of energy prices *per se*, but only for the effect of aggregate raw material and energy prices (intermediate input).[3] As far as the US is concerned, use will be made of JGF's own estimates of the parameters of the translog production function, which they fitted to 21 US manufacturing sectors over the period 1948–79, together with their data on prices and quantities of inputs in 1973 and 1979. Consideration will also be given to the earlier estimates of translog *price* functions (Jorgenson, 1984b) fitted to the same range of sectors but employing a more detailed breakdown of inputs. For the UK new estimates of the parameters of the translog production function, as applied to groups of manufacturing industries, will be employed.

To understand Jorgenson's argument that MFP growth is a variable influenced by economic decisions, in fact dependent on relative input prices, consider the production function for the ith industry ($i = 1, 2, \ldots, \mathcal{N}$):

$$Y_i = F^i(X_i, K_i, L_i, t).$$

where Y is output, X is intermediate input, K is capital, L is labour and t is time. The definition of MFP growth (v_t^i) is:[4]

$$v_t^i \equiv \partial \ln F^i / \partial t = f^i(X_i, K_i, L_i, t), \text{ say.}$$

That is to say, though MFP growth is defined as output growth, holding inputs constant, it is not necessarily independent of the *level* at which the inputs are held constant. But input levels are determined by input prices. Hence in general MFP growth is a decision variable. In the original model of Solow (1957), MFP growth *did* turn out to be exogenous, but this was because he argued that at the aggregate level technical progress was (approximately) neutral in the US, in which case the production function can be written in the separable form $Y_i = A(t) G^i(X_i, K_i, L_i)$, so that $v_t^i = \dot{A}(t)/A(t)$.

This point will now be illustrated for the case of the translog production function. As JGF show, this production function leads to the following equations describing input shares and MFP growth (assuming profit maximisation and that firms are price takers in all markets):

$$\begin{aligned}
v_X^i &= a_X^i + \beta_{XX}^i \ln X_i + \beta_{XK}^i \ln K_i + \beta_{XL}^i \ln L_i + \beta_{Xt}^i t \\
v_K^i &= a_K^i + \beta_{XK}^i \ln X_i + \beta_{KK}^i \ln K_i + \beta_{KL}^i \ln L_i + \beta_{Kt}^i t \\
v_L^i &= a_L^i + \beta_{XL}^i \ln X_i + \beta_{KL}^i \ln K_i + \beta_{LL}^i \ln L_i + \beta_{Lt}^i t \\
v_t^i &= a_t^i + \beta_{Xt}^i \ln X_i + \beta_{Kt}^i \ln K_i + \beta_{Lt}^i \ln L_i + \beta_{tt}^i t
\end{aligned} \qquad (6.1)$$

$$i = 1, 2, \ldots, \mathcal{N}$$

Here v_X^i, v_K^i and v_L^i are the value shares of intermediate, capital and labour input respectively. The αs and βs are parameters: β_{XX}^i, β_{XK}^i, β_{XL}^i, β_{KK}^i, β_{KL}^i and β_{LL}^i are called the share elasticities, and β_{Xt}^i, β_{Kt}^i and β_{Lt}^i are termed the biases of productivity growth. The last of these equations, for MFP growth, shows that, in general, MFP growth is not exogenous to economic decisions. It is *only* exogenous if the technology biases $\{\beta_{Xt}^i, \beta_{Kt}^i, \beta_{Lt}^i\}$ are all zero. If $\beta_{Xt}^i > 0$, then productivity growth is intermediate-using. Hence if the price of intermediate rises then X_i will fall, so that v_t^i will also fall.

The assumptions made by JGF in their study of US productivity – constant returns to scale, firms maximise profits and are price takers in all markets, all inputs are variable – enable estimates of MFP growth to be derived without requiring knowledge of the parameters of the production function. All that is needed to estimate average MFP growth over a discrete interval is data on prices and quantities of inputs and outputs. However, to assess the effect of input substitution on MFP growth we need to know in addition the parameters of the production function, which therefore have to be estimated econometrically.

In the next section some of the properties of the translog production function which are relevant to the analysis which follows will be discussed. Here an analytical expression for the effect on MFP growth of changing input prices will be derived. This is followed by a consideration of Jorgenson's claim that input substitution can explain the slowdown of MFP growth observed in the US after 1973. The problems of estimating the translog production function econometrically are then taken up and, finally, we present the estimates for British data and assess the role of input substitution in the UK.

PROPERTIES OF THE TRANSLOG PRODUCTION FUNCTION

The system of equations (6.1) is not immediately amenable to empirical analysis for several reasons. First, v_t^i is the *instantaneous* rate of MFP growth and hence is not directly observable. Only MFP growth over a discrete time period is observable. Second, quantities rather than prices appear on the right-hand side of each equation (in fact, prices only appear implicitly in the value shares), whereas we are interested in the effect of prices on quantities. It is therefore necessary to find a way to make the system observable, so that it can be estimated econometrically. This will assist in deriving an analytical expression for the effect of changes in factor prices on MFP growth.

Economic theory imposes a number of restrictions on the coefficients in equations (6.1) above, which econometric estimation must respect.[5] First, there are symmetry restrictions, which have already been implicitly imposed. The following additional restrictions hold, for each industry i, assuming constant returns to scale:

$a_j^i \geq 0, \quad j = X, K, L$ (shares must be non-negative, for example, if $X = K = L = 1$ and $t = 0$; the production function is increasing in the inputs)

$a_X^i + a_K^i + a_L^i = 1$ (shares must sum to 1, for example, if $X = K = L = 1$ and $t = 0$; constant returns to scale)

$\beta_{jj}^i \leq 0, \quad j = X, K, L.$ (concavity)

$\beta_{XX}^i + \beta_{XK}^i + \beta_{XL}^i = 0$ (shares must sum to 1 for all values of $\ln X$, $\ln K$, $\ln L$ and t; constant returns to scale)

$\beta_{KX}^i + \beta_{KK}^i + \beta_{KL}^i = 0$ ditto

$\beta_{LX}^i + \beta_{LK}^i + \beta_{LL}^i = 0$ ditto

$\beta_{Xt}^i + \beta_{Kt}^i + \beta_{Lt}^i = 0$ ditto

In the system (6.1) above, this means that in each equation the sum of the coefficients K, L and X is zero, as are the corresponding *column* sums of coefficients. The restrictions on the βs can be imposed by writing each equation as follows:

$$v_X^i = a_X^i + \beta_{XX}^i \ln(X_i/L_i) + \beta_{XK}^i \ln(K_i/L_i) + \beta_{Xt}^i t$$

$$v_K^i = a_K^i + \beta_{XK}^i \ln(X_i/L_i) + \beta_{KK}^i \ln(K_i/L_i) + \beta_{Kt}^i t$$

$$v_L^i = a_L^i + \beta_{XL}^i \ln(X_i/L_i) + \beta_{KL}^i \ln(K_i/L_i) + \beta_{Lt}^i t \tag{6.2}$$

$$v_t^i = a_t^i + \beta_{Xt}^i \ln(X_i/L_i) + \beta_{Kt}^i \ln(K_i/L_i) + \beta_{tt}^i t \qquad i = 1, 2, \ldots, N.$$

Note that there are cross-equation restrictions on the parameters (the symmetry and adding-up restrictions), so that there are only nine (not sixteen) parameters to estimate. One of the share equations can be derived from the other two, so there are three independent equations available to estimate these nine parameters.

Two other steps are necessary to arrive at an econometrically testable model. First, we must add a random error ϵ_j^i ($j = X, K, L$) to each equation (its properties will be discussed below). Second, v_t^i is not observable, since it would require us to compute instantaneous growth rates of outputs and inputs. However the average growth rate of MFP over a discrete interval *is* observable, hence observability can be achieved by averaging the equations over adjacent time periods (assumed u years apart). Application of these steps, dropping the labour share equation, yields:

$$\bar{v}_X^i = a_X^i + \beta_{XX}^i(\overline{\ln X_i} - \overline{\ln L_i}) + \beta_{XK}^i(\overline{\ln K_i} - \overline{\ln L_i}) + \beta_{Xt}^i \bar{t} + \bar{\epsilon}_X^i$$

$$\bar{v}_K^i = a_K^i + \beta_{XK}^i(\overline{\ln X_i} - \overline{\ln L_i}) + \beta_{KK}^i(\overline{\ln K_i} - \overline{\ln L_i}) + \beta_{Kt}^i \bar{t} + \bar{\epsilon}_K^i \qquad (6.3)$$

$$\bar{v}_t^i = a_t^i + \beta_{Xt}^i(\overline{\ln X_i} - \overline{\ln L_i}) + \beta_{Kt}^i(\overline{\ln K_i} - \overline{\ln L_i}) + \beta_{tt}^i \bar{t} + \bar{\epsilon}_t^i,$$

$$i = 1, 2, \ldots, N.$$

Here a bar over a variable denotes a time average:

$$\bar{v}_j^i \equiv (1/2)[v_j^i(t) + v_j^i(t - u)], \qquad j = X, K, L,$$

$$\overline{\ln X_i} \equiv (1/2)[\ln X_i(t) + \ln X_i(t - u)],$$

$$\overline{\ln K_i} \equiv (1/2)[\ln K_i(t) + \ln K_i(t - u)],$$

$$\overline{\ln L_i} \equiv (1/2)[\ln L_i(t) + \ln L_i(t - u)],$$

$$\bar{t} \equiv (1/2)[(t) + (t - u)] = t - (u/2),$$

$$\bar{\epsilon}_j^i \equiv (1/2)[\epsilon_j^i(t) + \epsilon_j^i(t - u)], \qquad j = X, K, L.$$

Now consider the problem of calculating the effect of input price changes on MFP growth. The strategy is to calculate what input intensities $(X_i/L_i$ and $K_i/L_i)$ would have been if input prices had remained constant over a given interval and hence what MFP growth would have been. Notice that we cannot simply assume that input intensities are unchanged if input prices are unchanged, unless technical progress happens to be neutral (which is not in general the case). The procedure for calculating hypothetical input intensities is as follows. We actually calculate the *growth rate* of input intensities, using equations (6.1). Define $x \equiv X_i/L_i$ and $k_i \equiv K_i/L_i$. Now divide the first and second of equations (6.1) by the third and rearrange, to obtain:

$$x_i = [p_L^i/p_X^i][a_X^i + \beta_{XX}^i \ln(x_i) + \beta_{XL}^i \ln(k_i) + \beta_{Xt}^i t]$$
$$\div [a_L^i + \beta_{XL}^i \ln(x_i) + \beta_{KL}^i \ln(k_i) + \beta_{Lt}^i t]$$

$$k_i = [p_L^i/p_X^i][a_K^i + \beta_{XK}^i \ln(x_i) + \beta_{KK}^i \ln(k_i) + \beta_{Kt}^i t]$$
$$\div [a_L^i + \beta_{XL}^i \ln(x_i) + \beta_{KL}^i \ln(k_i) + \beta_{Lt}^i t]$$

This derivation uses the fact that $v_X^i/v_L^i + x_i(p_X^i/p_L^i)$ and $v_K^i/v_L^i + k_i(p_K^i/p_L^i)$, where p_X^i, p_L^i and p_K^i are the prices of intermediate, capital and labour inputs. Totally differentiating these two equations with respect to time, while holding input prices constant, there results

$$\dot{x}_i/x_i = \{1 - (\beta_{XX}^i/v_X^i) + (\beta_{XL}^i/v_L^i)\}^{-1}\{(\beta_{Xt}^i/v_X^i) - (\beta_{Lt}^i/v_L^i)$$
$$+ [(\beta_{XK}^i/v_X^i) - (\beta_{KL}^i/v_L^i)](\dot{k}_i/k_i)\} \qquad (6.4)$$

$$\dot{k}_i/k_i = \{1 - (\beta^i_{KK}/v^i_K) + (\beta^i_{KL}/v^i_L)\}^{-1}\{(\beta^i_{Kt}/v^i_K) - (\beta^i_{Lt}/v^i_L)$$
$$+ [(\beta^i_{XK}/v^i_K) - (\beta^i_{XL}/v^i_L)](\dot{x}/x_i)\} \qquad (6.5)$$

Here a dot over a variable denotes the derivative with respect to time. Equations (6.4) and (6.5) are linear in the growth rates of the input intensities and hence can be readily solved, given knowledge of the parameters. The solution to these two equations is a pair of hypothetical growth rates of x_i and k_i, call them θ_{ix} and θ_{ik}. Letting a prime denote the hypothetical level of x_i and k_i in year t, we have (in logs):

$$\ln(x'(t)) = \ln(x(t-u)) + \theta_{ix}u$$

$$\ln(k'(t)) = \ln(k(t-u)) + \theta_{ik}u$$

Next to find the effect on MFP growth of the different assumptions about input prices, we use the last of equations (6.3), repeated here for convenience:

$$\bar{v}^i_t = a^i_t + \beta^i_{Xt}(\overline{\ln X_i} - \overline{\ln L_i}) + \beta^i_{Kt}(\overline{\ln K_i} - \overline{\ln L_i}) + \beta^i_{tt}t + \bar{\epsilon}^i_t.$$

Letting a prime again denote the situation where relative input prices are assumed to be constant, and absence of a prime the situation where input prices are assumed to follow their historical trajectory, we get by subtraction:[6]

$$\bar{v}^{i'}_t - \bar{v}^i_t = (1/2)\{\beta^i_{Xt}\ln[x'_i(t)/x_i(t)] + \beta^i_{Kt}\ln[k'_i(t)/k_i(t)]\} \qquad (6.6)$$

This last result is our equation for estimating the effect of changing input prices on MFP growth over the discrete interval from $t - u$ to t.

WHAT DOES US DATA REVEAL?

JGE found that in fifteen out of the 21 sectors into which they divided American manufacturing, productivity growth was intermediate-using ($\beta_{Xt} > 0$). This means that if the relative price of intermediate input were to rise, then these sectors would economise on intermediate input and MFP growth would be observed to slow down. The important question is, however, how big is such an effect likely to be? JGF have estimated the parameters of the translog production function for each of the 21 manufacturing sectors. We can use their estimates to calculate what input intensities would have been between 1973 and 1979 if all relative input prices had remained constant at their 1973 level. Then we can use the difference between these hypothetical input intensities and the actual intensities to calculate (from equation (6.6)) what the effect on MFP growth was from the change in input prices which actually occurred over this period.[7]

Turning to the results, we should note first of all that there was a substantial slowdown in MFP growth in most sectors, if we compare 1973–9 with the preceding period distinguished by JGF, 1969–73. Their estimates are as follows:

MFP growth rates in US manufacturing sectors, % p.a.

	1969–73	1973–9	Change, 1973–9 over 1969–73
Minimum	− 5.00	− 9.41	− 6.16
Maximum	3.59	2.97	5.54
Average	0.38	− 0.74	− 1.12

Source: JGF (1987, table 6.2). 21 sectors.

The difference in MFP growth rates caused by changing input prices, calculated as described above for nineteen out of the 21 manufacturing sectors,[8] was as follows:

Change in MFP growth rates due to changing factor prices (% p.a.)

Minimum	− 0.02
Maximum	+ 0.14
Average	+ 0.01

Source: Own calculations, using equation (6.6); parameter estimates and data from Jorgenson et al. (1987).

Clearly, therefore, input substitution due to changes in input prices accounts for a negligible proportion of the slowdown in productivity growth in the US. The reasons are not far to seek. First of all, the technology biases $(\beta_{Xt}, \beta_{Kt}, \beta_{Lt})$ tend to be fairly small. Second, the average rise in the price of intermediate input (relative to that of labour input) was in fact quite low – only 0.33 per cent per annum. Third, some sectors experienced changes in input prices which were favourable to MFP growth. For example, there were four intermediate-using sectors $(\beta_{Xt} > 0)$ which experienced *falls* in the relative intermediate price and five intermediate-*saving* sectors $(\beta_{Xt} < 0)$ which experienced *rises* in this price. Also, in seven capital-using sectors $(\beta_{Kt} > 0)$ the relative price of capital fell, while in two capital-using sectors $(\beta_{Kt} < 0)$ it rose.

The results so far relate to the whole of intermediate input, which aggregates both energy and non-energy inputs. Jorgenson has however stressed the role of *energy* prices in the slowdown: if the bias of technical progress is (non-energy) material-saving or if material prices do not rise by as much as energy prices, then the effect of the latter could be concealed in the estimates utilised so far. In other work he has given us evidence which allows a more refined test of the energy price hypothesis, since he has presented estimates of translog *price* functions for the same

range of sectors as in the production function estimates just discussed, but
with a five-fold breakdown of inputs – capital, labour, materials, electricity and non-electrical energy (Jorgenson, 1984b).

When the price function is assumed to be translog, the equation for
MFP growth is:

$$- \bar{v}_t^i = a_t^i + \beta_{Kt}^i \ln(\bar{p}_K^i) + \beta_{Lt}^i \ln(\bar{p}_L^i) + \beta_{Et}^i \ln(\bar{p}_E^i)$$
$$+ \beta_{Nt}^i \ln(\bar{p}_N^i) + \beta_{Mt}^i \ln(\bar{p}_M^i) + \beta_{tt}^i E, \qquad i = 1, \ldots, \mathcal{N}.$$

where $\{\bar{p}_K^i, \bar{p}_L^i, \bar{p}_E^i, \bar{p}_N^i, \bar{p}_M^i\}$ are the prices of capital, labour, electricity,
non-electrical energy and materials (averaged over adjacent time
periods), and where $\{\beta_{Kt}^i, \beta_{Lt}^i, \beta_{Et}^i, \beta_{Nt}^i, \beta_{Mt}^i\}$ are the technology biases. If for
example $\beta_{Et}^i > 0$, then a rise in the price of electricity reduces MFP
growth.

Jorgenson found that the technology bias for electricity was indeed
positive in fifteen out of 21 manufacturing sectors, and that the bias for
non-electrical energy was positive in nineteen out of 21 sectors; the sum of
the two biases was positive in sixteen sectors (Jorgenson, 1984b, table
7-2). However, the effects are again small. Even excluding the sectors for
which the bias was negative, it can be calculated that the average value of
the estimated β_{Et}^i was 0.0002, and of β_{Nt}^i was 0.0007; excluding sectors
where the sum of the biases was negative, the mean value of the sum of the
two biases was also 0.0007. The maximum values were, respectively,
0.0007, 0.0040 and 0.0040. This means that a doubling of all energy
prices would lead in these sectors to an average fall in MFP growth of
$(100 \times \ln 2 \times 0.0007 =)$ 0.05 percentage points per annum; in the worst
affected sector it would lead to a fall of 0.28 percentage points per annum.
The overall conclusion derived from price functions is therefore much the
same as the one derived from looking at the more aggregative production
function estimates.[9]

It seems then that we must look elsewhere for an explanation of the
slowdown in US productivity growth. However, though the hypothesis
does not seem to have fared very well for the US, it may prove to work
better for the UK, to which we now turn.

ECONOMETRIC ESTIMATION OF THE TRANSLOG PRODUCTION FUNCTION

In estimating production functions for the UK the methodology developed by JGF (1987, chapter 7) was followed. There are three potential
difficulties in estimating the system of equations (6.3). First, the restrictions on the parameters must be respected. Second, there is a simultaneity
problem, since some of the right-hand side variables are endogenous.
Third, if the original errors $\epsilon_X^i, \epsilon_K^i, \epsilon_L^i$ and ϵ_t^i are serially uncorrelated, as it

is natural to assume they are, then the averaging process will induce serial correlation in the transformed errors, $\bar{\epsilon}_X^i$, $\bar{\epsilon}_K^i$, $\bar{\epsilon}_L^i$, and $\bar{\epsilon}_t^i$.

Parameter restrictions

Inspection of (6.3) shows that the matrix of β coefficients is symmetric, so that there are three cross-equation restrictions. There are two other sets of restrictions, required by constant returns and by concavity. As stated above, constant returns implies that the constant terms are non-negative:

$$a_j^i \geq 0, \qquad j = X, K, L. \tag{6.7}$$

The production function is assumed to be concave in the inputs, that is, the matrix of second order partial derivatives of the production function with respect to the three inputs in negative semi-definite. For the 3-input translog case, necessary and sufficient conditions for concavity are that the 3×3 matrix of cross-partials $[F_{rs}^i] = [\beta_{rs}]$, $r,s, = K, L, X$, be negative semi-definite, which in turn can be shown to require that the parameters of the Cholesky factorisation of $[\beta_{rs}]$ have certain properties (JGF, chapter 7). The Cholesky factorisation of $[\beta_{rs}]$ is:

$$[\beta_{rs}] = ADA'$$

where A' is upper triangular and D is diagonal, with diagonal element δ_i. The symmetry and adding-up conditions on the βs imply that matrix A must have the form:

$$A = \begin{bmatrix} 1 & 0 & 0 \\ \lambda & 1 & 0 \\ -(1-\lambda) & -1 & 0 \end{bmatrix}$$

and that $\delta_3 = 0$. For the matrix of βs (the share elasticity matrix) to be negative semi-definite requires in addition that:

$$\delta_1 \leq 0, \ \delta_2 \leq 0.$$

Applying these conditions, we find that:

$$\begin{bmatrix} \beta_{XX}^i & \beta_{XK}^i & \beta_{XL}^i \\ \beta_{XK}^i & \beta_{KK}^i & \beta_{KL}^i \\ \beta_{XL}^i & \beta_{KL}^i & \beta_{LL}^i \end{bmatrix} = ADA'$$

$$= \begin{bmatrix} \delta_1 & \lambda\delta_1 & -(1+\lambda)\delta_1 \\ \lambda\delta_1 & \lambda^2\delta_1 + \delta_2 & -\lambda(1+\lambda)\delta_1 - \delta_2 \\ -(1+\lambda)\delta_1 & -\lambda(1+\lambda)\delta_1 - \delta_2 & (1+\lambda)^2\delta_1 + \delta_2 \end{bmatrix}$$

which implies

$$\beta_{jj}^i \leq 0, \qquad j = X, K, L. \tag{6.8}$$

Note that one way the concavity conditions (6.8) can be satisfied is if all the share elasticities are zero, that is, $\beta_{ij} = 0$ $(i, j = X, K, L)$. Note too, that though β_{LL} does not appear directly in the econometric model (6.3), from the adding-up restrictions it follows that

$$\beta_{LL} = \beta_{XX} + \beta_{KK} + 2\beta_{XK},$$

so concavity requires that

$$\beta_{XX} + \beta_{KK} + 2\beta_{XK} \leq 0. \tag{6.9}$$

A reasonable econometric strategy is to impose the cross-equation restrictions in the estimation process and then check whether the other restrictions (the non-negativity of the a_j^i and the non-positivity of the β_{jj}^i) are satisfied. If they are, all well and good; if not, the relevant set of coefficients can be set equal to zero, thus forcing the satisfaction of the restrictions.

Simultaneity

The econometric model (6.3) contains on the right-hand side some variables which are endogenous, namely the (logs of the) input intensities. Note that the value shares on the left-hand side can be thought of as the product of a variable which under the maintained hypothesis is exogenous (a real input price, where q^i denotes the ith industry's output price) and an endogenous one, the requirement of each input per unit of output:

$$v_X^i \equiv p_X^i X_i / q^i Y_i = (X_i / Y_i)(p_X^i / q^i)$$

$$v_K^i \equiv p_K^i K_i / q^i Y_i = (K_i / Y_i)(p_K^i / q^i)$$

[Also,

$$v_L^i \equiv p_L^i L_i / q^i Y_i = (L_i / Y_i)(p_L^i / q^i)].$$

An appropriate strategy to deal with simultaneity is to use instrumental variable (IV) techniques, employing the exogenous variables as instruments – the real input prices[10] (p_X^i / q^i, p_K^i / q^i and p_L^i / q^i) and time (t).

Serial correlation

On the assumption that the original errors ϵ_j^i $(j = X, K, L)$ are serially uncorrelated, with zero mean and constant variance σ_j^{i2}, the covariance matrix for each of the averaged equation errors $\bar{\epsilon}_j^i$ has the Laurent form:[11]

$$\Omega = \begin{bmatrix} 1/2 & 1/4 & 0 & \cdots & 0 \\ 1/4 & 1/2 & 1/4 & \cdots & 0 \\ 0 & 1/4 & 1/2 & \cdots & 0 \\ \cdot & \cdot & \cdot & & \cdot \\ \cdot & \cdot & \cdot & & \cdot \\ \cdot & \cdot & \cdot & & \cdot \\ 0 & 0 & 0 & \cdots & 1/2 \end{bmatrix} \sigma_j^{i2}.$$

Following JGF (1987, chapter 7) again, this matrix can be used to transform the system to remove the serial correlation, in the following way. Matrix Ω is positive definite and symmetric, so that there exists an upper triangular matrix R (that is, one with zeros below the main diagonal) such that

$$R\Omega R' = I$$

$$RR' = \Omega^{-1}.$$

JGF state that if each equation is transformed by matrix R then the resulting equations will have serially uncorrelated errors. Assume M observations originally; one observation is lost by the averaging process. Then in matrix notation the transformation for, for example, $\bar{v}_t^i$ is:

$$R\bar{v}_t = RZB + R\bar{\epsilon}_t$$

where

$$\bar{v}_t = (\bar{v}_t(2), \ldots, \bar{v}_t(N))'$$
$$B = (a_T^i, \beta_{Xt}^i, \beta_{Kt}^i, \beta_{tt}^i)'$$
$$\bar{\epsilon}_t^i = (\bar{\epsilon}_t^i(2), \ldots, \bar{\epsilon}_t^i(N))'$$

and where Z is the data matrix, whose first column is of ones, and whose other columns contain $M-1$ observations on each of $(\ln X_i - \ln L_i)$, $(\ln K_i - \ln L_i)$ and t. Analogous transformations can be applied to the other two equations of the econometric model.

In summary, the three potential difficulties discussed above – cross-equation restrictions on the parameters, simultaneity and serial correlation of the residuals – can be met by transforming the data prior to estimation and by the use of an appropriate estimation method, which employs the exogenous variables as instruments. JGF used non-linear 3SLS with instruments and we shall follow them in this respect.

A model with industry fixed effects

In the results to be described, the industry-level estimates described in earlier chapters will be employed. Estimates of outputs, inputs and the corresponding prices are available for 124 manufacturing industries for nine years (1954, 1958, 1963, 1968, 1973, 1976, 1979, 1982 and 1986); growth rates of MFP are consequently available for eight consecutive periods. Clearly, the fundamental problem is that we only have eight observations on each industry (JGF had 31 consecutive annual observations on each of their sectors). But there are 9 parameters to estimate in the system, with only (3 × 8 =) 24 observations to play with – plainly a hopeless task. The solution adopted here is to group the industries into Orders of the 1968 SIC and carry out panel regressions for each Order. This amounts to assuming that the production function is identical for each industry within a given Order, except for an industry effect, which can be captured by a dummy variable.[12] The primary aim of these tests is to see whether the productivity biases follow the same pattern as JGF find that they do in the US and hence whether this factor can explain the productivity slowdown in the UK. Hence this rather extreme assumption about industry production functions, which would in general be hard to defend, is worth pursuing.

The model to be estimated is therefore identical to the one estimated by JGF on US data, except that the constant term in each of equations (6.3) is allowed to differ between industries, by the addition of $M - 1$ industry dummies to each equation, where M is the number of industries in an Order. The method of estimation was non-linear 3-stage least squares. The instruments employed were the same in each equation, namely the exogenous variables in the model – the constant, the industry dummies, the (averaged) logs of real input prices (p_X/q, p_K/q and p_L/q), and time (t). Prior to estimation, the data were transformed to eliminate serial correlation, in the way described in the previous section.[13]

The 1968 SIC divided manufacturing into sixteen Orders (Orders III to XIX), with a varying number of industries in each order. Order X (Shipbuilding) consisted of only one industry. This Order was therefore dropped, as was also for similar reasons Order IV (Coal and petroleum products, three industries). Order XI (Vehicles) contained only four industries of extremely disparate size and nature (cars, motor cycles, aerospace and railway locomotives), so this too was omitted from the analysis. The small Order XIV (Leather, Leather Goods and Fur) was amalgamated with the larger Order XV (Clothing and Outerwear). From the original sixteen Orders, we thus obtain thirteen separate panels, comprisingintotal119industriesoutoftheoriginal124.Ineachpanelthereare eight time periods (1954–8, 1958–63, 1963–8, 1968–73, 1973–6, 1976–9, 1979–82, 1982–6). The Orders and the number of industries in each Order for which data were available were as follows:

Order number	Order name	Number of industries
III	Food, drink and tobacco	15
V	Chemicals & allied industries	15
VI	Metal manufacture	6
VII	Mechanical engineering	14
VIII	Instrument engineering	4
IX	Electrical engineering	5
XII	Metal goods n.e.s.	9
XIII	Textiles	14
XIV/XV	Leather, leather goods & fur and Clothing & footwear	12
XVI	Bricks, pottery, glass, cement, etc.	6
XVII	Timber, furniture, etc.	6
XVIII	Paper, printing & publishing	7
XIX	Other manufacturing industries	6
TOTAL		119

When the system (6.3) was fitted by the method described above, the results were found to be unsatisfactory from an econometric point of view. Why this was so will be briefly described, before the results of a slight generalisation of system (6.3), which turned out to be more satisfactory, are discussed.

The initial round of estimates produced results which violated concavity in eleven of the thirteen panels. Concavity was then imposed in these eleven cases (it was usually necessary to set all the β_{ij} equal to zero)[14] in a second round of estimates. In addition to concavity, production theory requires that the constant terms a^i_X, a^i_K and a^i_L be non-negative. The constants differ between industries in a given panel because of the presence of the industry dummies; the estimate of each industry-specific constant in the share equations is the estimated constant for the panel as a whole plus the estimated coefficient on the industry dummy. In the second round estimates after concavity had been imposed, 36 coefficients out of $(3 \times 119 =)$ 357, or 10 per cent, violated non-negativity – seventeen in the capital share equation, nineteen in the labour share equation and none in the intermediate share equation. The overall fit was found to be fairly good for the intermediate share, rather poor for the capital share, and extremely low for the MFP growth rate.

Accepting these coefficient estimates for the moment, the next step was to see how large a reduction in MFP growth rates could be explained by rising intermediate input prices in the UK case. When this was attempted using UK input data for 1973 and 1979 together with the parameter estimates just described, it was found that one or more of the estimated value shares required for equations (6.4) and (6.5) was negative in 43 out of the 119 industries.

The large number of industries with negative estimated value shares, the considerable number of negative estimated constants, together with the poor fit of the equation for MFP growth, suggest that this model should be rejected for the UK. These considerations also suggest however that it might be worthwhile to try a generalisation of the translog model, in which MFP growth is not constrained, as hitherto, to follow a linear time trend. Instead, the term $\beta^i_{ut}t$ in the last of equations (6.3) will be replaced by a set of seven time period dummies (one for each period except the first), so that the equation to be estimated is now:

$$\bar{v}^i_t = a^i_t + \beta_{Xt}(\overline{\ln X_i} - \overline{\ln L_i}) + \beta_{Kt}(\overline{\ln K_i} - \overline{\ln L_i}) + \Sigma^{j=8}_{j=2}\beta_{tj}D_j + \epsilon^i_t,$$

$$D_j = 1, \text{ if } j = t \text{ and } D_j = 0 \text{ if } j \neq t.$$

The other equations are as before. This modification leaves all the theoretical properties of the translog production function unchanged.

A model with industry and time period effects

This second model was estimated in a similar manner to the first. The instruments used were the same as in the first model, except that the time period dummies (D_j) replaced time (t). The initial round of estimates produced results which violated concavity in all thirteen Orders. The pattern was as follows:

$$\beta_{XX} > 0, \beta_{KK} > 0, \beta_{LL} > 0 - 2 \text{ Orders}$$

$$\beta_{XX} > 0, \beta_{KK} < 0, \beta_{LL} < 0 - 4 \text{ Orders}$$

$$\beta_{XX} > 0, \beta_{KK} < 0, \beta_{LL} > 0 - 7 \text{ Orders}$$

In the first of these three cases, all the share elasticities were set equal to zero (that is, $\beta_{ij} = 0$, $i,j = X, K, L$) and the equations re-estimated. This automatically ensured concavity. It also turned out that all the estimated constants were now positive. In the second case, the effect of setting only β_{XX} equal to zero in the second round was tried. This produced results consistent with concavity (that is, it was still the case that $\beta_{KK} < 0$ and $\beta_{LL} < 0$). However a large number of estimated constants were now negative in three out of these four orders. For these three Orders a third round of estimates was necessary, setting all the share elasticities equal to zero. The estimated constants were now found to be positive. Finally, in the third case above, the effect of setting both β_{XX} and β_{LL} equal to zero in the second round was tried; the new estimates satisfied concavity (that is, it was still the case that $\beta_{KK} < 0$), but again there were a large number of negative estimated constants in all seven Orders involved. So a third round of estimates was necessary for these Orders, setting all share elasticities equal to zero, which finally produced satisfactory results.

In the estimates finally accepted all $(119 \times 3 =)$ 357 constants in the share equations were positive. Somewhat disappointingly though, the share elasticities had to be zeroed in all except one Order (Order IX). These results appear in table 6.1. The principal point which springs out of this table is that technical progress in the UK is indeed biased towards intermediate input – β_{Xt} is positive and highly significant in all thirteen Orders. On the bias towards capital the evidence speaks less strongly: β_{Kt} is positive and significant in five Orders, insignificant in the other eight.

Since each of the productivity growth biases can be positive or negative (ignoring the remote possibility of an estimated coefficient being exactly zero), there are eight logically possible patterns for the three coefficients β_{Xt}, β_{Kt}, and β_{Lt}. But because the coefficients must sum to zero, two of these cases (when the coefficients are either all negative or all positive) are impossible economically. Of the six economically possible cases, only two are actually observed in table 6.1: there are eleven Orders where technology is intermediate-using, capital-using and labour-saving ($\beta_{Xt} > 0$, $\beta_{Kt} > 0$ and $\beta_{Lt} < 0$), and two Orders where technology is intermediate-using, capital-saving and labour-saving ($\beta_{Xt} > 0$, $\beta_{Kt} < 0$ and $\beta_{Lt} < 0$). It turns out that these were also the most frequent patterns found by JGF for the US.

Next equation (6.6) is re-estimated in order to gauge the effect of changing input prices in the more general model with period dummies. Negative estimated shares are now found in only four industries, a much improved result compared with the 43 industries where negative shares were found in the more restricted model. For the remaining 115 industries, the results are as follows:

Distribution of hypothetical changes in $\bar{v}_i^t$ by industry, 1973–9 (%)

Range	No. of industries
> -1.0 & ≤ -0.5	1
> -0.5 & ≤ 0.0	49
> 0.0 & ≤ 0.5	62
> 0.5 & ≤ 1.0	3
TOTAL	115

In more that half the industries therefore, changes in input prices are predicted to have *increased* MFP growth. The overall picture is as follows: Minimum, -0.52 per cent; Maximum, $+0.93$ per cent; Mean, $+0.03$

Table 6.1. *Translog production functions: panel regression results*

	III Coef.	t	V Coef.	t	VI Coef.	t	VII Coef.	t
				Order				
β_{XX}	–	–	–	–	–	–	–	–
β_{XK}	–	–	–	–	–	–	–	–
β_{KK}	–	–	–	–	–	–	–	–
β_{Xt}	0.00569	7.85	0.00718	11.58	0.00578	6.72	0.00726	12.70
β_{Kt}	0.00112	4.68	0.00026	0.60	0.00042	0.96	−0.00050	1.54
β_{t2}	−0.00519	0.34	0.00397	0.50	0.02104	1.04	0.03280	3.45
β_{t3}	−0.00478	0.22	0.00111	0.10	0.02513	0.88	0.02638	1.96
β_{t4}	0.00894	0.42	0.00661	0.59	0.00258	0.09	0.01728	1.29
β_{t5}	0.00080	0.04	−0.04092	3.64	−0.05886	2.06	−0.00175	0.13
β_{t6}	−0.02268	1.06	−0.03138	2.80	−0.00523	0.18	0.01241	0.93
β_{t7}	−0.01398	0.66	−0.03443	3.10	0.02020	0.71	0.00135	0.10
β_{t8}	−0.02226	1.10	−0.00943	0.89	0.03865	1.49	0.00728	0.58
NIND	15		15		6		14	
$R^2(\bar{v}_X)$	0.64542		0.69643		0.75108		0.69190	
$R^2(\bar{v}_K)$	0.85404		0.47111		0.09351		0.18607	
$R^2(\bar{v}_t)$	0.05600		0.51762		0.39986		0.33876	

	VIII Coef.	t	IX Coef.	t	XII Coef.	t	XIII Coef.	t
				Order				
β_{XX}	–	–	–	–	–	–	–	–
β_{XK}	–	–	−0.17009	2.57	–	–	–	–
β_{KK}	–	–	−0.11557	1.54	–	–	–	–
β_{Xt}	0.00988	11.01	0.01325	4.64	0.00400	6.86	0.00451	0.27
β_{Kt}	−0.00023	0.35	0.01450	2.99	0.00019	0.40	0.00073	2.03
β_{t2}	0.04522	2.58	0.02862	2.20	0.02817	1.89	−0.00394	0.27
β_{t3}	0.03218	1.30	0.01245	0.67	0.02628	1.25	−0.00134	0.07
β_{t4}	0.03075	1.24	0.00347	0.18	0.02629	1.25	−0.00269	0.13
β_{t5}	0.00170	0.07	−0.02396	1.24	−0.01258	0.60	−0.01985	0.97
β_{t6}	0.00182	0.07	−0.02287	1.16	0.00522	0.25	−0.02534	1.25
β_{t7}	0.01368	0.56	−0.01227	0.61	−0.01132	0.54	−0.00325	0.16
β_{t8}	0.00473	0.21	−0.02751	1.45	0.00874	0.45	0.00051	0.03
NIND	4		5		9		14	
$R^2(\bar{v}_X)$	0.79756		0.81739		0.87116		0.68221	
$R^2(\bar{v}_K)$	0.05226		0.17284		0.40048		0.27816	
$R^2(\bar{v}_t)$	0.36968		0.31944		0.39040		0.05013	

per cent. The actual change in MFP growth in these 115 industries, comparing 1973–9 with 1968–73, was − 2.34 per cent.[15] Once again therefore it seems that changing input prices can only account for a small proportion of the decline in MFP growth which actually occurred. But even if they under-predict the extent of the decline, do the estimates nonetheless predict its pattern? The answer is once again, no. If we

	XIV, XV Coef.	t	XVI Coef.	t	Order XVII Coef.	t	XVIII Coef.	t
β_{XX}	–	–	–	–	–	–	–	–
β_{XK}	–	–	–	–	–	–	–	–
β_{KK}	–	–	–	–	–	–	–	–
β_{Xt}	0.00569	7.55	0.00617	8.95	0.00731	7.98	0.00613	6.89
β_{Kt}	0.00041	1.80	0.00141	2.73	0.00068	2.51	0.00067	1.85
β_{t2}	0.01545	1.16	0.00159	0.13	0.00125	0.12	0.01760	1.47
β_{t3}	0.00810	0.43	0.00027	0.02	−0.01370	0.96	0.00685	0.41
β_{t4}	0.01768	0.94	0.00369	0.21	−0.02363	1.66	0.01664	0.99
β_{t5}	0.01820	0.97	−0.04251	2.44	−0.05226	3.67	−0.03369	2.00
β_{t6}	0.00754	0.40	−0.03666	2.11	−0.03496	2.46	−0.00696	0.41
β_{t7}	−0.01708	0.92	−0.04317	2.50	−0.02547	1.80	−0.02810	1.68
β_{t8}	0.00512	0.29	−0.00220	0.14	−0.01640	1.27	0.00346	0.23
NIND	12		6		6		7	
$R^2(v_X)$	0.40876		0.78913		0.63506		0.64061	
$R^2(v_K)$	0.50985		0.51042		0.28924		0.41292	
$R^2(v_t)$	0.14926		0.54843		0.35565		0.70982	

	Order XIX Coef.	t
β_{XX}	–	–
β_{XK}	–	–
β_{KK}	–	–
β_{Xt}	0.00588	6.43
β_{Kt}	0.00049	1.00
β_{t2}	0.00137	0.09
β_{t3}	0.00651	0.32
β_{t4}	0.00335	0.16
β_{t5}	−0.02020	0.98
β_{t6}	−0.03133	1.53
β_{t7}	−0.02847	1.40
β_{t8}	0.00642	0.35
NIND	6	
$R^2(v_X)$	0.55946	
$R^2(v_K)$	0.29170	
$R^2(v_t)$	0.22814	

Notes: Results are for equations (6.3), except that time period dummies have been added to, and t dropped from, the equation for $\bar{v}_t^i$. The β_{tj} $(j = 2, \ldots, 8)$ are the coefficients on the time period dummies in the latter equation. The method of estimation was non-linear 3SLS with cross-equation restrictions imposed. NIND is the number of industries in each Order of the 1968 SIC for which data were available. The number of observations in each panel was 8 × NIND. Each equation of (6.3) also contained a constant and (NIND − 1) industry dummies, for which the estimated coefficients are not reported. R^2 statistics are for the equations fitted after the data have been transformed to remove serial correlation.

correlate the predicted and the actual decline in MFP growth, the correlation coefficient turns out to be negligible (0.06).

A final consideration relates to the role of capacity utilisation. Is it possible that the role of energy or intermediate input is being swamped by the effect of varying capacity utilisation? If the latter is distorting our MFP measures, then energy could still be an important influence. It was to guard against such a possibility that the period 1973–9 was used, since in both countries these years were ones of high capacity utilisation. However, they were not necessarily years of *equal* utilisation – indeed, in the UK 1973 was certainly a stronger boom than 1979. Theory suggests that the way to adjust MFP estimates for differences in utilisation of quasi-fixed inputs is to adjust the valuation of these inputs, not their quantities: in fact, Berndt and Fuss (1986) show that if there is only one quasi-fixed input, and if expectations are realised, then use of the *actual* cost shares to weight all inputs is the correct method of adjustment. Jorgenson's estimates and the present ones for the UK use actual shares (actually, *revenue* shares, not *cost* shares);[16] this, coupled with the use of peak years, suggests that our estimates are not too seriously distorted by varying utilisation.[17]

CONCLUSION

We have examined the thesis that the slowdown in multi-factor productivity growth which has occurred since 1973 is due to the rise in intermediate input prices, or more specifically, to the rise in energy prices. Based on the econometric estimates of Jorgenson and his collaborators, we have found that only a small proportion of the US decline in productivity growth can be explained in this way. This is the case whether we look at intermediate input as a whole or just energy. Econometric estimates have been developed for UK manufacturing industries, based on a similar methodology to that of Jorgenson. These estimates were for a three-factor system (intermediate, capital and labour), so it was not possible to test whether it is specifically energy prices which are the culprit in the UK. However, we did find that, in the UK as in the US, the broader category of intermediate input prices can explain only a small part of the productivity slowdown.

One final comment is in order. As the introduction emphasised, many factors, including purely macro ones, may have been behind the slowdown. We have already seen (chapter 4) that MFP growth is positively correlated across industries with output growth; this is the case both over short (4–5)-year periods within the two halves of the overall span studied, 1954–73 and 1973–86, and also over longer periods (for example, the 19-year period 1954–73). Hence if, for whatever reason, *output* growth has slowed down since 1973, then we would expect, on the basis of previous experience, that MFP growth would slow down too. Of course, this explanation is of limited use, if we cannot identify the nature of the causal link between output and MFP growth. It is to this issue that the next chapter will be devoted.

7

INVESTMENT, INCREASING RETURNS, AND THE PATTERN OF PRODUCTIVITY GROWTH

INTRODUCTION

This chapter considers two related topics. First, do conventional growth accounting calculations understate the role of capital formation? Second, is there any evidence for increasing returns at the industry level? The new growth theory (Romer, 1986; Lucas, 1988) has brought externalities to the forefront of discussion. Also, some proponents of the new views (for example, Romer, 1987) have argued that capital investment itself creates externalities, so these topics are in fact related.

Much of the recent empirical work on the explanation of productivity growth has been at the aggregate or sectoral level. Here the data employed are at the industry level, the 124 UK manufacturing industries for which estimates are available for all eight time periods within the overall span of 1954–86. Aggregate data has the advantage that longer time series are usually available. By contrast, the present data set contains only eight time series observations: 1954–8, 1958–63, 1963–8, 1968–73, 1973–6, 1976–9, 1979–82, and 1982–6. Of these, four are periods in which capacity utilisation was roughly the same in the beginning and end years (though 1973 was a very strong peak),[1] two are periods of sharply falling capacity utilisation (1973–6 and 1979–82) and two are periods of sharply rising utilisation (1976–9 and 1982–6). To compensate for this paucity of time series information, the wealth of cross section information available in industry data allows illuminating tests of some of the main hypotheses discussed in the recent literature, as will be seen below.

The plan of the chapter is as follows. The following section discusses the arguments raised by those who consider that conventional calculations of MFP growth underestimate the role of capital formation and presents some tests of the 'capital is special' thesis. Issues discussed include the thesis of DeLong and Summer (1991) that within the total of capital investment it is investment in plant & machinery which is particularly important. The role of errors in measuring the capital stock is also treated. Next, by way of a prelude to an assessment of the role of increasing returns, we consider the important empirical regularity which was earlier (chapter 4) called Fabricant's Law: the positive cross-industry correlation between growth rates of output and growth rates of productivity (both labour and MFP). The evidence for increasing returns is then

discussed and whether alternative explanations based on labour hoarding
fit the facts better (Bernanke and Parkinson, 1991). The chapter closes
with a conclusion.

Is the weight given to capital formation too low?

Let us start by briefly recalling the theory of productivity measurement
set out in chapter 2. In the ith industry, production at time t is assumed to
be given by

$$Y_{it} = F^i(K_{it}, L_{it}, X_{it}, t) \qquad (7.1)$$

where Y is (gross) output, K is the capital stock, L is labour input and X is
intermediate input. By definition, the growth of multi-factor productivity
(MFP), μ_{it}, is

$$\mu_{it} \equiv \partial \ln Y_{it} / \partial t$$
$$= \Delta \ln Y_{it} - w_{Kit} \Delta \ln K_{it} - w_{Lit} \Delta \ln L_{it} - w_{Xit} \Delta \ln X_{it}, \qquad (7.2)$$

in a discrete-time approximation. Here w_{Kit}, w_{Lit} and w_{Xit} are the elasticities of output with respect to capital, labour and intermediate input
respectively. When MFP growth is actually being measured, these elasticities are assumed to be equal to the share of each input in the value of
output.[2]

Because the share of profits in gross output is fairly small – varying
between 13 and 17 per cent over 1954–86 when averaged across the
industries covered by the present study (table 4.2), the calculated contribution of capital stock growth to the growth of output or of output per
head is also fairly small. Many people believe that the true importance of
capital formation is in fact far greater than this calculation would suggest.
An extreme view is held by Scott (1989), who would attribute 100 per
cent of productivity growth to capital formation.[3] But others, in particular DeLong and Summers (1991), have claimed that the role of
investment, particularly investment in machinery, has been underestimated. A number of reasons are commonly given. First, new capital
goods may be of substantially higher quality than older ones, to an extent
not measured adequately by the deflators for capital goods; a variant of
this view is the vintage approach, that new technology must be embodied
in new capital goods and cannot be retrofitted to existing equipment.
Second, the process of investment may lead to 'learning by doing' effects
at the level of the individual firm. Third, learning by doing associated
with investment may be at the industry or the economy-wide level. In an
example of the latter view, Romer (1987), drawing on Arrow (1962), has
presented a model in which the growth of output depends on the growth

of inputs, but the coefficient on capital growth is higher than capital's share because of an externality associated with capital: capital goods are the bearers of knowledge, so that investment by one firm raises the productivity of others as the knowledge embodied in new equipment spills over into the public domain.

As far as the first of these arguments is concerned, it is relevant to recall that the capital stock estimates employed here include a substantial allowance for depreciation (they are 'net' stock estimates), the rates being based on rates of decline of second-hand asset prices observed in the US (see chapter 3). At any moment therefore the estimated stock will be smaller than would be the corresponding 'gross' stock, under which only retirements (scrapping) are allowed for. Hence if gross investment is high (low) in recent years, the estimated growth rate of the stock will be higher (lower) than the same pattern of gross investment would produce under the alternative, 'gross' stock convention. Since one reason for falling second-hand asset prices is obsolescence, it might be argued that the capital stock estimates used here already allow for the possibility that newer capital is superior to older capital. It should also be noted that the vintage capital theory has been tested on a similar data set to the present one in earlier work and found not to play an important role in explaining differences between industries in labour productivity growth rates (Oulton, 1989 and 1990).

Nevertheless, the issue remains worthy of further study. According to the 'capital is special' view, the measured contribution of capital to productivity growth is too small either because the weight accorded to capital is too low, or because capital growth is underestimated. These two possibilities will be dealt with in turn. In calculating MFP growth we subtract capital growth, weighted by its value share, but the value share underestimates capital's contribution, according to the Romer argument. The hypothesis that capital's share (or the share of any input) is under-estimated can be tested with cross-section data as follows. Suppose as above that the true weights to be applied to the input growth rates in calculating MFP growth are w_{Kit}, w_{Lit} and w_{Xit}. But the estimated MFP growth rates, μ^e_{it}, use weights equal to the input shares, w^e_{Kit}, w^e_{Lit} and w^e_{Xit}: the latter are only equal to the elasticities under certain assumptions, namely that firms are price-takers and that they are constant returns. Moreover, though the estimated weights sum to one by definition, this is not necessarily the case for the true weights, for example if increasing returns are important. While true MFP growth (defined to be inclusive of increasing returns, where present) in industry i at time t, μ_{it}, is given by equation (2), measured MFP growth is

$$\mu^e_{it} = \Delta \ln Y_{it} - [w^e_{Kit}\Delta \ln K_{it} + w^e_{Lit}\Delta \ln L_{it} + w^e_{Xit}\Delta \ln X_{it}]. \qquad (7.3)$$

Hence, subtracting (7.3) from (7.2):

Table 7.1. *Testing for errors in weighting of input growth rates*

	1954–8 Coef.	t	1958–63 Coef.	t	1963–8 Coef.	t	1968–73 Coef.	t	1973–76 Coef.	t
$\Delta \ln K$	− 0.0014	0.01	− 0.1114	1.48	− 0.0735	1.39	0.1653	1.83	0.2313	1.03
$\Delta \ln L$	0.1255	0.87	0.0986	1.49	0.0677	0.95	0.1567	1.35	0.3804	3.03
$\Delta \ln X$	− 0.0915	1.07	0.0432	1.05	0.0193	0.42	− 0.1826	2.11	− 0.2396	2.29
R^2	0.0180		0.0498		0.0212		0.1250		0.1381	

	1976–9 Coef.	t	1979–82 Coef.	t	1982–6 Coef.	t	1954–73 Coef.	t	1973–86 Coef.	t
$\Delta \ln K$	0.0739	0.58	− 0.2042	1.98	− 0.0426	0.51	0.0054	0.07	0.1531	1.37
$\Delta \ln L$	− 0.0474	0.50	− 0.1796	2.01	0.0216	0.28	− 0.0140	0.28	− 0.0516	0.55
$\Delta \ln X$	− 0.0305	0.47	0.1578	2.02	0.0069	0.13	0.0909	1.25	− 0.0689	1.00
R^2	0.0104		0.1290		0.0034		0.0697		0.0212	

Note: Dependent variable is MFP growth rate ($\Delta \ln \text{MFP}$). Regressions included a constant. 124 industries in sample. t ratios are heteroskedasticity-consistent.

$$\mu_{it}^e = \mu_{it} + (w_{Kit} - w_{Kit}^e) \Delta \ln K_{it} + (w_{Lit} - w_{Lit}^e) \Delta \ln L_{it}$$
$$+ (w_{Xit} - w_{Xit}^e) \Delta \ln X_{it}.$$

The μ_{it} differ across industries; a simple model to acount for this variation is:

$$\mu_{it} = \eta_i + \theta u_t + \epsilon_{it}, \tag{7.4}$$

where η_i varies across industries but is constant over time, θ_t is constant across industries but varies over time, and ϵ_{it} is a random error with zero mean. Substituting in the previous equation,

$$\mu_{it}^e = \eta_i + \theta_t + (w_{Kit} - w_{Kit}^e) \Delta \ln K_{it} + (w_{Lit} - w_{Lit}^e) \Delta \ln L_{it}$$
$$+ (w_{Xit} - w_{Xit}^e) \Delta \ln X_{it} + \epsilon_{it}. \tag{7.5}$$

Under the null hypothesis that MFP growth is correctly measured, the errors ϵ_{it} are independent of the three input growth rates which appear in this last equation; also, the coefficients on these growth rates are constant across industries and equal to zero.

Consider a cross-industry regression of the estimated MFP growth rate on the variables on the right-hand side of (7.5). Variation in the η_i will be absorbed into the error term; the constant will be $E(\eta_i) + \theta_t$. The coefficient on $\Delta \ln K$, if significantly positive, will indicate that the true weight for capital is (on average across industries) higher than the estimated weight. The results of this regression both for short time periods and for long ones appear in table 7.1. It will be seen that, over the eight short periods and the two long periods, the coefficient on $\Delta \ln K$ is significant only once, in 1979–82 (just), and on that occasion it is negative. It is never positive and significant. $\Delta \ln L$ and $\Delta \ln X$ are significant and of opposite sign in two periods, 1973–6 and 1979–82. In addition, $\Delta \ln X$ is significantly negative in 1968–73. However, over long periods none of the growth rates attracts a significant coefficient. These results therefore provide no support at all for the view that the role of capital has been understated.[4]

Some further tests

An alternative approach is to start with equation (7.2) and rearrange it to yield:

$$\Delta \ln y_{it} = \mu_{it} + w_{Kit}\Delta \ln k_{it} + w_{Xit}\Delta \ln x_{it}$$
$$+ [w_{Lit} + w_{Kit} + w_{Xit} - 1]\Delta \ln L_{it} \qquad (7.6a)$$

where $y_{it} \equiv Y_{it}/L_{it}, k_{it} \equiv K_{it}/L_{it}$ and $x_{it} \equiv X_{it}/L_{it}$. In a panel regression, we can model μ_{it} by a combination of fixed effects and time period dummies. If the theory underlying the calculation of MFP growth rates is correct, we would expect that the estimated coefficients on $\Delta \ln k_{it}$ and $\Delta \ln x_{it}$ in a panel regression would be approximately equal to the sample average of the value shares for capital and intermediate input respectively and that the coefficient on $\Delta \ln L_{it}$ would be equal to zero, since the value shares sum to one. On the other hand, if standard theory understates the role of capital and if increasing returns exist, then the sum of the elasticities exceeds one (that is, $w_{Lit} + w_{Kit} + w_{Xit} > 1$), and the coefficient on $\Delta \ln L_{it}$ is positive. Also, the coefficient on capital should be significantly larger than capital's value share.

It is also revealing to write equation (7.6a) in another form. By definition of an elasticity, the term involving capital growth in equation (7.2) can be written

$$w_{Kit}\Delta \ln k_{it} = [K_{it}/Y_{it}][\Delta Y_{it}/\Delta K_{it}][\Delta K_{it}/K_{it}] = [\Delta Y_{it}/\Delta K_{it}][I_{it}/Y_{it}],$$

where $I_{it} \equiv \Delta K_{it}$. Consequently (7.6a) can be written:

$$\Delta \ln y_{it} = \mu_{it} + [\Delta Y_{it}/\Delta K_{it}][I_{it}/Y_{it}] + w_{Xit}\Delta \ln x_{it}$$
$$+ [w_{Lit} + w_{Xit} - 1]\Delta \ln L_{it}. \qquad (7.6b)$$

Comparing (7.6a) and (7.6b), the growth of the capital stock has been replaced by the investment–output ratio; the coefficient on the latter is the social marginal product of capital. This is the same equation as the one estimated by DeLong and Summers (1991) in their cross-country study of growth and capital investment, with three differences: DeLong and Summers used a value added measure of output, so that no term in intermediate input (X) appeared in their equation; somewhat inconsistently,

Table 7.2. *Panel regression results: dependent variable is* $\Delta \ln(Y/L)$

| Variable | With fixed effects | | No fixed effects | |
	(1)	(2)	(3)	(4)
$\Delta\ln(K/L)$	0.0954	–	0.1435	–
	(2.24)		(3.97)	
$\Delta\ln(KP/L)$	–	0.0483	–	0.0878
		(1.23)		(2.64)
$\Delta\ln(KB/L)$	–	− 0.0063	–	0.0087
		(0.24)		(0.37)
$\Delta\ln(KV/L)$	–	− 0.0051	–	− 0.0050
		(0.33)		(0.34)
$\Delta\ln(X/L)$	0.5763	0.5832	0.5872	0.5991
	(27.96)	(28.34)	(29.50)	(30.31)
$\Delta\ln L$	− 0.0070	− 0.0441	0.0427	0.0156
	(0.19)	(1.12)	(1.46)	(0.53)
D5863	1.3379	1.4445	1.4625	1.5405
	(5.18)	(5.38)	(4.65)	(4.77)
D6368	0.9786	1.1026	1.0881	1.1859
	(4.11)	(4.59)	(3.40)	(3.63)
D6873	1.2182	1.2813	1.3811	1.4242
	(5.34)	(5.57)	(4.35)	(4.33)
D7376	− 1.4624	− 1.4906	− 1.2092	− 1.2536
	(6.53)	(6.60)	(3.80)	(3.82)
D7679	− 0.8679	− 0.8440	− 0.6519	− 0.6365
	(3.88)	(3.60)	(2.05)	(1.90)
D7982	− 0.6346	− 0.7602	− 0.2473	− 0.4210
	(2.31)	(2.67)	(0.67)	(1.10)
D8286	0.9803	0.8652	1.2853	1.1459
	(4.23)	(3.66)	(3.94)	(3.40)
SER	2.46	2.46	2.47	2.48
R^2	0.5578	0.5560	0.5551	0.5520

Notes: t statistics are in brackets. Number of observations is eight (time periods) × 124 (industries) = 992. Sample period covers 1954–86. D5863 is the dummy for 1958–63, D6368 that for 1963–8, and so on. The dummy for 1954–8 is omitted. Regressions (3) and (4) included a single constant, while (1) and (2) allowed a separate constant for each industry.

they employed gross, not net, investment; and they included a 'catch-up' variable, the initial gap in GDP per worker between countries.[5] It is certainly of interest that (7.6a) and (7.6b) are closely related since DeLong and Summers reached very strong conclusions about the importance of capital investment. However, from an empirical point of view, equation (7.6a) is superior when capital stock data are available, as is the case here, though not for DeLong and Summers.

Table 7.2 reports the results of running panel regressions based on equation (7.6a); μ_{it} is modelled in principle by a combination of fixed effects and time period dummies, as in equation (7.4). All regressions

Table 7.3. *Long-period regressions: dependent variable is Δ ln(Y/L)*

| Variable | 1954–73 | | 1973–86 | |
	(1)	(2)	(3)	(4)
$\Delta \ln(K/L)$	0.2410 (3.48)	–	0.2455 (2.20)	–
$\Delta \ln(KP/L)$	–	0.1636 (3.06)	–	0.0158 (0.19)
$\Delta \ln(KB/L)$	–	– 0.0405 (1.80)	–	0.1533 (1.67)
$\Delta \ln(KV/L)$	–	0.0303 (0.72)	–	– 0.0628 (1.06)
$\Delta \ln(X/L)$	0.6270 (8.28)	0.6959 (9.91)	0.5600 (7.92)	0.5990 (7.97)
$\Delta \ln L$	0.1229 (3.14)	0.0910 (2.51)	0.0601 (0.86)	0.0075 (0.10)
SER	0.97	0.98	1.45	1.47
R^2	0.6522	0.6505	0.4178	0.4146

Note: Heteroskedasticity-consistent t statistics are in brackets. Number of observations is 124. Regressions included a constant.

include time period dummies. Results are given for regressions with either fixed effects or with a common intercept. Regressions (1) and (3) use total capital, while regressions (2) and (4) split fixed capital up into plant & machinery (KP), buildings (KB) and vehicles (KV). The motivation for disaggregating the capital stock is that most of the arguments considered above for a special role for capital seem to relate to plant & machinery; also, DeLong and Summers (1991) in their cross-country study have claimed to find strong effects on labour productivity growth stemming from equipment investment, but weaker or non-existent effects from other types of investment.

With or without fixed effects, the equations all reject the hypothesis of a special role for capital. In fact the fixed effects turn out not to be significant: the F value for regression (1) versus regression (3) in table 7.2 is 1.11 and for (2) versus (4) it is 1.13. Without fixed effects, the coefficient on capital growth (equivalent to 14 per cent) is very close to the sample average of capital's share in the value of output; the coefficient on intermediate growth (equivalent to 59 per cent) is likewise close to the average share of intermediate input. Furthermore the coefficient on labour force growth is not significantly different from zero, which is consistent with the sum of the elasticities of the inputs with respect to output being equal to one, which in turn is consistent with constant returns. Disaggregating fixed capital also fails to reveal a special role for plant & machinery: the coefficient on $\Delta \ln(KP/L)$ is about half that on total capital growth, which is quite consistent with the share of such investment in the total, but not consistent with any uniquely important role for plant & machinery.[6]

DeLong and Summers looked at growth rates over long periods, so it is interesting to consider the result of running equation (7.6a) on the two long periods, 1954–73 and 1973–86 (table 7.3). Results are shown for both total capital and for the three types of fixed capital separately. For both 1954–73 and 1973–86, the coefficient on the growth of total capital (about 0.24) is substantially higher than the sample average of capital's share (about 0.15). However, the amount by which the coefficient exceeds the share is in both cases less than two standard errors (only one standard error in the case of 1973–86). In 1954–73, the coefficient on labour force growth is significantly different from zero, which could be taken as evidence of increasing returns. However, for 1973–86 the coefficient is not significant. When capital is disaggregated, plant & machinery is highly significant in 1954–73, but not in 1973–86. The period 1954–73 thus offers some weak support to the DeLong and Summers position, but the subsequent period does not.

Regressions were also run on each of the eight short periods. Total capital is significant only in 1968–73. Plant and machinery does somewhat better, being significant in 1954–8, 1968–73 and 1976–9, the latter providing the 'best' result (a coefficient of 0.2454, with a t value of 2.71). However in the other five periods the coefficient is small and even negative. All in all, these results are not very supportive of the 'capital investment is special' thesis.[7]

Errors in measuring the growth of the capital stock

As argued above, capital's role might be more important than MFP calculations allow either because the weight given to capital is too low or because the growth rate of capital has been underestimated for some reason. In addition, if there are errors in measuring capital stock growth, then the test based on equation (7.5) may be biased against acceptance of a special role for capital. The reason is that a positive error in measuring capital stock growth leads to a corresponding negative error in measuring MFP growth, so that even if the true coefficient on capital stock growth in (5) is zero, the estimated coefficient will be negative. But if the true coefficient is positive (a special role for capital), the presence of measurement error will bias the coefficient downwards, making us more likely to wrongly reject the 'capital is special' hypothesis.

Suppose that the true rate of growth of capital per unit of labour is related to the estimated rate $(\Delta \ln k_{it}^e)$ as follows:

$$\Delta \ln k_{it} = a_i + \beta_t + \gamma \Delta \ln k_{it}^e. \tag{7.7}$$

Here a_i is an industry-specific error and β_t is an error common to all industries in a given time period. The latter type of error might arise if technical progress is faster in some periods than in others but this fact is not reflected in the deflators used to calculate real investment. The kind of correction which has recently been made to US investment figures as a result of new deflators for computers which for the first time try to fully reflect their quality improvement is an example of this phenomenon (Cole *et al.*, 1986). The parameter γ could be of any size; a value greater than one could occur if industries which have rapid measured rates of capital growth are the ones who are in fact investing the most in new technology.

With the above model for measurement errors, equation (7.6a) becomes:

$$\Delta \ln y_{it} = w_{Kit}a_i + w_{Kit}\beta_t + w_{Kit}\gamma \Delta \ln k_{it}^e + w_{Xit}\Delta \ln x_{it}$$
$$+ [w_{Lit} + w_{Kit} + w_{Xit} - 1]\Delta \ln L_{it} + \mu_{it} \tag{7.6c}$$

Now suppose that in place of the true model as represented by equation (7.6c), equation (7.6a) is estimated on panel data but with measured capital growth $\Delta \ln k_{it}^e$ substituting for true growth $\Delta \ln k_{it}$. First of all, the industry specific errors a_i will tend to be absorbed into the fixed effects (since for a given industry w_{Kit} does not vary much over time). However, as already noted, F tests reject the hypothesis of significant fixed effects for both the regressions with aggregated capital and for the ones with disaggregated capital. Second, the hypothesis that $\gamma > 1$ can be tested by seeing whether the estimated coefficient on capital growth exceeds capital's average share by an economically significant amount. But we have already seen that this is not the case. Finally, the error which is constant across industries (the β_t) will probably be absorbed into the time period dummies, provided that the cross-industry variation in w_{Kit} is not too large (if the latter predominates, the β_t will show up in the fixed effects). In principle, there is no way of determining whether the time period dummies are proxying for the β_t in equation (7.7) or for the θ_t in equation (7.4). However, a (common-across-industries) measurement error in capital stock growth rates seems less plausible when one considers the pattern of the coefficients of the time period dummies: positive up to 1973, negative from 1973–82, and positive again in 1982–6. There seems no reason to think that measurement errors would follow this pattern. If they arise from failure to account adequately for technical progress, one would expect the time period dummies to be consistently positive in the 1970s and 1980s and perhaps rising, given the common view that the pace of technical progress has increased in recent years. All in all then, though there are undoubtedly errors in measuring capital stock growth rates, these errors do not seem to be related systematically to productivity

Table 7.4. *Output, productivity and prices: correlation coefficients between growth rates (124 industries)*

	$\Delta \ln Y$ with $\Delta \ln \mathrm{MFP}$	$\Delta \ln Y$ with $\Delta \ln[Y/L]$	$\Delta \ln Y$ with $\Delta \ln q$
Short periods			
1954–58	0.42	0.61	− 0.25
1958–63	0.45	0.62	− 0.32
1963–68	0.35	0.65	− 0.20
1968–73	0.52	0.70	− 0.45
1973–76	0.67	0.77	− 0.46
1976–79	0.46	0.64	− 0.09
1979–82	0.47	0.56	− 0.21
1982–86	0.40	0.51	0.00
Long periods			
1954–73	0.51	0.62	− 0.39
1973–86	0.39	0.49	− 0.31
1954–86	0.45	0.63	− 0.33

growth rates and the hypothesis that capital growth has been on average seriously underestimated finds no support.[8]

FABRICANT'S LAW

As chapter 4 noted, there is strong evidence for the presence of what was called there Fabricant's Law in the present data set. The first two columns of table 7.4 recapitulate these findings: in every period, short or long, there is a significant, positive correlation between the growth of labour productivity and the growth of output.[9] Though the relationship is somewhat weaker, there is also a significant positive correlation between MFP growth and output growth. As chapter 4 also noted, these correlations are too large to be explained as simply due to errors in the measurement of output. Do the same relationships hold in a multi-variate context? Table 7.5 attempts an answer. In these regressions, MFP growth is the dependent variable; output growth is entered as an explanatory variable, as would indeed be econometrically correct if economies of scale or externalities generated by rising industry were truly important.[10] Also, a large number of industry characteristic (IC) variables are added as controls; these variables are described in Appendix B. Briefly, there are nineteen variables, which can be divided roughly into six groups: labour force characteristics, industrial relations, product market characteristics, competition, technology and a catch-up variable, the productivity gap with the US.[11] In addition, fifteen dummies to represent the Order of the 1968 SIC to which each industry belongs are entered. The idea here is to

Table 7.5. *Coefficient on output growth, by period (124 industries): dependent variable is MFP growth*

	$\Delta \ln Y$	R^2
Short periods		
1954–48	0.2082	0.5369
	(7.30)	
1958–63	0.1206	0.5350
	(4.58)	
1963–68	0.0976	0.3739
	(3.59)	
1968–73	0.2870	0.4269
	(6.34)	
1973–76	0.4818	0.6017
	(9.09)	
1976–79	0.2401	0.4020
	(5.25)	
1979–82	0.2659	0.5190
	(5.31)	
1982–86	0.1404	0.4327
	(3.04)	
Long periods		
1954–73	0.1250	0.6516
	(4.83)	
1973–86	0.2292	0.5899
	(3.80)	

Note: For short periods, explanatory variables include (in addition to output growth) constant, fifteen Order dummies and nineteen industry characteristic variables; for long periods, seven change variables are also included for 1954–73, and thirteen for 1973–86. t ratios (in brackets) are heteroskedasticity-consistent.

allow for the possibility that high productivity and high output growth might both be caused by some third factor, which can be proxied by some measurable characteristic, such as low capital intensity, high unionisation, large plant size or a largely female labour force.

Despite the presence of this large number of control variables, table 7.5 makes clear that output growth is highly significant in all periods, short or long, thus confirming the impression created by the simple correlations of table 7.4.

Discussions of Fabricant's Law have focused on two possible explanations. The first, which until recently was the favoured one, argued that some industries (for accidental reasons) happened to enjoy more rapid productivity growth than others. With lower costs, producers in these industries were motivated to expand output, prices fell and the extra output was absorbed by the market. According to this view, causation runs from autonomous technical progress to output via prices (Salter, 1966, chapter X, though he did allow a subsidiary role for economies of scale). Though this view was originally couched in terms of labour productivity, the argument in fact works better for MFP, as will be seen in a moment. A macro level version of Salter's view has been espoused by the real business cycle school (Prescott, 1986).

The second explanation is increasing returns. If increasing returns genuinely exist then (part of) what has been measured as MFP growth is really the effect of increasing returns. Here causation runs the other way, from demand to lowered costs and hence to expanded supply.

Postponing the discussion of increasing returns to the next section, we now discuss the case for the first explanation, which turns out to be not without difficulties. There are two legs to the argument: first, differences in MFP growth lead to changes in relative prices, and second, changes in prices lead to different growth rates of output. As to the first leg, there are certainly reasons for expecting MFP growth to be negatively correlated with price growth. Assume constant returns and competitive conditions in factor and product markets. Wages and capital costs will then be equalised across industries. If relative input prices are unchanged, then, by duality (Jorgenson, 1986), the price of output will fall (relative to the average price level) at the same rate as MFP is rising. It is not contended of course that technology changes are the *only* cause of relative price changes,[12] it is enough that they are one possible cause. Turning to the second leg of the argument, the demand for the ith industry's output can be written (in terms of changes) as follows, assuming a constant elasticity form:

$$\Delta \ln Y_i = \eta_{iq} \Delta \ln(q_i/\bar{q}) + f_i(t),$$

where q_i is the price of the ith industry's output, $\bar{q}$ is some cross-industry index of output prices, $f_i(t)$ is an industry-specific function of time (added to take care of income effects or taste changes), and η_{iq} is the price elasticity of demand for the ith industry. It is clear from this equation that sufficient variability across industries in the price elasticity or in the industry-specific functions of time would wipe out the correlation between output and price growth. Nevertheless, the correlation is in fact negative and quite high in absolute value, as column 3 of table 7.4 shows. So if this explanation of Fabricant's Law is correct, the cross-industry variability in income and price elasticities is perhaps surprisingly low.

However, in accordance still with this explanation of Fabricant's Law, we would expect that the correlation between the growth of output and the growth of MFP (or of labour productivity) would be lower than the correlation of output growth with price growth. For according to this explanation, MFP growth works not directly but indirectly, via its effect

Table 7.6. *Panel regression results: dependent variable is output growth ($\Delta \ln Y$)*

	(1)	(2)	(3)
$\Delta \ln q$	− 0.4037 (7.84)	–	− 0.0326 (0.61)
$\Delta \ln \text{MFP}$	–	0.9096 (16.51)	0.8905 (14.05)
SER	4.40	3.97	3.97

Note: 124 industries and eight time periods. *t* statistics are in parentheses. All regressions include fixed effects and seven time period dummies.

on relative prices, but the latter are influenced by other forces as well. Turning to the data, we find the opposite: the correlations of output with MFP (or with labour productivity) are invariably higher than those with prices (table 7.4).

A somewhat more formal test is also possible. The equation for industry demand leads to a panel regression model in which output growth is regressed on price growth, industry fixed effects, and time period dummies (there are eight periods in the data set, so seven period dummies are employed). This regression is justified since, under the null hypothesis, price changes are largely due to exogenous technical progress: what we are allegedly observing is the demand curve traced out by exogenous shifts in the supply curve. Alternatively, the same panel regression can be run, with MFP growth replacing or supplementing price growth. The results are in table 7.6. It will be seen that MFP growth is a far more significant variable than price growth, and when both variables are included together, price growth ceases to be significant. These results are inconsistent with the view that MFP growth exerts only an indirect effect through relative prices and in fact constitute a refutation of this explanation of Fabricant's Law.

Fabricant's Law and the relationship between aggregate output and productivity growth

On average, MFP growth tends to be high when output growth in manufacturing as a whole is high, as is documented in table 7.7 (columns 1 and 3). This time series relationship between output and productivity growth at the aggregate level, sometimes misleadingly called Verdoorn's Law, has been frequently observed.[13] Also, as we have already seen, there are important 'period effects' revealed by our data set: the time period dummies in table 7.2 are all significant, except for 1976–9. In other words, after controlling for the effects of growing capital intensity and intermediate input intensity, which differ between industries, there are

Table 7.7. *Period effects and growth of manufacturing value added,* %, *p.a.*

Period	Mean MFP growth	Period effects	$\Delta \ln V$
1954–58	− 0.15	− 0.14	0.86
1958–63	1.23	1.32	4.85
1963–68	0.99	0.95	4.19
1968–73	1.23	1.24	3.51
1973–76	− 1.52	− 1.35	− 4.55
1976–79	− 0.85	− 0.79	− 2.39
1979–82	− 0.71	− 0.39	− 7.42
1982–86	0.96	1.15	1.53

Source: Mean MFP growth is the sample average of the 124 industries. Period effects are the period dummies from regression (3) of table 7.2, plus the constant from this regression (− 0.14). $\Delta \ln V$ is the growth of manufacturing value added, from table 5.1.

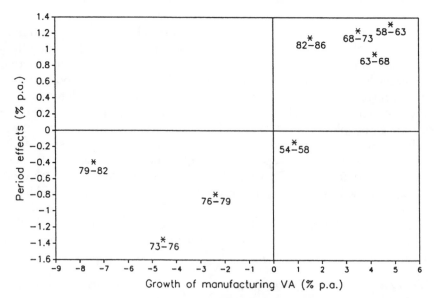

Chart 7.1   Period effects and aggregate growth
Source: Table 7.7.

some periods in which there is a common positive stimulus to productivity growth and others in which the common stimulus is negative. It is also the case that the size of the stimulus is positively related to the rate at which manufacturing as a whole is growing, as table 7.7 shows (comparing columns 2 and 3). Table 7.7, and the corresponding chart 7.1, make clear that the higher the growth of aggregate manufacturing, the higher the period effect.[14] In passing, we may note that though there are only eight data points, chart 7.1 strongly suggests the anomalous nature of the 1979–82 period.

Whatever the mechanism behind Fabricant's Law may be, the same force may be generating the positive relationship between output growth and productivity growth which we seem to observe at the aggregate level. Suppose that MFP growth at the industry level follows the model of chapter 4 and is affected by both idiosyncratic and common, economy-wide shocks

$$\mu_{it} = \eta_i + \theta_t + \epsilon_{it},$$

where η_i is an industry fixed effect, θ_t is a common shock and ϵ_{it} is the idiosyncratic shock. We assume that the idiosyncratic shocks are independent of each other and of the economy-wide shocks:

$$\mathrm{E}\theta_t = 0; \ \mathrm{E}\epsilon_{it} = 0; \ \mathrm{E}\epsilon_{it}\epsilon_{jt} = 0 \ (i \ne j); \ \mathrm{E}\epsilon_{it}\theta_t = 0.$$

θ_t and each ϵ_{it} are assumed to have finite variances, denoted by $\sigma^2(\cdot)$.

The intuitive argument for a link between Fabricant's Law and the time series correlation between aggregate output and productivity growth is as follows. Suppose there is a favourable economy-wide shock. Then MFP growth will tend to be higher in all industries. Because of Fabricant's Law, output growth will also tend to be higher in all industries. Since aggregate output growth is an average of industry output growth, the link is demonstrated. This proposition will now be proved more formally.

By definition, the growth rate of output in the ith industry is

$$\hat{Y}_{it} = \hat{W}_{it} + \mu_{it},$$

where W is total input and a 'hat' denotes a growth rate. Fabricant's Law (an empirical finding) says that $\mathrm{Cov}(\hat{Y}_{it}, \mu_{it}) > 0$. Now

$$\mathrm{Cov}(\hat{Y}_{it}, \mu_{it}) = \mathrm{Cov}(\hat{W}_{it}, \mu_{it}) + \sigma^2(\mu_t),$$

so the truth of Fabricant's Law depends on the second term, which is positive, swamping the effect of the first which may be negative: this turns out to be always the case with the present data set. We may therefore assume in addition that $\mathrm{Cov}(\hat{Y}_{it}, \theta_t) > 0$ and that $\mathrm{Cov}(\hat{Y}_{it}, \epsilon_{it}) > 0$. Now consider the effect on the ith industry's output of productivity growth in the jth industry:

$$\mathrm{Cov}(\hat{Y}_{it}, \mu_{jt}) = \mathrm{Cov}(\hat{Y}_{it}, \theta_t) + \mathrm{Cov}(\hat{Y}_{it}, \epsilon_{jt}).$$

The first term on the right-hand side is positive. The second term might be either positive or negative: for example, it might be negative if the ith and jth industries produce products which are substitutes. However, it seems more likely to be positive (a favourable shock to one industry raises demand elsewhere, either through income effects or because industry i supplies inputs to j). So we will assume that $\text{Cov}(\hat{Y}_{it}, \mu_{jt}) > 0$.

The growth rate of aggregate final output $(\hat{Y}_t)$ is a weighted average of the industry output growth rates, where the weights are the ratios of industry to total final output:[15]

$$\hat{Y}_t = \Sigma_i v_{it} \hat{Y}_{it}, \qquad v_{it} > 0, \ \Sigma_i v_{it} = 1.$$

Following the theory set out in chapter 5, the growth rate of aggregate MFP (μ_t) is a weighted sum of industry MFP growth rates, where the weights are the ratios of industry gross output to total final output:

$$\mu_t = \Sigma_i w_{it} \mu_{it}, \qquad w_{it} > 0, \ \Sigma_i w_{it} \geq 1.$$

Suppose that Fabricant's Law holds. Will the aggregate time series correlation be observed as well? The answer is yes. Consider the covariance between output and productivity growth at the aggregate level:

$$\begin{aligned}
\text{Cov}(\hat{Y}_t, \mu_t) &= \text{Cov}(\Sigma_i v_{it} \hat{Y}_{it}, \ \Sigma_i w_{it} \mu_{it}) \\
&= \Sigma_i v_{it} \ \Sigma_j w_{jt} \text{Cov}(\hat{Y}_{it}, \mu_{jt}) \\
&= \Sigma_i v_{it} w_{it} \text{Cov}(\hat{Y}_{it}, \mu_{it}) + \Sigma_{i \neq j} v_{it} \ \Sigma_j w_{jt} \text{Cov}(\hat{Y}_{it}, \mu_{jt}).
\end{aligned}$$

With N industries, there are N covariances in the first term and $N^2 - N$ covariances in the second. The weighted sum of the N covariances in the first term goes to zero as N increases (an instance of the law of large numbers). However, the $N^2 - N$ covariances in the second term are all positive by assumption because of the common shocks, and their weighted sum does *not* approach zero. Hence

$$\text{Cov}(\hat{Y}_t, \mu_t) > 0,$$

as asserted.

This argument is not conclusive, since alternative explanations for the aggregate relationship are possible. But it does at any rate suggest that it is important to establish the true explanation for Fabricant's Law and in particular whether increasing returns have anything to do with the matter.

INCREASING RETURNS

Types of increasing returns and alternative explanations

Two types of true increasing returns are possible. First, there are static economies of scale (for example, in a Cobb-Douglas production function when the exponents on the inputs add up to more than one). Second, there are dynamic increasing returns, ascribed usually to learning effects of one sort or other. The latter may be wholly internal to the firm, or they may give rise to spillover effects. Hitherto unexploited static economies of scale, which are then revealed by demand expansion, are possible in principle if there is imperfect competition, but seem unlikely to have been important in practice in our period. The fact that the size distribution of plants in manufacturing shows little change from the 1950s at least till the 1980–81 recession (Oulton, 1987), coupled with the well-known fact that a substantial proportion of manufacturing output is in the hands of a 100 or so giant companies,[16] each of whom typically owns a large number of plants, militates against this possible type of increasing returns. In one sense, static economies of scale may be very important. For example, they may help to explain why Britain has a steel industry and Liechtenstein does not. But it is quite a different matter to argue that some significant part of the expansion of output in British industry over 1954–86 has been due to the exploitation of static economies of scale. For these reasons, most interest attaches to dynamic increasing returns.

Three other effects may give rise to the *appearance* of increasing returns. First, if there are fixed costs due to short-run indivisibilities, then a demand expansion may lead to an apparent rise in MFP; this rise is spurious, since at least one input was not being fully utilised. Second, there may be labour hoarding (Rotemberg and Summers, 1990; Bernanke and Parkinson, 1991). If labour hoarding occurs because labour has an overhead character, then this effect reduces to the first. Alternatively, labour hoarding may be due to costs of adjustment of the labour force, leading to firms smoothing the pattern of employment over the cycle. The third effect concerns technology shocks, as emphasised by real business cycle theorists in a macro context (for example, Prestcott, 1986). If on average technology shocks are positive, then intertemporal substitution of labour by workers will lead to employment and consequently output expanding particularly rapidly.

Fixed costs due to specificity of capital are undoubtedly an important feature of many industries, and the phenomenon of labour hoarding is also well-attested. It might be thought that these factors can only help to explain a relationship between productivity growth and output growth over cyclical frequencies (peak-to-trough or trough-to-peak). However, as we have seen (table 7.4), the relationship is just as strong over long periods; and anyway four out of our eight short periods have start and end dates of roughly equal capacity utilisation. Nevertheless, cyclical effects cannot be entirely excluded, since it is possible that even in a period when capacity utilisation was *on average* the same at the beginning and end, the industries which have expanded faster may finish up with above average capacity utilisation, or may have started with below average utilisation.

Hall (1990), building on Hall (1988), has claimed that US sectoral data do show evidence of increasing returns, while Caballero and Lyons (1989, 1990, and 1991) have gone further and claimed that not only do increasing returns exist but that they are due to external effects on productivity generated by overall growth in the economy. Their results, taken at face value, suggest that such effects exist at the 2-digit level (roughly, the 'Order' level of the 1968 SIC) for a number of countries, including the UK.

The type of evidence assembled above in table 7.7 and chart 7.1, showing that productivity grows rapidly in manufacturing as a whole when output is also growing rapidly, suggests that if we wanted to construct a case for aggregate output growth generating externalities at the industry level, in the manner of Caballero and Lyons, then the materials are ready to hand. However, as we have just seen, an alternative explanation which has the causation running the other way, from a micro relationship (Fabricant's Law) to the macro level correlation, is also possible. Moreover, as others have noted (for example, Bernanke and Parkinson, 1991), it is difficult to think of a plausible mechanism which is capable of generating significant externalities over such short periods of time (Caballero and Lyons offer no suggestions). Nevertheless, ultimately the issue is an empirical one, which requires us to test directly for the presence of externalities.

Testing for learning effects

How might one test whether increasing returns due to learning effects are important?[17] This sort of increasing returns is usually thought of as irreversible in nature. An industry can learn, but it cannot forget, or at least forgetting takes place at a slower rate, unless some disaster (such as war or revolution) intervenes. So one would expect that increasing returns would show up in industries where output growth is positive, but be absent, or at least occur at a different rate, in industries where output growth is negative. This possibility can be tested by splitting the sample into high and low growth industries. Ideally, the former should have positive growth and the latter negative. But in order to get adequate sample numbers in every period, the actual dividing line was set at 0.75 per cent per annum growth, with those growing faster than this rate being classified as 'high growth', the rest as 'low growth' (the latter includes a large number of industries with negative output growth). The identical regression, of MFP growth on output growth plus the IC controls, was then run for every period on the high and low growth samples separately. The coefficient and t statistic on $\Delta \ln Y$, together with other statistics, are reported in table 7.8.[18]

It will be seen that in short periods there is only a slight tendency for the coefficient on output growth in high growth industries to exceed the

Table 7.8. *Split sample results: coefficient on* $\Delta \ln Y$ *(dependent variable is* $\Delta \ln MFP$)

	Low output growth industries [< = 0.75%, p.a.]		High output growth industries [> = 0.75%, p.a.]	
	Coef.	NOB	Coef.	NOB
Short periods				
1954–58	0.2093 (4.90)	45	0.3081 (5.49)	79
1958–63	− 0.1032 (0.40)	26	0.1187 (3.52)	98
1963–68	0.2570 (1.78)	26	0.1060 (3.72)	98
1968–73	0.8397 (3.79)	27	0.2052 (3.94)	97
1973–76	0.4719 (7.40)	80	0.5610 (3.12)	44
1976–79	0.0079 (0.07)	66	0.3508 (4.75)	58
1979–82	0.2139 (4.41)	110	NA NA	14
1982–86	0.0085 (0.17)	50	0.2945 (3.49)	74
Long periods				
1954–73	0.4386 (5.45)	25	0.1306 (3.33)	99
1973–86	0.2429 (4.34)	95	0.1492 (1.65)	29

Notes: Regressions are of $\Delta \ln MFP$ on constant, $\Delta \ln Y$, and nineteen IC variables (Order dummies were omitted and levels only, not changes, of IC variables were included). t ratios are heteroskedasticity-consistent. NOB is number of industries.

corresponding coefficient in low growth industries. In long periods, the opposite is found: the coefficient in low growth industries is larger and more significant in both halves of the time span. This latter result in particular is strong evidence against the increasing returns hypothesis.

An alternative test is to estimate the same regression as in table 7.8 over the whole sample of industries, but adding a dummy variable (LOWG) which is equal to one when output growth is less than or equal to 0.75 per cent per annum; an interaction term, LOWGDY, the product of LOWG and $\Delta \ln Y$, is also added to allow for a different response of productivity to output growth when the latter is low. (Note that this is not quite the same model as in table 7.8 since the coefficients on the IC variables are now constrained to be equal in the high and low growth industries). The

Table 7.9. *Whole sample results: coefficient on LOWGDY (dependent variable is Δ ln MFP)*

	Coefficient
Short periods	
1954–58	− 0.1272
	(1.46)
1958–63	− 0.2284
	(2.70)
1963–68	− 0.1718
	(2.11)
1968–73	0.4777
	(1.60)
1973–76	− 0.1525
	(0.90)
1976–79	− 0.2972
	(2.36)
1979–82	0.0426
	(0.20)
1982–86	− 0.1559
	(1.38)
Long periods	
1954–73	− 0.1359
	(1.74)
1973–86	− 0.07
	(0.56)

Notes: Regressions are of $\Delta \ln$ MFP on constant, LOWG, $\Delta \ln Y$, LOWGDY, and nineteen IC variables) (Order dummies were omitted and levels only, not changes, of IC variables were included). t ratios are heteroskedasticity-consistent. Number of industries is 124.

coefficients and heteroskedasticity-consistent t ratios on LOWGDY are in table 7.9. Although they are predominantly negative, neither of the two long-period coefficients is significant, and only three out of eight short-period coefficients are significant.[19] In summary, the results detailed in tables 7.8 and 7.9, though not overwhelmingly decisive, on the whole go against the increasing returns hypothesis.

Labour hoarding

As discussed above, an alternative explanation for Fabricant's Law is labour hoarding. Here again industry data allows a test which would not be possible using only macro data. It is well known that the layoff rates of blue-collar workers are systematically higher than those of white-collar workers; blue-collar workers are also more subject to short-time working, and to overtime working. Presumably therefore the importance of labour

Table 7.10. *Test of labour hoarding hypothesis*

	$\Delta \ln Y$	DYBLU
Short periods		
1954–58	1.0453	− 0.0103
	(3.68)	(2.99)
1958–63	0.7411	− 0.0079
	(3.07)	(2.61)
1963–68	− 0.2269	0.0042
	(0.49)	(0.69)
1968–73	0.1769	0.0015
	(0.66)	(0.38)
1973–76	− 0.3199	0.0106
	(0.77)	(1.87)
1976–79	0.4652	− 0.0031
	(1.27)	(0.61)
1979–82	0.6096	− 0.0050
	(1.43)	(0.84)
1982–86	0.4444	− 0.0043
	(2.00)	(1.31)
Long periods		
1954–73	0.4876	− 0.0044
	(2.09)	(1.58)
1973–86	0.2371	− 0.0001
	(0.74)	(0.03)

Note: Regressions are of $\Delta \ln$ MFP on constant, $\Delta \ln Y$, DYBLU, and nineteen IC variables (order dummies were omitted and levels only, not changes, of IC variables were included). t ratios (in brackets) are heteroskedasticity-consistent. Number of industries is 124.

hoarding should be greater the higher the share of white-collar labour in an industry's labour force, since for whatever reason employers prefer not to vary too much the employment and hours worked of their white-collar workers. In other words, the response of productivity growth to output growth should depend negatively on the labour force share of blue-collar workers (Rotemberg and Summers, 1990). The blue-collar share is fortunately available for every year in the study from the Census of Production.[20] It varies substantially across industries, for example, in 1973 its mean was 74.9 per cent and standard deviation 8.5 per cent, with a minimum of 51.3 per cent and a maximum of 90.5 per cent (see table B.1 in Appendix B).

Table 7.10 reports the results of testing this hypothesis. The same basic regression, of MFP growth on output growth plus controls, is carried out for the whole sample of 124 industries as in table 7.5, but with the addition of an interaction term, DYBLU, which is equal to the product of

$\Delta \ln Y$ and BLU, where BLU is the blue-collar proportion (measured as a percentage). The coefficient on the interaction term, DYBLU, is expected to be negative. It is in fact negative in five out of eight short periods, and in both long periods. But it is only significant twice (in 1954–8 and 1958–63). However, one interesting fact does emerge. If one calculates what the response of MFP growth to output growth would be in a hypothetical industry which was 100 per cent blue collar, one finds that in most periods it would be roughly zero (since the coefficient on DYBLU is about one hundredth of that on $\Delta \ln Y$ and of opposite sign). On the whole, though, we must conclude that the labour hoarding hypothesis does *not* receive strong support. This does not of course mean that labour hoarding as a general phenomenon has been discredited, only that over predominantly non-cyclical frequencies it does not appear to be important. An additional reason is perhaps that in the 1970s the combination of employment protection legislation and union militancy destroyed the usual link between labour hoarding and the blue-collar share.

CONCLUDING REMARKS

It is time to sum up the main conclusions. First, we have found no support for the 'capital is special' view. The weight given to capital growth in the MFP calculations seems to have been correct on average, and no evidence was found to suggest that the growth rate of the capital stock has been systematically underestimated (table 7.1). The DeLong–Summers thesis, that investment in plant & machinery (rather than investment in general) is uniquely important for economic growth, also found no support using industry data (tables 7.2 and 7.3).[21] It follows that Romer's claim, that capital investment generates externalities, is also not supported by these data.

However, this does not mean that other sorts of externality might not be important. The empirical regularity known as Fabricant's Law – the cross-industry correlation between output growth and productivity growth – is certainly *prima facie* evidence for increasing returns (tables 7.4 and 7.5). The fact that the alternative explanation for the Law, in which causation runs from (exogenous) technical progress via changes in relative prices to output growth, is not supported by the evidence adds weight to this suspicion (table 7.6).

In support of the view that increasing returns matter, we can cite the evidence that rapid growth in manufacturing as a whole (or domestic output as a whole, since the two are highly correlated) produces on average higher productivity growth in individual industries (table 7.7). This phenomenon, which at the macro level has been labelled procyclical labour productivity or short-run increasing returns to scale, is on one view a statistical artefact due to labour hoarding. However a test for the presence of labour hoarding based on the proportion of blue-collar workers in each industry's workforce yielded inconclusive results (table 7.10).

But when direct tests are made for the presence of increasing returns, the picture which emerges is not altogether clear. It was argued that if increasing returns are of the dynamic kind, involving some kind of learning effects, then they should show up much more readily in those industries where growth is rapid than in those where it is slow or even negative (a common occurrence in our sample); the argument is that industries can learn but (usually) do not forget. In fact, no strong differences emerged between slow-growing and fast-growing industries (tables 7.8 and 7.9). This test assumes that firms learn from their rivals in the same industry. Of course, learning might take many different forms, including learning from one particularly dynamic sector or learning from abroad. These negative results on increasing returns leave the true explanation for Fabricant's Law still unclear.

Finally, we may recall a conclusion reached in chapter 4: though the majority of the variation in productivity growth is both industry- and period-specific, strong evidence emerged of economy-wide shocks. The nature and mechanism of propagation of these shocks remain to be determined.

APPENDIX A

LIST OF INDUSTRIES COVERED BY THE CENSUS OF PRODUCTION, CLASSIFIED BY THE 1968 SIC

MLH	INDUSTRY

Order II – Mining and Quarrying

101	Coal mining**
102/103	Stone and slate quarrying and mining; chalk, clay, sand and gravel extraction*
104	Petroleum and natural gas**
109	Other mining and quarrying*

Order III – Food, drink and tobacco

211	Grain milling
212	Bread and flour confectionery
213	Biscuits
214	Bacon curing, meat and fish products
215	Milk and milk products
216	Sugar
217	Cocoa, chocolate and sugar confectionery
218	Fruit and vegetable products
219	Animal and poultry foods
221	Vegetable and animal oils and fats
229/1	Margarine
229/2	Starch and miscellaneous foods
231	Brewing and malting
232	Soft drinks*
239/1	Spirit distilling and compounding
239/2	British wines, cider and perry*
240	Tobacco

Order IV – Coal and petroleum products

261	Coke ovens and manufactured fuel*
262	Mineral oil refining*
263	Lubricating oils and greases*

Order V – Chemicals and allied industries

271	General chemicals
272	Pharmaceutical chemicals and preparations
273	Toilet preparations
274	Paint
275	Soap and detergents
276	Synthetic resins and plastics materials and synthetic rubber
277	Dyestuffs and pigments
278	Fertilisers
279/1	Polishes
279/2	Formulated adhesives, gelatine, etc.
279/3	Explosives and fireworks
279/4	Formulated pesticides, etc.
279/5	Printing ink
279/6	Surgical bandages, etc.
279/7	Photographic chemical materials

Order VI – Metal manufacture

311	Iron and steel (general)
312	Steel tubes
313	Iron castings, etc.
321	Aluminium and aluminium alloys
322	Copper, brass and other copper alloys
323	Other base metals

Order VII – Mechanical engineering

331	Agricultural machinery (except tractors)
332	Metal-working machine tools
333	Pumps, valves and compressors
334	Industrial engines
335	Textile machinery and accessories
336	Construction and earth-moving equipment
337	Mechanical handling equipment
338	Office machinery
339/1	Mining machinery
339/2	Printing, bookbinding and paper goods machinery
339/3/4	Refrigerating machinery (except domestic type refrigerators); space-heating, ventilating and air-conditioning equipment
339/5–9	Scales and weighing machinery; portable power tools; food and drink processing machinery; packaging and bottling machinery; other machinery except electrical machinery*
341	Industrial (including process) plant and steelwork
342	Ordnance and small arms
349	Other mechanical engineering not elsewhere specified

Order VIII – Instrument engineering

351	Photographic and document copying equipment
352	Watches and clocks
353	Surgical instruments and appliances
354	Scientific and industrial instruments and systems

Order IX – Electrical engineering

361	Electrical machinery
362	Insulated wires and cables
363	Telegraph and telephone apparatus and equipment
364	Radio and electronic components*
365	Broadcast receiving and sound reproducing equipment*
366	Electronic computers*
367	Radio, radar and electronic capital goods*
368	Electric appliances primarily for domestic use
369	Other electrical goods

Order X – Shipbuilding and marine engineering

370	Shipbuilding and marine engineering

Order XI – Vehicles

380	Wheeled tractor manufacturing*
381	Motor vehicle manufacturing
382	Motor cycle, tricycle and pedal cycle manufacturing
383	Aerospace equipment manufacturing and repairing
384/385	Locomotives and railway track equipment; railway carriages and wagons and trams

Order XII – Metal goods not elsewhere specified

390	Engineers' small tools and gauges
391	Hand tools and implements
392	Cutlery, spoons, forks and plated tableware, etc.
393	Bolts, nuts, screws, rivets, etc.

394	Wire and wire manufactures
395	Cans and metal boxes
396	Jewellery and precious metals
399/1	Metal furniture
399/2–12	Metal industries not elsewhere specified (except metal furniture)

Order XIII – Textiles
411	Production of man-made fibres
412	Spinning and doubling on the cotton and flax systems
413	Weaving of cotton, linen and man-made fibres
414	Woollen and worsted
415	Jute
416	Rope, twine and net
417	Hosiery and other knitted goods
418	Lace
419	Carpets
421	Narrow fabrics (not more than 30 cm. wide)
422/1	Household textiles and handkerchiefs
422/2	Canvas goods and sacks and other made-up textiles
423	Textile finishing
429	Other textile industries

Order XIV – Leather, leather goods and fur
431	Leather (tanning and dressing) and fellmongery
432	Leather goods
433	Fur

Order XV – Clothing and footwear
441	Weatherproof outerwear
442	Men's and boy's tailored outerwear
443	Women's and girl's tailored outerwear
444	Overalls and men's shirts, underwear, etc.
445	Dresses, lingerie, infant's wear, etc.
446	Hats, caps and millinery
449/1/3/4	Corsets and swimwear; umbrellas and walking sticks; other
449/2	Gloves
450	Footwear

Order XVI – Bricks, pottery, glass, cement, etc.
461	Bricks, fireclay and refractory goods
462	Pottery
463	Glass
464	Cement
469/1	Abrasives
469/2	Building materials, etc. not elsewhere specified

Order XVII – Timber, furniture, etc.
471	Timber
472	Furniture and upholstery
473	Bedding, etc.
474	Shop and office fitting
475	Wooden containers and baskets
479	Miscellaneous wood and cork manufactures

Order XVIII – Paper, printing and publishing
481	Paper and board
482/1	Cardboard boxes, cartons and fibre-board packing cases
482/2	Packaging products of paper and associated materials
483	Manufactured stationery
484	Manufactures of paper and board not elsewhere specified

| 485/486 | Printing, publishing of newspapers; printing, publishing of periodicals |
| 489 | Other printing, publishing, bookbinding, engraving, etc. |

Order XIX – Other manufacturing industries

491	Rubber
492	Linoleum, plastics floor-covering, leathercloth, etc.
493	Brushes and brooms
494/1/2	Toys and games; children's carriages*
494/3	Sports equipment*
495	Miscellaneous stationers' goods
496	Plastics products not elsewhere specified
499	Miscellaneous manufacturing industries

Order XX – Construction

| 500 | Construction** |

Order XXI – Gas, electricity and water

601	Gas**
602	Electricity**
603	Water supply**

Notes: On the SIC 1968 definition, manufacturing comprises Orders III–XIX, that is MLH 211–499 (137 industries). To obtain the SIC 1980 definition (approximately), MLH 261–263 are *excluded* and MLH 102/103 and 109, from Order II, are *included*, to give a total of 136 industries in manufacturing.
*Indicates an industry for which estimates of MFP were possible for some but not all eight periods. Fifteen industries in the above list fall into this category.
**Indicates an industry for which no MFP estimates for any period were possible. Six industries in the above list fall into this category.

APPENDIX B

DATA SOURCES

INTRODUCTION

In the description of the sources in this and the following appendices the following abbreviations have been used:

AAS   *Annual Abstract of Statistics* (CSO, HMSO, London)
BB   'Blue Book', that is, *United Kingdom National Accounts* (CSO, HMSO, London)
BrBu   *British Business* (Department of Trade and Industry)
BLSHA   *British Labour Statistics: Historical Abstract 1886–1968*, Department of Employment and Productivity (HMSO, London, 1971).
BLSYB   *British Labour Statistics Year Book* (Department of Employment)
EG   *Employment Gazette* (Department of Employment)
ETAS87   *Economic Trends Annual Supplement 1987* (CSO, 1987)
MDS   *Monthly Digest of Statistics* (CSO)
HRCP   *Historical Record of the Census of Production 1907 to 1970* (Business Statistics Office, 1978)
NES   *New Earnings Survey* (Department of Employment)
RCP   *Report on the Census of Production: summary tables, PA1002* (BSO, various years)

DATA FROM THE CENSUS OF PRODUCTION

Data on output, wages, employment, investment and stocks were derived from the Census of Production. All monetary values in the Census are in current prices; the sources for the deflators are described below. These variables were extracted for the following years: 1954, 1958, 1963, 1968 and 1973, 1976, 1979, 1982 and 1986. Up to and including 1979, the Census of Production was classified in accordance with the 1968 SIC; in subsequent years, it was classified in accordance with the 1980 SIC. (For 1979, the Census was published on both bases, which is the essential foundation for the reclassification algorithm described in Appendix C). The 1968 SIC divided the economy up into 'Minimum List Headings' (MLH); in some cases data was also published for 'sub-headings' of an

MLH. In the 1980 SIC the basic unit is the 'Activity Heading' (AH). For further details, see Appendix C.

Output

Three concepts of output are to be found in the Census of Production – 'net output', 'gross output' and 'gross value added'. The relations between them are as follows:

Gross output = Sales and work done
                plus
                Increase during the year, stocks of work in progress and goods on hand for sale
Net output = Gross output
                minus
                Purchases
                plus
                Increase during the year, stocks of materials, stores and fuel
                minus
                Cost of industrial services received
Gross value
added   = Net output
                minus
                Cost of non-industrial services received

Net output, unlike gross output, can be aggregated over industries covered by the Census without double counting; gross value added, since it excludes services purchased outside the Census sector, can be aggregated over industries inside and outside the Census. All three concepts, however, suffer from the defect of being gross of stock appreciation. Aggregate gross value added in manufacturing, as recorded in the Census, will therefore differ, for this reason alone, from the contribution of manufacturing to GDP as recorded in the Blue Book ('value added' in the ordinary sense). Output on all three measures has therefore been adjusted for stock appreciation by a method conceptually analogous to the method used by the CSO for estimating stock appreciation at the aggregate level (see Appendix D).

Prior to 1970, the published figures for net output were on a different definition; in particular, payments to other organisations for transport were included in the 'Cost of industrial services received' and hence subtracted in arriving at net output; from 1970 onwards such payments are included in the 'Cost of *non-industrial* services' and so not subtracted in arriving at net output. To improve comparability, our net output figures for years prior to 1970 have been augmented by adding in payments for transport (from HRCP, table 1; the few cases of missing values were set to zero).

Gross output has also been adjusted to exclude (net) payments of excise duties/receipt of subsidies, in cases where excise duties are included in the value of sales. The effect of this exclusion is that gross output is valued at the prices received by producers, not paid by purchasers. The industries affected were MLH 214, 216, 217, 231, 239/1, 239/2, 240 and 263. Excise duties (net of subsidies) were taken from the individual reports (see Appendix D).

Net output and gross output have always been available from the Census, but gross value added only from 1973.

Intermediate input

The Census of Production allows us to distinguish only three types of intermediate input: materials and fuel; industrial services and non-industrial services. The first two types will be considered together as the same deflator has to be used for both (see below). In nominal terms, these two types are measured by the difference between gross output (GO) and net output (NO), after adjusting both gross and net output for stock appreciation. Denoting stock appreciation in work in progress and goods on hand for sale by SAWGS and stock appreciation in materials stores and fuel by SAMSF, then in nominal terms:

Intermediate input =   Cost of non-industrial services
$$+ \left[(GO - SAWGS) - (NO - SAMSF) \right].$$

See Appendix D for the derivation of SAWGS and SAMSF.

The Census of Production tabulates the cost of non-industrial services received by each MLH from 1973 onwards. Our measure of non-industrial services, NIS, equals the Census definition *minus* payments for rents, hire of plant and machinery and vehicles, bank charges and commercial insurance payments. Prior to 1973 payments for non-industrial services were not published but one large component, payment for transport, was included separately from 1954–72. Payments for non-industrial services before 1973 were estimated using both payments for transport and a residual component; the latter includes payments for communications, royalties and professional services.

In detail, the estimation procedure was as follows. The ratio of NIS to gross output was first calculated for each MLH in 1973. This ratio was then applied to 1972 gross output to get an estimate of NIS for 1972. Payments for transport were then excluded and the ratio of the residual to gross output was applied back to 1954 to get estimates of 'other' non-industrial services. Payments for transport were then added to this residual category to get total NIS for the benchmark years from 1954–68.

The calculation therefore allows part of NIS to be determined freely from the data but assumes that the ratio of the residual category to gross output was constant over time.

Wages and employment

Three types of worker are distinguished in the Census – operatives; administrative, technical and clerical (ATC) employees; and working proprietors. The third category is nearly always very small. The Census gives the total wage bill, the wage bill of operatives and the wage bill of ATC employees; also, wages per head for operatives and ATC employees. The numbers of operatives and of ATC employees were derived by dividing the wage bill by the wage per head for each group; though the numbers employed are given in the Census, this procedure reduces rounding error, as the published figures for numbers employed are often only given to two significant figures. Total employment was taken directly from the Census.

The year 1986 presented a particular problem since neither the wage bills for operatives (WOPERT) and for ATC employees (WATCT) nor the numbers of employees of the two sorts (EOPER and EATC) were given by AH in the Summary Report but only by group (3-digit level); however, the total wage bill (WTOT) *was* given by AH. The individual reports gave wages per head for operatives and ATC employees (WOPERH and WATCH) and the ratio of operatives to ATC employees (R) by AH. The procedure was to estimate WOPT, WATCT, EOPER and EATC by the following equations. Since WTOT = WOPERT + WATCT, then

$$\text{WTOT/WOPERT} = [\text{WOPERT} + \text{WATCT}]/\text{WOPERT}$$
$$= 1 + [\text{WATCH}/[\text{WOPERH*R}]],$$

whence

$$\text{WOPERT} = \text{WTOT}/[1 + [\text{WATCH}/[\text{WOPERH*R}]]].$$

Then, by definition,

$$\text{WATCT} = \text{WTOT} - \text{WOPERT}.$$

Finally, as before,

$$\text{EOPER} = \text{WOPERT/WOPERH}$$
and $$\text{EATC} = \text{WATCT/WATCH}.$$

The methods used to go from numbers employed to hours worked (the basic unit of labour input) by different types of worker are more fully described in Appendix F. For manual workers, the main source on weekly hours was the Department of Employment's 'Annual Inquiry' into earnings and hours (EG, various issues). For non-manuals, the NES was used. Weeks worked per year are derived mainly from Matthews *et al.* (1982).

Inventories (stocks)

The Census records the book value of three sorts of stocks at the end of the firm's year (which is usually though not invariably the end of the calendar year in which the Census is taken): 'materials, stores and fuel' (MSF); 'work in progress' (WP); and 'goods on hand for sale' (GS). In addition, it records the increase over the course of the year in the book value of MSF (IMSF) and the increase in the book value of (usually) the *sum* of work in progress and goods on hand for sale (IWGS). It is for this reason that we have aggregated together work in progress and goods on hand for sale, the resulting stock being labelled WGS. Some firms may have used the 'standard cost' method of accounting for inventories (under which additions to inventory are recorded at a fixed price during the accounting period), particularly during the inflationary 1970s. It was probably uncommon before then and seems likely to have become so again subsequently, going the way of its conceptual sister, current cost accounting. Most firms probably record additions to inventory at the prices current at the time the additions are made, which means that the increases in book value recorded in the Census are a mixture of price increases and quantity increases. In other words, we need to calculate a conceptual analogue of what the CSO in the Blue Book calls the 'Value of the physical increase in stocks at current prices'; see Appendix D for more on this.

Sources for Census data

The sources for the series derived from the Census were as follows:

1954–68   HRCP (by MLH)
1973–9   RCP, various issues (by MLH), principally PA 1002 for 1973, 1976 and 1979.
1979–86   RCP, various issues (by AH), supplemented by unpublished data supplied by BSO for 1980–83, when the published Censuses were less detailed. The 1979 data, classified by AH, comes from *Census of Production and Purchases Inquiry: Analysis of production industries by Standard Industrial Classification Revised 1980* (PA 1002.1, BSO, 1983).

SOURCES FOR CAPITAL STOCK ESTIMATES

Investment

A. Industry-level series

Investment in current prices is available at the industry level from the Census for four types of asset: 'Land and existing buildings', 'New building and works', 'Plant & machinery' and 'Vehicles'. Data on the first of these is available only since 1968 but on the others since 1948. The Census records 'Acquisitions' and 'Disposals' separately for each asset except 'New building and works' (since only a second-hand building can be disposed of). Note that 'Disposals' do *not* include assets sold for scrap. Prior to 1970, at which date the Census became annual, the years for which data is available differ between industries (see below for the interpolation and extrapolation procedures, necessary to construct the continuous investment series employed in the estimation of capital stocks by industry). In a few cases investment figures have been suppressed by the BSO for confidentiality reasons; these have been estimated using data from adjacent years by the RAS method. Except for 'New buildings and works', the investment series are for 'Acquisitions' *less* 'Disposals'.

The sources were as follows:

1948–68	HRCP, table 4 (by MLH); available years differ between industries
1970–79	RCP, table 5, various years (by MLH)
1980–83	unpublished data supplied by BSO (by AH)
1984	RCP 1984, table 5a (by AH)
1985	RCP 1985, table 5 and individual reports (by AH)
1986	RCP 1986, table 5 and individual reports (by AH).

B. Annual group-level series (current prices)

Prior to 1948, the CSO has unpublished annual series in current prices on investment in plant & machinery (from 1888), buildings (from 1852) and vehicles (from 1936), for twelve industry groups in manufacturing. From 1948–71, series on 25 industry groups in manufacturing were employed. Of these, 23 were unpublished CSO series. The other two series were for MLH 370 (Shipbuilding) and MLH 383 (Aerospace) which were taken from various issues of the Blue Book. The unpublished series, with one exception, conformed to the 1968 SIC, and are the ones used by the CSO in their perpetual inventory model of the capital stock before they switched their estimates to a SIC 1980 basis. We are very grateful to RJ Allard for making these data available to us. The exceptional series was the iron and steel group which was obtained direct from the CSO. This series was on the 1980 SIC basis and had to be reclassified.

C. Financial leasing adjustment

As described in the text, the basis for the adjustment is two unpublished CSO series on gross investment in plant & machinery and in vehicles, 1980 prices, 1967–85. Prior to 1967 financial leasing is generally agreed to have been negligible. Tony Smith kindly supplied these series. The series used to apportion the total amongst the industries was 'Hire of vehicles, plant & machinery' from RCP 1979 (PA 1002.1), table 1b. This was reclassified from an AH to a MLH basis using the method outlined in Appendix C.

Deflators for investment

(a) Plant & machinery

Before 1956 — One deflator for all manufacturing (CSO, unpublished)

1956–79 — Separate deflators for ten industry groups in manufacturing (CSO, unpublished)

1980–86 — Separate deflators for 27 industry groups in manufacturing from *Price index numbers for current cost accounting* (BSO, various issues)

(b) Land and buildings

Before 1980 — One deflator for manufacturing (CSO, unpublished)

1980–86 — Private sector industrial construction deflator from *Price index numbers for current cost accounting* (DE, various issues)

(c) Vehicles

Before 1984 — One deflator for manufacturing (CSO, unpublished)

1984–6 — Deflator for passenger cars from *Price index numbers for current cost accounting* (DE, various issues).

(a) Plant and Machinery Prior to 1956 it is only possible to derive a single price index for manufacturing investment. From 1956–80 separate indices were available for ten industries within manufacturing and for mining and quarrying. The industries covered were food, drink, chemicals and allied industries, metals, mechanical engineering and allied industries, electrical engineering, vehicles, textiles, printing and publishing and other manufacturing. The food index was also used for tobacco, the mechanical engineering index for instrument engineering, shipbuilding and other metal goods, and the other manufacturing index was used for leather, clothing, footwear, bricks etc. and timber and furniture. The above price indices were unpublished data which were supplied by the CSO.

From 1980–85 average annual deflators were obtained from various issues of the BSO publication, *Price index numbers for current cost accounting*. These data were available for a much larger number of industry groups which covered the 1980 classification of production industries. The industries for which separate series were available were: coal extraction, coke ovens, extraction of mineral oil and gas, mineral oil processing, and twenty seven manufacturing industry groups, a full list of which is given in the above mentioned publications.

Although the later, more detailed series are available back to 1974, they refer to the 1980 SIC, and hence were only used from that date. The investment data from 1980 to 1985 were first deflated and then reclassified to the 1968 SIC using the method described in Appendix C.

(b) New Buildings Price data disaggregated by industry are not available for new buildings, hence a single deflator is used. Up to 1970 the deflator is for new construction excluding dwellings and from 1970–80 it refers to private industrial construction. Both series were unpublished data from the CSO. The deflator from 1980–85 is again taken from *Price Index Numbers for Current Cost Accounting* and refers to private sector industrial construction. These two indices are very close for the overlapping period 1974–80. The former was used prior to 1980 because this facilitated comparisons with the CSO's estimates of the capital stock.

(c) Vehicles As in the case of building investment, a single price index for vehicles is used for all industry groups. Up to 1983 the deflator is an unpublished price index for road vehicles from the CSO. *Price Index Numbers for Current Cost Accounting* presents four price series from 1974, that is, passenger cars and three types of commercial vehicles distinguished by their tonnage. However, there is no information on the relative weights of the four types of vehicles in total manufacturing investment. Therefore, the passenger car series was used to complete the series for 1984–6 but was spliced with the road vehicle series in 1983 to maintain consistency.[1]

Capital/output ratios

The 'output' part of these ratios was derived as follows. The indices of industrial production at constant factor cost were used to measure real output by industry. The industry groups were in most cases equal to the industry order group of the 1968 SIC, the single exception being that shipbuilding and vehicles were aggregated. These indices were available in BB on a consistent classification from 1952–82, thereafter the indices were classified according to the 1980 SIC. In general, the post 1982 indices were set equal to the SIC 1980 group which most closely matched the SIC 1968 Order so that firms omitted from or added to the SIC 1980 group were assumed to have experienced the same output growth as those in the SIC 1968 classification. Man-made fibres, a separate SIC 1980 group, were added to textiles using the 1980 weights used in constructing the index as detailed in the relevant table in BB. Mineral oil refining was added to the SIC 1980 total manufacturing index again using the published 1980 weights. The two series were spliced in 1982.

DEFLATORS

Deflators for output

In most cases producer price indices (PPI), formerly wholesale price indices, for 'home sales' were employed as deflators. The main source was various issues of BrBu and its predecessors. A number of unpublished indices were specially supplied by the BSO. Producer price indices with reference years 1954, 1963, 1970, 1975 and 1980 were spliced together using overlapping years. For 1980 and after indices are for Activity Headings and for other years they are for Minimum List Headings; see Appendix C for the reclassification procedure. In a few cases, producer prices were estimated by means of retail prices. Where no alternative was available, the price index for the order to which the industry belonged was used, the source again being BrBu.

In general, the number of industries for which no output deflator is available increases the further back in time one attempts to go. Thus PPIs are available for 177 out of 218 AH in divisions 1–4 of the 1980 SIC from 1979 onwards; they are available for 112 industries (MLH) in manufacturing, mining and the utilities out of a possible 144 in 1973; in 1968, they are available for 88 industries and in 1954 for 67. See Appendix E for further details of the construction of the indices.

Deflators for inputs

Intermediate input is divided in the Census of Production into three parts – 'Purchases' (of materials, components, energy, and so on), 'Cost of industrial services' (mainly payment to other firms for work done on materials supplied by the establishment and payments for repairs and maintenance) and 'Cost of non-industrial services' (rents of buildings and hire charges for plant, machinery and vehicles; transport and other business services).

Materials and fuel These were deflated using the BSO's 'Price index numbers of materials and fuels purchased' for each industry, from BrBu. These indices have been published on an AH basis since 1979; unpublished figures back to 1974 were obtained from the BSO (back to 1979 only for the food industries, AH 4115–4239). The indices were reclassified to an MLH basis using 'Purchases' from the 1979 Census as the weights (see Appendix C). Prior to 1974 very little data is available by industry, hence special procedures had to be adopted – see Appendix E.

Cost of industrial services No official deflator is available for this item. In

1986, 'Cost of industrial services received' was 5.9 per cent of 'Purchases' in manufacturing. In the absence of any better alternative, this item also was deflated by the price index for 'Purchases', described above.

Cost of non-industrial services   Once again, no official deflator is available for this item. A single price index, assumed invariant across industries, was constructed from the implicit deflators for transport, communication, and financial services (the source was various issues of BB). These three indices were averaged using purchases of each of these services by aggregate manufacturing as weights; the weights were derived from the 1979 input–output tables (table D) and were respectively 0.65, 0.10 and 0.25.

Deflators for stocks

For MSF, each industry's price index for materials and fuel (see above) was employed; for WGS, each industry's PPI for home sales. See Appendix D on stock appreciation for the treatment of missing values.

THE INDUSTRY CHARACTERISTIC (IC) VARIABLES

The Industry Characteristic (IC) variables can be classified for convenience into seven broad groups: Labour force characteristics; Industrial relations; Product market characteristics; Competition; Technology; Other; and Order dummies. The groups are only meant to be suggestive. Some variables might well have been classified in a different group; for example, plant size is put in the technology group, but might have been considered as an industrial relations variable, since there is evidence that labour relations have been worse in large plants (Prais, 1981, chapter 7). The variables in each group and their sources were as follows.

Labour force characteristics (three variables)

FEMBLU: per cent of total labour input (annual hours) which is *FEM*ale *BLU*e-collar.
FEMWH: per cent of total labour input which is *FEM*ale *WH*ite-collar.
BLU: per cent of total labour force which is *BLU*e-collar.
[The omitted categories, which can be derived from the three above, are the male blue and male white-collar percentages.]
Source: Annual Inquiry into Earnings and Hours of Manual Workers (DEG, various issues).

Industrial relations (three variables)

NSCA: per cent of male manual workers covered by both a *N*ational and a *S*upplementary *C*ollective *A*greement.
NCA: per cent of male manual workers covered by *N*ational *C*ollective *A*greement *only*.

COCA: per cent of male manual workers covered by a *C*ompany *A*greement only.

[The omitted category, derivable from the above as a residual, is the per cent not covered by *any* collective agreement]

Source: *New Earnings Survey*, 1973, 1978 and 1985.

Product market characteristics (four variables)

CONP: per cent of *domestic* sales to *CON*sumers (in 1974).

GOVP: per cent of *domestic* sales to *GOV*ernment (in 1974).

INVP: per cent of *domestic* sales to fixed capital formation (in 1974).

[The omitted category is per cent of domestic sales to intermediate use.]

WGY: *W*ork in progress and *G*oods on hand for sale as per cent of *G*ross output.

Source: CONP, GOVP and INVP from 1974 Input–Output Tables (BSO), table D; WGY from Census of Production.

Competition (three variables)

C_5: per cent of sales held by five largest firms (where size is measured by employment), that is, the *C*oncentration ratio.

IMPORT: *IMPORT*s as a per cent of home demand (import competition).

EXPORT: *EXPORT*s as a per cent of total sales (export propensity).

Source: C_5 from Census of Production; IMPORT and EXPORT from Business Monitor, MQ12 (DTI).

Technology (five variables)

ENINT: Expenditure on fuel and electricity as a percentage of gross output (1974), that is, *EN*ergy *INT*ensity. Source: 1974 Purchases Inquiry.

CAPINT: Fixed capital (sum of plant, buildings & land, and vehicles) as per cent of gross output (that is, *CAP*ital *INT*ensity). Source: Census of Production plus own estimates.

RDINT: R & D spending as per cent of gross output (in 1978), i.e. *R & D INT*ensity. Source: Business Monitor, MO14 1978 (BSO, 1980).

MSFY: (*R*eal) stocks of *M*aterials, *S*tores and *F*uel as per cent of (real) gross output. (Source: Census of Production).

PLSZ: per cent of employment in plants employing 500 or more, that is, *PL*ant *SIZ*e. (Source: Census of Production).

Other (one variable)

GAPUS: US output per person as a per cent of UK output per person (in 1967–68).

Source: Smith *et al.* (1982, table 6.1).

Table B.1. *Descriptive statistics of IC variables, 1973 (124 industries), %*

	MEAN	S.D.	MIN	MAX
FEMBLU	22.7	18.6	0.8	77.4
FEMWH	7.1	4.0	0.8	24.2
BLU	74.9	8.5	51.3	90.5
NSCA	36.8	17.6	1.9	90.1
NCA	25.5	11.8	2.1	63.2
COCA	14.9	11.5	0.8	63.9
CONP	28.2	32.2	0.0	99.6
GOVP	5.3	10.6	0.0	89.4
INVP	10.1	19.6	0.0	83.9
WGY	13.5	11.0	0.6	70.7
C5	49.7	24.1	8.0	99.0
IMPORT	20.7	16.1	0.0	94.0
EXPORT	21.4	16.6	1.0	95.0
CAPINT	53.9	26.8	17.5	135.4
RDINT	0.9	1.8	0.0	16.9
ENINT	2.9	3.3	0.7	26.9
MSFY	9.5	5.3	1.5	45.9
PLSZ	50.8	26.0	0.0	97.2
GAPUS	272.8	92.1	114.0	669.0

Note: For explanation and sources, see text.

Order dummies (fifteen variables)

ORD3–19: *ORD*er dummies for Orders III (3) to XIX (19) of the 1968 SIC. In regressions, Order III is omitted and Order IV has no observations, so ORD5–ORD19 are the ones used.

Though the reasons for inclusion of most of these variables is fairly clear, and many of them are hallowed by tradition, a few may require explanation. MSFY is included as an indicator of the length of the production process. On the other hand, the other stock variable (WGY) measures the extent to which an industry produces to order. If WGY is high, it suggests first that the industry does not produce to order and second that the industry is sensitive to consumer requirements, in the sense of being concerned at the possibility of lost sales due to stockouts. GAPUS is included in order to measure the scope for catch-up. Finally, the Order dummies are included on the grounds that there may be features unique to each sector (for example, a 'chemical' effect) which are not captured by the explicit measures which it has been possible to quantify.

Note that, except for the order dummies, all these variables are expressed as percentages. In order to employ a consistent set of variables in the analysis of each time period, it was sometimes necessary to extrapolate forwards and backwards and to interpolate. In some cases, this meant applying the value for one period to another. For example, the industrial relations variables are not available prior to 1973, so the 1973 values are used for all earlier periods. Three of the product market variables (CONP, GOVP and INVP) are only available for 1974 (due to the limitations of the input–output tables), so this year's values are used throughout. For similar reasons we use the 1978 R & D intensities (RDINT) and the 1974 energy intensities (ENINT) for every period.

To illustrate orders of magnitude, descriptive statistics (mean, standard deviation, minimum and maximum) of the nineteen IC variables for the year 1973 in the sample of 124 manufacturing industries appear in table B.1.

In principle, as well as including the beginning-of-period value of each IC variable, it would be desirable to include also the change in each variable over the period. This was done wherever the data allowed, which led to some differences in the variable set applied to the two long periods studied. For example, the change in the three industrial relations variables is available for 1973–86 but not for 1954–73, since (owing to their unavailability prior to 1973) these three variables are assumed to be constant at their 1973 value over the 1954–73 period.

The change variables which were employed in the two long periods were (in obvious notation):[2]

DFEMBLU:	Both periods
DFEMWH:	Both periods
DBLU:	Both periods
DNSCA:	1973–86 only
DNCA:	1973–86 only
DCOCA:	1973–86 only
DWGY:	Both periods
DC_5:	1973–86 only
DIMPORT:	1973–86 only
DEXPORT:	1973–86 only
DCAPINT:	Both periods
DMSFY:	Both periods
DPLSZ:	Both periods

APPENDIX C

THE RECLASSIFICATION OF THE STANDARD INDUSTRIAL CLASSIFICATION FROM THE 1980 TO THE 1968 BASIS

INTRODUCTION

1980 was the 'Year Zero' of official statistics, when a new and quite different Standard Industrial Classification (SIC) was introduced. From then on all industrial statistics, such as the Census of Production, have been produced on the new basis. Though the previous 1968 SIC was itself the latest revision of a classification first introduced in 1948, these revisions had created no radical break in continuity. With the aid of the Business Statistics Office's own retrospective volume (BSO, 1978), it is possible to examine industrial statistics on an essentially consistent basis from 1948–79. But the 1980 SIC does represent a radical break in continuity and one which the BSO has done very little to bridge. It is true that producer prices on the new basis have been carried back to 1974 and on the old basis have been brought forward to 1983. Also, and crucially for the work to be reported here, the 1979 Census of Production, originally published on the old basis, was later reworked on the new one. But apart from this there has been little official attempt to produce industry-level statistics on a consistent basis before and after the change in classification.

The work reported here involved the writing of computer programs which can reclassify industry-level data published on the new basis to the old one. By means of these programs, one can take as input any industrial series, such as gross output, net output, employment or price, which is classified on the new basis and receive as output the same series reclassified on the old basis. Thus the continuity of industrial statistics can be preserved and it is possible to study the evolution of economic performance at the industry level from 1948 (in practice, 1954) to the present day.

The plan of this appendix is as follows. The next section compares the two classification systems and discusses the nature of the reclassification problem. A discussion of reclassification from a mathematical point of view follows. Then in the final section the main algorithm is described.

Table C.1. *Structure of the Census sector of the 1968 SIC*

Name of Order		Number of industries
Order II	Mining and quarrying	4
Order III	Food, drink and tobacco	17
Order IV	Coal and petroleum products	3
Order V	Chemicals and allied industries	15
Order VI	Metal manufacture	6
Order VII	Mechanical engineering	15
Order VIII	Instrument engineering	4
Order IX	Electrical engineering	9
Order X	Shipbuilding and marine engineering	1
Order XI	Vehicles	5
Order XII	Metal goods not elsewhere specified	9
Order XIII	Textiles	14
Order XIV	Leather, leather goods and fur	3
Order XV	Clothing and footwear	9
Order XVI	Bricks, pottery, glass, cement, etc.	6
Order XVII	Timber, furniture, etc.	6
Order XVIII	Paper, printing and publishing	7
Order XIX	Other manufacturing industries	8
Order XX	Construction	1
Order XXI	Gas, electricity and water	3
TOTAL		145

Source: CSO (1968).

THE RECLASSIFICATION PROBLEM

The 1968 and the 1980 SIC: a comparison

The first SIC was issued in 1948. It was revised in 1958 and again in 1968. The 1968 revision is described in CSO (1968). It divides economic activity into 27 'Orders' of which twenty, Orders II–XXI, fall within the scope of the Census of Production. Of these twenty Orders, seventeen (Orders III–XIX) fall within manufacturing. Orders are divided into one or more Minimum List Headings (MLH), denoted by a 3-digit number, which may in turn be sub-divided. The degree to which data were published at a sub-MLH level increased to some extent over time. There is a choice whether to descend to the lowest possible level (where data are available for only the most recent years) or to stay at the MLH level. In order to maximise comparability with earlier periods, the list of industries chosen for the reclassification exercise is not the longest possible, but is nearly so. The resulting list comprises a total of 145 industries covering the Census of Production sector of the economy, of which 137 are in manufacturing. No MLH in the Census sector has been omitted. Of the 145 industries, 27 are sub-divisions of complete MLHs and three are

Table C.2. *Structure of the Census sector of the 1980 SIC*

Division	Number of AH	Corresponding Orders
Energy and water supply	12	II (part), IV, XXI
Extraction of minerals and ores other than fuels; manufacture of metals, mineral products and chemicals	43	II (part), V, VI, XVI
Metal goods, engineering and vehicles industries	75	VII–XII
Other manufacturing industries	88	III, XIII–XV, XVII–XIX
Construction	5	XX
TOTAL	223	

Source: CSO (1979)

combinations of two MLHs. Despite this, for simplicity all these industries will be referred to as MLHs. The complete list is in Appendix A but the main breakdown is shown in table C.1.

The 1980 SIC is described in CSO (1979). It divides economic activity into ten Divisions, numbered 0–9, of which Divisions 1–5 fall within the Census of Production. The numbering system is quite different from that of the 1968 SIC, being decimal, and the order in which the industries occur is somewhat different too. But these differences are superficial. What matters is the degree of correspondence between the industries of the two classifications – the MLH of the 1968 classification and what are called Activity Headings (AH), which are the lowest (4-digit) level of the 1980 classification. There are 223 AH within the Census sector and 145 MLH so obviously we can only hope to convert AH to MLH, not the reverse.

The complete list of AH in Divisions 1–5 can be found in CSO (1979). An outline of the system is in table C.2. It should be noted that in three cases what is called an AH is actually a combination of two or three AH. These cases are: AH 2330 and 2396; AH 4180 and 4239; and AH 4811, 4812 and 4820. The reason for this is that the published data are for the combination, not the individual AH.

The nature of the reclassification problem

Since there are more AH than MLH, one might hope that the correspondence between the two would be many-one (each MLH made up of one or more *complete* AH). However, this is not the case – the correspondence is many-many as is made clear by the CSO's *Standard Industrial Classification Revised 1980: Reconciliation with Standard Industrial Classification 1968* (CSO, 1980), hereafter referred to as the 'Reconciliation'. This lists the

AH and against each gives the MLH or subdivision of an MLH to which it corresponds. A glance at this publication shows that in numerous cases more than one MLH (or sub-division of an MLH) corresponds to a given AH. In other words, to reclassify the SIC it is necessary to split up many AH.

The 'Reconciliation' is rather like a French-English dictionary when what is required is an English-French one. The first step in the reclassification process was to reorder the information in the 'Reconciliation' so as to produce a list of MLH, against each of which is to be shown a list of one or more corresponding AH, together with an indication as to whether the whole or only a part of each AH goes to the given MLH. This reordering is in table C.3. Here the lines come in pairs. The first number in the first row is the code number of the MLH; the next, 4-digit, numbers are the code numbers of the corresponding AH. On the next line a 'one' beneath an AH code number indicates that the whole of this AH goes into the corresponding MLH; a zero indicates that only a part does so. This is all the information that can be gleaned from the 'Reconciliation'.[1]

The problem then is that though we know that, to take one example, a proportion of AH 4832 goes to MLH 276 (along with the whole of AH 2514 and 2515), we do not know how large a proportion. Furthermore, the proportion clearly need not be the same for net output as it is for, say, employment – in fact in general we would expect it to be different for every Census variable.

Fortunately, the 1979 Census of Production was published on the basis of both SIC, the 1968 basis in BSO (1982) and the 1980 basis in BSO (1983), and this provides us with the means to discover the unknown proportions. To see in general how this can be done, consider again MLH 276 (see table C.3) and take the example of net output. From BSO (1982), net output of MLH 276 in 1979 was £690.9 million and from BSO (1983) net outputs of AH 2514, 2515 and 4832 were £476.5 million, £34.3 million and £295.7 million respectively. If we add together the whole of AH 2514 and 2515's net output and 60.9 per cent of AH 4832's, we will get a total which agrees with the figure for MLH 276. Therefore, 60.9 per cent is the proportion we seek. A similar exercise could be carried out for gross output, employment or any other Census variable to solve for the unknown proportions; in general we would not expect to get 60.9 per cent as the answer for any other variable.

RECLASSIFICATION: A MATHEMATICAL FORMULATION

The example just given is a very simple one. In reality the problem is rather more complex, as a mathematical formulation may help to explain. For any Census variable (for example, net output), we can write:

$$y = Ax \qquad (\text{C.}1)$$

where

$$y = [y_i], \text{ an } N \times 1 \text{ column vector}$$
$$x = [x_j], \text{ an } M \times 1 \text{ column vector}$$
$$A = [a_{ij}], \text{ an } N \times M \text{ matrix}$$

Here y_i is net output of the ith MLH, x_j is net output of the jth AH and the a_{ij} are the proportions which we wish to find. In our case, $N = 145$ and $M = 223$. In addition,

$$\Sigma_i a_{ij} = 1, \qquad j = 1, 2 \ldots M, \qquad (\text{C.}2)$$

that is, the elements in each column of the A matrix sum to one, since every part of an AH must go to *some* MLH. Assuming the data to be consistent and error-free,[2]

$$\Sigma_i y_i = \Sigma_j x_j. \qquad (\text{C.}3)$$

In this problem, the x_j and y_i are known (from the two Census reports); some of the a_{ij} are known to be zero ($a_{ij} = 0$ means that none of the jth AH goes to the ith MLH) and some are known to be one ($a_{ij} = 1$ means that the whole of the jth AH goes to the ith MLH). We seek the conditions under which it is possible to solve for the remaining unknown a_{ij}.

There are NM coefficients in the A matrix (most of which are in practice equal to zero). The system described by (C.1) and (C.2) consists of $M + N$ equations. However it is readily shown that one of these $M + N$ equations can be derived from the rest, using (C.3). Hence there are $M + N - 1$ independent equations. It follows that for the system to be soluble the number of unknown a_{ij} cannot exceed $M + N - 1$, or 367 in our case.

To illustrate, consider a highly simplified example where $N = M = 2$:

$$y_1 = a_{11}x_1 + a_{12}x_2$$

$$y_2 = a_{21}x_1 + a_{22}x_2$$

$$a_{21} = 1 - a_{11}$$

$$a_{22} = 1 - a_{12}$$

Here there are three independent equations, but four unknowns (a_{11}, a_{12}, a_{21} and a_{22}). If for example a_{11} were known to be 1, then the first equation would contain only one unknown (a_{12}). Once this was found, the remaining unknowns (a_{21} and a_{22}) could be found from the 'adding-up' restrictions.

COMPUTER PROGRAMS TO RECLASSIFY THE CENSUS OF PRODUCTION

Three computer programs have been written to reclassify the Census. The first program, RECLASS, solves the mathematical problem described in the previous section. The second, SIC68, uses the results of RECLASS to reclassify any Census variable (real or nominal) initially classified by the 1980 SIC to the 1968 SIC. For example, net output by the 223 AH in 1984 can be reclassified to the 145 MLH by this program. The third program, P68, reclassifies producer price indices from an AH to an MLH basis.[3]

The RECLASS program

The algorithm which RECLASS uses can best be described by means of an example. Consider the following one, where $N = 3$ and $M = 4$:

$$y_1 = x_1 + a_{12}x_2 \qquad\qquad + x_4 \qquad\qquad (C.4)$$

$$y_2 = \qquad\quad a_{22}x_2 + a_{23}x_3 \qquad\qquad (C.5)$$

$$y_3 = \qquad\qquad\qquad a_{33}x_3 \qquad\qquad (C.6)$$

$$a_{22} = 1 - a_{12} \qquad\qquad (C.7)$$

$$[a_{33} = 1 - a_{23}] \qquad\qquad (C.8)$$

Here there are four unknowns and four independent equations, so the system is soluble. (The fifth equation, which will be dropped, has been bracketed). Presented with this problem, RECLASS would proceed as follows:

Step 1   Read in initial values for the coefficients known to be equal to one and for the coefficients known to be less than one but greater than zero (that is, ignore the coefficients known to be zero).

In the example above, six coefficients are known to be zero and are ignored, two are known to be one and four (a_{12}, a_{22}, a_{23} and a_{33}) are unknown. RECLASS sets the unknown coefficients initially equal to zero. So here RECLASS would read in the following row vectors of coefficients (one for each MLH):

$$(1, 0, 1)$$
$$(0, 0)$$
$$(0)$$

Step 2   Taking each equation in the $y = Ax$ system in turn, check if there is only one unknown coefficient (that is, count the number of zeros in each row vector) and if so solve for it. Update the row vectors of coefficients with the new values.

In the example, the first and third equation contain only one unknown so we can solve them to find

$$\alpha_{12} = (y_1 - x_1 - x_4)/x_2$$
$$= \alpha \text{ say,}$$

and

$$\alpha_{33} = y_3/x_3$$
$$= \beta \text{ say.}$$

The row vectors of coefficients now become:

$$(1, \alpha, 1)$$
$$(0, 0)$$
$$(\beta)$$

Step 3   Solve the adding-up restrictions and update the row vectors of coefficients with the new values.

Here there is only one adding-up restriction to apply, so we find

$$\alpha_{22} = 1 - \alpha_{12}$$
$$= 1 - \alpha.$$

The row vectors of coefficients are now:

$$(1, \alpha, 1)$$
$$(1 - \alpha, 0)$$
$$(\beta)$$

Step 4   If all coefficients are non-zero, then stop. If not, return to Step 2.

In the example, the second-row vector contains a single zero so RECLASS would return to Step 2 and find

$$\alpha_{23} = (y_2 - (1 - \alpha)x_2)/x_3$$
$$= \gamma \text{ say.}$$

The row vectors of coefficients are now

$$(1, \alpha, 1)$$
$$(1 - \alpha, \gamma)$$
$$(\beta)$$

Thus a second pass through the algorithm would complete the solution.

In general, if the system is soluble, the algorithm will find the solution in a finite number of steps. In fact for the problem under study, three passes proved sufficient.

The program carries out a number of consistency checks, both of the data and of the computed coefficients:

(1) Does $\Sigma_i y_i = \Sigma_j x_j$? The answer, for the aggregates so far tested, is yes, very nearly. For example, for net output, gross output and employ-

ment, the percentage differences between the MLH totals and the AH totals are respectively 0.33 per cent, 0.08 per cent and 0.06 per cent.

(2) Do the calculated values of the a_{ij} fall in the permitted range $(0 \leq a_{ij} \leq 1)$? If there are errors in the data or if there have been mistakes made in the concordance derived from the 'Reconciliation' (table C.3), then it is possible that the calculated value of an a_{ij} (Step 2 of the algorithm) might produce a value outside the permitted range. The program checks if this is so. If a value exceeds one it is set equal to one; if it is less than zero, it is set equal to zero.

(3) How close are the calculated MLH values to the actual MLH values? Let $\hat{A}$ be the estimated matrix of proportions and $\hat{y} = [\hat{y}_i]$ be the column vector of calculated MLH values. Then

$$\hat{y} = \hat{A}x.$$

The program calculates the proportional error $(\hat{y}_i - y_i)/y_i$. In many cases this is necessarily zero, because of the way the program works, but not always. For gross output, net output and employment, the industries which produced an absolute error of 5 per cent or more on this test were as follows:

	Absolute percentage error (E)	
$5 \leq E \leq 10$	$10 < E \leq 20$	$20 < E$
MLH 213	MLH 279/4	MLH 331
332	279/7	422/1
339/1	413	446
354	418	449/2
479	429	
496		

The industries producing errors exceeding 20 per cent accounted for about 0.6 per cent of net output in 1979. In some cases it is clear that the error is due to anomalies in the data. The following MLH which feature in the table above are supposed to correspond exactly, according to the 'Reconciliation', to a single AH:

MLH	AH
213	4197
279/7	2591
331	3211
339/1	3251
418	4395
446	4537
449/2	4538

In these cases, the weights produced by RECLASS are correct, but the data are wrong.

A final consistency check would be to see whether $\Sigma_i a_{ij} = 1$. RECLASS does not actually make this check, though in most cases it will automatically be satisfied.

The SIC68 and P68 programs

As the previous sub-section showed, RECLASS solves for the matrix A in the system

$$y^{79} = Ax^{79}$$

where superscripts indicate the year. Here y^{79} and x^{79} are given. The program SIC68 takes the matrix A from RECLASS and solves for y^T in the system

$$y^T = Ax^T.$$

Here A and x^T (for example, net output in 1984 by AH) are known, y^T unknown. For the results to be meaningful, a basic assumption must be satisfied. When an AH is split between two or more MLH it must be assumed that the constituent parts of the AH are homogeneous in terms of growth rates. By this is meant the following. Suppose an AH has to be split into two parts. For it to be justifiable to use the proportions correct for 1979 in some other year T, the two parts of the AH must have been growing at the same rate between then and year T. Since the AH is the lowest level on which data are collected, there seems to be no way of testing this assumption. Obviously, it cannot be literally true; we can only hope that it is approximately true.

The program P68 takes price indices classified by AH and reclassifies them to an MLH basis. It does so by calculating a weighted average of AH price indices, where the weights are gross output. If P_i represents price, GO_j represents gross output and superscripts indicate whether MLH or AH,

$$P_i^{\text{MLH}} = \Sigma_j a_{ij} GO_j^{\text{AH}} P_j^{\text{AH}} / \Sigma_j a_{ij} GO_j^{\text{AH}}$$

Note that the denominator is

$$\Sigma_j a_{ij} GO_j^{\text{AH}} = GO_i^{\text{MLH}},$$

that is, the sum of the weights is gross output in the MLH in question.

One might quarrel with the use of gross output as weights. Sales of the product concerned would be more appropriate. But the Census only gives sales of the *industry*, which is not the same: an industry is defined by its 'principal product', which may be produced by other industries too. But given the other uncertainties, such as errors in the underlying AH price indices, the choice of gross output seems reasonable.

Price indices do not exist for all 223 AH and P68 employs a parameter MINCVR (expressed in per cent) for dealing with this. For any MLH, if the available AH price indices represent gross output (or whatever is the weighting variable) which is less than MINCVR per cent of the total gross output in this MLH, then the price index for this MLH is recorded as a missing value. If price indices for more than MINCVR per cent but less than 100 per cent of gross output are available, the MLH price index is calculated as a weighted average of the available AH price indices. To produce the estimates, MINCVR was set to 33 per cent.

Table C.3. *Concordance between MLH and AH*

MLH	AH				
101	1113 I				
102/103	2310 I	2330/2396 o	2450 o		
104	1300 I				
109	2100 I	2330/2396 o			
211	4160 I	4180/4239 o			
212	4196 o				
213	4197 I				
214	4121 o	4122 I	4123 I	4126 o	4150 I
215	4130 I	4213 I			
216	4200 I				
217	4214 I				
218	4147 I	4180/4239 o			
219	4221 I	4222 o			
221	4116 I	4126 o			
229/1	4115 I				
229/2	4180/4239 o				
231	4270 I				
232	4283 I				
239/1	4240 I				
239/2	4261 I				
240	4290 I				

261	1115 (1)	1200 (1)					
262	1401 (1)						
263	1402 (1)						
271	1520 (1)	2511 (1)	2512 (1)	2551 (0)	2564 (1)	2567 (1)	2599 (0)
272	2570 (0)	4222 (0)					
273	2582 (1)						
274	2551 (0)						
275	2563 (1)	2581 (1)	2599 (0)				
276	2514 (1)	2515 (1)	4832 (0)				
277	2516 (1)						
278	2513 (1)						
279/1	2599 (0)						
279/2	2562 (1)						
279/3	2565 (0)	3290 (0)					
279/4	2568 (1)	2570 (0)	2599 (0)				
279/5	2552 (1)						
279/6	2570 (0)	4722 (0)					
279/7	2591 (1)						
311	2210 (1)	2235 (1)	3111 (0)				
312	2220 (1)						
313	3111 (1)						
321	2245 (1)	3112 (0)					
322	2246 (0)	3112 (0)	3120 (0)				
323	2247 (0)						
331	3211 (1)						
332	3221 (1)	3289 (0)	3435 (0)				
333	3283 (1)	3287 (1)	3288 (1)				
334	3281 (0)						
335	3230 (1)						

336	3254_1				
337	3255_1				
338	3276_0	3301_1			
339/1	3251_1				
339/2	3276_0				
339/3&/4	3284_0				
339/5–/9	3244_1	3245_0	3275_1	3285_1	3286_1
341	3142_0	3204_1	3205_1	3245_0	3246_1 3435_0
342	3290_0				
349	3261_1	3262_1	3284_0	3289_0	3620_0
351	3733_0				
352	3740_0				
353	3720_1	3731_1			
354	3442_1	3453_0	3710_1	3732_1	3733_0 3740_0
361	3420_0				
362	3410_1				
363	3441_1				
364	3302_0	3444_1	3453_0		
365	3452_1	3454_0			
366	3302_0				
367	3433_1	3435_0	3443_1	3454_0	
368	3435_0	3460_1			
369	3420_0	3432_1	3434_1	3470_1	3740_0
370	3281_0	3289_0	3610_1		
380	3212_1				
381	3510_1	3521_1	3522_1	3523_1	3530_1
382	3633_1	3634_1	3650_0		
383	3640_1				
384/385	3620_0				

390	3222_1	3710_0							
391	3161_1								
392	3162_1	3167_0							
393	3137_0								
394	2234_1	2246_0							
395	3164_0								
396	2247_0	4910_1							
399/1	3166_0								
399/2–/12	3120_0	3137_0	3138_1	3142_0	3163_1	3164_0	3165_1	3166_0	3167_0
	3169_1	3650_0	4959_0						
411	2600_1								
412	4321_1	4336_1	4340_0						
413	4322_1	4340_0							
414	4310_1	4399_0							
415	4350_1								
416	4396_1								
417	4363_1	4364_1							
418	4395_1								
419	4384_1								
421	4398_1								
422/1	4556_0	4557_1							
422/2	4556_0								
423	4370_1								
429	2440_1	4385_1	4399_0						
431	4410_1								
432	4420_1								
433	4560_1								
441	4531_1								
442	4532_1								

443	4533_1			
444	4534_1	4535_1		
445	4536_1			
446	4537_1			
449/1/3/4	4539_1			
449/2	4538_1			
450	4510_1			
461	2410_1	2481_1		
462	2489_1			
463	2471_1	2478_1	2479_1	
464	2420_0			
469/1	2460_1			
469/2	2420_0	2436_1	2437_1	2450_0
471	4610_1	4620_1	4630_0	4650_0
472	4671_0			
473	4555_1	4671_0		
474	4630_0	4672_1		
475	4640_0			
479	4640_0	4650_0	4664_1	
481	4710_1			
482/1	4724_0	4725_1		
482/2	4724_0	4835_0		
483	4723_1			
484	4721_1	4722_0	4728_1	
485/486	4751_1	4752_1		
489	4753_1	4754_1		
491	2569_1	$4811/4812/4820_1$		
492	4831_1	4832_0	4833_1	
493	4663_1			

494/1/2	3650 0	4941 1			
494/3	4942 1				
495	4954 1				
496	4832 0	4834 1	4835 0	4836 1	
499	4920 1	4959 0			
500	1114 1	5000 1	5010 0	5020 0	5030 0	5040 0
601	1620 1				
602	1610 1	1630 1			
603	1700 1				

Source: CSO (1980)

Note: A '1' below an AH denotes that the whole of that AH belongs in the corresponding MLH; a '0' denotes that only a part does.

APPENDIX D

THE ESTIMATION OF GROSS OUTPUT

INTRODUCTION

In this appendix we discuss the adjustments we made to the published 'gross output' figures (from the Census of Production) in order to arrive at an economic definition of nominal gross output for each industry, valued at producer prices. These adjustments were, first, the removal of stock appreciation; second, the elimination of intra-industry purchases; and third, the adjustment to a producer price basis (elimination of excise taxes and subsidies). In going from nominal to real gross output, deflators purged of the influence of excise taxes and subsidies are also required.

STOCK APPRECIATION

The Census of Production concept of output is gross of stock appreciation. An adjustment conceptually identical to the one in the national accounts, which turns the increase in the value of stocks into what is called 'Value of the physical increase in stocks at current prices', is required also at the industry level. The Census distinguishes three kinds of stocks – materials and fuel, work in progress and goods on hand for sale (the last two usually being aggregated) and records both the value of the stocks at a reference date and the increase in value over the preceding year. For most, though not all, respondents the reference date is the end of the Census year. Ideally, separate price indices should be used for each stock. Also, while output is deflated by an index which is an annual average, calculating stock appreciation requires an index appropriate to the time interval over which stocks are held (generally considerably less than a year).

Let us consider first the correct theoretical treatment, before turning to questions of data availability. Suppose that items enter a stock at a steady rate and remain in the stock for an interval of length m. In general, m will vary over time, so we can write $m = m(t)$, where t is time. Then under the FIFO convention the historic cost value of a stock at time t, that is, at the *end* of the interval $[t - 1, t]$, $V(t)$, is the physical quantity of the stock, $S(t)$, times the average price over the interval $[t - m, t]$; call the latter $\bar{P}(t, m)$. So

$$V(t) = S(t) . \bar{P}(t, \mathrm{m}(t))$$
(D.1)

where

$$\bar{P}(t, m(t)) = m(t)^{-1} \int_0^{m(t)} P(t - v)\, dv \qquad (D.2)$$

and where $P(t - v)$ is the price at the instant $t - v$.

To save on notation, write $\bar{P}(t)$ for $\bar{P}(t, 1)$, the average price prevailing over the interval $[t - 1, t]$. Then, always assuming that firms employ the FIFO convention, stock appreciation (SA) is:

$$
\begin{aligned}
\mathrm{SA}(t) &= [\bar{P}(t) - \bar{P}(t - 1)] \cdot S(t - 1) \\
&= [\bar{P}(t) - \bar{P}(t - 1)] \cdot V(t - 1) / \bar{P}(t - 1, m(t - 1)) \qquad (D.3)
\end{aligned}
$$

using (D.1).

Two special cases are worth considering. First, $m = 1$, when the denominator becomes simply $P(t - 1)$. Second, $m = 0$, Now the denominator is $P(t - 1)$, that is, the price at the end of $(t - 1)$, which may be approximated by:

$$P(t - 1) = [\bar{P}(t) \cdot \bar{P}(t - 1)]^{1/2}. \qquad (D.4)$$

How large is m in practice? Assuming that firms follow the FIFO convention, and that there is a steady inflow into stocks at one end matched by a steady outflow at the other end, then $m(t) = S(t)/Y(t)$, where $Y(t)$ is the inflow. For finished goods and work in progress, $Y(t)$ is gross output; for materials and fuels, $Y(t)$ is purchases. A glance at the Census suggests that manufacturers typically hold no more than a couple of months of output (or purchases) in the form of stocks. So the case $m = 0$ considered above is not so far from the truth. In view of the fact that not all establishments in the Census report their stocks for the end of the year (though most do so, a sizeable fraction report for the end of the quarter following the Census year and others' reporting dates are spread throughout the year), great precision seems unattainable.

In summary, stock appreciation was calculated assuming stocks are valued at end-of-period prices, the case $m = 0$ considered above, with end-of-period prices approximated by (D.4) above. The formula is then

$$\mathrm{SA}(t) = [\bar{P}(t) - \bar{P}(t - 1)] \cdot V(t - 1) / [\bar{P}(t) \cdot \bar{P}(t - 1)]^{1/2}. \qquad (D.5)$$

In practice, the main difficulty with estimating SA is the absence of price data for many industries. The strategy was to produce *some* estimate of SA, whenever the basic data on stocks existed. If no estimate was possible, then SA was set to zero, in order to avoid creating additional missing values. This was in fact necessary in only a handful of cases. The procedure for prices was as follows. For WGS, we used the PPI (home sales); if this was unavailable, we used the order or class price (homes sales); if *this* was unavailable too, we used the index for total manufacturing (home sales). For MSF, we used the price index for materials, stores

Table D.1. *Stock appreciation in manufacturing (£m, current prices)*

| | | MSF | | | WGS | |
	Actual	Calc.	Diff.	Actual	Calc	Diff.
1954	19	11	8	41	15	26
1958	− 21	− 4	− 17	5	3	2
1963	71	23	48	39	38	1
1968	137	101	36	210	191	19
1970	246	233	13	469	435	34
1971	225	289	− 64	372	532	− 160
1972	279	204	75	500	414	86
1973	814	303	511	764	548	216
1974	1683	1126	557	2021	1832	189
1975	1234	1220	14	2038	2289	− 251
1976	1838	1312	526	2253	2154	99
1977	752	1367	− 615	2000	2754	− 754
1978	737	633	104	1637	1772	− 135
1979	1968	1441	527	3124	2411	713
1979	1606	1167	439	2900	2223	677
1980	591	1375	− 784	2222	3052	− 830
1981	835	636	199	1640	1763	− 123
1982	597	808	− 211	1281	1710	− 429
1983	727	696	31	1197	1279	− 82
1984	759	822	− 63	1393	1531	− 138
1985	− 5	462	− 467	1373	1563	− 190
1986	55	− 273	328	1000	1152	− 152

Sources: 'Actual' columns from Blue Book (various issues); SIC 1968 definition of total manufacturing for 1954–79, SIC 1980 definition for 1979–86. 'Calc.' columns are own calculations – for explanation, see text. 'Diff.' is actual *less* calculated.

and fuel; if this was unavailable, we used the PPI (home sales); if this was unavailable, we used the order or class price (home sales); if this was unavailable, we used the index for total manufacturing (home sales). Notice that the order or class price (materials, stores and fuels) is *never* used as this nets out all intra-order or intra-class purchases; for most industries, the output price is likely to move in line with the input price.

Table D.1 compares our estimates (aggregated up from the industry level) with those produced by the CSO for total manufacturing. It will be noted that there is fairly good agreement for the earlier years when SA was small, but that there are some quite large discrepancies for the later years when SA was much larger. However, there does not seem to be any consistent pattern to the differences, though some of them may be due to timing, since as just noted the end of the 'year' differs between firms. Our estimates assume that all firms use a FIFO, historic cost system of accounting for inventories. However, some firms, particularly in the 1970s, may have used the 'standard cost' method, under which stock

Table D.2. *Stock appreciation as a proportion of gross and net output by industry: summary statistics (%)*

	GO 1973	NO 1973	GO 1979	NO 1979
Minimum	− 0.5	− 5.8	0	0.6
Maximum	3.6	19.6	8.6	24.6
Mean	0.8	3.2	1.5	5.9
SD	0.7	2.7	1	3.4

Note: GO = Gross output; NO = Net output. For GO, stock appreciation is only for WGS; for net output it includes also MSF.

appreciation would be automatically excluded from the recorded increases in the value of stocks. If so, and since the CSO's estimates supposedly take account of the proportion of firms who use this method, we would expect our estimates to be above the CSO's. The fact that there is no such tendency apparent suggests that firms do not in fact use the 'standard cost' method of accounting to any great extent.

How important is SA in relation to net output and gross output? Table D.2 shows SA (for WGS only) as a proportion of *gross* output (GO) and total SA (for WGS and MSF) as a proportion of *net* output (NO), for the years 1973 and 1979. On average in manufacturing, SA was 0.8 per cent of GO in 1973 and 1.5 per cent in 1979; as a proportion of NO it was 3.2 per cent in 1973 and 5.9 per cent in 1979. That the proportion is higher for NO than GO is inevitable since there are two sorts of SA relevant for NO and NO is smaller than GO. In the case of GO there is only one case (MLH 370) where there is a big difference between the proportion in the two years. For NO however, there are fourteen industries where there is a difference of 5 percentage points or more between the proportion in the two years, so that in these cases one would expect a substantial effect on the calculated productivity growth rate as a result of making the SA adjustment.

Let SAWGS be estimated stock appreciation in work in progress and goods on hand for sale and let SAMSF be stock appreciation in materials, stores and fuel; let GO, NO and GVA be gross and net output and gross value added as recorded in the Census. Then gross output adjusted for stock appreciation is

$$GO - SAWGS,$$

net output adjusted for stock appreciation is

$$NO - SAWGS - SAMSF,$$

and gross value added adjusted for stock appreciation is
GVA − SAWGS − SAMSF.

INTRA-INDUSTRY PURCHASES

This section considers the problems raised by the fact that the Census of production definition of gross output of an industry includes purchases of materials by the industry from itself, that is, it includes intra-industry purchases (or 'own purchases'). The nominal value of gross output as given in the Census of Production is, in that case, overstated since the value of the input is included both independently and in the value of sales of the final product. The input–output tables, which are published periodically by the CSO, do not include intra-industry purchases in the definition of gross output but fortunately provide separate estimates of own purchases for a large number of industries; these data form the basis of the adjustment to the Census gross output figures presented below.

Prior to presenting the methodology and estimates of the adjustment to gross output we first ask what is the effect of inclusion in intra-industry purchases on the measurement of multi-factor productivity. For illustrative purposes assume that an industry is composed of two firms, one of which, V, produces vehicles and the second, C, produces components for assembly in V. For simplicity the material input of V is assumed to equal the entire output of C. This, plus labour, L_V, and capital, K_V, are used to produce output in V whereas production in C requires labour, L_C, capital, K_C, and materials purchased outside the industry, M.

Real gross output in the industry, as measured by the Census of Production, is given by:

$$Q^* = Q_V + Q_C \tag{D.6}$$

It is obvious that the Census gross output figure will be sensitive to changes in the industrial structure of the industry. If the industry integrates vertically, producing its previous output of both vehicles and components in the same establishment, then the Census will record the nominal value of Q_V rather than Q^*. Since inputs are unchanged the exclusion of Q_C in the recorded output figures will obviously affect productivity estimates. This productivity change does not reflect any actual change in the production capabilities of the industry. The rate of change of output in the vehicles industry will also be sensitive to changes in the proportion of components imported from abroad.

We now turn to the effects of intra-industry purchases on the growth rate of multi-factor productivity, MFP. Net output, the difference between gross output and materials is given, for vehicles and components respectively, by

$$Y_V = Q_V - Q_C$$

and

$$Y_C = Q_C - M$$

so that industry net output is

$$Y = Y_V + Y_C = Q_V - M \tag{D.7}$$

This is equivalent to the definition of net output recorded in the census. If (D.7) is subtracted from the Census definition of gross output in (D.6) then the resulting material input is given by

$$M^* = Q - Y = Q_C + M \tag{D.8}$$

Letting L and K denote, respectively, industry labour and capital, then the estimate of the growth rate of MFP will be

$$\mu^* = \dot{Q}^*/Q^* - s_M^*(\dot{M}^*/M^*) - s_L^*(\dot{L}/L) - s_K^*(\dot{K}/K), \tag{D.9}$$

where s_x^* is the share of input x in the value of total industry output, that is,

$$s_x^* = P_x x/(P_V Q_V + P_C Q_C), \quad x = K, L, M.$$

An alternative, preferable, measure of MFP growth can be derived as follows. Let the production functions for vehicles and components be given respectively by:

$$Q_V = f^V(L_V, K_V, Q_C, t)$$
$$Q_C = f^C(L_C, K_C, M, t) \tag{D.10}$$

If Q_C is substituted into Q_V in equation (D.10) and labour and capital in both sectors are assumed to grow at the same proportionate rate over time, then it is easy to show that the growth rate of MFP in the integrated industry is given by:

$$\mu = (\partial \ln f^V/\partial t) + (p_c Q_c/p_v Q_v)(\partial \ln f^c/\partial t)$$
$$= \dot{Q}_v/Q_v - s_L(\dot{L}/L) - s_K(\dot{K}/K) - s_M(\dot{M}/M) \tag{D.11}$$

where the share of input x is now given by:

$$s_x = P_x X/P_V Q_V \quad x = K, L, M.$$

The left-hand side of (D.11) is the rate at which the production function for vehicles is shifting over time plus the rate of shift of the components production function, the latter weighted by its contribution to the output change in vehicles, and hence can be interpreted as the rate of technical progress originating in the industry. The MFP calculation in equation (D.11) is a reduced form with labour, capital and outside materials only appearing as inputs. It is equivalent to the *ring-fence* method discussed by Paige and Bombach (1959), that is, only products sold and materials purchased *outside* the industry are included in the calculation.

Comparing equations (D.9) and (D.11) shows that the difference in the two measures depends not only on the growth rates of outputs and materials but also on the share weights. Even in the special case where the growth rates of the two outputs and material inputs are equal, there will be a discrepancy between the two measures of MFP growth due to differences in the value shares of inputs. In fact the Census-based measure will overestimate the share of materials at the expense of the shares of both capital and labour. In equation (D.9) the cost of components to the vehicles producer is included both directly in the share of materials and indirectly in the shares of labour and capital; hence there is an element of double counting in this calculation.

Therefore, we decided to attempt to estimate the extent of own purchases. The basis for these estimates are data for both the *Input–Output Tables* and the *Purchases Inquiries* published by the CSO which are available for the years 1968, 1974, 1979 and 1984. As will be explained below, the former source does not provide sufficient information to calculate the importance of intra-industry purchases for all industries so that we need to use the more detailed information in the purchases inquiries. In the discussion below, the definition of an industry is the minimum list heading, MLH, of the 1968 Standard Industrial Classification.

Table D of the input–output tables shows domestic purchases by each industry group from all industries including itself and hence can be used to give an idea of the importance of intra-industry purchases. If intra-industry purchases were negligible then equation (D.9) can be correctly used to measure MFP growth. However, it is quite obvious that this is not the case in a significant number of MLH. To take the example of vehicles used in the above discussion, intra-industry purchases were 33 per cent in 1968, 19 per cent in 1974 and declined to 7 per cent in 1979. Therefore, in this industry, the error in MFP measurement is probably large and not constant over time.

One difficulty with the input–output tables is that they are not disaggregated by MLH but by a smaller sample of about 90 industries. In this case some of the intra-industry purchases using the input–output classification are inter-industry when the industry unit is MLH. An important example is the aggregation of MLH 311 (Iron and steel), with MLH 312 (Steel tubes). The intra-industry purchases proportion for MLH 311 plus 312 was 34 per cent in 1974. Obviously within each MLH intra-industry purchases are important but MLH 312 also purchases quantities of steel from the iron and steel industry.

The estimation techniques for all four years are similar but 1979 and 1984 present additional difficulties because of the need to reclassify from the 1980 SIC to 1968 SIC. Therefore, the general estimation technique is first presented and then the additional problems due to reclassification are considered.

Let X_i equal purchases by industry i from itself and let Y_i^C and Y_i^{IO} denote gross output from the Census of Production and the input–output tables respectively, where the latter includes the value of own purchases. Table D of the input–output tables yields a value for X_i/Y_i^{IO}. This ratio can then be used to adjust the Census figure to give the corrected gross output value

$$Y_i^* = Y_i^C(1 - X_i/Y_i^{IO}).$$

If input–output group i corresponds to an individual MLH then the adjustment in equation (7) is sufficient. The input–output measure adjusts for stock appreciation so that the Census figure adjusted for stock appreciation is used in the above calculation. The adjustment for intra-industry purchases is carried out using nominal output figures. The CSO producer price indices exclude own purchases so that the adjustment should be to nominal, rather than real, output. Since the input–output gross output figure differs from that of the Census for reasons other than the inclusion of intra-industry purchases (for example, the definition of an industry differs between the two measures), it was considered inappropriate to use $Y_i^{IO} - X_i$ as an estimate of Y_i. Therefore, it is assumed that the value of own purchases relative to gross output from the input–output tables are representative of firms covered by the Census of production.

A significant number of input–output groups correspond to two or more MLH so that it is not possible to use the input–output tables to estimate own purchases. Instead, we have attempted to identify each MLH's own purchases from the purchases inquiry. The value of commodities bought by industries as given in the purchases inquiry include materials from both domestic sources and imports. Therefore it is necessary to exclude intra-industry imports in calculating the ratio of own purchases to gross output.

Let M_j be intra-industry imports, that is, imports by input–output group j from commodity group j, where j includes two or more MLH. Data on M_j were derived from the commodity-by-commodity intermediate import flow matrix, table M, of the input–output tables. The ratio of imports to total intra-industry purchases was then calculated as

$$m_j = M_j/(M_j + X_j),$$

where again X_j are own purchases by input–output group j. The purchases inquiry yields an estimate of $X_i + M_i$, for MLH i, for the firms covered by the inquiry. If it is assumed that the ratio of imports to total intra-industry purchases is identical for all MLH i within input–output group j, it is possible to estimate X_i as

$$X_i = (X_i + M_i)(1 - m_j).$$

Then the corrected gross output figure can be calculated as

$$Y_i^* = Y_i^c(1 - X_i/Y_i^c)$$

where again Y_i^c is adjusted for stock appreciation. Note, in the earlier years, 1968 and 1974, the purchases inquiry total referred only to firms within an industry employing greater than a minimum number of employees (usually 50 or 100) so that purchases required factoring up by the ratio of purchases in the inquiry to those in the census.

The most difficult step in the above procedure is of course to identify each MLH's own purchases from the inquiry. The task is made somewhat easier by the fact that the inquiry does tend to identify products of the industry bought for further processing in many cases. However, the procedure does involve some element of judgement, for example, in the mechanical engineering industries we include the category '*machinery and plant bought for installation and erection*' but not '*second hand machinery bought for reconditioning*', since the latter is more likely to have been bought outside the industry than the former.

In a small number of cases own purchases were grouped together with those from other MLH. In these cases the purchases were broken down by the ratios of gross output of the MLHs included in the group. Finally, if own purchases were not identified, either separately or in a group, then they were assumed to equal zero.

The main problem with the 1979 and 1984 input–output tables and purchases inquiries is the need to reclassify to the 1968 SIC. Since many MLH include all or part of more than one AH it is necessary not only to estimate own purchases but also some cross-industry purchases at the AH level. The easiest way to illustrate the methodology used is to examine a number of special cases.

If an MLH corresponds to an input–output group, then, as in 1974, the input–output ratio of own purchases to gross output was used. This occurred only for nineteen MLH. In the case where MLH i consists of two complete AH, l and k, then own purchases were calculated as

$$X_i = (\bar{X}_l + \bar{X}_{lk} + \bar{X}_{kl} + \bar{X}_k)(1 - m_j)$$

where $\bar{X}_{lk}$ are purchases (both domestic and imports) by industry l from industry k. In the above formulation both l and k belong to the same input–output group j. If l and k belong to different input–output groups, j and s, respectively, then own purchases are calculated as

$$X_i = (\bar{X}_l + \bar{X}_k)(1 - m_j) + (\bar{X}_{kl} + \bar{X}_k)(1 - m_s)$$

so that the products of industry l are multiplied by l's import ratio.

In many cases MLH include only parts of activity headings. Let P_{il}, P_{ik} be the proportion of AH l and k included in MLH i and again assume both l and k belong to input–output group j. Then

$$X_i = (1 - m_j)[P_{il}\tilde{X}_l + P_{ik}\tilde{X}_k + P_{il}P_{ik}(\tilde{X}_{lk} + \tilde{X}_k)].$$

The first two terms in the square brackets are purchased by each AH from itself. Since only a proportion of AH l is included in MLH i, these own purchases need to be factored downwards by that proportion. Since only a proportion of AH k belongs to MLH i, purchases by l and k need to be multiplied by P_{ik}; the remainder, $(1 - P_i)\tilde{X}_{lk}$ is bought from some other MLH. But since only a proportion of AH l is in MLH i, these purchases require multiplying by its proportion P_{il}, hence the double multiplication in the final two terms. The proportions P_{ik} were derived from the weights used to reclassify 1979 and 1984 gross output from AH to MLH using the program outlined in Appendix C.

For the majority of industries, approximately 80 per cent in all four years, the estimated ratio of own purchases to gross output was less than 5 per cent. Only in about 4 per cent of industries were own purchases very large, that is, greater than 20 per cent of gross output; this occurred primarily in motor vehicles, iron and steel, non-ferrous metals, aerospace and woollen and worsted.

There is evidence of substantial movements over time in some industries but the cross-section correlations, shown in the matrix below, are reasonably high. The factors which alter the importance of intra-industry purchases such as the technology and the structure of industries and the import content of purchases are unlikely to be similar across industries. On the other hand, a correlation close to zero would cast some doubt on the estimates. In particular, given that a large number of the 1974 figures were taken directly from the input–output tables whereas most of the 1979 ratios were estimated, the high correlation between these two series would seem to support the plausibility of the results. The correlations are smaller the further the series are apart in time which is to be expected if industries were experiencing some structural change.

Correlations of X_i/Y_i, 1968 to 1984

	1968	1974	1979	1984
1968	1	0.87	0.69	0.57
1974		1	0.78	0.65
1979			1	0.72
1984				1

The next step was to examine more closely the changes in the importance of intra-industry purchases over time. To do so the per cent change in the adjustment to gross output, that is, $1 - X_i/Y_i$, was calculated for adjacent periods. The largest changes were experienced in aluminium and copper, shipbuilding, motor vehicles, sugar, oils and fats, and general chemicals. However, again the majority of industries showed little change in the adjustment to gross output. In many cases where the change was large this was readily apparent from the input–output tables – either the entire MLH or the greater part of it are complete input–output groups and so the change is unlikely to be due to the estimation method.

In some industries it is possible to see the source of the change in own purchases. For example, data on the value of imports of motor vehicles' components, derived from *Overseas trade statistics of the UK* (DTI), suggest that in this particular industry the decline in the importance of intra-industry purchases was most likely due to a substitution of imports for domestically produced components: the value of imports showed substantial increases in the period 1974–84 at a time when output was falling. There was a large fall in imports of refined sugar between 1979 and 1984 which is consistent with the significant rise in own purchases in that period. In general, it seems to be the case that changing shares of imported materials probably account for a substantial part of the changing importance of own purchases in some industries.

Changes in the structure of industries should also account for some of the observed change in the importance of own purchases. For example, MLH 365 (Broadcast receiving and sound reproducing equipment), which includes televisions, video recorders, radios and records and tapes, showed one of the largest rises in the proportion of own purchases to gross output, from virtually zero up to 1979 to over 20 per cent in 1984. This is obviously a rapidly changing new technology industry. Some indication of industrial structure can be obtained by looking at the change in the number of establishments relative to employment size. In MLH 365, the number of establishments rose from 332, employing on average 110 workers in 1979, to 726, employing on average 33 workers in 1984. Therefore, it is likely that this represents a splitting up of the industry with final goods produced in some establishments and components in others.

Finally, the effect of intra-industry purchases on the shares of materials in output was examined. The share of materials calculated using the original Census data were compared with the share using the adjusted gross output figures above and the differences were found to be non-negligible in a number of industries which correspond to the MLH with large proportions of own purchases to gross output just listed.

EXCISE TAXES AND SUBSIDIES

The Census of Production definition of gross output includes excise payments and excludes subsidies. In our multi-factor productivity framework it is necessary to measure output at factor cost. It is also necessary, when calculating real gross output, to use deflators which have been purged of the influence of excise taxes and subsidies. Fortunately the Census publishes most of the necessary information on the values of excise payments and subsidies.

All available information on excise payments and subsidies were extracted for the Census years from 1954–86. For the most important industries affected, that is, drink and tobacco, the series are reasonably complete although it was necessary to derive an estimate for tobacco for 1958.[1] A number of the Food industries were also affected. Complete series were available for MLH 214 (Bacon curing, meat and fish products), MLH 216 (Sugar) and MLH 217 (Cocoa and chocolate confectionery). In the case of sugar the industry received large subsidies in the mid 1970s but made net payments in the 1960s and 1980s. MLH 212 (Bread and flour confectionery), received a bread subsidy from 1974–8.

The remaining industries affected by excise payments/subsidies were in Coal and Petroleum products and Chemicals but data are available only for a small number of years for most of these industries. Surprisingly, the net excise payment by MLH 262 (mineral oil refining) was very small, of the order of 1–2 per cent of gross output in the years for which data were available. By 1979 this seemed to have decreased to zero. With the exception of MLH 263, excise payments were less than 1 per cent of gross output for all the industries affected. Therefore, it was decided not to adjust gross output rather than attempt to estimate the missing values. Finally, in the case of MLH 263 (Lubricating oils and greases), excise payments were substantial in the mid-1970s but are lumped together with those for MLH 262 from 1980. The data for 1979 on both the SIC 1968 and SIC 1980 basis show that about 98 per cent of excise payments by AH 1400 (MLH 262 + MLH 263) was by MLH 263. Therefore we can assume that all excise payments from 1980 recorded in AH 1400 were by MLH 263.

The wholesale price indices include revenue duties on tobacco and alcohol since it is argued that revenue duties are paid by the manufacturer as part of input costs (*Wholesale price index: principles and procedures*, CSO, 1980b, p. 9). In a study of productivity it does not seem sensible to include these taxes – it puts far too large a weight on material input. Jorgenson *et al.* (1987) exclude excise and sales taxes from nominal output and then adjust the deflators by dividing by one plus the indirect tax rate.

We decided to use the excise payments from the Census to adjust the output deflators rather than using indirect tax rates which are not, in any case, available in a usable form. The procedure adopted is as follows. Let P denote the producer price excluding excise payments and d be the per unit duty. The official PPI equals the producer price plus the duty, that is,

$$\text{PPI} = P + d$$

Gross output of the industry is given by

$$\text{GO} = (P + d)Q$$

where Q is quantity of units sold. Excise payments (E) are given by

$$E = dQ.$$

Therefore,

$$(1 - E/\text{GO})\,\text{PPI} = (1 - d/(P + d))(P + d) = P$$

yields an estimate of the producer price excluding duties. Since the producer price index is normalised to equal 1 at 1980 it is necessary in the above calculation of P to first set $(1 - E/\text{GO})$ equal to 1 at the same base year.

In the Food industries the deflators for Bacon curing and Chocolate are not very different but the sugar index is significantly affected by the large subsidies in the period 1973–6 and to a lesser extent by the excise payments in the 1980s. The drink and tobacco deflators show more substantial differences particularly in the 1980s where the rate of increase of duties far exceeded the increase in the marginal cost of production. The annual average rates of increase of duties for tobacco and beer were 18 per cent and 12 per cent, respectively, between 1980 and 1986 (Customs and Excise Report, 1988) which far exceeded the general rate of producer price increases.

APPENDIX E

CONSTRUCTION OF PRICE INDICES

In most cases producer price indices (PPI), formerly wholesale price indices, for 'home sales' were employed as deflators. The main source was various issues of *British Business* (DTI) and its predecessors. A number of unpublished indices were specially supplied by what was then the Business Statistics Office (BSO), particularly for the earlier years, when it was not the policy to publish as many indices as in more recent years. In some cases, particularly for the earlier years, a possible deflator is only partially representative of the products of the MLH for which it might be used; judgement had to be exercised as to whether it was sufficiently representative to be acceptable and in general a conservative strategy was adopted. Unfortunately, as we were informed, the BSO has destroyed some of the earlier price data which it used to hold. Producer price indices with reference years 1954, 1963, 1970, 1975 and 1980 were spliced together using overlapping years. For 1980 and after, indices are for Activity Headings and for other years they are for Minimum List Headings; see Appendix C for the reclassification procedure. As we go back further in time, MLH indices cease to be available for an increasing number of industries. Where the MLH price index is missing for an industry, but a price index for the Order of the SIC to which the industry belongs is available, we have used the latter. For recent years, in the smaller number of cases for which a price index of an AH is not available, we have used, wherever possible, the price index of the 2-digit class of the 1980 SIC to which the AH belongs.

In a few cases where PPI were not available the corresponding Retail Price Index was used instead. This was the case for MLH 485/486 (Newspapers and periodicals). Use was also made of the RPI in the food industries.

For industries in the food sector (MLH 211–229), PPI on an AH basis were obtained back to 1974 (the earliest available year) from the BSO, and were then reclassified to an MLH basis for the years 1974–86. The resulting indices were extrapolated backwards to the earlier benchmark years by means of the corresponding retail price indices (RPI), of which ten are available for this group of industries. The procedure was to regress each PPI on the corresponding RPI (or RPIs) and on the PPI for the food *order* (excluding drink and tobacco), together with a constant, for the period 1974–86. The estimated equations were then used to generate the indices for 1954–73, since data on the right-hand side variables is available for the earlier period.[1] Obviously, the reliability of the estimates must diminish the further away they are from the sample period.

Retail price indices are available for the following sub-groups within the food sector for the whole of our study period (1954–86):

1. Bread, flour, cereals and cakes
2. Meat and bacon
3. Fish
4. Butter, margarine, lard and other cooking fats
5. Milk, cheese and eggs
6. Tea, coffee, cocoa, soft drinks etc.
7. Sugar, preserves and confectionery
8. Vegetables, fresh, canned and frozen
9. Fruit, fresh, dried and canned
10. Other food

There is no one-to-one correspondence between the food industries in the 1968 SIC and the food sub-groups of the RPI. However the following rough equations were made:

MLH	*RPI sub-group no.*
211	1
212	1
213	1
214	2,3
215	4,5
216	7
217	7
218	7,8,9
219	10
221	4
229/1	4
229/2	6

The equation of MLH 221 (Vegetable and animal oils and fats) with 'Butter, margarine, lard and other cooking fats' is just a guess; it is clear that this industry sells little to the final consumer. It turned out that results were in fact worse for this industry than for the others, which sell largely to final consumers.

The RPIs came from *Retail Prices* (DE, various issues); the PPI for the food industries as a whole (*not* the PPI for the food, drink and tobacco Order, which covers a somewhat wider group of industries) came from

British Business (various issues). The PPI for food industries was usually not significant (in the equation for MLH 221 its coefficient was negative), but was nevertheless retained in the 'backcasting' equation. The RPI(s) were usually highly significant.

In the case of the utilities – gas, electricity and water – since no PPI was available, and because of the homogeneous nature of the products of these industries, it was decided to estimate prices by dividing gross output by a quantity indicator. For gas, the quantity indicator was 'Total sales', in therms, from AAS (various issues). For electricity, it was 'Electricity generated', in gigawatt hours, from AAS. For water, from 1963 onwards, it was water supplied in England and Wales, in megalitres per day, from *Water Facts* (Water Authorities Association, 1985 and 1988); prior to 1963, the total quantity of water supplied in the UK was taken from the Census report for MLH 603. With regard to water, note that although the water authorities are responsible for sewage treatment as well as water supply, only the latter activity is counted as part of the water industry (AH 1700, formerly MLH 603), therefore the quantity indicator chosen is a representative one.

The price indices were also adjusted in a few cases to remove the effects of excise payments, where these were included (usually taxes on consumption are excluded from the price indices; this is invariably the case with VAT but for some industries excise duties are included). The formula employed was:

Adjusted price = official price × [1 − (Excise payments/Gross Output)].

The industries affected were MLH 214, 216, 217, 231, 239/1, 239/2 and 263. Further details on excise taxes are in the fourth section of Appendix D.

DEFLATORS FOR INPUTS

The official 'Price index numbers of materials and fuels purchased' have been published on an AH basis since 1979; unpublished figures back to 1974 were obtained from the BSO (back to 1979 only for the food industries, AH 4115–4239). The indices were reclassified using 'Purchases' from the 1979 Census as the weights (see Appendix C).

Prior to 1974 very little data is available by industry. Price indices of materials and fuels purchased exist at the Order level, but these are unsuitable for our purposes since the Order level indices net out all intra-Order purchases. It was decided instead to construct price indices of materials and fuels purchased, for years prior to 1974, from the *output* price indices, making use of weights derived from the 1974 input–output tables. (*1974 Input–Output Tables for the United Kingdom*, PA1004, BSO,

1981). The 1974 tables were chosen since these were the fullest ever produced on the basis of the 1968 SIC (the 1979 tables were based on the 1980 SIC) and were derived from the 1974 Purchases Inquiry.

The procedure was to derive a price index for domestic purchases and one for purchases from abroad and then to average the two indices. However, for 1954, 1958 and 1963 the indices are based only on domestic prices; the reason is partly that import price data are harder to come by, partly that the rate of price increase does not justify the extra effort. For domestic purchases, the weights used were taken from table D (the industry-by-industry flow matrix, showing each industry's purchases from every other industry). Where an output price was missing, we used the output price index for the corresponding Order. (For the food industries, MLH 211–229/2, it was necessary to derive estimates for 1974–8 in addition, using the same method).

The methodology for imports is similar to that used for domestic purchases, that is, import price indices are weighted by their corresponding shares of imports purchased, taken from table C of the 1974 input–output tables. The main alteration in constructing import prices was that purchases from agriculture and industry own purchases were treated differently. Rather than use a single price index for agriculture for all industries, the price of the primary input from agriculture was used, where available. For example, purchases by the sugar industry from agriculture were assumed to consist entirely of raw sugar; similarly for the wool and cotton industries. If price indices were not available for the primary input from agriculture then an aggregate agricultural price index was used. In the case of *own purchases* (included for imports, but not for domestic purchases), it was possible in some industries to derive price indices for components – these were used instead of the price indices constructed for general imports. A full list of the prices used is in tables E.1–E.3.

Where possible, the import price indices were taken from the series 'Price indices of commodities wholly or mainly imported into the UK', from the Annual Abstract of Statistics. However, these data were not as detailed in the early 1970s as they are in the current period. Therefore, it was necessary to use unit values of imports from the DTI's *Overseas trade statistics of the UK*. Where an input–output group referred to more than one imported commodity, the price index was constructed by using a weighted average of the commodities' unit values, with weights equal to their share in the value of that category of imports.

For commodity groups where neither price indices of imported inputs nor unit values were available, domestic producer prices were used. This occurred mostly in the engineering and clothing industries. This was necessary to ensure that the shares of each industry's purchases were consistent with total purchases, that is, from domestic sources and imports.

The final step (for 1968 and 1973) was to combine the import price indices with those for domestic purchases. This was achieved by weighting imports and domestic purchases by their shares in total purchases.

In the case of the food industries, MLH 211–229, import price indices using the above methodology were also constructed for the years 1975–9 and combined with price indices for domestic purchases. In the case of coal mining (MLH 101) and the utilities (MLH 601–603), no official materials and fuel index is published.

Obviously, the figures for the earlier years, being based on weights which refer to a much later year, cannot be regarded as very accurate. Also, the 1974 input–output tables only distinguish 89 industries within the production sector, so for some industries our estimates are really an average over several MLH.

Table E.1. *Import price indices for purchases from input–output groups*

	Input–output group		Description of import price index
3.	Stone, slate etc.	UV	stone, gravel and sand
4.	other mining and quarrying	UV	ores and concentrates of iron and non-ferrous metals
5.	Water	PP	
6.	Gas	PP	
7.	Electricity	PP	
8.	Coal	UV	coal
9.	Petroleum	UV	crude petroleum
10.	Coke ovens etc.	UV	coke
11.	Mineral oil refinining	PP	
12.	Grain milling	PP	
13.	Bread & flour confectionery	PP	
14.	Meat & fish products	UV	meat and fish, fresh or chilled
15.	Milk & milk products	PP	
16.	Sugar	UV	sugar and honey
17.	Cocoa, chocolate & sugar	PP	
18.	Animal & poultry foods	AA	index of feeding stuffs
19.	Oils & fats	UV	animal and vegetable oils & fats
20.	Other food	PP	
21.	Soft drinks	PP	
22.	Alcoholic drinks	PP	
23.	Tobacco	UV	tobacco, unmanufactured
24.	General chemicals	PP	
25.	Pharmaceutical preparations	PP	
26.	Toilet preparations	PP	
27.	Paint	PP	
28.	Soap	PP	
29.	Synthetic resins etc.	UV	plastic materials, synthetic resin etc.

30.	Dyestuffs & pigments		PP
31.	Fertilisers	UV	fertilisers
32.	Other chemicals		PP
33.	Iron castings etc.	UV	iron and steel castings
34.	Other iron & steel	UV	iron and steel products (exclud. wire & castings)
35.	Aluminium	UV	aluminium products
36.	Other non-ferrous metals	UV	other non-ferrous metals
37.	Agricultural machinery		PP
38.	Machine tools		PP
39.	Pumps, valves etc.		PP
40.	Industrial engines		PP
41.	Textile machinery		PP
42.	Mech. handling equip.		PP
44.	Other non-electrical machinery		PP
45.	Industrial plant & steelwork		PP
46.	Other mechanical engineering		PP
47.	Instrument engineering		PP
48.	Electrical machinery		PP
49.	Insulated wires & cables	UV	insulated wires and cables
50.	Telegraph		PP
51.	Radio & electronic components		PP
52.	Television equipment		PP
53.	Electronic computers		PP
54.	Electronic capital goods		PP
55.	Domestic electric appliances		PP
56.	Other electrical goods		PP
57.	Shipbuilding		PP
58.	Wheeled tractors		PP
59.	Motor vehicles		PP
60.	Aerospace		PP
61.	Other vehicles		PP
62.	Engineers small tools		PP
63.	Cutlery, precious metals		PP
64.	Bolts, nuts, screws	UV	bolts, nuts, screws
65.	Wire	UV	wire
66.	Metal, cans etc.		PP
67.	Other metal goods		PP
68.	Man-made fibres	UV	yarn of synthetic fibres
69.	Cotton	UV	cotton yarn and thread
70.	Woolen & worsted	UV	yarn of wool
71.	Hosiery etc.		PP
72.	Carpets		PP
73.	Household textiles		PP
74.	Textile finishing		PP
75.	Other textiles		PP
76.	Leather	UV	leather goods
77.	Clothing		PP
78.	Footwear		PP
79.	Bucks, fireclay & refractory goods		PP
80.	Pottery & glass	UV	pottery and glass
81.	Cement	UV	cement
82.	Other building materials	UV	clay construction material & other mineral manufact.
83.	Furniture		PP
84.	Timber	AA	average of indices for hardwood, softwood and plywood

85.	Paper & board	UV	paper and board
86.	Packaging products of paper	PP	
87.	Other paper products	PP	
88.	Printing & publishing	PP	
89.	Rubber	PP	
90.	Plastics products	PP	
91.	Other manufacturing	PP	

Notes: In the list below the following abbreviations are used: PP = producer price index for domestic sales; AA = price index from Annual Abstract; UV = unit value of imports. Purchases by the metals industries from 'other mining' was broken down as follows: Iron & steel – ores of iron; Aluminium – ores of aluminium; Other non-ferrous metals – ores of other non-ferrous metals.

Table E.2. *Agricultural products*

Input–output group		Price index of agricultural products	
12.	Grain milling	UV	wheat
14.	Meat & fish products	UV	meat and fish
16.	Sugar	UV	raw sugar
17.	Cocoa, chocolate etc	UV	cocoa
18.	Animal & poultry foods	AA	index of feeding stuff
19.	Oils & fats	UV	animal and vegetable oils & fats
23.	Tobacco	UV	tobacco, unmanufactured
69.	Cotton	AA	index of raw cotton
70.	Wool & worsted	AA	index of raw wool
75.	Other textiles	AA	index of raw jute
76.	Leather	AA	index of hides and skins
89.	Rubber	AA	index of natural rubber

Note: For most industries the price index for agricultural products was the index for all agricultural products from the Annual Abstract. The industries where the price of the primary input from agriculture was available are those above.

Table E.3. *Own purchases*

Input–output group		Price index for own purchases	
38.	Machine tools	UV	parts and accessories for machine tools
59.	Motor vehicles	UV	parts for motor vehicles
61.	Other vehicles	UV	parts for motor cycles
68.	Man-made fibres	UV	discontinuous and continuous synthetic fibre
69.	Cotton	AA	index of price raw cotton

Notes: The price index for own purchases is as in table 1a except for the above groups. The share of imports by the cotton industry from agriculture was very small and probably does not include raw cotton – therefore raw cotton is assumed to be included in own purchases.

APPENDIX F

LABOUR INPUT

Labour input, for each type of worker, is measured by annual hours, which are computed as numbers employed × weekly hours × weeks worked per year. The share of each type of worker is the wage bill of that type (hourly earnings × annual hours) divided by the total wage bill of all types of workers. Nine types of workers, five manual and four non-manual, have been distinguished and for each type in each benchmark year labour input and share have been calculated. The five manual types are: full-time males, aged 21 and over; full-time females, aged eighteen and over; part-time females, aged eighteen and over; males aged less than 21 and females aged under eighteen. The four non-manual types are: males; full-time females; part-time females and working proprietors. The overall split between manual and non-manual workers for each industry comes from the Census of Production, which gives us the wage bill and the employment level of 'operatives' and 'administrative, technical and clerical' (ATC) workers. 'Working proprietors' are a small, residual category. The Census of Production figures for wage bills and employment served as control totals.

Manual workers were split into their five groups using information from the *Annual Inquiry into earnings and hours of manual workers*, carried out by the Department of Employment; earnings and hours of each group were derived from the same source. Unfortunately, much less information is available for non-manuals. These were split into types using proportions derived from the Census of Employment. To achieve comparability with the earlier years, it was necessary to use a single hourly earnings series and a single weekly hours series for each type of non-manual workers, that is, no variation across industries was possible. These series, which are averages over all index of production industries, were taken from the *New Earnings Survey* from 1973 onwards and extrapolated backwards using *manual* earnings and hours, except that working proprietors were assumed to earn the average wage of ATC workers (taken from the Census of Production). For lack of data a single series for annual weeks worked was also used, that is, no variation across industries or across types of worker. This series draws on the work of Matthews *et al.* (1982); it allows for time lost due to strikes, sickness and holidays. It shows a steady decline in weeks worked per year from 46.3 in 1954 to 42.3 in 1986.

Numbers, weekly earnings and weekly hours of manual workers

The Department of Employment has carried out a regular inquiry into the earnings and hours of manual workers throughout our period and the results are published every year in the *Gazette*. In earlier years the survey was bi-annual, nowadays it is annual; where there was a choice, the October figures were used. This large-scale survey gives the numbers, the average wage paid and the average weekly hours worked of each type of worker in each industry. The types, five in number, are those listed above. Until 1982 the survey used the 1968 SIC. After then the 1980 SIC has been employed, but, unfortunately, so we were informed, the survey is now coded only at the 3-digit level, hence there is no way to reclassify the results to the 1968 SIC, for which the 4-digit figures would be required (except in those cases where a 1968 MLH happens to be identical with a 3-digit group of the 1980 SIC). Therefore it was not possible to employ this survey after 1982.[1]

The survey relating to each of our benchmark years was employed. The surveys for 1954 and 1958 were done on the basis of the 1948 SIC and those of 1963 and 1968 on the 1958 SIC. The 1958 SIC is very similar to the 1968 one, the 1948 SIC less so. All these surveys were reclassified to a 1968 SIC basis. The basic procedure to estimate the number of workers of each type was to apply the proportions of each type of worker in the sample to the Census totals of operatives in each industry. The reclassification necessary for 1954 and 1958 produced some large jumps in the proportions of some types of workers in some industries, so where these were judged unacceptable the 1963 proportions were projected backwards. Total weekly hours for each type of worker were obtained by multiplying the estimated numbers (of workers of each type) by the average weekly hours per worker (of each type).

Because the 1986 survey was no help, for the reason just given, it was assumed that the proportions of each type were the same as in 1982. 1986 hours and earnings were extrapolated from 1982 using the ratio of hours (earnings) in 1986 to that in 1982 in manufacturing as a whole.

The 1954 survey did not give figures for part-time women. These were assumed to be in the same ratio to full-time women as in 1958. Where the survey did not report a value for earnings or hours the figure for the corresponding order was used. Missing values usually occurred where the numbers in the sample were very small. Since the sample was a very large one (covering several million workers) this usually meant that the number of workers in this category was in reality negligible. An exception is coal mining (MLH 101) which for some obscure administrative reason has never been covered by the survey. Here it was assumed that all manual workers are adult males (which is not far from the truth). In this industry we can estimate *annual* hours worked per worker directly from the relationship [Output per man-year] ÷ [Output per man-shift] = Shifts per man-year, assuming that a shift lasts eight hours. Output per man-year and per man-shift come from the National Coal Board's (now British Coal) accounts (National Coal Board, 1979, *Statistical Tables, 1978/79*, table 2, and *Report and Accounts 1982/3*, p. 20). Earnings in coal mining were estimated as the wage bill of operatives divided by the number of operatives, from the Census of Production.

The annual surveys employed came from the following sources: 1954, EG, March 1955; 1958, EG, December 1958 (for PT women) and February 1959; 1963, EG, February 1964; 1968, EG, February 1969; 1973, EG, February 1974; 1976, EG, March 1977; 1979, EG, February 1980; 1982, EG, February 1983.

Numbers, weekly earnings and hours of non-manual workers

There is no survey of non-manual workers comparable to the one available for manuals. Non-manuals are of course included in the *New Earnings Survey* but because the sample size is fairly small there is often little industry detail available, at least prior to 1979. To preserve comparability over time, it was therefore decided not to attempt a detailed breakdown by industry of earnings and hours. But it was thought desirable to break the non-manual labour force down at least by sex and whether or not part-time. The Census of Employment gives a breakdown of each industry's *total* labour force between full-time males, full-time females and part-time females. In principle, it would have been possible to use these proportions, in conjunction with the proportions of the *manual* workforce of various types (from the annual inquiry into manual workers discussed above) and the overall manual/non-manual split (from the Census of Production), to estimate the proportions of the *non-manual* labour force of each type. Attempts to do this however produced unsatisfactory results, whether because of differences of definition between the various sources or because of sampling error. Eventually therefore it was decided simply to apply the Census of Employment proportions (which as stated apply to the whole labour force, manual plus non-manual) to the total of ATC employees given for each industry in the Census of Production.

Weekly earnings and hours of non-manual workers for 1973–86 were taken from the *New Earnings Survey*. The three types we used were full time males (21 and over), full-time females (eighteen and over) and part-time females (eighteen and over). The earnings and hours were the average of all index of production industries (those whose pay was not affected by absence). Years prior to 1973 were extrapolated back from 1973 using the corresponding figures from the annual inquiry into manual workers.

Obviously this assumes that earnings and hours of each type of non-manual worker grew at the same rate as his or her manual counterpart.

The Census of Production allows us to distinguish a third category of worker, 'working proprietors', derived as a residual by subtracting operatives and ATCs from total employment. Because the employment figures are given in thousands to one decimal place, it is possible that the residual figure for working proprietors is simply due to rounding error. Where this could have been the case, the estimate of working proprietors was set to zero. In other cases the number of working proprietors was found to be nearly always very small. The weekly hours worked by working proprietors were assumed to be those of adult non-manual males. Their wage was assumed to be the average wage of ATC workers given in the Census. The Census itself, though it records implicitly the number of working proprietors, does not attribute any payments to them, their remuneration being counted as part of profits. We have treated them as an additional, non-manual type of labour and priced them accordingly.

Weeks worked per year

No attempt was made to estimate weeks worked per year by industry or by type of worker. Instead a single series was applied to all industries and all types of worker, based on the work of Matthews *et al.* (1982). In their Appendix D, table D.1, they give the average number of weeks lost per year due to holidays, sickness and strikes for, amongst others, the years 1951, 1955, 1960, 1964, 1968 and 1973. Benchmark years up to 1973 were estimated by linear interpolation between their figures. For the years after 1973 similar sources to theirs were used. Basic holidays of *manual* workers were estimated from figures given in EG, March 1987, p. 132. Non-manual workers were assumed to enjoy the same growth rate of basic holidays as manuals. Public holidays were assumed to be eight days per year after 1973. Total weeks lost to holidays were then estimated as basic holidays plus public holidays. Weeks lost due to sickness came from *Social Security Statistics* and weeks lost due to strikes (a much smaller number) came from EG.

Weeks worked per year were then calculated as 52 *less* weeks lost due to holidays, sickness and strikes, and were as follows:

	Weeks worked per year
1954	46.27
1958	46.13
1963	46.10
1968	45.82
1973	44.98
1976	44.20
1979	43.42
1982	42.82
1986	42.34

Shares of each type of labour

To construct the Törnqvist index of total labour input we need the shares of each of our nine types of labour (five manual and four non-manual) in the total wage bill. The total wage bill is defined as the wage bill of operatives, of ATC workers and of working proprietors *plus* employers' National Insurance contributions and their contributions to private pension schemes (*employees'* contributions to National Insurance, and so on, are included in wages). Employers' contributions are assumed to be proportional to the wage bill of each type of worker, so they do not affect the calculation of total labour input; however they do affect the calculation of labour's contribution to MFP growth.

The numerator of each share for each type of worker was annual hours worked *times* the hourly wage, but in calculating the shares care was taken to ensure consistency with Census of Production totals. Thus the sum of the wage bills of the five types of manual worker was constrained to be equal to the wage bill of operatives, given in the Census for each industry. This control amounted to a uniform scaling up or down of the hourly wage assumed to be paid to each type of labour; an alternative would have been to scale weekly hours worked up or down, but there seems to be much less cross-industry variability in hours (for a given type of labour) than in wages, hence less violence is done to the data by scaling wages rather than hours (recall that numbers employed are already controlled to equal Census totals). In a similar way the sum of the non-manual wage bills (except for that of working proprietors) was controlled to be equal to the wage bill recorded for ATC workers in the Census.

Employers' National Insurance Contributions

The Census of Production identified the costs to employers of National Insurance contributions from 1973 onwards but not before that date. The following outlines the method employed to estimate these contributions for the Census years up to 1973. Since the National Insurance system involved both flat and graduated payments, each is considered in turn below.

Flat payments

Table F.1 shows the flat rate employers' National Insurance contributions for the benchmark years 1954–68 and for the years 1970–73. The table shows the ordinary rates and the rates for adult men and women who were contracted out of the system. The source for these data were various issues of the *Annual Abstract of Statistics*. The published data were converted to annual figures by multiplying each flat-rate contribution by the proportion of the year for which it was applicable.

Table F.1. *Employers' National Insurance contributions: flat rates (£ per person per week)*

Year	Ordinary				Self-employed Men	Contracted out	
	Men	Women	boys	Girls		Men	Women
1954	0.25	0.20	0.15	0.12	0.37	—	—
1958	0.40	0.33	0.24	0.19	0.57	—	—
1963	0.46	0.40	0.33	0.26	0.77	0.56	0.45
1968	2.28	1.42	1.25	0.90	1.09	2.30	1.50
1970	3.32	1.98	1.79	1.30	1.24	3.44	2.05
1971	2.76	1.71	1.53	1.13	1.31	2.88	1.79
1972	2.17	1.42	1.24	0.95	1.55	2.29	1.50
1973	1.39	1.07	0.87	0.73	1.74	1.51	1.15

Source: Annual Abstract of Statistics (various issues).

The ordinary flat-rate payments per week for each category of worker (men, full-time women, part-time women, boys and girls) were multiplied by the number of workers in that category to yield employers' weekly contribution bills. This was then multiplied by 52 to give an annual total; the average number of actual weeks worked was not used as employers were required to contribute to the system even if their employees were on holiday, sick leave or on strike, and so on. Separate calculations were carried out for manual and non-manual workers and for working proprietors. The number of white-collar workers in manufacturing who contracted out of the system was considered to be small so no attempt was made to calculate separately payments on behalf of those workers. Also, it is clear from table F.1 that the difference between the ordinary and contracted out payments was marginal.

Graduated payments

From 1961, in addition to the flat payment, employers also paid a graduated payment which was a percentage of employees earnings between lower and upper cut-off points. The details of the system were as follows: 1963: up to 3rd June, 4.25 per cent of earnings between £9–15; from 3rd June, 4.25 per cent of earnings between £9–18. 1968: 4.75 per cent of earnings btween £9–18; 0.5 per cent of earnings between £18–30. 1970: 4.75 per cent of earnings between £9–18; 3.25 per cent of earnings between £18–30. 1971: Up to 21 September, as for 1970; from 21 September, 4.75 per cent of earnings between £9–18; 4.35 per cent of earnings between £18–42. 1972: up to 2nd October, as for September 1971; from 2nd October: 4.75 per cent of earnings between £9–42. 1973: up to 1st October, as for October 1972; from 1st October, 5.0 per cent of earnings between £9–54.

These graduated rates were applied to the average weekly earnings for each type of worker, summed over all employees and multiplied by 52. They were then combined with flat-rate payments to yield employers' total National Insurance contributions.

The next step was to calculte the ratio of the *actual* payments to the *estimated* payments for 1973; the ratio was positive for all MLH and substantially greater than one for a few. This in turn suggests that the discrepancy is not so much due to the estimation method but rather to the fact that the Census figures include not just National Insurance contributions but also commercial insurance premiums to provide pensions, superannuation, sickness, disability and death benefits, and so on (*Report on the Census of Production, 1979, introductory notes*). In this context it is interesting that there is a significant positive relationship between the ratio of actual to estimated contributions and the average wage bill per head in 1973; the correlation was 0.58. Workers in industries which paid above-average wages were also likely to be in receipt of higher non-wage benefits such as pension schemes. Data on firms' contributions to pension schemes, and so on, are not readily available. Therefore, it was decided to factor up the pre-1973 estimates by the ratio of actual to estimated contributions in 1973.

APPENDIX G

RENTAL PRICES OF CAPITAL SERVICES

INTRODUCTION

The standard neoclassical approach to estimating the rental prices of capital services is to infer their values from the assumed correspondence between the purchase price of an asset and the present discounted value of all future services from the asset; this inference is necessary because of the lack of data on market rental prices of assets. The neoclassical approach most often forms the basis for estimation of rental prices but in empirical applications rental prices vary according to the assumed structure of depreciation, the nature of expectations of capital gains and the assumed nominal rate of return or discount rate. Unfortunately, as discussed below, the various empirical assumptions yield very different estimates of rental prices. Also, the theoretical formula does not constrain the rental prices to be non-negative, which is necessary to be consistent with the full equilibrium framework implicit in the calculation of multi-factor productivity.

The following section presents a brief discussion of the theoretical approach and the alternative empirical assumptions. The next section contains information on the data used and the impact of the tax system on rental prices. This section also looks at some experiments using two alternative empirical methods of estimating expected capital gains and discusses our final estimates of rental prices.

THE THEORY OF RENTAL PRICE DETERMINATION

The rental price of asset i, in discrete time, was derived in Christensen and Jorgenson (1969) and, ignoring tax terms, is given by:

$$p_i^K(t) = \{r(t)\,q_i(t-1) + \delta_i q_i(t) - [q_i^*(t) - q_i(t-1)]\} \qquad (\text{G.1})$$

where p_i^K = rental price of asset i
r = nominal, post-tax rate of return
δ_i = depreciation rate of asset i
q_i = purchase price of asset i
q_i^* = *expected* purchase price of asset i

In our capital stocks estimates we assume geometric depreciation, as discussed in chapter 3, so to preserve internal consistency between capital stocks and rental prices we include the same constant depreciation rate in the calculation of rental prices. The remaining unknowns in (G.1) are therefore the nominal rate of return, $r(t)$, and expected capital gains, $q_i^*(t) - q_i(t-1)$.

There are basically two approaches to measuring the nominal rate of return. The first sets it equal to an external market rate such as the yield on long term bonds, the second uses an internal measure which equates the value of the marginal product of aggregate capital in an industry to the realised profits in that industry. Both options have been used extensively, for example, Kelly and Owen (1985) use an external rate based on the cost of financing debt and equity whereas Jorgenson and his collaborators use an internal measure. Economic theory has little to say on the relative merits of the two measures, but in the context of MFP measurement the internal one has the advantage of preserving the accounting identity between the total value of capital services (sum over all assets of rental price times asset quantity) and total profits, hence its popularity among researchers primarily interested in productivity measurement. Assuming equalisation of nominal rates of return across all asset types, the internal measure can be estimated by summing rental prices in (G.1) multiplied by the corresponding capital stocks across asset types and setting the result equal to gross profits. Letting Π denote gross profits and K_i the real stock of asset i, the nominal rate of return is given by:

$$ r = \frac{\Pi - \sum_i \delta_i q_i(t) K_i(t-1) + \sum_i [q_i^*(t) - q_i(t-1)] K_i(t-1)}{\sum_i q_i(t-1) K_i(t-1)} $$

$$ = \{\text{Gross Profits} - \text{Depreciation} + \text{Capital gains}\} \div \text{Value of capital.} $$

$$ \text{(G.2)} $$

Harper, Berndt and Wood (1989) have examined alternative specifications of both the nominal rate of return and expected capital gains using a sample of two-digit US manufacturing industries from 1948 to 1981. They conclude that in the case of the former, the use of an external rate of return performs badly relative to internal measures, both in terms of the number of negative rental prices and the very wide divergence between the *ex ante* implied return to aggregate capital and *ex post* profits. We carried out some experiments with various external rates and found a similar problem of negative outcomes and excess volatility. Therefore, in our rental price calculations we used the internal measure as given by (G.2), modified to include tax terms.

We now turn to an examination of the specification of expected capital gains. A thorough discussion of the issues involved are presented in Harper, Berndt and Wood (1989) where they conclude that whereas it is generally accepted that some form of capital gains should be included in the rental price formula, its exact specification is largely an empirical issue. An important contribution of that paper is that they show that with an internal measure, the use of average capital gains over all asset types gives an identical rental price to one with zero capital gains. Therefore, it is variations in *relative* purchase prices of capital assets which yield differences in rental prices. Since the Törnqvist index of aggregate capital weights each asset by its contribution to the value of the marginal product of capital, theoretical consistency requires the use of asset specific capital gains. Therefore, we again follow their lead by only looking at rental prices where prices vary across assets.

It remains to specify the form of expected capital gains by asset type; as suggested above the choice between alternatives is primarily an empirical issue. Jorgenson, Gollop and Fraumeni (1987) assume that expectations are fully realised so that the expected purchase price at the end of period t is replaced by its actual value in equation (G.1). An alternative attempted by Harper, Berndt and Wood (1989) is to include a three-year moving average of capital gains. In the fourth section below we present results on average values of rental prices using both these alternatives. First we discuss some further calculations necessary to implement equations (G.1) and (G.2) empirically.

EMPIRICAL IMPLEMENTATION

Here we distinguish three types of fixed capital assets – plant & machinery, building & land and vehicles – and two types of inventories – materials & fuel and the sum of work in progress and goods on hand for sale. The purchase prices of fixed assets are the investment deflators discussed in Appendix B and for inventories are the price indices for materials and fuel and output prices, respectively, discussed in Appendix E.

When account is taken of the tax system, the rental price of capital asset i, as shown in Christensen and Jorgenson (1969), is given by:

$$p_i^K(t) = \{r(t)\,q_i(t-1) + \delta_i q_i(t) - [q_i^*(t) - q_i(t-1)]\}$$
$$\times [(1 - u(t)\,z_i(t))/(1 - u(t))] \qquad (G.3)$$

where u = corporation tax rate

z_i = present value of depreciation allowances per £ spent on i

and $r(t)$ is now the *post-tax* nominal rate of return.

If the firm can borrow at rate r' and if interest is tax deductible, then $r = (1 - u)r'$. $q_i(1 - uz_i)$ may be thought of as the effective price of an asset.

Every pound spent on i gives rise to a stream of depreciation charges whose present value is z_i; these can be set against tax, so the firm is better off to the tune uz_i. In the case of inventories both δ_i and z_i are zero but the tax treatment of inventories is more complicated than (G.3) because of the introduction of 'stock relief' in the 1970s which implies that the formula changes with time. The tax treatment of stocks are discussed at the end of this section.

Since the nominal rate of return is post-tax, gross profits in the internal measure of the rate of return (G.2) are replaced by gross after-tax profits. Gross after tax profits in our accounting framework are equal to:

Net Output — Wages and salaries — Employers National Insurance Contributions — Corporation tax — 'other' non-industrial services.

where the last item includes the cost of professional services, payments for transport and communications and royalty payments. The remainder of the census definition of non-industrial services, that is, payments for the hire of plant and equipment, rent of buildings, bank charges and commercial insurance premiums, as well as licensing of motor vehicles and rates, are deemed to be part of profits.

The value of corporation tax paid is not given in the Census. Ideally we would like to include the proportion of profits actually paid in tax but data at the industry level are not readily available. Instead we use the actual marginal tax rate but, following Kelly and Owen (1985), we discount the marginal tax rate for seven quarters to reflect lags in payment of the tax. The remaining unknown in (G.3) is the present value of tax allowances and grants, to which we now turn.

The present value of tax allowances and grants on a unit of investment in different asset types have been calculated by Melliss and Richardson (1975) for the period 1946–74 and by Kelly and Owen (1985) for the period 1966–84. Apart from their treatment of investment grants and their use of different discount rates the formulas are identical. (Mellis and Richardson's sum of investment allowances plus initial allowances plus one year writing down allowance correspond exactly to Kelly and Owen's first year allowance). The alternative discount rates which can be used in the calculation in (G.1) are discussed below.

In our calculations of the present value of tax allowances we basically follow Kelly and Owen's methodology except that we ignore the regional investment grants. The amount of the regional grants obviously varies across industries according to their location but since time series on the regional dispersion of production are not readily available at the MLH level, it was deemed appropriate to ignore this item altogether. The formulas for calculating the present value of tax allowances by asset type are given as follows.

The present value of tax allowances and grants for plant and machinery was calculated as

$$ZP = \frac{T}{(1 + p)^{1.75}} \left[\frac{\rho FP + DP}{\rho + DP} \right] (1 - GP) + GP$$

where

T = corporation tax rate
ρ = discount rate
FP = first year capital allowances on plant and machinery
DP = annual writing down allowance on plant and machinery (reducing balance basis).
GP = national investment grant on plant and machinery

Since taxes are paid with a lag, the effective marginal corporation tax rate is the actual rate, T, discounted for a period L, $T/(1 + p)^L$; Kelly and Owen set L equal to seven quarters. FP, DP and GP are all expressed as proportions of the asset price.

The writing-down allowance for new industrial buildings (DB) is on a straight-line rather than a reducing balance basis so that the formula for the present value of allowances and grants is given by

$$ZB = \frac{T}{(1 + p)^{1.75}} \left[FB + \frac{DB}{\rho} \left(1 - (1 + p)^{\frac{-(1 - FB)}{DB}} \right) \right]$$

Since the writing down allowance on vehicles (DV) is on a reducing balance basis, the formula for ZV is identical to that for ZP with FV replacing FP and so on. Investment grants were zero for both new buildings and vehicles in the period 1954–86.

Data on first-year and annual writing-down allowances and investment grants for plant and machinery are available from Melliss and Richardson and the Inland Revenue Statistics; the national investment grants operated only between 1966–70 for plant and machinery. The corporation tax rate from 1966 is available in *Inland Revenue Statistics, 1988*. Prior to 1966 company taxation was based on a combination of profits and income taxes. Melliss and Richardson (1975) calculate the appropriate company tax rates back to 1946.

Ideally the nominal discount rate in the estimation of the present value of tax allowances should equal the interest rate, r, in equation (G.1) above. However, the estimate of r as outlined above was dependent on given values of z_i. Hence it is not possible to use the same nominal rate of return in both parts of the calculation. Instead we opted for a market rate of interest in the calcultaion of z_i. In the choice of nominal discount rate we experimented with a number of rates, that is, the annual average per cent redemption yield on long dated British government stocks, as used by Melliss and Richardson, the yield on 3-month Treasury bills and an average of the long and short rates. These interest rates were taken from *Annual Abstract of Statistics*. The calculations of investment allowances were found to be not very sensitive to the choice of interest rate so we opted for the long rate.

Finally, in this section, we briefly discuss the tax treatment of inventories; a full discussion of the system is presented in Kay and King (1986). Up to 1974, firms paid corporation tax on the value of additions to stocks, both on the increase in the physical value of stocks and stocks appreciation. With the large rises in the prices of materials in 1973, a liquidity crisis developed since firms recorded large accounting profits on their stocks of materials. This led to the introduction of 'stock relief' in 1974 where firms could deduct any change in the book value of stocks greater than 10 per cent of gross trading profits. A second liquidity crisis developed in 1980 when firms ran down their volume of stocks since sales of stocks were taxable. The government then modified the scheme to restrict relief to stock appreciation. In 1984, stock relief was abolished entirely. Therefore, the taxation of stocks of inventories was subjected to three different tax regimes in the period covered by this study so that the rental price calculation for stocks must vary according to regime.

The rental price formulae for each tax regime, with the benchmark years for which they were applicable in parentheses, are as follows:
(i) taxation of both nominal stock appreciation and the value of the physical increase in stocks (1954, 1958, 1963, 1968, 1973 and 1986):

$$P_j^K(t) = 1/(1 - u)\{r(t)\,q_j(t-1) - (1-u)[q_j(t) - q_j(t-1)]\}$$

(ii) relief against tax for both nominal stock appreciation and the value of the physical increase in stocks (1976, 1979):

$$P_j^K(t) = \{r(t)\,q_j(t-1) - [q_j(t) - q_j(t-1)]\}$$

(iii) relief only for nominal stock appreciation (1982):

$$P_j^K(t) = 1/(1-u)\{r(t)\,q_j(t-1) - [q_j(t) - q_j(t-1)]\}.$$

These formulae are equivalent to those presented in Kelly and Owen (1985).

Kelly and Owen ignore the 10 per cent of profits threshold for stock relief arguing that it is difficult to handle analytically. The same problem applies to our rental price measure since they do not depend in a simple way on profits, therefore, we also chose to ignore the tax relief threshold.

Table G.1. *Means of rates of return and asset shares, 1973–86*[*]

| | | | Value shares in total profits | | | | |
| | | Nominal rate of return | Inventories | | Fixed capital | | |
			Materials	Goods	Plant	Buildings	Vehicles
1973	(1)	0.23	0.15	0.20	0.62	− 0.02	0.06
	(2)	0.21	0.12	0.17	0.52	0.11	0.05
1976	(1)	0.24	0.03	0.06	0.32	0.53	0.07
	(2)	0.24	0.04	0.06	0.51	0.33	0.07
1979	(1)	0.21	0.05	0.07	0.78	0.01	0.10
	(2)	0.19	0.05	0.06	0.62	0.19	0.09
1982	(1)	0.07	− 0.11	− 0.37	0.24	1.10	0.15
	(2)	0.12	0.01	− 0.11	0.77	0.18	0.15
1986	(1)	0.12	0.10	0.13	0.53	0.19	0.05
	(2)	0.12	0.08	0.12	0.53	0.22	0.05

Notes:

(1) Capital gains estimated by Δq_t.

(2) Capital gains estimated by $\frac{1}{3} \sum_{i=0}^{2} \Delta q_{t-i}$.

(*) 139 industries.

AN EVALUATION OF ALTERNATIVE RENTAL PRICES

We estimated rental prices for each of the five types of assets for our benchmark years from 1963 under two assumptions on capital gains. Letting $\Delta q_t = q_t - q_{t-1}$, the assumptions are:

(1) perfectly anticipated capital gains, that is, Δq_t,
(2) 3-year moving average of price changes, backward from the current period, that is,

$$\frac{1}{3} \sum_{i=0}^{2} \Delta q_{t-i}.$$

We computed a number of descriptive statistics such as the mean and standard deviation across industries for value shares (rental prices times capital stocks as a proportion of profits) and for the nominal rate of return for each time period and type of asset. The results for 1973–86 are in table G.1. Table G.2 tabulates the corresponding number of negative outcomes. Note that the occurrence of negative rental prices implies that the 'shares' are not restricted by equation (G.1) to lie between zero and one.

The following are a few general comments on the results:
(i) The nominal rates of return do not appear, on average, to be overly sensitive to the capital gains specification in the 1970s but shows some variation in 1982. The occurrence of some negative nominal rates is

Table G.2. *Number of negative outcomes**

| | | Value shares in total profits | | | | |
| | Nominal rate of return | Inventories | | Fixed capital | | |
		Materials	Goods	Plant	Buildings	Vehicles
1973 (1)	0	2	2	0	55	0
(2)	0	0	0	0	14	0
1976 (1)	0	36	24	9	1	0
(2)	0	26	21	0	3	0
1979 (1)	2	26	18	2	49	1
(2)	1	20	22	1	10	0
1982 (1)	10	75	74	7	0	0
(2)	0	39	40	0	11	0
1986 (1)	4	4	9	0	10	0
(2)	3	8	8	0	6	0

Notes:

(1) Capital gains estimated by Δq_t.

(2) Capital gains estimated by $\frac{1}{3} \sum_{i=0}^{2} \Delta q_{t-i}$.

(*) 139 industries.

disturbing, although most can be explained by negative gross profits in the industries concerned. This is not, however, true of the majority of negative outcomes in 1982 under assumption (1).

(ii) In contrast, the shares are very sensitive to the expectations assumption and also vary greatly over time. Again the problem is most acute in 1982 but the mean shares differ significantly in all years, with buildings showing the greatest changes. The shares under assumption (1) are considerably more volatile; this was also found to be the case by Harper, Berndt and Wood for US manufacturing.

(iii) On the criterion of smallest number of negative values, the 3-year moving average is a clear winner. Also the negative values under assumptions (2) are, in general, much closer to zero than under (1). Negative shares in the 1970s occur because of the large capital gains; in 1982 they occur because profits, and hence the nominal rates of return are abnormally low. Again a similar result was found by Harper, Berndt and Wood for US manufacturing.

Given the above remarks, we decided to opt for the three-year moving average of capital gains in our rental price calculations.[1] It is obvious from table G.1 that this reduces the negativity problem but it does not eliminate it entirely. Since the shares of each asset type in the MFP calculation are assumed to equal the value of their marginal products, it does not seem sensible to retain any negative outcomes. One possibility

Table G.3. *Mean and standard deviation of value shares in total profits, by asset type, 1954–86*

		Inventories		Fixed capital		
		Materials	Goods	Plant	Buildings	Vehicles
1954	Mean	0.13	0.13	0.42	0.27	0.05
	SD	0.08	0.09	0.14	0.09	0.04
1958	Mean	0.16	0.12	0.42	0.25	0.05
	SD	0.09	0.08	0.14	0.09	0.03
1963	Mean	0.11	0.15	0.48	0.27	0.05
	SD	0.06	0.10	0.16	0.08	0.04
1968	Mean	0.11	0.16	0.43	0.26	0.05
	SD	0.06	0.10	0.15	0.09	0.04
1973	Mean	0.12	0.17	0.53	0.13	0.05
	SD	0.07	0.11	0.18	0.09	0.03
1976	Mean	0.04	0.06	0.51	0.33	0.07
	SD	0.04	0.06	0.13	0.09	0.04
1979	Mean	0.05	0.06	0.61	0.19	0.09
	SD	0.08	0.06	0.17	0.10	0.05
1982	Mean	0.05	0.06	0.59	0.20	0.10
	SD	0.07	0.07	0.16	0.10	0.06
1986	Mean	0.07	0.10	0.56	0.22	0.06
	SD	0.05	0.07	0.13	0.08	0.04

would be to smooth prices even more by for example using a five or six years moving average. Experiments suggest that even a seven year moving average is not sufficient to eliminate all negative outcomes; the problem arises because the rate of inflation in asset prices was so large and persistent in the 1970s that further smoothing tends merely to shift the problem across time periods.

Therefore, for industries with positive gross profits, we simply set the rental prices equal to zero whenever there was a negative outcome. The MFP calculation involves the average share of an asset in adjacent time periods. In only a small number of cases was the average share set to zero, that is, there were few persistent negative outcomes across both industries and asset types.

There are persistent negative gross profits for four industries, – iron and steel (MLH 311), shipbuilding (MLH 370), railway track equipment (MLH 384/5) and photographic and document copying equipment (MLH 351). In the case of the first three there were hidden government subsidies, that is, subsidies which were not on a per unit of output basis and hence do not appear in the census.

In the case of iron and steel we added the subsidy received by the British Steel Corporation, from 1979–86, to the value of output and estimated capital's share using the residual method outlined above. These subsidies were not merely capital grants but were given to cover operating expenses as well as investment. Data on the payments by government under section 18 (1) of the 1975 Iron and Steel Act were obtained from the BSC annual accounts. These amounted to over five billion pounds between 1976 and 1986.

It was not possible to estimate directly subsidies in other industries. Therefore, for the remaining three industries we set the nominal rate of return equal to the average for their industry order group and calculated implied profits from equation (G.2) which was then added to gross output. Ths calculation was carried out for each time period, rather than just for the years for which negative profits occurred, to ensure we did not introduce artificial jumps in the data.

Finally, in table G.3 we show the mean shares when all negative rental prices have been eliminated, for the complete sample period, 1954–86. The long-term movements in relative shares approximate the changes in the relative shares of each asset in nominal investment, that is, the long-term decline in buildings' share of fixed assets and the decline in inventories from the late 1970s. The former has been counteracted, to some extent, by the more favourable tax treatment of plant and vehicles since the 1960s. Large changes in shares now only occur in the early to mid-1970s when relative prices showed substantial movements, in particular the price of buildings increased considerably relative to all other assets in the early 1970s but general inflation in output and material input prices was greater than in fixed assets in the mid-1970s. Also the shares in 1982 are now much closer to those for adjacent time periods, which seems reasonable when we recall that the problem in that year was primarily one of low profits, whose main impact should have been on the share of aggregate capital rather than on the relative value of shares of different types of assets.

APPENDIX H

DETAILED TABLES

NOTE

All growth rates are exponential, expressed as per cent per annum, for example, the growth of some variable Z between time T and $T - u$ is $(100/u) \, [\ln Z(T) - \ln Z(T - u)]$. Growth rates of input quantities are Törnqvist indices of growth rates of components – see text for details. Growth rates of input prices are derived as implicit deflators: that is, the growth of nominal value *minus* the growth of quantity.

If desired, the growth rates of prices and quantities can be used, in conjunction with the nominal values for 1986 given in table H.9, to recover the real or nominal *level* of output and of each of the three inputs, in any of the eight other years studied, from 1954–82.

In addition to the industries classified to manufacturing (MLH 102/3, 109, and 211–499), estimates are presented, when available, for the other industries covered by the Census of Production (with the exception of Construction, MLH 500), namely: MLH 101, 104, and 601–603.

A list of the industries, showing the official names corresponding to the MLH number, will be found in Appendix A.

For sources and methods, see the text.

Table H.1. *Growth rates of real gross output, selected periods, 1954–86, %, p.a.*

MLH	1954–8	1958–63	1963–8	1968–73	1973–6	1976–9	1979–82	1982–6
101	− 1.72	− 1.89	− 5.56	− 7.22	4.42	− 0.06	− 4.97	− 9.30
102/103	− 1.15	4.43	7.83	4.69	− 9.77	− 2.55	− 4.37	− 4.56
104	NA	NA	NA	NA	NA	47.54	8.66	− 6.26
109	NA	NA	NA	NA	− 2.03	8.30	− 7.99	− 3.16
211	3.01	− 2.41	0.42	− 2.19	7.20	0.23	− 3.95	0.70
212	8.62	3.08	1.02	0.54	1.23	− 3.79	− 2.01	3.92
213	3.92	1.49	2.75	− 1.49	7.13	− 1.21	− 1.21	− 2.92
214	6.58	2.94	6.85	8.93	1.30	1.73	1.87	− 0.23
215	8.19	− 3.18	20.46	0.48	− 5.03	− 0.43	− 2.74	− 3.04
216	3.09	0.07	− 3.46	− 1.56	− 0.95	− 2.24	− 8.22	− 3.57
217	0.09	− 1.49	1.90	1.80	− 1.73	4.03	− 4.99	2.44
218	8.33	5.00	2.71	3.50	− 4.56	0.95	0.26	0.66
219	7.64	6.60	1.49	3.40	4.54	5.30	− 0.03	− 4.10
221	7.12	− 4.28	− 1.37	7.34	19.08	− 0.51	5.74	6.07
229/1	− 0.87	− 3.48	− 5.18	6.35	12.91	− 2.66	3.49	1.25
229/2	4.86	2.53	16.07	2.24	2.69	− 5.03	1.74	2.79
231	6.08	3.13	2.39	3.23	− 0.53	2.09	− 9.97	− 1.86
232	13.65	6.59	0.98	13.16	− 0.83	3.97	− 3.87	2.55
239/1	8.52	8.49	5.41	9.27	− 2.50	7.95	− 13.25	0.92
239/2	10.16	0.04	4.59	11.00	− 7.20	8.10	− 1.04	4.21
240	2.44	1.50	− 1.23	3.89	− 3.06	− 2.01	− 7.22	− 6.45
261	8.92	− 2.06	2.99	− 11.66	9.82	− 8.56	− 12.83	− 7.81
262	4.11	3.05	6.57	8.26	5.40	− 1.63	− 10.66	− 8.87
263	6.72	0.42	0.75	7.17	2.33	1.49	− 4.07	− 5.28
271	8.19	8.48	6.68	7.26	2.84	0.58	− 0.07	5.14
272	10.30	6.76	8.50	12.18	2.17	5.52	− 0.13	5.99
273	6.95	6.75	5.44	7.11	1.06	3.75	− 2.49	9.62
274	4.03	1.39	2.27	3.90	− 0.62	4.83	− 4.93	− 1.07
275	4.00	1.94	1.06	2.46	5.22	9.09	− 3.34	2.52
276	15.52	12.27	13.38	5.20	3.29	− 3.25	− 8.55	14.35
277	− 1.53	6.50	2.62	8.29	− 1.13	− 2.29	− 7.28	4.63
278	8.70	3.87	11.47	0.46	3.86	− 0.35	− 3.93	0.30
279/1	4.18	5.29	6.71	4.71	− 3.88	− 0.32	3.06	9.97
279/2	1.53	9.74	11.37	4.18	3.78	2.61	− 10.40	0.95
279/3	− 4.03	2.76	1.07	3.46	11.88	− 2.61	− 2.80	1.52
279/4	10.97	1.77	5.39	16.65	3.89	7.17	2.63	13.77
279/5	3.73	5.90	5.73	7.25	− 3.92	1.95	− 5.31	4.73
279/6	− 0.63	2.40	5.63	5.45	− 3.71	3.36	− 0.79	3.82
279/7	5.65	4.35	4.03	9.47	2.08	− 1.10	− 4.76	6.27
311	1.71	− 0.22	2.79	0.76	− 7.23	− 8.32	− 7.69	3.08
312	5.78	0.74	3.07	− 2.71	− 7.36	− 7.46	− 4.64	− 0.15
313	− 1.99	1.63	− 0.39	− 2.59	− 3.94	− 4.38	− 16.68	− 4.97
321	− 1.96	6.12	6.59	5.17	2.97	3.35	− 13.89	0.94
322	− 7.55	5.97	9.60	0.56	− 19.41	3.62	− 2.77	− 4.39
323	− 1.39	3.25	10.48	0.17	− 3.53	3.68	− 10.07	0.10
331	− 5.52	4.30	3.67	4.59	− 3.78	− 0.84	− 12.46	− 2.72
332	3.17	6.66	2.58	− 1.79	− 5.04	− 0.04	− 10.95	− 0.30
333	4.24	2.61	7.25	2.14	3.92	2.11	− 6.74	0.61
334	3.79	− 5.83	3.43	− 2.56	4.75	3.43	2.15	− 6.89
335	− 6.09	7.44	3.89	− 1.14	− 18.59	− 9.52	− 15.41	3.62
336	− 0.01	14.73	6.32	4.26	3.88	− 6.70	− 8.28	− 1.25
337	1.81	7.06	8.21	3.01	2.87	− 0.08	− 8.71	2.71
338	6.96	3.31	8.01	− 0.73	− 6.31	− 5.21	− 3.57	8.71

339/1	6.91	4.84	4.14	3.94	8.70	10.97	− 9.81	− 6.87
339/2	1.67	6.27	10.10	2.39	0.65	7.74	− 11.38	4.64
339/3/4	6.76	1.24	8.87	4.49	− 1.09	4.02	− 6.28	0.60
339/5/9	NA	NA	4.37	0.59	− 1.15	0.34	− 7.76	− 1.10
341	6.02	0.54	8.85	2.57	− 3.73	3.32	− 4.15	− 3.38
342	− 18.28	− 2.83	− 0.16	1.51	9.18	10.82	− 4.74	− 0.82
349	3.67	0.94	5.21	2.51	− 0.30	0.26	− 7.91	1.77
351	− 3.41	12.84	26.63	6.05	− 4.77	5.23	3.75	− 12.76
352	− 4.01	4.72	6.81	8.21	2.63	− 3.87	− 0.56	− 20.66
353	− 0.35	8.19	6.36	4.93	3.03	2.33	− 0.74	0.82
354	2.06	14.79	8.82	0.86	3.35	6.70	0.97	5.33
361	3.48	3.92	0.97	0.63	6.65	− 2.82	− 1.04	− 0.82
362	− 2.64	6.55	7.16	1.67	− 5.55	− 0.83	− 9.80	1.63
363	0.96	7.72	5.83	6.47	− 1.76	− 3.65	10.55	1.53
364	NA	NA	13.63	8.62	− 4.26	2.97	− 0.39	6.46
365	NA	NA	0.32	21.98	− 7.83	0.49	− 1.79	6.10
366	NA	NA	19.11	15.66	2.76	9.61	− 3.32	16.92
367	NA	NA	4.94	5.79	7.95	7.32	7.92	4.37
368	7.60	15.59	5.35	5.40	− 0.61	− 0.60	− 3.03	6.78
369	2.08	5.15	5.90	2.26	− 2.59	0.77	− 7.79	3.07
370	− 1.88	− 3.91	0.84	2.52	− 5.09	0.92	0.19	− 9.21
380	NA	NA	4.57	3.80	3.94	− 13.93	− 14.09	− 3.63
381	3.98	7.67	3.36	3.63	− 1.93	2.78	− 8.46	3.98
382	− 6.84	− 9.17	0.39	− 0.37	− 8.78	− 6.01	− 13.02	− 12.06
383	3.08	0.15	6.03	4.43	− 4.87	1.24	8.56	6.46
384/385	− 0.94	− 10.95	− 4.27	0.04	− 2.66	6.88	− 0.62	− 9.22
390	0.03	6.80	6.88	4.53	− 5.30	1.29	− 6.25	− 1.34
391	0.91	1.00	− 0.56	1.10	0.32	− 0.66	− 13.04	− 0.23
392	− 3.86	11.67	3.40	− 2.06	− 1.42	− 0.05	− 11.95	− 4.67
393	2.41	1.59	3.29	2.05	− 9.21	− 6.90	− 14.26	3.21
394	2.28	2.97	1.99	3.32	− 1.06	− 0.89	− 8.79	− 5.09
395	0.12	5.07	4.68	2.46	1.99	0.25	− 5.14	0.44
396	− 0.81	18.45	− 13.00	− 5.65	5.30	5.00	− 32.29	0.36
399/1	− 4.32	8.44	5.01	5.02	− 8.75	4.92	− 4.03	5.32
399/2/12	0.23	3.34	5.26	2.26	1.28	− 0.87	− 3.41	0.90
411	1.97	12.22	12.51	6.83	− 3.11	− 3.74	− 17.64	3.29
412	− 6.47	− 1.19	1.53	− 3.74	− 2.99	− 4.19	− 12.90	1.33
413	− 4.40	− 3.07	− 2.99	− 3.34	− 1.06	− 0.46	− 13.44	3.19
414	2.11	− 0.07	0.20	− 3.13	− 1.52	− 3.89	− 9.46	2.74
415	− 0.43	− 0.24	− 3.28	1.00	− 6.74	− 4.68	1.11	− 0.09
416	− 0.23	0.77	− 2.18	− 1.23	− 10.24	0.38	− 7.07	0.39
417	0.77	6.59	10.27	2.14	1.69	− 1.70	− 5.23	1.30
418	1.09	− 0.33	− 4.43	1.49	− 18.88	− 1.07	− 7.26	1.52
419	2.30	6.54	8.55	4.52	− 2.12	− 5.64	− 13.00	4.05
421	− 0.48	3.64	3.13	1.02	− 8.52	1.17	− 6.89	− 0.67
422/1	5.13	4.13	3.65	5.17	0.52	2.69	− 6.49	1.72
422/2	1.92	0.18	− 1.60	− 2.28	− 1.97	4.31	− 1.01	− 3.79
423	0.21	− 0.54	2.11	2.55	4.25	− 3.11	− 10.53	2.59
429	6.42	− 1.20	5.56	5.98	− 2.03	− 0.94	− 13.45	6.10
431	− 2.31	1.00	− 0.97	− 0.76	7.21	− 6.83	− 6.72	1.36
432	0.22	3.53	2.11	3.79	0.73	− 1.42	− 6.94	3.83
433	− 0.39	6.56	− 2.63	− 4.27	5.40	0.59	− 14.94	− 19.97
441	− 2.47	3.28	− 1.70	2.53	5.49	3.41	− 9.31	7.72
442	− 1.19	1.03	1.61	3.25	− 7.20	− 2.25	− 10.98	3.93
443	− 1.28	2.71	0.55	4.01	2.06	11.10	− 12.08	− 1.82
444	1.81	2.43	1.55	7.32	− 1.07	7.87	− 2.01	6.73
445	3.66	1.63	5.02	6.83	3.61	5.63	− 2.68	4.86
446	− 7.91	− 2.12	− 5.01	− 3.01	− 0.74	1.70	− 8.87	0.46

449/1	5.09	3.53	4.16	2.58	− 3.88	7.07	− 8.94	1.47
449/2	− 6.83	4.00	− 0.04	2.79	− 0.37	2.89	− 11.13	1.16
450	0.13	3.17	1.64	1.60	− 1.09	0.69	− 10.00	3.22
461	1.02	1.76	2.85	3.05	− 7.53	− 3.84	− 9.29	1.44
462	− 1.74	2.54	0.90	4.00	5.03	1.93	− 10.85	3.80
463	5.17	3.36	5.50	5.87	− 3.21	− 0.11	− 7.22	5.02
464	− 0.37	4.41	2.45	5.37	− 5.42	0.33	− 9.75	1.38
469/1	4.04	3.31	2.25	5.57	0.90	1.09	− 14.16	− 2.63
469/2	4.04	6.50	8.12	3.13	− 4.15	− 0.75	− 2.80	0.72
471	1.98	4.34	7.33	6.25	− 1.60	− 3.35	1.52	− 2.30
472	0.79	3.13	3.17	7.02	− 1.58	3.20	− 5.44	2.76
473	1.06	4.98	8.80	3.64	− 2.75	− 1.85	− 3.71	3.28
474	7.36	9.11	5.60	5.04	− 3.46	1.05	− 1.53	6.79
475	− 2.51	0.88	0.23	8.09	− 8.30	− 1.79	− 5.99	− 2.37
479	4.07	1.38	3.58	4.21	− 0.33	6.86	− 8.73	0.23
481	2.03	4.24	1.20	1.15	− 3.46	0.26	− 10.61	4.63
482/1	3.96	6.97	6.70	3.07	− 3.28	1.26	− 6.55	2.68
482/2	4.21	8.72	6.70	8.34	− 5.47	− 0.66	− 6.84	− 1.79
483	5.64	4.56	6.94	6.87	− 7.31	5.19	− 7.62	4.11
484	8.29	1.87	5.49	5.09	− 6.38	6.02	− 7.05	1.14
485/486	6.00	5.61	4.22	3.11	− 7.20	3.47	− 6.93	3.54
489	2.03	4.32	2.56	1.64	2.21	5.55	1.72	4.93
491	1.00	5.78	5.67	1.97	2.51	− 4.12	− 10.10	1.70
492	− 1.87	5.74	− 2.50	6.52	− 1.32	− 12.35	− 10.47	3.88
493	1.91	− 0.93	− 0.12	2.14	− 4.08	− 2.99	− 7.30	− 1.31
494/1/2	NA	NA	NA	NA	3.46	− 1.55	− 13.05	− 5.80
494/3	NA	NA	NA	NA	− 0.02	3.67	− 3.48	− 3.24
495	3.61	3.58	7.42	3.81	− 3.35	5.90	− 8.43	8.38
496	11.32	17.42	15.09	10.56	3.05	4.78	− 3.82	8.13
499	3.83	0.55	9.01	6.89	− 0.82	2.30	− 7.48	16.06
601	0.49	2.31	8.43	18.05	8.74	2.97	2.22	2.57
602	7.34	8.82	5.36	4.87	− 0.42	3.05	− 3.38	2.10
603	1.83	4.68	2.38	3.15	− 0.88	3.40	0.26	0.98

Table H.2. *Growth rates of intermediate input, selected periods, 1954–86, %, p.a.*

MLH	1954–8	1958–63	1963–8	1968–73	1973–6	1976–9	1979–82	1982–6
101	NA	NA	NA	NA	NA	NA	NA	NA
102/103	3.72	3.11	8.50	7.91	2.09	5.01	− 0.44	− 1.13
104	NA	NA	NA	NA	NA	NA	NA	NA
109	NA	NA	NA	NA	19.34	12.48	− 8.09	4.17
211	2.83	− 2.20	0.49	− 3.63	8.85	6.09	− 3.89	1.92
212	8.58	2.17	0.12	1.12	4.03	− 0.75	− 0.35	5.91
213	3.78	0.44	2.52	− 0.03	10.27	3.48	− 4.93	− 1.71
214	5.91	2.12	7.06	8.60	− 13.32	4.39	3.60	− 0.81
215	8.83	− 2.35	20.87	− 6.81	4.19	7.40	− 2.48	− 2.36
216	0.92	3.38	− 10.74	9.21	9.29	− 5.43	− 6.83	− 5.08
217	− 1.72	− 2.67	2.51	3.82	1.70	7.94	− 1.98	2.84
218	7.42	4.27	3.03	2.68	0.93	1.54	0.62	2.56
219	8.02	6.98	2.47	3.06	6.01	4.34	0.09	− 4.36
221	7.20	− 4.18	− 0.98	8.29	8.45	0.50	3.44	4.59
229/1	− 1.74	− 2.55	− 5.03	4.48	7.62	− 1.61	8.47	3.76
229/2	3.53	2.38	18.79	− 0.70	7.16	− 0.33	3.29	6.34
231	14.24	3.32	6.60	− 3.89	− 8.34	5.71	− 5.90	1.65
232	NA	NA	NA	NA	NA	NA	NA	NA
239/1	7.98	6.74	10.88	− 0.45	− 7.56	5.39	− 8.29	5.68
239/2	NA	NA	NA	NA	NA	NA	NA	NA
240	11.04	2.84	2.17	− 0.16	− 4.00	7.82	− 10.06	0.59
261	NA	NA	NA	NA	NA	NA	NA	NA
262	NA	NA	NA	NA	NA	NA	NA	NA
263	NA	NA	NA	NA	NA	NA	NA	NA
271	6.23	5.62	7.52	7.13	11.62	2.77	0.05	5.48
272	8.84	3.37	6.49	12.00	2.50	5.06	3.09	5.38
273	9.37	6.60	8.83	9.01	7.35	8.91	1.94	8.39
274	5.05	1.65	1.31	3.58	3.88	5.09	− 0.29	0.36
275	4.14	0.24	1.66	3.73	9.98	6.98	− 0.92	4.44
276	13.09	7.84	11.08	2.66	14.44	− 1.27	− 9.14	16.57
277	− 2.57	5.06	3.10	9.97	− 1.05	6.10	− 6.99	2.09
278	8.35	3.00	10.94	− 1.53	6.61	− 0.42	− 1.60	2.67
279/1	1.67	5.36	5.76	4.02	5.01	1.30	3.69	11.24
279/2	3.04	7.49	11.83	3.28	7.81	5.68	− 7.70	5.55
279/3	− 7.39	4.55	0.21	9.33	11.52	− 1.81	− 2.88	0.70
279/4	8.54	4.88	6.79	16.98	3.86	9.91	0.90	14.83
279/5	4.80	5.30	5.23	6.37	1.92	2.43	− 4.22	4.49
279/6	− 3.21	− 0.30	5.07	5.89	− 6.68	9.82	3.69	3.29
279/7	4.56	7.94	9.03	6.39	2.00	3.13	0.15	2.62
311	4.85	− 1.64	1.97	2.95	− 0.78	− 3.44	− 8.87	− 2.56
312	7.98	0.73	2.35	1.33	− 2.35	− 2.28	− 2.78	− 0.22
313	1.40	0.60	− 0.37	0.70	2.55	− 4.82	− 12.39	− 4.66
321	− 0.85	4.18	7.87	5.40	7.65	7.86	− 19.67	− 0.75
322	− 7.55	5.47	10.95	− 1.67	− 5.95	6.59	− 0.02	− 5.36
323	0.36	2.37	11.47	0.13	4.33	7.16	− 6.23	− 7.18
331	− 5.43	2.75	4.51	5.78	− 2.62	2.66	− 14.37	− 1.82
332	8.55	4.57	3.53	0.48	− 0.58	2.51	− 8.02	2.45
333	6.67	1.39	11.85	4.44	4.47	2.70	− 4.64	3.03
334	7.32	− 7.62	3.23	− 1.25	6.15	4.35	5.08	− 8.47
335	− 3.08	9.38	5.83	0.28	− 9.41	− 9.26	− 14.27	2.76
336	3.03	13.86	7.34	5.57	4.83	− 5.56	− 10.72	0.20
337	3.85	5.24	8.50	3.54	7.32	3.15	− 9.38	1.18

338	11.53	4.51	9.14	0.97	− 5.74	− 10.46	− 0.18	8.66
339/1	9.99	2.85	5.44	4.78	7.84	9.98	− 12.21	− 5.55
339/2	2.33	5.99	14.43	4.83	− 0.98	10.53	− 2.63	3.89
339/3/4	4.52	0.53	8.49	4.48	− 1.32	6.64	− 1.70	2.73
339/5/9	NA	NA	4.43	1.66	2.39	2.82	− 3.17	− 0.25
341	8.64	− 0.93	9.64	2.39	− 4.78	0.76	− 0.66	− 2.96
342	− 19.39	− 4.58	1.66	7.93	11.59	10.33	− 4.34	− 0.03
349	8.07	− 1.30	5.15	2.27	0.38	0.20	− 5.23	3.98
351	1.67	18.53	27.80	5.05	− 3.77	8.89	− 0.95	− 15.69
352	0.44	1.39	8.53	6.32	10.11	− 3.16	14.45	− 28.52
353	2.58	10.45	8.63	4.86	5.17	8.23	1.01	2.38
354	5.19	15.23	8.88	1.33	3.09	8.60	2.90	8.18
361	4.86	5.60	0.19	2.29	6.86	− 3.08	− 3.03	− 0.99
362	− 1.75	5.45	9.47	2.40	− 5.12	− 0.67	− 7.97	2.50
363	3.88	6.87	7.36	5.27	5.53	− 8.43	11.33	6.55
364	NA	NA	17.82	9.75	− 1.61	2.83	0.93	9.90
365	NA	NA	− 0.61	21.89	− 16.67	− 1.44	− 7.20	0.64
366	NA	NA	NA	NA	NA	NA	NA	NA
367	NA	NA	6.91	4.04	10.04	9.57	8.23	6.54
368	4.99	13.52	5.06	4.66	− 0.15	1.99	− 4.13	6.59
369	4.58	3.97	5.56	3.63	2.65	4.83	− 6.14	6.89
370	− 1.03	− 6.57	0.59	3.86	2.56	0.49	− 0.50	− 6.06
380	NA	NA	2.90	6.83	8.51	− 11.46	− 12.61	− 0.51
381	8.10	5.04	2.53	5.84	0.36	5.66	− 6.33	4.93
382	− 2.98	− 12.93	0.31	− 2.45	− 4.21	− 2.86	− 9.86	− 5.09
383	7.61	− 4.14	5.80	7.98	12.19	6.88	8.58	6.39
384/385	2.85	− 14.61	− 4.00	− 2.49	2.30	7.54	− 2.77	− 3.91
390	2.34	6.69	6.19	3.54	− 2.93	10.76	− 2.61	− 0.64
391	2.60	2.15	1.03	2.85	5.97	2.14	− 5.88	1.04
392	− 1.99	13.28	5.01	1.60	2.92	5.05	− 6.94	− 1.18
393	5.29	− 0.68	3.72	2.40	0.01	− 5.74	− 11.17	3.90
394	3.78	1.30	1.48	1.95	− 0.58	1.32	− 7.83	− 5.56
395	0.66	5.33	4.00	− 11.81	8.86	1.60	− 4.12	2.11
396	2.58	20.09	− 15.87	− 5.77	12.73	NA	NA	NA
399/1	− 1.75	5.44	6.51	6.51	− 11.01	7.00	− 3.97	7.45
399/2/12	3.07	1.45	4.96	5.11	− 0.38	1.87	− 1.47	2.31
411	4.95	9.94	9.77	3.21	0.63	− 4.53	− 16.37	− 0.10
412	− 8.93	− 3.06	3.98	− 4.10	3.38	− 3.36	− 13.83	1.86
413	− 6.06	− 3.72	− 0.22	− 1.47	0.61	− 0.44	− 11.72	2.85
414	− 4.89	0.87	− 2.22	5.80	− 10.87	− 1.61	− 10.48	− 0.28
415	− 0.79	− 0.75	2.86	3.39	− 7.74	− 3.83	− 4.96	− 0.47
416	− 2.00	5.08	− 5.14	1.26	− 1.53	0.29	− 6.29	2.66
417	− 0.26	5.70	9.75	− 0.78	− 1.58	2.67	− 5.83	1.03
418	0.57	− 1.06	− 3.13	− 2.72	− 9.81	9.18	− 9.26	2.49
419	4.52	7.18	11.62	3.81	− 2.72	− 1.32	− 11.36	4.93
421	0.89	4.13	4.52	2.91	− 5.53	2.77	− 4.16	1.12
422/1	3.08	5.28	5.69	2.45	8.04	5.32	− 5.39	0.18
422/2	− 2.20	2.81	− 2.15	1.10	− 2.36	9.07	− 1.99	− 3.94
423	− 1.04	− 2.20	1.87	8.31	2.01	− 3.28	− 14.33	3.74
429	8.65	3.41	7.24	5.19	− 2.82	4.48	− 9.27	7.50
431	− 6.69	2.70	1.26	5.60	− 10.28	− 11.12	− 0.61	6.85
432	1.01	5.68	2.62	4.95	0.82	− 0.15	− 5.11	0.02
433	3.31	8.10	− 0.84	− 8.07	6.49	− 5.06	− 9.84	− 21.78
441	− 3.13	2.59	− 2.98	− 0.20	6.25	5.86	− 8.33	7.96
442	1.40	− 0.79	1.32	2.00	− 5.83	0.02	− 12.33	2.82
443	0.62	1.55	1.72	0.02	3.66	13.51	− 13.17	− 3.03
444	3.37	1.74	1.75	6.30	− 1.25	8.80	− 0.88	4.86
445	6.36	0.13	5.75	3.83	1.97	5.21	− 0.61	3.31

446	− 0.94	− 2.73	− 3.45	− 2.85	− 0.59	6.18	− 6.67	− 2.83
449/1	7.10	2.74	4.73	− 0.36	− 0.89	9.81	− 4.68	2.24
449/2	− 4.88	3.47	2.07	2.47	4.97	2.32	− 11.53	0.04
450	− 0.99	2.42	1.08	2.01	− 5.80	2.06	− 7.89	1.69
461	0.49	0.77	3.79	1.54	4.83	4.88	− 7.77	1.41
462	0.03	5.20	3.99	3.40	6.88	6.49	− 9.03	4.57
463	6.94	3.43	5.74	5.27	− 0.52	1.57	− 7.57	0.26
464	0.54	1.42	2.77	7.34	1.27	3.90	− 5.92	0.78
469/1	2.07	4.50	1.71	10.96	2.31	1.62	− 9.01	0.48
469/2	0.90	5.46	9.07	2.71	0.49	3.17	− 2.20	1.24
471	0.95	5.43	10.57	10.28	− 1.57	− 0.36	2.28	− 2.85
472	1.15	2.23	4.37	7.04	0.64	4.42	− 3.94	3.00
473	0.57	3.95	9.96	4.00	1.85	2.32	− 2.26	1.81
474	9.74	7.08	9.12	8.82	− 1.72	1.15	0.58	10.26
475	− 2.45	0.13	1.12	9.19	− 3.37	− 1.16	− 8.64	− 2.81
479	2.53	1.32	4.90	9.39	6.53	9.58	− 6.90	0.71
481	3.33	2.13	2.27	2.64	0.97	3.17	− 10.86	2.72
482/1	4.57	7.19	7.40	3.03	0.08	2.64	− 2.69	2.58
482/2	4.97	7.62	6.88	7.29	− 1.94	1.97	− 7.59	− 2.99
483	6.63	4.32	7.16	5.34	− 3.41	10.14	− 0.01	5.33
484	11.08	2.11	8.60	1.87	− 1.76	8.98	− 0.31	2.62
485/486	6.40	2.98	2.36	3.55	− 1.14	7.28	2.86	6.97
489	6.41	4.56	4.49	− 0.25	2.58	11.60	2.72	4.30
491	4.96	4.02	4.35	3.16	3.11	2.95	− 8.99	2.50
492	− 0.42	5.63	0.28	3.73	0.12	− 9.75	− 7.17	3.47
493	0.45	4.69	− 0.66	1.43	− 2.98	1.44	− 4.32	− 0.54
494/1/2	NA	NA	NA	NA	1.54	4.91	− 8.53	− 3.82
494/3	NA	NA	NA	NA	− 1.30	10.41	1.67	− 1.35
495	4.00	4.27	8.28	5.06	− 2.19	6.66	− 5.80	5.34
496	13.82	17.88	13.79	10.84	2.34	8.18	− 2.26	8.87
499	0.70	− 4.44	7.13	5.95	− 0.33	7.95	− 5.48	15.76
601	NA	NA	NA	NA	NA	NA	NA	NA
602	NA	NA	NA	NA	NA	NA	NA	NA
603	NA	NA	NA	NA	NA	NA	NA	NA

Notes: Growth rates are Törnqvist indices of total intermediate input. Components are (1) purchases of materials, stores & fuel, and of industrial services; and (2) non-industrial services.

Table H.3. *Growth rates of capital input, selected periods, 1954–86, %, p.a.*

MLH	1954–8	1958–63	1963–8	1968–73	1973–6	1976–9	1979–82	1982–6
101	NA	NA	NA	NA	NA	NA	NA	NA
102/103	2.82	6.29	8.40	5.03	1.21	2.94	− 1.73	− 0.38
104	NA	NA	NA	NA	NA	NA	NA	NA
109	NA	NA	NA	NA	3.82	1.87	− 4.31	− 3.17
211	3.57	3.29	1.78	1.48	0.19	2.15	− 0.78	0.80
212	1.22	2.84	2.30	0.78	− 0.07	− 1.05	− 1.66	0.87
213	8.13	3.08	4.46	1.91	2.04	1.08	− 2.43	0.00
214	6.63	6.37	6.95	8.11	4.53	7.11	2.84	4.20
215	5.43	3.29	4.82	4.02	4.03	3.45	1.75	2.25
216	5.17	3.46	− 1.90	3.90	− 0.08	5.49	0.31	0.75
217	1.67	3.04	2.19	1.60	1.46	5.15	1.61	2.18
218	7.56	7.61	4.36	2.81	2.27	2.29	1.22	2.48
219	5.25	7.89	4.07	3.66	0.60	4.25	0.89	1.30
221	2.91	1.46	2.19	4.53	4.76	1.55	− 2.38	1.26
229/1	6.06	− 0.83	1.12	3.73	3.21	− 0.30	− 0.11	0.13
229/2	5.27	5.99	9.50	2.61	1.73	2.41	2.11	4.49
231	3.20	8.41	6.83	6.21	3.34	2.84	− 0.47	− 0.25
232	2.70	4.93	4.24	1.72	4.97	2.97	1.41	0.52
239/1	4.06	8.52	7.32	4.07	1.12	3.66	0.48	− 4.98
239/2	4.82	3.79	5.82	2.62	2.88	5.30	3.13	2.64
240	11.54	1.71	2.72	3.40	1.26	1.07	− 0.67	− 1.74
261	14.14	0.27	− 0.88	0.01	− 1.23	− 1.98	− 3.00	− 3.46
262	5.81	− 0.59	6.73	6.41	− 0.78	0.41	3.48	− 1.83
263	7.23	0.51	5.30	0.76	0.89	2.03	− 1.47	2.53
271	7.98	5.26	6.00	3.70	2.71	3.96	1.76	2.58
272	6.48	6.25	5.83	9.60	5.25	5.21	4.37	4.65
273	8.79	6.31	8.70	8.20	3.20	6.62	2.39	4.25
274	4.71	2.21	0.80	1.22	2.41	3.38	0.35	1.18
275	2.29	3.64	2.19	2.94	− 0.57	2.56	0.62	2.95
276	7.20	7.58	8.62	4.25	1.61	2.54	− 1.67	− 0.97
277	2.16	4.45	6.39	5.55	2.20	4.53	− 2.85	− 1.07
278	9.68	8.53	5.03	2.79	4.24	4.63	− 0.86	1.20
279/1	5.42	7.16	4.53	4.27	2.32	2.24	2.99	4.07
279/2	3.91	4.30	5.04	6.32	4.20	3.61	2.16	1.49
279/3	4.93	1.78	1.87	3.84	0.86	2.97	2.37	2.79
279/4	6.72	3.19	9.17	7.24	7.79	4.36	5.44	10.45
279/5	4.36	7.08	8.75	6.23	2.14	3.15	− 0.58	1.17
279/6	4.41	8.89	7.68	2.08	2.33	1.96	2.68	3.04
279/7	9.41	7.23	5.91	5.06	1.13	1.78	− 1.55	− 1.29
311	7.31	6.92	− 0.71	3.07	6.25	0.60	− 3.83	− 2.47
312	6.03	4.68	2.69	1.65	0.62	0.91	− 3.53	− 1.63
313	3.16	4.72	0.69	1.33	0.03	1.20	− 2.51	− 2.76
321	5.44	6.04	7.19	10.11	0.66	− 0.62	− 2.81	− 2.43
322	1.60	2.89	4.21	2.28	− 2.22	− 0.34	− 3.57	− 2.49
323	2.20	3.13	3.06	3.28	0.96	1.52	− 1.05	− 2.30
331	− 0.79	1.17	0.95	0.45	1.54	2.28	− 4.28	− 1.51
332	5.00	2.68	4.28	− 0.31	− 0.50	3.20	− 2.06	− 1.76
333	4.86	2.84	6.58	1.75	5.12	4.94	− 0.73	0.62
334	5.07	− 1.85	− 1.37	1.19	3.83	6.19	0.79	− 1.63
335	− 0.66	2.96	2.65	1.68	− 1.86	− 1.51	− 6.06	− 2.92
336	10.01	6.36	7.02	1.64	5.47	4.02	− 1.00	− 1.97
337	5.64	3.95	7.81	− 0.74	4.34	5.37	− 0.67	1.45
338	6.36	3.46	6.21	4.20	0.62	− 2.02	− 2.85	0.07

339/1	6.67	4.24	3.87	1.56	4.75	6.93	− 1.63	− 1.21
339/2	4.24	6.07	6.78	− 0.79	0.20	4.51	2.24	1.48
339/3/4	4.33	2.95	6.97	4.51	1.81	4.30	0.02	1.68
339/5/9	NA	NA	4.17	1.66	1.65	2.28	− 1.70	− 0.71
341	6.01	0.65	15.87	0.93	3.27	2.65	1.51	1.86
342	− 6.56	− 1.99	0.61	3.87	2.99	0.87	1.93	1.04
349	5.19	2.64	3.49	3.06	1.68	2.94	− 1.33	− 0.18
351	− 0.27	6.84	22.08	11.65	8.78	1.96	− 1.72	− 2.64
352	0.50	2.30	4.91	9.56	0.29	− 0.35	− 3.05	− 3.90
353	1.92	7.20	8.38	7.26	4.86	5.81	1.89	4.06
354	3.56	11.17	9.61	3.38	1.96	6.50	1.22	5.94
361	3.76	3.01	2.01	− 0.28	3.53	2.13	− 0.96	− 0.77
362	2.94	5.19	2.64	2.56	1.11	1.24	− 1.30	0.28
363	6.34	7.40	3.74	2.42	1.71	1.81	4.03	3.17
364	NA	NA	11.77	10.05	4.84	5.66	3.22	6.98
365	NA	NA	− 7.03	15.67	3.81	4.13	0.13	5.05
366	NA	NA	15.47	7.21	0.08	10.14	4.13	11.68
367	NA	NA	5.81	1.88	5.14	7.11	3.75	5.83
368	6.21	8.69	6.45	2.41	2.61	3.35	− 1.21	2.36
369	4.92	4.69	6.30	3.99	1.80	3.08	− 1.14	0.41
370	2.28	− 0.73	3.76	5.99	4.02	1.65	0.68	1.13
380	NA	NA	4.27	6.73	8.46	3.36	− 1.82	− 0.66
381	1.67	3.47	3.24	1.58	0.86	5.52	3.63	1.00
382	− 2.71	− 2.23	− 2.83	− 2.01	− 3.23	− 1.48	− 4.98	− 2.77
383	2.80	1.28	1.32	− 0.08	2.06	3.58	4.75	2.45
384/385	0.35	− 4.77	− 0.00	− 4.71	1.26	1.01	0.33	− 3.55
390	4.18	4.98	4.81	3.01	1.48	3.96	− 0.90	− 0.52
391	0.69	1.75	1.54	2.56	1.73	1.04	− 3.11	− 1.23
392	− 0.34	11.23	4.51	0.45	− 0.01	0.48	− 2.83	− 0.61
393	4.38	3.21	1.19	1.59	1.07	− 0.38	− 4.04	− 1.19
394	3.18	4.75	2.99	2.47	2.62	2.37	− 3.23	− 1.66
395	3.92	6.07	5.66	2.26	3.94	1.85	− 2.06	− 1.71
396	− 3.55	4.13	8.87	2.55	5.27	− 2.30	7.32	− 10.92
399/1	− 0.77	5.64	3.70	3.29	2.57	3.57	− 0.84	2.95
399/2/12	2.99	3.62	4.00	3.99	2.42	3.31	− 1.25	0.64
411	4.00	2.65	5.09	3.92	0.68	− 1.88	− 3.66	− 2.87
412	− 1.31	0.62	3.08	0.40	− 0.82	− 3.43	− 5.17	− 3.57
413	− 0.05	− 0.36	0.90	0.17	3.29	− 1.78	− 4.34	− 1.55
414	0.12	2.26	1.51	0.80	0.10	− 0.39	− 3.71	− 0.89
415	3.75	− 0.60	1.53	− 0.38	0.64	1.96	− 4.11	− 1.20
416	4.07	1.16	− 0.95	2.48	0.54	− 1.50	− 4.32	− 1.43
417	1.35	2.74	5.98	3.80	0.07	− 0.26	− 2.69	− 0.63
418	1.63	− 0.14	− 0.48	0.84	− 3.25	− 0.19	− 4.15	0.82
419	3.64	6.34	6.86	5.89	1.90	− 0.28	− 4.24	− 1.04
421	1.16	2.99	4.79	2.23	0.35	1.01	− 2.39	− 0.74
422/1	5.86	7.83	7.58	5.26	1.85	5.72	− 3.17	1.46
422/2	1.15	1.65	0.95	2.05	0.43	1.05	− 5.86	− 1.03
423	1.79	1.96	3.69	2.97	0.36	− 0.10	− 3.35	− 0.79
429	5.89	1.68	4.80	4.19	1.82	1.13	− 1.40	1.26
431	− 2.71	0.43	1.13	2.16	1.95	− 0.13	− 3.61	0.17
432	− 2.50	7.08	5.09	3.68	3.21	4.11	− 2.85	4.22
433	0.58	2.40	− 2.58	3.53	− 0.32	1.24	− 3.13	− 4.47
441	− 0.38	1.03	0.11	3.76	3.24	3.71	− 2.62	1.58
442	− 0.51	0.97	3.39	3.21	0.26	0.99	− 2.79	0.97
443	− 0.50	2.57	2.33	3.67	2.00	3.29	− 1.70	3.25
444	1.46	3.75	4.21	6.64	0.81	5.56	− 1.19	4.03
445	2.90	3.47	4.54	5.37	4.34	4.36	0.22	4.64
446	− 4.06	− 1.05	− 2.54	− 0.73	1.86	− 0.34	− 5.76	0.46

449/1	2.23	2.03	3.21	1.28	0.36	2.62	− 0.72	1.61
449/2	− 2.99	− 0.11	− 1.26	− 0.54	− 2.30	2.09	− 3.94	− 1.69
450	1.62	3.79	2.93	3.43	0.53	2.47	− 0.65	3.12
461	4.39	4.32	5.02	3.16	1.99	1.76	− 1.22	1.18
462	1.90	5.13	4.85	3.65	3.74	2.16	− 0.62	0.47
463	5.39	6.05	6.29	4.81	2.62	3.08	0.34	− 0.77
464	3.85	7.42	7.62	4.00	− 0.46	1.78	− 0.17	1.84
469/1	3.60	2.69	2.17	4.56	1.22	0.73	− 0.63	− 1.27
469/2	8.68	7.58	6.54	4.05	0.92	3.47	0.71	2.29
471	2.10	4.85	6.04	7.80	2.54	2.20	− 1.93	1.46
472	1.21	3.20	3.59	7.54	1.16	4.95	− 1.31	2.26
473	− 1.15	2.10	5.66	5.39	1.67	4.08	− 4.23	2.10
474	3.84	5.75	5.89	6.40	0.99	3.65	0.34	4.94
475	− 0.38	2.17	3.57	5.11	1.76	0.61	− 5.18	− 2.63
479	3.30	1.41	3.39	5.85	1.58	4.40	− 2.03	0.43
481	9.14	3.05	3.33	0.66	0.61	1.74	− 0.21	0.27
482/1	3.78	5.35	4.59	3.90	1.78	3.90	0.11	1.68
482/2	3.19	5.95	7.10	6.72	3.78	4.18	1.17	1.85
483	4.80	7.57	8.01	7.34	3.18	3.46	0.40	3.57
484	7.21	6.37	6.39	4.19	1.49	3.49	3.16	3.23
485/486	7.00	5.13	4.08	3.60	2.05	3.08	2.60	5.55
489	1.74	4.59	3.92	2.97	2.12	4.14	1.12	3.70
491	4.64	3.17	6.81	5.02	− 1.34	− 0.33	− 1.84	− 1.20
492	0.21	4.76	1.34	3.28	− 1.16	0.82	− 4.09	− 2.38
493	0.43	2.21	2.71	2.30	− 1.54	0.43	− 2.05	− 2.34
494/1/2	NA	NA	NA	NA	5.60	4.88	− 0.32	− 1.95
494/3	NA	NA	NA	NA	3.02	1.50	− 1.50	0.14
495	0.56	3.08	6.55	4.73	1.08	2.35	− 0.51	2.43
496	5.74	14.43	13.60	10.04	4.92	5.84	1.75	5.90
499	4.11	3.38	4.33	3.70	2.02	2.90	− 2.24	5.43
601	NA	NA	NA	NA	NA	NA	NA	NA
602	NA	NA	NA	NA	NA	NA	NA	NA
603	NA	NA	NA	NA	NA	NA	NA	NA

Notes: Growth rates are Törnqvist indices of total capital input. Components of total are (a) stocks of inventories, comprising (1) Materials, stores and fuel; (2) Work in progress and finished goods, and (b) fixed capital, comprising (3) Plant & machinery; (4) Buildings & land; and (5) Vehicles.

Table H.4. *Growth rates of labour input, selected periods, 1954–86, %, p.a.*

MLH	1954–8	1958–63	1963–8	1968–73	1973–6	1976–9	1979–82	1982–6
101	− 1.64	− 5.92	− 8.59	− 7.92	2.10	− 1.12	− 3.16	− 11.89
102/103	NA	NA	− 0.55	− 1.91	− 4.71	− 2.64	− 4.72	− 8.07
104	NA	NA	NA	NA	NA	NA	NA	NA
109	NA	NA	NA	NA	11.46	0.56	− 6.86	− 4.30
211	0.69	− 3.02	− 4.49	− 3.74	− 4.78	− 3.49	− 5.87	− 2.23
212	2.63	2.15	− 1.25	0.01	− 5.04	− 2.76	− 6.03	1.22
213	− 0.45	− 4.24	0.21	− 2.40	2.47	− 4.94	− 8.34	− 5.13
214	5.62	2.69	2.98	3.68	2.14	0.13	− 1.29	− 1.12
215	6.11	− 3.83	19.18	− 1.86	− 6.83	0.90	− 4.09	− 4.82
216	1.71	− 3.97	− 0.79	− 3.28	− 2.14	− 1.55	− 9.24	− 3.98
217	1.21	− 2.29	− 2.97	− 2.60	− 2.60	− 0.72	− 5.66	− 5.62
218	0.83	1.43	− 1.89	0.55	− 6.50	0.98	− 5.92	− 2.19
219	4.36	2.32	− 2.98	− 1.76	− 0.76	− 0.55	− 6.89	− 5.89
221	0.21	− 3.77	− 2.40	0.03	− 1.66	− 2.87	− 3.80	− 1.57
229/1	− 1.21	− 4.94	− 1.22	− 1.71	2.35	− 0.16	− 5.85	− 4.20
229/2	− 0.16	− 1.39	4.57	1.85	2.75	− 3.38	− 1.61	0.15
231	3.93	1.36	− 1.95	− 2.24	− 6.18	− 3.38	− 10.36	− 4.68
232	0.75	3.86	− 2.21	− 0.94	− 6.26	− 2.69	− 4.23	− 3.17
239/1	4.35	1.97	2.81	3.98	0.88	1.70	− 7.85	− 7.40
239/2	5.82	− 3.79	0.03	2.06	0.83	− 0.23	− 3.21	− 2.64
240	0.87	− 0.98	− 0.70	− 1.82	− 1.83	− 0.78	− 6.17	− 10.01
261	0.53	− 4.84	− 1.11	− 9.22	− 2.76	− 4.43	− 13.49	− 14.28
262	4.07	− 0.29	− 4.17	0.51	− 2.17	− 0.56	− 4.89	− 11.30
263	0.57	− 4.22	− 3.56	− 0.05	− 1.65	0.51	− 5.43	− 4.69
271	3.86	0.04	− 2.28	− 0.78	0.62	1.05	− 4.55	− 2.63
272	4.68	2.09	− 1.21	1.40	1.47	0.70	− 2.87	0.28
273	3.04	6.93	2.88	− 0.71	− 2.72	2.45	− 4.25	1.73
274	1.61	− 1.83	− 4.16	− 2.57	− 1.26	− 2.14	− 2.63	− 4.55
275	0.08	− 0.87	− 6.90	− 2.89	2.97	− 1.62	− 5.36	− 3.34
276	8.63	1.89	5.25	− 5.57	3.28	− 2.58	− 16.47	− 0.24
277	− 1.47	0.28	− 1.98	− 0.70	− 4.52	− 3.36	− 12.91	− 0.24
278	3.54	1.07	0.67	− 1.30	1.76	− 7.04	− 3.56	− 7.38
279/1	− 0.37	2.91	− 0.82	− 3.23	− 5.40	− 6.05	− 4.00	1.94
279/2	− 0.36	4.35	2.07	− 3.74	− 2.43	6.66	− 8.97	0.99
279/3	− 8.63	− 6.97	− 3.26	− 6.74	8.25	− 1.17	− 8.19	− 2.75
279/4	2.31	− 3.17	− 2.10	− 8.30	5.47	9.40	− 5.99	3.06
279/5	1.16	0.67	− 0.49	0.07	− 4.05	− 0.83	− 3.71	− 1.84
279/6	− 1.10	− 5.38	0.03	0.35	− 3.13	− 0.29	− 2.29	− 0.82
279/7	4.09	4.06	− 3.87	− 2.17	− 0.96	− 4.97	− 5.02	− 1.88
311	− 0.27	− 0.55	− 1.36	− 1.27	− 3.17	− 5.39	− 23.78	− 8.72
312	2.78	1.16	0.31	− 3.63	− 3.60	− 3.94	− 15.27	− 5.21
313	− 2.01	0.35	− 2.94	− 4.66	− 2.57	− 4.32	− 16.44	− 9.80
321	0.34	1.83	0.05	− 2.66	− 0.48	− 2.27	− 12.31	− 3.39
322	− 0.62	− 1.19	− 1.02	− 0.67	− 6.16	− 3.49	− 12.93	− 7.89
323	1.19	− 0.13	− 3.98	− 6.28	− 1.21	0.25	− 3.17	− 7.28
331	− 4.71	1.04	− 0.35	0.41	− 1.15	− 2.55	− 13.77	− 4.14
332	0.96	3.34	− 0.95	− 4.34	− 1.27	− 3.09	− 14.14	− 2.89
333	4.23	− 0.79	4.99	− 0.46	0.37	− 0.68	− 9.66	− 2.91
334	2.98	− 7.11	− 2.83	− 5.62	1.98	4.99	− 7.92	− 7.34
335	− 6.70	0.84	− 1.41	− 4.30	− 7.86	− 11.02	− 22.15	− 4.66
336	3.75	6.66	− 0.31	− 0.24	− 1.63	1.78	− 12.66	− 11.27
337	1.63	4.88	1.91.	− 1.10	0.75	− 1.13	− 9.47	− 3.41
338	5.86	− 1.17	− 0.28	− 3.29	− 11.14	− 11.86	− 6.66	− 4.32

339/1	5.03	2.27	1.74	− 2.29	4.36	2.29	− 5.34	− 4.44
339/2	− 1.74	1.73	3.27	− 5.92	2.80	− 1.08	− 10.29	− 4.44
339/3/4	0.87	− 0.73	3.23	0.64	− 1.04	− 1.09	− 15.70	4.19
339/5/9	NA	NA	− 0.20	− 2.19	− 2.90	− 3.54	− 10.10	− 5.34
341	4.10	− 1.87	2.31	− 1.32	1.79	− 0.49	− 8.57	− 4.75
342	− 13.61	− 5.86	− 7.08	− 3.62	− 2.37	3.01	− 9.09	− 3.29
349	2.36	− 2.95	0.94	− 2.35	− 2.03	− 1.23	− 8.71	− 5.26
351	− 4.26	1.25	16.72	0.81	− 2.37	1.21	− 14.28	− 9.74
352	− 1.59	− 1.20	1.89	0.84	− 2.58	− 2.69	− 13.62	− 26.66
353	− 1.85	1.68	1.41	0.72	− 0.32	− 3.68	− 1.14	− 2.83
354	2.09	8.96	2.76	− 5.59	1.45	0.04	− 4.23	2.38
361	2.61	0.70	− 6.17	− 4.55	0.32	− 1.97	− 7.38	− 3.97
362	− 1.26	2.42	− 0.36	− 3.18	− 4.97	− 3.28	− 12.07	4.36
363	2.77	1.68	− 1.22	1.60	− 7.03	− 9.88	− 1.65	− 5.45
364	NA	NA	3.94	2.28	− 5.87	0.40	− 9.51	1.67
365	NA	NA	− 6.96	3.19	− 5.79	− 7.69	− 18.12	4.02
366	NA	NA	12.22	7.00	− 0.02	− 1.88	− 9.82	7.67
367	NA	NA	1.14	1.85	2.22	2.71	− 1.09	1.24
368	3.47	7.73	0.45	− 3.85	− 5.05	− 2.82	− 10.61	− 0.33
369	4.31	− 1.40	1.09	− 2.15	− 3.38	0.88	− 8.51	− 1.70
370	− 1.13	− 6.50	− 1.91	− 1.64	− 1.58	− 4.64	− 4.12	− 8.56
380	NA	NA	0.39	1.21	4.82	− 12.68	− 18.84	− 5.32
381	0.90	5.54	0.32	0.98	− 2.13	− 0.56	− 14.71	− 5.39
382	− 7.19	− 8.38	− 5.04	− 2.10	− 10.01	− 3.31	− 15.06	− 14.46
383	2.55	− 2.17	− 2.07	− 2.82	− 2.34	− 2.48	− 1.62	− 1.95
384/385	− 2.71	− 10.69	− 9.45	− 4.77	1.02	− 0.99	− 4.27	− 12.48
390	1.85	1.42	2.85	0.11	− 5.11	− 0.43	− 8.44	− 5.02
391	− 2.03	− 2.95	− 2.67	− 2.89	0.43	− 2.31	− 11.21	− 5.86
392	− 4.44	12.12	− 3.77	− 2.01	− 4.49	− 1.13	− 10.08	− 7.61
393	1.28	− 1.92	− 1.24	− 1.67	− 3.06	− 7.69	− 13.44	− 0.80
394	1.99	1.65	− 2.01	− 0.07	− 3.50	− 3.06	− 10.86	− 7.35
395	− 0.78	− 0.58	− 0.75	0.50	− 0.32	− 1.02	− 9.37	− 7.05
396	− 2.35	− 5.30	− 1.11	− 2.33	3.39	0.01	− 18.09	− 0.29
399/1	− 5.61	5.59	− 0.69	0.33	− 9.82	0.54	− 7.02	1.02
399/2/12	0.01	− 0.54	− 0.69	0.13	− 0.85	− 1.62	− 8.51	− 1.83
411	− 0.33	− 0.57	1.59	1.50	− 3.75	− 7.19	− 28.14	− 6.40
412	− 6.83	− 7.26	− 3.27	− 5.58	− 7.13	− 8.11	− 21.67	− 3.44
413	− 6.88	− 6.72	− 6.55	− 5.98	− 3.36	− 4.37	− 18.39	− 3.26
414	− 2.08	− 1.15	− 4.44	− 5.40	− 7.72	− 6.31	− 14.89	− 2.36
415	− 4.15	− 0.91	− 3.13	− 6.72	− 6.38	− 5.12	− 19.66	− 2.57
416	− 2.64	− 3.49	− 5.54	− 5.82	− 9.78	− 1.25	− 12.07	− 3.94
417	− 2.15	1.03	1.29	− 0.52	− 3.37	− 4.88	− 5.47	− 2.60
418	− 5.00	− 5.81	− 8.74	− 1.89	− 12.13	2.61	− 7.32	3.47
419	1.78	3.64	3.07	− 0.39	− 6.39	− 5.45	− 20.03	1.14
421	− 2.13	0.14	− 1.22	− 1.83	− 9.40	− 2.13	− 7.34	− 5.91
422/1	0.60	− 0.09	− 2.68	3.33	− 6.30	0.41	− 11.99	− 0.91
422/2	− 3.56	− 3.29	− 4.00	− 0.59	− 3.70	0.41	− 9.83	− 1.82
423	− 4.09	− 4.06	− 3.82	− 4.09	− 2.41	− 5.02	− 15.17	− 1.61
429	2.28	1.53	1.07	− 1.93	0.68	− 0.73	− 11.62	− 1.59
431	− 5.23	− 2.78	− 3.62	− 3.71	− 1.03	− 8.64	− 9.95	− 3.70
432	− 4.88	− 0.24	0.80	− 0.61	− 2.75	− 0.47	− 10.37	0.96
433	− 5.18	0.25	− 6.57	− 4.33	− 3.77	3.03	− 15.47	− 20.79
441	− 4.95	− 2.01	− 6.22	− 2.54	0.98	− 2.09	− 7.62	0.61
442	− 2.53	− 2.46	− 3.05	− 2.76	− 9.04	− 5.98	− 17.15	− 1.29
443	− 2.89	− 1.97	− 3.91	− 0.15	− 1.39	− 3.30	− 12.12	− 2.76
444	− 0.70	− 1.72	− 1.95	1.46	− 1.67	− 0.42	− 7.15	4.25
445	− 1.22	− 2.38	− 1.19	1.07	− 0.67	1.14	− 6.90	2.00
446	− 9.02	− 4.04	− 8.46	− 6.71	− 7.77	− 1.69	− 15.36	2.61

449/1	1.45	−0.73	−1.17	−2.04	−4.09	−0.12	−8.80	−0.82
449/2	−8.34	−1.61	−4.92	−4.89	−4.63	−1.10	−15.10	−0.06
450	−2.43	−1.23	−3.37	−2.63	−5.37	−2.55	−9.54	−0.34
461	−3.51	−1.65	−2.97	−4.51	−7.58	−3.69	−10.42	−1.51
462	−3.46	−0.94	−2.05	0.68	−0.26	0.82	−11.79	2.14
463	1.68	0.17	−0.58	−1.49	−4.47	−2.49	−11.28	−1.80
464	−0.07	1.74	−1.87	0.96	−1.39	−2.79	−7.36	−9.28
469/1	0.84	1.37	−1.82	0.18	−1.00	0.43	−9.04	−8.35
469/2	−0.88	0.62	0.13	−1.43	−5.00	−1.67	−5.84	−2.35
471	−3.90	0.99	1.73	0.62	−2.97	−4.51	−5.29	−5.08
472	0.20	−0.65	−3.80	1.23	−1.05	−0.87	−7.89	−0.62
473	−3.69	0.28	2.13	3.52	−0.83	−0.95	−6.25	3.21
474	2.30	4.26	1.58	0.04	−3.25	−1.82	−3.94	2.10
475	−6.71	−3.23	−2.42	1.51	−7.82	−3.26	−10.35	−7.52
479	−2.53	−4.86	−1.58	0.00	0.48	1.40	−9.88	−2.64
481	2.44	1.09	−3.12	−4.92	−3.36	−2.74	−13.33	−2.80
482/1	1.33	2.00	2.92	−0.44	−3.16	0.02	−8.10	−2.29
482/2	1.79	5.44	5.05	6.88	−4.15	−4.37	−8.90	−3.75
483	2.66	0.45	2.95	3.69	−3.91	−2.46	−7.31	−0.58
484	4.64	−2.24	2.52	1.09	−6.72	3.55	−7.11	−1.49
485/486	2.34	0.93	1.14	−0.15	−2.34	−2.18	−2.17	−1.91
489	1.46	1.26	−0.95	−2.21	0.10	−0.57	−7.44	0.25
491	0.04	1.98	0.70	−1.12	−2.36	−2.81	−12.38	−4.06
492	−2.71	4.60	−3.36	−1.95	−3.87	−15.08	−15.41	−1.51
493	−3.09	−3.69	−2.93	−0.98	−4.33	−3.51	−6.71	−3.42
494/1/2	NA	NA	NA	NA	2.54	−1.39	−17.34	−9.58
494/3	NA	NA	NA	NA	2.04	−1.23	−9.28	−5.17
495	3.01	−2.64	−1.59	−2.01	−1.68	−3.87	−7.43	−0.59
496	4.39	10.25	6.68	2.75	1.02	2.57	−6.74	2.30
499	1.82	−0.04	−0.80	−0.97	2.54	−1.14	−9.69	10.77
601	−2.05	−1.50	−1.14	−4.04	−3.92	0.53	−1.95	−3.87
602	1.33	2.70	−1.80	−4.51	−3.28	−1.18	−5.23	−2.20
603	0.20	1.91	−0.63	−2.08	0.95	−2.42	4.06	−3.02

Notes: Growth rates are Törnqvist indices of aggregate labour input (annual hours), constructed from five types of manual labour (full-time males, aged 21 and over; full-time females, aged eighteen and over; part-time females, aged eighteen and over; males aged under 21; females aged under eighteen) and four types of non-manual labour (males; full-time females; part-time females; working proprietors).

Table H.5. *Growth of output prices, selected periods, 1954–86, %, p.a.*

MLH	1954–8	1958–63	1963–8	1968–73	1973–6	1976–9	1979–82	1982–6
101	7.98	2.21	2.43	8.65	30.76	13.05	15.00	4.20
102/103	7.98	2.21	2.42	7.38	25.90	16.06	14.48	6.70
104	1.67	2.51	4.54	8.02	34.72	14.65	21.08	− 1.95
109	7.98	2.21	2.43	8.65	30.76	13.05	12.68	6.15
211	1.20	1.70	2.71	7.80	13.16	11.90	7.94	5.00
212	1.20	1.70	2.71	7.80	17.02	14.35	9.51	5.72
213	1.20	1.70	2.71	7.80	18.36	14.75	7.13	4.29
214	0.25	1.45	2.53	7.47	18.00	11.42	8.25	3.41
215	1.20	1.70	2.71	7.80	26.10	16.17	10.98	3.56
216	− 1.89	5.47	− 2.70	16.96	22.41	6.09	10.55	2.35
217	1.20	1.76	2.73	7.76	20.97	15.40	7.22	5.17
218	1.20	1.70	2.71	7.80	21.78	11.24	8.42	5.84
219	1.20	1.70	2.71	7.80	14.58	9.47	7.10	2.24
221	1.20	1.70	2.71	7.80	3.73	9.94	− 3.30	− 2.12
229/1	1.20	1.70	2.71	7.80	13.09	12.64	1.75	3.72
229/2	1.20	1.70	2.71	7.80	20.06	14.99	7.21	7.64
231	7.55	2.21	5.06	4.00	17.12	11.30	12.95	6.01
232	1.24	0.23	5.31	1.94	21.57	10.46	10.55	5.93
239/1	1.24	0.23	5.31	1.94	18.42	9.46	13.96	6.80
239/2	3.82	0.02	1.52	4.78	21.86	9.72	14.77	5.68
240	9.35	2.62	6.76	5.10	18.27	13.95	12.18	5.30
261	1.37	− 0.19	1.06	4.55	20.00	12.11	9.10	3.32
262	1.67	2.51	4.54	8.02	34.72	14.65	21.08	− 1.95
263	1.37	− 0.32	2.46	2.77	25.46	12.67	15.04	4.47
271	1.85	− 1.58	0.57	3.51	24.88	13.05	7.89	2.03
272	0.13	− 0.46	− 0.96	2.75	16.25	11.30	10.85	4.03
273	2.72	2.92	3.85	5.92	13.91	12.51	11.13	4.36
274	2.15	0.79	0.77	6.20	19.38	12.40	9.95	5.12
275	2.61	0.88	2.16	6.14	17.51	10.08	7.90	4.86
276	− 2.14	− 3.49	− 0.88	2.02	23.54	12.49	4.14	3.45
277	2.54	− 0.91	2.50	6.94	18.92	11.91	6.31	4.87
278	1.37	− 0.19	1.05	5.90	19.86	11.47	10.09	− 0.22
279/1	1.37	− 0.19	1.06	4.55	20.00	12.11	9.10	3.32
279/2	1.37	− 0.19	1.06	4.55	20.00	12.12	11.53	8.10
279/3	1.37	− 0.19	1.06	4.55	20.00	12.11	9.10	3.32
279/4	− 0.23	3.37	1.07	4.21	21.95	10.61	8.67	2.86
279/5	1.37	− 0.19	1.06	4.55	20.00	12.11	9.10	3.32
279/6	1.36	− 0.19	1.06	5.26	17.04	12.27	12.04	5.06
279/7	2.15	2.53	3.24	3.37	17.01	10.27	12.14	5.95
311	6.52	0.49	1.18	8.39	25.25	11.25	5.32	3.16
312	6.65	1.23	2.52	9.09	26.68	13.24	7.41	1.86
313	6.75	1.75	2.53	8.01	24.54	12.72	9.01	5.82
321	6.55	0.57	1.37	5.75	22.58	12.05	3.69	5.93
322	6.55	0.57	1.37	5.75	22.58	12.05	3.86	3.64
323	6.55	0.57	1.37	5.75	22.58	12.05	5.78	1.43
331	6.54	0.58	2.34	7.80	19.55	15.26	7.45	4.94
332	6.55	0.57	2.81	7.54	22.32	14.15	9.80	7.42
333	6.55	0.57	5.17	8.04	18.77	11.73	11.19	6.06
334	6.55	0.57	2.81	7.67	20.54	14.24	11.32	3.79
335	5.58	2.31	3.24	8.23	23.96	11.45	8.17	3.00
336	6.55	0.57	3.00	7.17	20.27	13.09	8.43	3.91
337	6.55	0.57	2.71	6.94	18.69	13.09	9.10	3.89
338	6.55	0.57	2.81	6.81	14.98	10.92	7.92	3.74

339/1	6.55	0.57	2.81	7.51	16.06	10.94	10.24	6.70
339/2	3.21	1.42	1.20	6.39	18.14	13.63	11.58	5.81
339/3/4	3.21	1.42	1.20	6.39	18.14	13.63	11.58	5.81
339/5/9	6.55	0.57	2.81	7.13	18.25	13.92	10.98	5.59
341	6.55	0.57	2.81	7.34	20.23	12.50	9.58	5.39
342	6.55	0.57	2.81	7.34	20.23	12.50	9.58	5.39
349	6.55	0.57	2.12	5.67	17.42	12.36	9.24	5.29
351	6.55	0.57	1.37	4.82	16.82	11.31	7.05	1.33
352	6.55	0.57	1.37	4.92	18.64	12.10	7.00	2.31
353	6.55	0.57	3.60	6.31	16.22	14.03	12.23	4.42
354	6.55	0.57	1.37	4.87	16.49	10.54	9.85	5.95
361	6.54	0.58	2.33	5.98	17.26	10.73	7.84	3.65
362	6.54	0.58	2.33	5.98	16.67	11.37	10.74	6.33
363	6.54	0.58	2.33	5.98	17.26	10.73	7.84	4.48
364	6.54	0.58	2.33	5.98	17.26	10.73	7.84	4.48
365	2.54	3.89	0.78	2.04	10.66	7.17	0.98	1.94
366	6.54	0.58	2.33	5.98	17.26	10.73	7.84	4.48
367	6.54	0.58	2.33	5.98	17.26	10.73	7.96	5.50
368	1.00	− 0.86	0.82	3.89	14.59	13.38	5.31	3.70
369	6.54	0.58	2.33	5.98	19.07	14.27	9.76	5.48
370	6.55	0.57	2.81	7.34	20.23	12.50	9.58	5.29
380	6.55	0.56	1.38	8.23	25.16	15.01	8.34	6.72
381	6.55	0.56	1.38	7.21	20.83	14.89	8.31	5.33
382	6.55	0.56	1.38	7.21	20.83	14.89	8.31	5.33
383	6.55	0.56	1.38	7.21	20.83	14.89	8.31	5.33
384/385	6.55	0.56	1.38	7.21	20.83	14.89	7.81	5.41
390	6.56	0.57	1.37	6.37	16.93	16.72	10.20	5.71
391	6.15	1.53	3.28	8.21	21.80	15.00	12.68	4.98
392	5.26	1.06	3.24	6.73	17.82	13.77	12.08	5.78
393	6.56	0.57	1.37	7.44	25.93	13.28	10.81	4.79
394	6.56	0.57	1.37	7.35	19.81	11.15	6.61	4.57
395	6.56	0.57	1.37	7.59	22.61	14.50	7.48	5.01
396	6.56	0.57	1.37	7.92	20.35	13.80	11.13	8.35
399/1	6.56	0.57	1.37	7.17	17.71	13.36	7.99	5.38
399/2/12	6.56	0.57	1.37	8.59	17.68	13.48	8.21	5.41
411	0.96	− 0.21	− 2.95	1.86	16.21	7.38	5.26	5.80
412	− 1.36	− 0.60	3.50	7.53	16.30	8.15	3.95	3.34
413	− 0.84	1.03	3.05	8.39	16.45	10.49	5.80	4.69
414	− 4.72	2.64	− 1.43	10.88	12.19	10.13	5.69	3.78
415	− 0.61	1.69	6.70	7.01	15.11	10.42	− 5.59	6.80
416	0.45	3.47	− 0.90	6.87	21.06	9.93	7.08	6.16
417	− 0.94	− 0.06	− 0.53	3.37	12.81	12.14	6.33	5.07
418	− 2.03	0.39	1.37	3.34	23.93	18.46	4.98	7.58
419	2.06	1.88	1.92	6.87	15.04	12.29	7.05	5.57
421	2.02	0.90	1.94	7.31	18.81	10.95	8.20	5.46
422/1	− 0.52	1.19	2.66	9.37	14.14	12.17	5.20	5.02
422/2	− 1.63	1.82	0.76	9.26	15.21	12.17	3.74	6.94
423	− 0.52	1.19	1.50	6.72	14.90	11.54	6.68	5.23
429	2.15	5.37	2.18	3.57	19.73	14.04	11.45	5.44
431	− 2.00	2.48	4.30	11.40	7.15	14.05	5.36	9.05
432	1.74	2.57	2.80	7.02	16.65	13.43	6.51	4.18
433	1.74	2.57	2.80	7.02	16.65	13.43	6.51	4.18
441	− 0.79	1.03	1.07	3.71	14.41	10.79	7.02	5.91
442	2.25	0.38	1.45	5.52	14.31	10.15	5.95	4.35
443	1.22	0.53	2.23	4.15	13.84	8.97	6.02	5.05
444	1.34	0.96	1.71	5.23	15.00	12.01	4.09	4.96
445	1.36	0.54	1.47	3.91	11.46	11.74	5.00	4.05
446	4.20	2.04	2.44	7.41	12.09	11.16	10.32	6.69

449/1	1.34	0.96	1.71	4.86	15.80	11.91	9.25	4.97
449/2	1.34	0.96	1.71	5.92	15.79	13.51	5.24	5.95
450	0.96	1.54	1.82	6.32	13.66	13.17	9.21	5.13
461	0.69	2.74	2.03	7.53	21.73	14.76	13.64	6.25
462	3.43	3.26	4.38	7.31	17.99	13.58	12.31	5.72
463	4.29	1.16	1.78	5.93	20.55	13.00	7.90	1.24
464	3.56	1.16	1.72	8.07	22.00	16.08	16.28	1.48
469/1	1.20	3.87	2.59	5.73	20.79	13.96	11.59	7.71
469/2	0.79	1.19	1.91	5.87	23.20	15.03	12.54	5.08
471	1.27	2.57	4.08	11.02	12.91	12.12	5.68	5.44
472	2.31	1.20	3.26	7.06	15.43	12.74	8.62	5.79
473	0.59	1.27	2.78	8.04	18.90	15.28	7.96	5.09
474	1.57	1.08	3.43	8.99	16.50	12.57	8.73	5.45
475	2.41	0.96	3.16	7.53	17.33	11.97	5.36	3.42
479	1.57	1.08	1.98	10.18	19.18	12.38	8.73	4.70
481	2.56	−0.16	2.43	6.27	23.83	8.89	8.53	4.91
482/1	1.83	0.50	2.67	8.03	23.23	10.78	9.77	5.43
482/2	1.83	0.50	2.66	7.52	24.59	10.69	7.56	4.00
483	2.22	1.38	2.46	8.15	21.90	12.25	13.92	6.90
484	4.52	1.85	5.20	5.82	22.87	9.99	13.14	7.35
485/486	2.33	0.34	2.46	8.41	22.20	12.34	17.38	6.80
489	6.27	2.62	3.85	7.02	17.87	10.91	8.52	4.54
491	3.93	0.34	1.24	7.01	18.91	14.34	8.84	5.47
492	3.73	2.12	4.76	4.72	15.82	11.13	9.24	5.19
493	1.85	4.50	2.07	6.65	19.72	13.08	9.24	5.17
494/1/2	2.59	1.46	2.73	7.86	18.70	13.11	7.36	6.58
494/3	2.59	1.46	2.73	7.86	18.70	13.11	8.44	6.08
495	3.93	0.57	2.32	5.80	16.28	10.23	6.37	4.32
496	0.81	0.02	−0.69	4.78	18.17	13.53	7.57	4.16
499	0.81	0.02	−0.69	4.78	18.17	13.53	8.06	5.69
601	4.45	2.00	−1.86	−8.96	8.47	14.82	18.26	4.06
602	2.34	0.73	2.81	2.05	23.89	9.69	16.31	2.04
603	3.90	2.42	5.03	8.52	26.62	6.30	16.90	4.23

Table H.6. *Growth rates of price of intermediate input, selected periods, 1954–86,* %, p.a.

MLH	1954–8	1958–63	1963–8	1968–73	1973–6	1976–9	1979–82	1982–6
101	NA	NA	NA	NA	NA	NA	NA	NA
102/103	1.83	1.72	2.81	5.21	15.54	9.37	9.45	3.72
104	NA	NA	NA	NA	NA	NA	NA	NA
109	NA	NA	NA	NA	17.70	10.80	10.03	3.33
211	− 0.01	0.79	2.18	9.98	12.39	6.95	7.44	3.62
212	1.44	1.38	2.46	7.12	16.30	11.51	7.80	3.94
213	1.43	1.46	2.50	7.00	15.75	11.24	6.70	3.63
214	− 0.16	0.71	2.13	8.74	32.22	9.41	5.48	3.11
215	− 0.19	0.70	2.10	13.25	18.51	10.26	9.23	2.06
216	0.77	0.86	1.96	7.84	10.50	9.03	7.94	2.38
217	1.59	1.15	2.37	7.13	18.33	12.18	2.49	3.91
218	1.71	1.32	2.41	8.79	17.76	9.97	6.78	3.88
219	0.66	0.93	2.14	7.98	14.64	10.16	6.17	1.97
221	1.86	0.72	1.99	7.02	15.45	11.34	− 5.09	− 1.08
229/1	1.75	1.19	2.35	9.05	18.59	10.25	− 3.82	− 0.20
229/2	1.72	1.31	2.40	8.93	18.18	10.05	4.48	4.59
231	1.79	0.97	2.24	8.42	28.64	10.28	9.04	2.41
232	1.24	0.50	5.14	2.17	20.02	10.06	9.83	5.84
239/1	1.77	1.06	2.28	8.29	27.32	11.19	8.68	2.56
239/2	3.34	0.61	1.83	4.74	18.80	8.65	11.70	5.49
240	2.73	0.77	2.70	7.24	18.41	6.94	5.79	1.93
261	1.36	0.00	1.14	4.55	19.43	11.85	8.76	3.37
262	1.67	2.51	4.53	7.99	34.56	14.60	20.97	− 1.90
263	1.36	− 0.15	2.49	2.84	24.52	12.27	14.16	4.50
271	2.65	1.11	1.64	4.27	20.11	12.22	9.34	− 0.45
272	1.98	0.39	1.80	5.69	17.16	8.77	6.03	4.67
273	2.01	0.67	1.53	4.75	13.43	9.64	5.91	4.20
274	1.22	− 0.43	1.44	6.01	18.87	10.95	6.33	3.62
275	1.53	1.34	2.37	5.63	12.98	10.09	4.01	2.56
276	2.06	− 0.54	1.35	4.55	18.75	11.08	6.77	0.39
277	2.53	− 0.44	1.19	4.59	20.67	10.00	8.40	3.29
278	2.24	− 0.18	1.37	4.55	18.59	11.25	9.56	0.84
279/1	1.40	− 0.09	1.48	5.03	17.95	10.86	8.25	3.27
279/2	1.40	− 0.08	1.48	5.06	18.37	10.22	6.83	2.62
279/3	1.41	− 0.17	1.41	5.11	22.31	11.76	8.30	4.33
279/4	1.78	− 0.55	1.39	5.11	20.65	11.26	7.58	2.95
279/5	1.41	− 0.25	1.40	5.07	19.88	10.89	7.69	4.51
279/6	1.41	− 0.13	1.46	5.05	19.68	7.62	6.81	4.38
279/7	1.41	− 0.30	1.35	5.09	20.08	9.97	7.75	4.67
311	4.18	0.99	1.97	4.94	24.08	9.81	6.50	3.72
312	4.23	0.97	1.96	4.95	23.46	10.43	6.40	3.24
313	4.01	0.79	1.73	5.05	21.25	11.49	3.60	4.57
321	4.44	0.83	1.81	5.19	21.41	10.09	7.97	5.69
322	5.01	0.79	1.89	5.44	10.67	9.44	2.18	2.66
323	5.03	0.78	1.88	5.45	16.68	7.39	4.67	4.51
331	5.45	0.92	2.10	7.39	20.56	11.29	7.75	4.17
332	5.60	0.93	2.16	5.44	20.63	11.71	8.68	4.33
333	5.33	0.94	2.04	5.94	19.56	11.82	7.69	4.83
334	5.87	0.82	2.24	7.14	20.22	12.51	8.76	5.09
335	5.26	0.90	2.16	6.32	19.00	11.50	7.84	4.54
336	5.83	0.84	2.34	7.10	20.24	12.17	8.55	4.73
337	5.86	0.84	2.35	7.06	19.44	11.60	8.24	4.55

338	5.39	0.69	2.10	6.32	17.99	11.13	7.50	4.28
339/1	5.40	0.80	2.07	7.10	21.33	11.15	7.50	4.25
339/2	5.16	0.91	2.11	7.05	18.41	11.35	6.78	4.79
339/3/4	5.28	0.87	2.10	7.01	18.91	11.31	7.13	4.37
339/5/9	NA	NA	2.11	6.99	18.91	11.19	7.87	4.49
341	5.51	0.93	2.07	7.43	19.86	9.75	6.51	3.77
342	4.94	0.87	1.84	6.50	21.36	12.03	8.25	4.33
349	4.86	0.91	1.87	6.44	20.15	11.49	7.56	4.03
351	4.34	0.78	1.86	6.45	19.39	11.22	7.60	4.53
352	4.44	0.68	1.88	6.41	16.41	11.21	6.00	3.81
353	4.43	0.67	1.85	6.41	17.72	11.60	6.82	4.42
354	4.26	0.79	1.93	6.34	17.28	10.23	6.56	4.36
361	5.20	0.80	1.99	6.98	18.58	10.96	7.24	4.37
362	4.79	0.34	1.36	5.88	15.45	11.19	3.65	3.89
363	5.04	0.59	1.92	5.96	17.75	9.95	6.76	4.44
364	NA	NA	1.65	6.13	17.60	10.71	6.27	3.97
365	NA	NA	2.02	5.41	18.86	9.35	6.86	3.87
366	NA	NA	2.35	5.96	16.84	10.45	7.45	4.50
367	NA	NA	2.17	6.45	17.85	10.02	7.44	4.77
368	4.20	0.64	1.80	5.89	17.70	10.66	6.46	4.27
369	4.48	0.61	1.74	6.00	16.05	10.92	6.10	4.05
370	5.50	0.78	2.28	6.42	19.26	11.68	8.86	4.42
380	NA	NA	1.91	6.97	21.15	12.90	9.09	4.78
381	4.95	0.92	1.86	6.60	20.89	12.07	7.58	4.39
382	5.05	0.88	1.91	7.06	20.19	11.25	6.98	4.01
383	5.29	0.84	2.15	6.59	19.18	11.88	8.93	4.70
384/385	5.17	0.81	1.85	7.17	20.52	12.28	8.89	4.41
390	5.20	1.02	1.94	7.19	19.76	10.75	6.42	3.89
391	4.89	0.87	1.73	6.58	19.76	11.21	6.89	4.35
392	4.13	1.00	1.85	6.26	16.69	10.59	5.34	4.31
393	5.66	0.82	1.75	7.30	20.02	10.99	6.91	4.09
394	5.61	0.81	1.74	7.43	21.53	10.32	4.46	3.61
395	5.46	0.86	1.70	21.57	17.57	11.63	6.82	4.00
396	4.57	0.71	1.65	6.45	14.07	16.95	4.03	2.24
399/1	4.83	0.90	1.75	6.56	21.08	10.48	6.14	3.71
399/2/12	4.91	0.86	1.73	6.59	20.16	10.83	5.93	3.80
411	1.19	− 0.75	1.21	4.69	20.73	9.84	8.02	1.88
412	0.04	1.10	− 0.30	6.55	11.90	8.07	5.34	2.41
413	0.04	1.10	− 0.30	6.56	15.75	8.90	4.46	4.43
414	1.22	0.24	− 0.75	5.03	19.92	8.08	4.61	4.24
415	0.50	− 0.10	0.26	4.95	14.99	8.74	4.67	4.25
416	0.48	0.02	0.35	4.94	14.84	9.19	4.95	3.52
417	− 0.82	0.95	− 0.38	6.02	16.54	8.35	5.34	4.30
418	0.52	0.01	0.34	4.94	16.09	8.34	4.94	4.71
419	− 1.30	1.08	− 0.22	6.86	17.73	9.09	5.37	4.33
421	0.51	− 0.04	0.31	4.94	17.09	8.81	5.67	4.66
422/1	0.06	0.27	0.98	10.39	9.54	8.65	5.58	4.29
422/2	0.50	− 0.08	0.25	4.95	15.15	9.71	4.32	5.09
423	1.99	0.09	1.89	4.42	19.82	11.25	10.79	3.27
429	0.53	0.05	0.38	4.94	19.18	9.95	7.43	3.81
431	1.24	0.22	1.77	7.12	24.95	19.21	− 3.32	3.94
432	1.24	0.35	1.84	7.00	17.23	12.97	6.25	6.11
433	1.24	0.18	1.76	7.13	23.76	17.26	1.80	2.83
441	− 1.18	1.08	0.54	6.50	13.78	10.02	4.87	6.04
442	− 1.20	1.06	0.50	6.54	14.27	10.02	5.22	6.28
443	− 1.17	1.08	0.54	6.51	14.11	10.44	4.93	6.40
444	− 1.18	1.08	0.55	6.50	13.63	9.93	3.75	6.10
445	− 1.19	1.06	0.51	6.53	13.36	9.71	4.16	5.56

446	− 1.20	1.06	0.52	6.52	13.89	8.71	4.98	5.05
449/1	− 1.11	1.14	0.61	6.44	13.41	9.66	5.06	5.17
449/2	− 1.16	1.09	0.53	6.53	14.58	12.96	5.46	7.28
450	0.97	1.04	1.95	5.30	18.87	12.73	6.19	6.31
461	2.89	1.49	2.25	9.65	12.62	9.26	11.45	3.58
462	2.94	0.92	1.60	5.58	20.17	11.91	10.12	3.85
463	2.88	0.98	1.63	5.56	21.44	12.36	11.36	3.25
464	3.89	1.35	2.19	5.62	18.50	10.25	11.78	3.74
469/1	3.55	1.07	2.12	5.68	21.17	11.88	9.20	5.15
469/2	3.37	1.18	2.17	5.58	21.30	12.49	12.14	3.64
471	2.18	0.67	1.96	6.96	14.42	10.12	5.96	5.49
472	1.48	0.99	1.93	7.13	15.16	12.48	8.09	5.12
473	1.48	0.93	1.90	7.19	15.25	11.54	6.90	5.31
474	2.19	0.65	1.96	6.97	16.08	11.68	7.12	4.66
475	2.16	0.75	2.01	6.82	12.18	11.05	5.49	5.22
479	2.17	0.70	1.97	6.92	14.14	10.97	5.51	4.99
481	2.70	0.71	1.71	5.43	22.41	5.05	10.22	3.12
482/1	2.05	− 0.09	2.03	7.65	20.65	8.93	7.14	4.91
482/2	2.05	− 0.11	2.02	7.68	21.24	8.07	7.21	4.82
483	2.12	0.19	1.99	10.06	19.99	8.84	6.82	5.41
484	2.09	0.30	2.03	9.88	19.46	7.05	7.17	4.18
485/486	2.43	1.02	2.76	6.91	20.26	7.81	6.09	4.66
489	2.51	0.88	2.72	7.11	21.56	8.77	6.79	4.87
491	0.99	− 0.44	1.19	5.83	20.51	10.25	6.35	3.64
492	2.24	0.21	1.57	6.51	19.56	10.09	5.50	3.93
493	2.22	0.25	1.60	6.46	17.97	11.01	5.94	5.42
494/1/2	NA	NA	NA	NA	19.02	10.11	6.46	4.12
494/3	NA	NA	NA	NA	20.25	10.23	6.01	4.39
495	2.23	0.24	1.59	6.51	19.07	10.15	6.30	4.46
496	− 0.21	− 1.69	0.39	5.32	21.74	10.34	4.72	4.11
499	2.29	0.09	1.52	6.56	18.44	10.65	6.08	4.83
601	NA	NA	NA	NA	NA	NA	NA	NA
602	NA	NA	NA	NA	NA	NA	NA	NA
603	NA	NA	NA	NA	NA	NA	NA	NA

Note: Growth rates of price are derived as implicit deflators: that is, growth of nominal value *minus* growth of quantity.

Table H.7. *Growth rates of price of capital input, selected periods, 1954–86, %, p.a.*

MLH	1954–8	1958–63	1963–8	1968–73	1973–6	1976–9	1979–82	1982–6
101	NA	NA	NA	NA	NA	NA	NA	NA
102/103	9.41	4.25	2.15	7.24	13.52	10.23	14.19	3.09
104	NA	NA	NA	NA	NA	NA	NA	NA
109	NA	NA	NA	NA	9.60	19.94	11.53	− 2.81
211	9.18	− 2.10	3.29	0.17	15.83	3.63	3.51	7.16
212	8.34	2.97	− 1.10	9.42	13.07	9.63	10.02	11.73
213	− 5.57	6.88	− 1.46	− 2.79	25.88	14.84	23.58	− 0.85
214	4.94	3.17	1.03	4.78	11.13	− 2.36	17.14	0.78
215	9.31	− 6.34	14.52	16.97	12.16	− 0.24	16.76	2.58
216	− 31.99	33.54	3.70	8.05	34.63	− 7.13	6.91	2.12
217	− 0.36	0.74	− 2.18	5.81	15.79	18.24	0.27	13.92
218	4.55	3.41	0.05	7.69	10.86	10.01	12.09	5.91
219	3.46	2.66	− 4.06	10.92	4.82	13.83	12.64	− 1.13
221	− 1.49	0.68	− 0.76	13.01	11.53	− 30.98	49.06	4.15
229/1	− 5.80	− 8.52	− 16.98	26.67	25.72	19.51	7.44	12.33
229/2	4.08	− 0.73	2.28	14.51	8.91	8.26	10.54	5.07
231	8.17	− 2.47	− 2.25	4.81	8.71	6.04	0.62	6.63
232	14.51	− 0.58	0.80	18.99	5.61	18.84	4.33	1.69
239/1	5.00	2.14	− 2.05	12.71	6.17	15.94	− 2.03	15.05
239/2	14.04	− 5.17	− 3.98	19.41	− 27.49	21.66	24.23	10.76
240	− 2.60	3.09	3.59	8.91	13.24	2.66	19.01	− 6.27
261	− 1.60	− 11.21	14.37	− 1.66	− 2.09	− 2.71	− 14.92	19.07
262	− 15.01	15.33	6.33	17.93	21.98	46.25	− 29.02	13.24
263	− 0.47	0.57	− 7.39	10.25	12.69	23.10	− 6.25	14.00
271	4.41	2.73	− 2.53	6.63	17.74	1.31	− 8.36	20.37
272	2.67	2.59	0.76	4.06	7.84	17.57	6.97	6.13
273	− 1.36	5.69	− 3.00	6.04	− 2.24	0.83	10.31	16.86
274	0.69	1.54	0.74	13.35	1.27	23.59	− 6.04	4.66
275	8.98	2.97	− 1.54	2.44	23.40	30.92	5.16	7.96
276	0.90	5.52	2.69	4.20	7.37	0.28	− 22.27	40.19
277	− 0.29	2.48	− 1.34	15.55	13.04	− 14.76	− 14.09	31.67
278	− 2.75	− 2.94	9.64	12.77	16.32	5.83	1.31	− 19.39
279/1	5.45	− 4.54	3.74	6.82	− 5.08	10.98	14.60	6.80
279/2	− 13.06	15.42	6.05	6.39	11.20	− 2.03	4.92	13.16
279/3	− 0.72	2.75	− 3.07	− 6.85	21.65	− 7.36	10.99	1.31
279/4	7.02	5.43	− 9.26	18.74	20.35	2.89	14.61	5.60
279/5	− 2.81	− 1.96	− 2.80	8.74	− 1.71	15.10	0.91	7.73
279/6	2.99	2.79	− 2.19	8.16	5.82	11.04	10.93	9.62
279/7	− 1.20	− 7.51	− 9.30	19.22	5.94	− 41.30	− 7.17	75.88
311	17.69	− 7.90	− 0.26	10.33	− 33.78	− 11.91	75.19	20.77
312	9.55	− 5.68	2.94	4.07	9.82	− 21.27	9.11	− 15.45
313	− 0.06	1.06	− 3.95	5.10	13.85	0.14	− 5.92	18.98
321	0.36	5.16	− 6.59	9.07	19.02	3.03	− 24.97	32.47
322	− 0.58	5.53	− 0.02	14.71	− 23.58	26.31	− 3.93	16.19
323	− 1.51	3.99	5.08	7.08	0.96	24.53	− 2.92	9.34
331	4.38	5.58	− 0.52	12.64	− 3.09	19.55	− 5.00	2.48
332	− 3.07	7.43	− 3.24	6.65	0.35	20.20	− 13.17	18.86
333	2.09	1.57	− 0.26	8.86	17.97	5.77	10.70	5.77
334	− 7.53	− 1.79	13.35	2.13	23.95	7.59	22.46	− 4.20
335	− 7.57	13.39	1.98	7.97	− 26.82	− 10.41	7.59	19.27
336	− 16.47	15.66	1.98	6.37	19.69	− 15.39	12.34	1.67
337	− 2.87	5.68	3.85	10.33	− 1.96	− 4.97	− 0.77	20.63

338	0.91	− 3.63	7.53	0.22	− 13.17	31.92	− 2.67	24.41
339/1	2.31	5.64	− 4.16	14.28	− 4.34	30.19	10.73	0.29
339/2	− 2.29	2.64	− 6.80	10.82	12.93	26.82	− 31.51	31.82
339/3/4	7.86	0.74	− 0.11	6.29	8.78	17.78	− 18.32	21.84
339/5/9	NA	NA	2.73	4.54	− 3.26	21.51	− 1.15	11.12
341	3.05	− 0.44	− 3.53	11.20	4.44	31.39	0.61	2.64
342	− 5.67	− 0.17	4.77	− 12.41	33.30	43.96	3.44	4.86
349	1.17	1.70	0.52	5.53	2.12	10.26	− 7.61	12.14
351	0.33	− 1.02	0.51	4.53	9.16	11.31	8.82	2.70
352	− 8.72	14.45	− 8.17	12.29	15.53	2.21	− 134.08	94.90
353	5.82	− 2.26	0.26	6.63	− 1.49	10.90	19.79	− 0.13
354	3.36	3.81	− 2.10	1.08	13.40	9.88	14.91	3.87
361	7.48	− 8.28	7.79	2.17	19.98	− 9.47	23.80	1.60
362	3.29	8.79	0.40	2.87	6.90	2.72	30.76	11.41
363	− 9.02	6.73	5.64	9.79	− 3.43	26.71	22.68	− 2.59
364	NA	NA	2.32	4.09	− 0.78	5.41	9.87	− 1.60
365	NA	NA	5.23	5.93	− 15.98	2.57	1.67	16.89
366	NA	NA	− 5.35	23.95	14.35	23.15	3.66	5.89
367	NA	NA	− 9.07	15.02	19.52	6.41	18.78	0.57
368	− 4.87	10.18	− 5.18	8.07	− 13.97	14.57	9.88	13.93
369	− 1.01	5.93	1.47	− 1.84	10.53	5.26	11.19	4.97
370	0.08	10.40	0.79	4.91	2.83	− 0.58	− 105.20	91.64
380	NA	NA	1.74	− 1.10	22.52	− 2.72	− 28.37	− 2.81
381	2.54	10.13	− 3.30	− 4.03	14.12	26.06	− 9.98	21.64
382	− 8.16	− 2.58	− 9.48	26.41	5.54	2.62	− 56.78	− 3.68
383	2.47	− 0.81	7.02	16.73	− 74.58	33.24	34.68	33.01
384/385	− 4.80	21.36	0.45	3.08	12.40	3.27	11.35	− 37.31
390	− 2.37	4.09	− 1.22	10.39	− 7.85	12.45	5.53	12.34
391	9.24	1.24	− 4.03	11.97	10.19	20.84	− 4.84	8.47
392	0.00	− 3.99	3.95	− 3.58	8.30	9.25	6.44	− 3.59
393	0.12	3.32	− 4.36	10.15	2.21	12.72	− 1.12	14.68
394	2.40	2.01	− 3.67	16.62	7.13	− 3.65	0.27	10.66
395	6.17	− 5.36	0.57	5.47	11.84	18.83	− 3.29	16.98
396	− 2.11	− 3.21	4.18	7.43	14.24	21.50	− 6.08	22.33
399/1	1.10	8.45	− 4.42	9.73	0.81	20.40	8.17	8.94
399/2/12	0.01	3.75	− 0.66	7.08	13.50	8.11	6.69	9.43
411	− 11.87	19.73	1.28	4.51	− 23.34	− 24.95	− 8.37	56.23
412	− 11.62	− 1.41	9.06	8.38	4.70	− 2.15	− 1.61	12.84
413	− 3.75	1.11	− 1.07	7.63	0.25	24.01	− 8.50	22.53
414	− 5.03	4.67	− 5.02	− 0.91	13.80	4.10	6.75	19.12
415	− 16.94	9.99	− 2.99	16.40	4.99	0.62	− 26.58	29.52
416	− 0.16	2.33	− 2.84	3.23	− 5.42	13.68	6.72	18.79
417	− 3.67	5.00	4.36	− 2.77	8.15	7.76	4.80	15.56
418	− 11.99	7.45	− 10.65	13.29	− 7.94	19.39	− 16.11	24.07
419	0.84	1.72	− 3.02	11.46	− 8.85	− 2.01	12.06	14.18
421	− 1.29	2.61	− 2.47	8.95	6.31	10.78	− 0.88	7.72
422/1	3.79	− 2.41	− 4.31	18.67	− 0.99	12.75	− 13.68	22.18
422/2	12.99	− 5.09	− 1.45	8.65	6.23	3.61	12.34	7.96
423	− 9.04	3.77	− 1.50	4.36	16.82	6.56	− 2.94	14.42
429	0.95	1.31	1.56	5.21	13.25	3.90	− 9.85	25.06
431	− 1.20	8.72	1.36	1.23	− 1.71	− 2.01	21.88	21.76
432	2.14	− 0.25	− 5.50	9.02	12.41	− 2.85	− 18.68	25.63
433	− 11.29	16.74	− 1.97	4.67	11.87	20.27	− 46.86	6.24
441	− 4.16	8.37	− 0.16	2.51	13.48	3.09	− 12.59	28.53
442	− 1.05	4.22	− 1.99	10.81	− 11.16	− 27.42	30.77	8.26
443	− 3.13	5.14	− 1.04	11.82	2.86	21.60	− 7.25	− 1.32
444	2.66	5.39	− 3.65	8.28	9.32	30.27	− 4.59	11.96
445	1.56	1.51	1.44	9.98	0.89	25.92	− 10.04	6.26

446	− 5.45	3.52	− 2.81	12.51	− 0.44	3.24	19.21	17.90
449/1	3.85	5.14	1.19	10.33	1.95	21.98	− 4.22	− 0.39
449/2	− 5.53	5.78	− 1.25	14.89	2.79	14.37	− 9.52	12.13
450	− 3.60	6.54	− 4.15	8.98	6.74	14.39	− 5.78	11.80
461	− 7.30	6.57	− 3.15	12.30	8.94	− 1.25	8.79	17.44
462	− 2.65	1.78	− 4.84	15.29	13.65	8.18	6.65	13.64
463	5.04	− 3.67	− 1.17	12.36	10.51	4.53	− 9.19	20.69
464	− 4.27	2.02	− 6.58	14.45	5.41	21.54	7.71	0.38
469/1	− 0.53	6.96	1.52	− 2.63	20.63	18.21	− 28.64	21.56
469/2	− 1.81	5.59	1.59	6.70	14.77	7.64	11.01	6.83
471	4.01	4.96	3.76	17.03	− 2.90	1.70	0.70	7.54
472	0.10	5.22	4.03	11.57	0.65	11.11	− 1.70	11.51
473	− 1.10	12.26	5.92	6.43	9.06	3.17	9.93	11.51
474	− 1.00	9.90	− 1.64	8.16	− 2.64	22.19	2.43	− 0.27
475	1.23	2.83	− 4.01	19.28	− 5.48	11.02	5.08	3.60
479	3.79	1.92	− 0.85	10.83	5.82	21.05	− 3.25	− 2.96
481	− 12.47	3.15	− 3.70	6.93	6.52	6.59	− 17.84	38.43
482/1	− 3.77	2.96	1.11	11.02	18.46	4.74	− 12.24	16.97
482/2	− 3.78	11.55	− 1.55	10.51	18.87	5.18	− 3.10	1.77
483	0.59	1.97	− 2.89	8.87	3.39	15.79	− 0.48	15.08
484	6.23	1.57	3.92	2.90	11.30	8.52	− 3.31	16.81
485/486	− 1.99	5.54	1.93	11.07	4.56	14.98	5.39	8.94
489	3.90	5.28	0.81	11.11	10.25	5.23	14.11	8.18
491	− 7.56	11.24	− 0.41	4.29	21.36	− 4.38	3.37	19.65
492	− 0.50	8.86	− 1.75	14.30	− 3.41	− 10.94	3.21	23.78
493	8.57	− 5.13	− 5.81	13.98	14.60	0.99	− 8.14	5.72
494/1/2	NA	NA	NA	NA	18.28	− 5.05	− 21.14	12.73
494/3	NA	NA	NA	NA	5.56	9.91	− 3.66	5.62
495	6.82	1.19	6.11	2.84	− 7.20	16.96	− 30.42	38.29
496	4.99	8.88	− 0.09	6.81	9.61	12.30	2.71	7.69
499	1.35	2.99	4.09	10.84	6.95	4.57	1.94	24.41
601	NA	NA	NA	NA	NA	NA	NA	NA
602	NA	NA	NA	NA	NA	NA	NA	NA
603	NA	NA	NA	NA	NA	NA	NA	NA

Note: Growth rates of price are derived as implicit deflators: that is, growth of nominal value *minus* growth of quantity.

Table H.8. *Growth rates of price of labour input, selected periods, 1954–86, %, p.a.*

MLH	1954–8	1958–63	1963–8	1968–73	1973–6	1976–9	1979–82	1982–6
101	0.64	4.92	7.59	6.92	− 3.10	15.58	12.34	10.89
102/103	NA	NA	8.41	11.31	19.58	14.39	13.32	7.48
104	NA	NA	NA	NA	NA	NA	NA	NA
109	NA	NA	NA	NA	25.03	16.67	13.89	7.34
211	7.12	6.04	8.40	9.03	23.01	14.32	15.46	7.12
212	6.79	5.04	8.48	7.69	21.58	13.72	13.33	6.66
213	7.12	5.93	8.62	11.29	20.54	13.77	13.67	7.14
214	6.41	7.14	8.42	10.25	21.51	13.80	11.79	7.22
215	6.61	6.45	9.27	11.84	21.31	10.73	15.47	6.89
216	5.77	7.29	7.25	10.82	19.82	15.43	13.63	5.90
217	5.69	5.42	9.90	9.52	20.44	15.27	13.99	9.65
218	8.47	6.12	8.26	10.76	20.91	14.11	15.84	7.17
219	6.83	7.04	8.55	10.01	19.05	15.03	15.58	7.18
221	8.82	5.54	7.06	9.55	21.46	14.99	14.72	7.55
229/1	7.37	7.08	8.43	12.50	18.83	12.74	13.79	9.83
229/2	6.32	7.02	8.79	9.84	20.75	14.13	13.46	8.23
231	5.83	6.65	9.75	11.40	19.30	14.64	16.89	5.94
232	6.90	5.20	9.41	9.52	22.77	14.99	13.11	8.06
239/1	8.27	5.85	8.94	11.23	17.83	14.95	14.98	6.91
239/2	5.67	4.76	9.87	8.54	21.30	16.46	13.37	9.05
240	6.15	6.67	8.19	12.44	21.73	16.11	16.79	10.23
261	7.66	5.17	7.62	9.97	25.57	12.65	13.92	8.82
262	8.12	8.34	8.49	10.58	26.13	12.69	15.82	6.79
263	4.82	5.33	8.51	10.82	23.78	13.34	12.97	8.75
271	6.23	5.72	9.28	10.08	20.76	15.60	15.94	6.23
272	6.72	5.67	8.76	9.18	21.41	15.04	16.18	8.55
273	5.82	5.34	10.17	9.51	20.23	14.88	11.80	8.13
274	5.08	5.71	9.41	9.79	21.16	14.84	13.45	7.54
275	7.73	6.17	8.69	10.37	18.25	15.72	16.67	6.92
276	5.45	6.44	9.02	11.26	20.28	14.53	13.74	7.03
277	4.40	6.30	8.94	10.13	21.48	16.50	14.30	6.07
278	6.79	5.01	10.70	9.62	21.10	20.22	9.89	7.89
279/1	7.16	5.39	9.54	10.50	19.48	14.79	10.29	7.60
279/2	6.62	5.02	8.68	9.65	20.93	13.41	13.54	6.93
279/3	6.49	6.05	8.13	9.61	22.54	13.04	14.90	7.33
279/4	5.88	5.29	12.43	10.11	23.68	12.54	14.92	3.30
279/5	5.30	7.10	8.29	9.47	20.14	13.75	10.77	6.89
279/6	5.36	4.95	8.77	10.33	22.70	13.99	13.28	8.78
279/7	7.49	6.61	9.75	12.40	19.79	15.92	12.32	7.19
311	25.27	4.20	8.02	10.97	22.92	12.15	16.58	7.89
312	7.76	3.98	8.45	10.63	23.17	11.61	15.42	6.28
313	6.37	5.20	8.11	9.35	20.73	16.66	10.30	7.53
321	6.04	6.17	7.67	10.28	19.96	15.99	12.17	7.21
322	5.58	7.51	8.03	10.23	19.97	13.99	13.60	7.16
323	6.49	5.15	9.22	9.90	20.53	16.48	13.31	7.50
331	6.49	5.35	8.88	9.70	20.05	15.11	14.20	6.52
332	6.47	5.14	7.93	9.63	20.11	14.37	13.92	7.82
333	7.23	4.48	8.47	10.15	19.95	14.83	13.77	7.62
334	7.30	4.33	8.15	10.09	19.91	16.18	15.37	6.52
335	6.50	5.08	8.70	10.62	19.29	14.60	12.48	8.00
336	5.32	6.19	8.78	10.16	21.46	13.88	14.82	8.05
337	7.85	4.08	8.71	10.27	20.53	14.33	13.05	7.12

338	7.72	5.42	9.18	8.53	22.12	15.77	11.36	8.52
339/1	6.84	4.22	8.53	10.19	21.02	14.95	13.63	6.94
339/2	6.04	6.11	7.73	9.80	20.37	17.47	13.36	10.11
339/3/4	8.06	4.95	7.85	9.26	20.28	16.17	28.55	−4.64
339/5/9	NA	NA	8.45	9.37	20.67	14.94	12.90	7.92
341	7.11	5.74	8.91	10.26	21.22	15.30	15.43	6.89
342	5.26	4.98	7.87	10.67	23.87	12.29	15.85	7.55
349	6.71	5.22	8.37	9.81	20.34	14.71	11.50	10.09
351	6.16	6.83	10.30	10.14	20.44	16.27	17.21	2.88
352	5.90	4.80	8.82	9.61	21.09	13.46	11.98	8.61
353	6.55	6.65	8.56	9.29	21.51	15.18	13.85	6.48
354	6.52	5.91	8.01	9.60	19.48	15.39	14.75	7.74
361	6.68	5.74	8.30	9.46	21.14	15.01	13.04	6.78
362	7.23	4.98	9.34	9.61	20.46	16.27	14.05	4.64
363	7.22	5.35	7.76	12.16	20.27	14.89	14.63	8.21
364	NA	NA	9.32	10.82	20.10	14.97	14.17	7.21
365	NA	NA	9.36	10.19	21.54	14.85	14.23	7.91
366	NA	NA	8.76	13.21	19.00	15.08	15.49	7.49
367	NA	NA	8.51	9.62	19.72	15.00	14.22	7.92
368	8.73	5.58	7.31	9.88	21.28	14.35	10.31	6.62
369	6.76	5.71	9.03	11.95	18.29	15.68	10.44	7.59
370	6.60	4.99	8.50	10.96	22.07	13.21	13.63	7.11
380	NA	NA	9.24	9.94	21.09	12.75	16.74	5.61
381	7.87	4.39	7.66	11.34	17.62	14.29	13.39	8.55
382	5.96	5.12	9.12	8.04	19.40	14.79	13.07	1.73
383	6.74	5.39	8.85	10.28	20.73	14.11	14.79	7.11
384/385	5.96	6.12	9.29	10.21	20.86	15.02	11.89	7.00
390	6.58	4.84	7.61	9.88	18.89	15.83	12.35	8.16
391	7.11	4.56	7.90	9.46	21.67	14.32	12.58	8.23
392	7.39	4.67	8.38	8.63	20.62	13.54	11.48	7.67
393	7.02	4.72	9.00	9.83	19.83	13.82	11.94	6.46
394	6.78	5.13	8.10	9.36	21.71	14.69	12.49	6.53
395	6.99	7.57	7.93	11.59	22.73	18.21	13.36	6.21
396	4.01	8.20	8.36	9.53	20.05	13.14	18.07	6.71
399/1	7.19	5.37	7.58	9.80	19.01	16.83	12.77	8.15
399/2/12	6.56	5.56	8.89	9.17	19.71	14.59	13.66	6.71
411	7.43	6.86	9.21	9.79	21.93	13.81	15.17	7.40
412	4.67	5.59	8.88	9.87	20.86	14.04	10.79	7.21
413	4.30	5.78	8.59	9.87	19.60	15.27	11.45	6.92
414	4.83	5.10	8.43	9.69	21.08	12.94	13.01	7.55
415	6.81	4.90	9.06	10.51	18.71	13.86	14.11	8.82
416	6.37	5.28	8.39	9.85	21.05	13.27	14.81	5.72
417	5.58	4.49	8.97	8.94	19.40	15.15	9.22	7.60
418	5.51	3.59	10.33	6.37	23.90	13.82	13.14	3.62
419	6.39	5.54	8.81	10.25	23.54	11.69	9.13	7.85
421	5.10	4.76	8.38	9.53	19.25	15.55	10.46	7.61
422/1	6.54	4.58	9.29	11.10	19.97	15.57	12.52	6.77
422/2	4.77	5.77	7.48	8.77	21.57	13.28	12.59	9.44
423	5.64	5.11	7.93	10.82	19.14	14.90	11.90	7.93
429	6.38	5.10	7.80	10.45	21.06	15.22	12.41	7.34
431	5.34	5.28	8.49	9.78	19.35	14.36	13.50	6.57
432	7.35	6.14	8.51	8.69	19.40	14.14	10.66	6.21
433	6.30	5.67	7.94	10.57	16.14	10.82	19.60	6.38
441	4.78	5.58	8.96	8.66	19.98	15.83	10.35	7.71
442	6.38	4.79	8.71	10.03	19.60	15.23	10.97	8.05
443	5.09	4.86	8.21	8.15	18.62	13.35	12.25	6.20
444	6.07	4.28	8.48	9.65	20.19	15.45	11.69	6.73
445	6.13	5.57	8.37	8.20	19.82	14.76	12.63	6.20

446	5.21	5.67	7.62	8.82	20.90	14.74	17.46	5.21
449/1	6.32	4.91	9.19	9.50	20.65	15.06	11.98	7.78
449/2	5.72	6.99	6.75	9.99	17.59	20.48	12.35	5.58
450	6.92	5.62	9.41	9.64	19.43	13.83	12.22	6.60
461	5.31	5.68	8.12	11.57	19.25	15.27	14.25	5.84
462	5.12	6.06	8.90	9.65	22.46	13.99	11.95	6.40
463	6.72	5.78	8.85	11.35	19.98	16.95	11.77	4.74
464	5.03	6.73	8.54	5.21	27.52	16.05	14.22	7.55
469/1	5.75	6.11	9.01	9.25	19.14	15.31	12.45	6.25
469/2	5.78	5.58	8.62	10.69	19.88	14.46	13.24	7.94
471	6.11	6.16	7.97	10.85	19.33	13.23	13.49	6.88
472	4.34	5.20	9.92	10.04	17.75	15.07	11.70	7.88
473	5.94	5.67	8.63	9.47	17.53	16.10	8.80	5.90
474	5.66	6.50	7.16	11.35	19.50	12.48	12.12	8.07
475	6.72	6.02	7.55	9.78	22.71	13.54	13.99	6.25
479	9.00	7.58	6.44	9.94	19.52	12.02	15.52	8.29
481	5.89	5.25	8.84	10.26	21.56	15.64	12.37	7.82
482/1	6.32	5.90	8.27	10.50	20.98	15.10	14.72	7.67
482/2	4.43	5.31	9.08	11.01	20.38	14.89	14.56	6.15
483	5.23	5.56	9.68	10.04	19.49	16.14	15.74	8.06
484	6.63	5.84	8.71	10.85	22.57	14.97	14.43	7.31
485/486	7.02	5.23	7.90	11.00	17.28	17.71	15.63	8.42
489	7.27	6.10	7.22	10.12	19.42	14.93	16.52	8.40
491	6.67	5.29	9.04	9.87	20.59	14.03	12.80	7.46
492	6.52	4.50	8.88	9.93	20.26	14.02	15.34	7.86
493	6.16	7.86	8.98	8.56	22.30	12.50	12.40	5.54
494/1/2	NA	NA	NA	NA	21.24	14.17	11.04	7.04
494/3	NA	NA	NA	NA	22.45	13.28	12.24	6.26
495	6.77	6.16	8.53	9.76	19.68	16.72	10.15	7.65
496	5.95	5.99	8.69	10.05	18.97	15.36	12.80	7.61
499	6.20	5.56	8.64	9.56	18.82	16.52	10.57	9.01
601	7.10	5.54	9.44	11.53	22.50	17.05	17.77	5.26
602	7.06	6.28	10.58	10.69	22.95	15.28	17.68	5.62
603	6.99	5.24	9.35	9.49	23.82	13.96	15.11	6.72

Note: Growth rates of price are derived as implicit deflators: that is, growth of nominal value *minus* growth of quantity.

Table H.9. *Capital stocks in 1986, by industry (£m, 1980 prices)*

MLH	MSF	WG	PMC	BL	V
101	NA	194.3	NA	NA	NA
102/103	11.1	28.0	769.2	302.9	26.9
104	NA	NA	7389.7	19 115.5	43.2
109	5.9	8.0	143.8	125.9	3.0
211	73.7	32.4	336.4	299.5	13.8
212	51.5	13.9	612.4	583.4	44.3
213	31.4	35.0	294.2	204.6	7.3
214	153.4	165.0	944.7	651.4	57.8
215	66.7	252.2	845.8	517.4	36.3
216	19.9	49.6	344.4	211.9	4.5
217	121.7	176.0	704.4	313.4	17.8
218	145.1	235.9	545.6	349.4	17.9
219	45.6	50.4	460.6	321.6	32.0
221	84.8	24.0	156.8	93.7	2.8
229/1	4.1	1.2	68.8	33.7	1.0
229/2	129.7	57.3	585.7	264.8	15.2
231	286.8	253.6	1391.1	1559.0	44.9
232	19.5	27.4	288.1	191.6	15.4
239/1	296.6	535.7	358.2	416.8	8.2
239/2	16.3	25.6	89.4	49.2	6.3
240	355.9	134.6	489.3	226.1	11.5
261	20.5	70.1	317.6	112.3	1.9
262	370.4	784.7	2785.0	540.0	10.2
263	25.8	32.3	131.1	109.0	7.2
271	425.8	544.5	6982.3	1882.8	68.0
272	270.5	493.1	1455.2	1138.9	35.4
273	76.7	77.4	225.9	180.3	9.9
274	67.9	114.6	283.1	206.4	15.6
275	59.6	61.9	334.2	132.4	8.0
276	106.3	165.4	1497.8	483.4	14.5
277	78.4	133.2	654.0	229.3	5.3
278	42.7	134.3	718.3	149.8	10.7
279/1	14.8	10.6	85.3	58.4	2.7
279/2	28.1	35.5	102.7	49.4	4.8
279/3	51.7	128.2	215.5	203.1	2.5
279/4	49.1	102.6	177.6	64.2	3.0
279/5	12.4	18.7	43.1	29.4	3.1
279/6	26.8	29.6	117.4	48.6	7.0
279/7	29.3	21.8	193.1	138.4	1.9
311	411.0	395.6	5137.0	2226.0	55.5
312	41.8	180.5	446.8	227.7	8.1
313	79.3	123.8	553.5	361.0	10.9
321	57.6	104.2	670.0	308.9	11.7
322	0.3	111.3	362.0	205.6	6.6
323	88.1	110.2	309.6	205.9	4.8
331	38.1	68.8	98.9	100.9	6.1
332	71.6	240.4	312.7	224.4	10.1
333	154.5	134.8	560.8	258.7	20.7
334	40.7	139.8	286.2	152.9	5.0
335	39.4	83.4	118.7	110.9	4.1
336	100.2	142.0	313.4	339.9	11.1
337	92.5	339.1	265.8	189.0	20.7
338	80.6	114.5	152.6	106.5	2.6

339/1	51.8	81.3	134.7	86.0	6.3
339/2	7.6	40.0	123.7	46.3	6.0
339/3/4	75.0	110.7	234.8	172.0	18.7
339/5/9	128.8	432.7	578.9	439.6	27.2
341	110.2	2903.4	976.1	666.5	54.6
342	61.4	93.3	191.7	132.4	2.5
349	112.9	287.9	1039.4	477.9	35.2
351	31.4	61.9	83.7	45.2	1.3
352	9.1	12.4	51.8	42.8	1.5
353	58.7	60.2	134.7	63.4	7.8
354	218.8	419.1	607.2	239.8	28.3
361	164.9	471.0	695.7	510.2	22.4
362	50.3	124.0	416.5	250.1	6.2
363	82.5	146.1	555.5	248.3	9.6
364	163.6	257.6	1062.8	395.6	16.6
365	127.8	199.6	234.8	129.1	4.8
366	98.0	157.2	437.5	250.6	9.9
367	196.3	636.0	750.7	299.1	26.9
368	95.3	146.4	361.2	160.9	18.4
369	124.3	208.7	546.3	316.8	16.2
370	75.5	1792.3	688.8	1300.6	14.2
380	3.6	110.3	212.7	95.2	2.3
381	335.6	1278.5	4519.7	2439.1	108.4
382	24.1	3.9	91.3	106.0	1.9
383	369.8	2762.6	1475.7	944.7	45.4
384/385	139.4	72.5	151.4	228.7	3.1
390	45.4	87.0	376.2	159.2	13.1
391	11.8	30.0	65.4	53.9	2.8
392	6.5	11.4	74.0	53.9	1.9
393	22.8	66.2	186.2	91.0	4.6
394	39.4	58.7	268.3	173.2	7.4
395	47.3	59.4	235.2	128.3	4.1
396	115.0	64.5	105.2	90.3	5.1
399/1	29.1	34.9	91.5	68.2	9.0
399/2/12	385.0	469.7	1455.0	871.1	87.6
411	33.6	61.0	784.0	327.4	4.9
412	49.1	103.8	422.7	167.7	3.8
413	48.8	164.5	399.5	184.3	2.9
414	173.1	281.6	581.0	308.3	10.4
415	5.1	14.1	70.3	29.0	0.6
416	3.1	14.0	35.8	16.5	1.5
417	88.4	238.9	710.0	282.6	14.0
418	6.3	16.5	23.3	13.5	0.8
419	52.3	113.0	240.0	146.2	6.3
421	18.0	20.2	80.9	40.8	2.3
422/1	18.4	41.1	77.0	59.6	3.0
422/2	11.0	11.4	21.9	20.9	2.6
423	32.2	40.0	379.3	188.0	5.7
429	19.0	48.2	197.3	90.7	6.4
431	75.8	82.5	79.0	108.5	2.9
432	17.4	12.6	30.9	24.9	4.1
433	15.7	15.0	7.9	8.8	0.7
441	23.9	36.3	30.2	33.6	2.0
442	58.7	92.7	104.8	93.3	6.2
443	33.4	79.0	67.4	63.3	7.8
444	38.1	79.7	96.1	65.3	5.9
445	70.4	132.0	174.5	142.8	15.1
446	6.2	4.5	8.7	8.0	0.8

449/1	33.8	47.9	50.9	64.2	4.4
449/2	5.4	13.7	9.7	57.3	0.9
450	66.7	97.6	194.4	107.8	13.8
461	40.3	109.5	441.6	290.5	15.2
462	42.5	121.7	233.4	391.3	7.5
463	74.9	117.5	671.7	231.5	11.2
464	64.6	24.5	496.6	321.4	19.9
469/1	9.8	11.1	52.6	33.4	2.5
469/2	134.6	218.0	997.0	478.7	59.2
471	217.9	262.7	412.5	437.6	41.5
472	104.9	150.5	342.7	367.0	38.8
473	24.8	17.6	48.0	51.0	8.2
474	29.9	77.3	76.2	82.7	15.6
475	12.6	3.1	30.8	51.6	3.7
479	28.8	14.4	66.3	58.3	5.6
481	176.8	131.4	1219.2	596.6	13.6
482/1	75.8	77.2	585.2	230.6	17.2
482/2	48.4	33.3	213.6	78.8	5.2
483	46.9	60.9	332.2	111.4	14.2
484	59.0	52.5	421.1	180.2	15.5
485/486	89.8	41.3	1070.2	517.7	57.0
489	170.7	400.6	1780.5	695.3	81.4
491	122.9	215.6	838.0	525.1	21.5
492	16.7	35.8	112.1	112.0	1.8
493	10.1	17.6	31.6	44.1	2.1
494/1/2	40.7	49.0	124.7	100.5	4.4
494/3	11.2	27.2	38.9	27.7	3.0
495	26.6	18.9	79.4	49.9	2.8
496	190.9	216.0	1301.1	469.2	45.9
499	38.1	26.5	81.3	59.5	7.7
601	NA	NA	NA	NA	NA
602	NA	NA	NA	NA	NA
603	NA	NA	NA	NA	NA

Total Manufacturing (1968 SIC): MLH 211–499

11 488.4	25 461.7	70 613.4	38 084.8	2010.0

Source: Fixed capital estimates derived by PIM, using 'short' lives from table 3.3 and depreciation rates from table 3.4.

Key   MSF: Materials, stores and fuel
       WG: Work in progress and goods on hand for sale
       PMC: Plant & machinery
       BL: Buildings and land
       V: Vehicles

Table H.10. *Nominal values of gross output and inputs in 1986 (£m)*

MLH	Labour	Capital	Inter- mediate	Gross output
101	2639.9	− 153.2	1204.5	3691.3
102/103	236.1	568.7	777.6	1582.5
104	NA	NA	NA	11216.3
109	59.4	48.1	125.5	233.0
211	159.0	171.6	1441.8	1772.4
212	824.4	398.7	1821.6	3044.7
213	211.3	197.7	582.9	991.9
214	920.8	480.3	3739.3	5140.4
215	440.9	618.8	3716.4	4776.1
216	101.6	133.8	525.9	761.2
217	458.8	429.7	1534.7	2419.3
218	396.9	399.1	1628.7	2424.8
219	240.2	331.8	2562.8	3134.8
221	84.1	115.7	735.6	935.4
229/1	38.9	65.1	306.7	410.7
229/2	310.7	420.0	2097.1	2827.8
231	453.9	735.4	1808.9	2998.2
232	177.8	273.7	1025.6	1477.2
239/1	174.3	506.7	1089.0	1770.0
239/2	48.2	72.6	184.6	305.3
240	324.2	410.2	822.0	1556.4
261	47.3	18.2	262.2	327.7
262	171.7	1406.0	6638.1	8215.8
263	66.4	142.1	422.4	630.9
271	1403.1	1642.6	6190.1	9235.8
272	810.5	1275.8	1767.0	3853.3
273	201.1	337.5	838.2	1376.9
274	241.4	183.1	814.2	1238.7
275	148.4	289.8	892.7	1330.9
276	403.0	531.0	2430.6	3364.6
277	185.1	227.4	559.8	972.3
278	174.9	91.4	747.6	1014.0
279/1	41.4	66.5	280.7	388.6
279/2	73.6	60.1	240.9	374.6
279/3	142.7	32.6	309.1	484.4
279/4	57.0	310.5	795.6	1163.1
279/5	46.6	35.4	127.8	209.8
279/6	90.2	101.8	219.8	411.8
279/7	140.7	150.6	427.2	718.4
311	962.3	789.4	2578.5	4330.2
312	240.7	24.6	666.6	931.9
313	301.2	119.8	388.5	809.6
321	339.5	195.7	926.2	1461.4
322	206.1	137.9	744.3	1088.2
323	157.7	148.6	889.1	1195.4
331	119.9	40.0	247.9	407.9
332	355.5	126.0	632.0	1113.5
333	647.8	369.9	1229.9	2247.6
334	226.8	125.2	478.1	830.1
335	106.0	29.9	191.1	327.0
336	231.2	127.7	887.4	1246.3
337	457.3	186.3	838.1	1481.8

338	103.7	94.9	224.4	423.0
339/1	212.7	116.8	388.0	717.4
339/2	148.0	88.5	297.8	534.3
339/3/4	359.3	189.8	703.4	1252.4
339/5/9	715.4	341.3	1440.4	2497.1
341	1409.6	863.6	1799.4	4072.6
342	166.5	124.5	396.2	687.2
349	1064.3	291.6	1282.8	2638.8
351	52.3	− 1.1	140.1	191.3
352	21.6	9.4	32.9	63.9
353	214.9	98.9	326.0	639.7
354	1074.0	467.6	1599.1	3140.7
361	947.0	355.4	1443.9	2746.3
362	337.0	276.2	806.6	1419.8
363	516.6	403.4	937.0	1856.9
364	789.3	441.4	1603.5	2834.2
365	229.8	176.7	713.3	1119.8
366	375.7	974.1	1780.7	3130.5
367	1252.6	598.0	2248.3	4098.9
368	339.5	218.9	1102.2	1660.6
369	685.4	305.9	1304.1	2295.4
370	1109.4	− 193.8	1094.4	2010.0
380	135.8	37.1	590.0	763.0
381	3031.9	2029.4	9367.6	14429.0
382	29.7	− 4.3	67.2	92.6
383	2126.6	1251.7	4359.8	7738.0
384/385	234.5	12.7	373.1	620.3
390	398.3	145.9	375.4	919.6
391	79.3	43.7	144.4	267.4
392	57.7	24.8	107.9	190.4
393	155.6	76.6	266.8	499.0
394	189.9	100.0	495.6	785.5
395	173.0	100.3	646.2	919.5
396	123.5	146.9	449.0	719.4
399/1	150.3	88.7	306.0	545.0
399/2/12	1872.3	991.4	3549.6	6413.3
411	156.2	189.7	504.1	850.0
412	136.1	63.7	354.3	554.1
413	147.8	96.8	511.5	756.2
414	335.6	236.0	648.3	1219.9
415	31.1	14.1	61.1	106.3
416	20.4	15.0	62.2	97.6
417	529.0	236.8	926.4	1692.2
418	22.5	8.8	28.2	59.4
419	164.8	93.9	567.6	826.3
421	51.9	28.0	115.6	195.5
422/1	85.2	56.7	262.1	404.0
422/2	46.8	16.4	119.6	182.7
423	194.2	97.7	249.4	541.3
429	174.6	109.2	348.6	632.3
431	84.2	63.7	423.9	571.8
432	73.5	24.4	148.4	246.3
433	13.5	3.5	18.3	35.2
441	85.4	36.8	163.5	285.7
442	203.0	47.2	337.6	587.8
443	154.5	57.8	306.0	518.3
444	242.7	131.8	481.1	855.6
445	464.3	190.5	841.5	1495.3

446	23.9	15.7	29.0	68.6
449/1	116.4	46.8	218.0	381.1
449/2	18.5	6.8	45.6	71.0
450	380.5	179.4	555.9	1115.9
461	265.5	259.0	471.7	996.2
462	359.2	178.8	343.4	881.4
463	419.4	318.9	643.5	1381.7
464	106.1	217.8	419.9	743.8
469/1	49.8	30.5	121.6	201.9
469/2	612.4	654.4	1994.0	3260.7
471	512.9	294.1	1634.8	2441.8
472	670.5	306.8	1289.6	2267.0
473	133.3	74.3	352.4	560.1
474	298.1	86.3	556.7	941.1
475	65.7	21.2	120.9	207.7
479	125.0	33.5	270.1	428.5
481	386.8	422.9	1345.0	2154.7
482/1	509.6	259.6	1207.7	1976.9
482/2	139.5	83.3	367.1	589.9
483	328.7	220.1	711.8	1260.6
484	263.7	217.7	721.7	1203.1
485/486	1822.3	1164.4	2443.6	5430.4
489	1956.6	1084.0	2948.0	5988.6
491	678.6	469.6	1436.3	2584.5
492	64.2	53.1	192.2	309.5
493	40.3	8.7	76.3	125.3
494/1/2	91.0	51.7	218.2	360.9
494/3	55.0	25.0	148.2	228.2
495	63.9	53.5	160.8	278.2
496	1092.9	799.2	2527.8	4419.9
499	205.6	119.9	339.0	664.5
601	1231.5	1432.7	4430.7	7094.9
602	2139.3	3174.3	6823.7	12137.3
603	533.0	882.9	409.1	1825.0

Notes: 'Labour' is the wage bill *plus* employers' National Insurance contributions. 'Intermediate' is purchases of materials, stores and fuel *plus* cost of industrial services *plus* cost of non-industrial services. Gross output equals the sum of the three inputs (the value of capital services is the residual). Nominal value added can be derived as the sum of labour and capital services.

Table H.11. *Growth rates of MFP, selected periods, 1954–86, %, p.a.*

MLH	1954–8	1958–63	1963–8	1968–73	1973–6	1976–9	1979–82	1982–6
101	NA	NA	NA	NA	NA	NA	NA	NA
102/103	NA	NA	1.46	− 0.23	− 10.29	− 5.51	− 2.77	− 2.61
104	NA	NA	NA	NA	NA	NA	NA	NA
109	NA	NA	NA	NA	− 14.06	1.72	− 1.28	− 3.32
211	0.24	− 0.88	0.17	0.73	0.53	− 4.70	− 0.17	− 0.73
212	2.46	0.82	1.00	− 0.19	0.43	− 2.42	0.15	− 0.05
213	0.37	1.56	0.37	− 1.15	− 0.15	− 2.46	3.99	− 0.85
214	0.64	0.30	0.39	1.09	10.82	− 2.19	− 0.89	0.18
215	− 0.19	− 1.23	1.00	5.65	− 8.11	− 6.89	− 0.53	− 1.01
216	1.97	− 2.75	5.34	− 8.74	− 8.05	1.28	− 2.11	0.43
217	0.82	0.21	0.73	− 0.23	− 2.48	− 1.88	− 2.73	1.41
218	1.90	0.68	0.27	1.16	− 4.49	− 0.60	0.67	− 1.08
219	0.15	− 0.15	− 0.73	0.62	− 0.53	1.28	0.26	− 0.21
221	0.74	− 0.67	− 0.62	0.10	11.67	− 0.87	3.26	2.41
229/1	0.09	− 0.93	− 0.79	2.52	6.09	− 1.29	− 2.73	− 1.26
229/2	1.46	− 0.07	0.39	2.14	− 3.11	− 4.74	− 0.82	− 2.56
231	− 3.15	− 1.42	− 2.88	3.88	3.93	− 1.44	− 4.62	− 2.05
232	NA	NA	NA	NA	NA	NA	NA	NA
239/1	2.05	1.58	− 3.74	7.94	1.53	3.44	− 7.38	− 0.30
239/2	NA	NA	NA	NA	NA	NA	NA	NA
240	− 7.59	− 0.67	− 3.21	3.26	− 0.95	− 6.68	− 0.59	− 4.18
261	NA	NA	NA	NA	NA	NA	NA	NA
262	NA	NA	NA	NA	NA	NA	NA	NA
263	NA	NA	NA	NA	NA	NA	NA	NA
271	1.97	4.05	1.41	2.36	− 5.16	− 2.13	0.44	1.38
272	3.06	2.74	4.01	3.14	− 0.92	1.32	− 2.36	1.95
273	− 1.30	0.20	− 2.27	0.09	− 3.51	− 3.60	− 3.42	3.18
274	− 0.34	0.30	2.19	2.05	− 3.24	1.35	− 4.30	− 0.57
275	0.59	1.36	0.53	− 0.28	− 2.63	3.76	− 2.19	− 0.68
276	4.55	5.56	3.98	3.70	− 6.70	− 2.26	1.22	2.32
277	− 0.23	2.66	− 0.03	1.91	− 0.43	− 6.18	0.43	3.54
278	0.81	0.41	2.97	1.08	− 1.40	0.03	− 2.15	− 0.44
279/1	1.89	− 0.12	2.47	1.93	− 6.58	− 0.63	0.53	1.09
279/2	− 0.99	3.33	2.60	1.54	− 2.52	− 2.96	− 3.61	− 3.09
279/3	1.55	2.84	1.70	0.19	2.32	− 1.32	1.32	1.70
279/4	3.88	− 1.48	− 0.66	4.87	− 1.18	− 1.32	1.16	0.84
279/5	− 0.16	1.29	1.18	2.48	− 4.48	0.15	− 1.84	2.29
279/6	1.04	1.66	0.83	1.64	0.09	− 2.45	− 2.91	1.50
279/7	0.05	− 2.37	− 0.82	5.53	0.93	− 2.09	− 3.54	5.12
311	− 2.52	− 0.19	2.07	− 1.01	− 6.75	− 4.87	4.23	7.04
312	− 0.85	− 0.73	1.16	− 2.77	− 5.06	− 4.98	1.63	1.44
313	− 2.58	0.51	0.79	− 1.27	− 4.31	− 0.30	− 3.42	1.51
321	− 2.17	2.35	1.08	1.30	− 1.84	− 1.55	2.89	2.50
322	− 2.11	1.96	1.25	1.57	− 13.85	− 0.32	0.00	1.17
323	− 2.06	1.13	1.71	0.29	− 7.04	− 2.39	− 4.65	6.77
331	− 1.06	2.25	1.01	0.99	− 2.05	− 2.13	0.64	− 0.25
332	− 2.25	2.80	0.49	− 0.43	− 4.22	− 0.64	− 1.40	− 0.57
333	− 1.29	1.63	− 1.38	− 0.23	0.68	0.14	− 1.13	− 0.24
334	− 2.00	1.04	2.68	− 0.32	0.10	− 1.35	1.26	0.20
335	− 2.00	2.23	1.02	− 0.21	− 10.75	− 0.05	1.43	3.86
336	− 4.30	3.57	0.63	0.43	0.12	− 3.63	1.92	1.19
337	− 1.70	2.16	2.03	1.76	− 1.95	− 2.08	0.10	3.01
338	− 1.29	1.14	2.81	− 0.83	0.45	4.56	− 0.76	5.42

339/1	−1.34	1.88	−0.07	1.50	2.08	3.05	−0.81	−2.35
339/2	0.55	1.99	1.58	2.16	0.21	1.92	−6.83	3.58
339/3/4	3.32	0.62	2.29	1.20	−0.32	0.14	−0.03	−2.49
339/5/9	NA	NA	1.54	0.23	−1.66	−0.34	−2.61	0.73
341	−0.99	1.51	0.51	1.47	−2.13	2.67	−1.26	−0.77
342	−3.09	1.92	2.09	−1.41	2.94	3.64	−0.34	−0.18
349	−1.73	2.07	2.04	1.97	0.10	0.32	−1.60	2.11
351	−2.64	1.55	2.31	1.04	−3.30	−0.88	7.66	−0.57
352	−3.54	4.34	1.99	3.89	−0.47	−1.33	−3.11	5.40
353	−0.93	1.94	0.67	1.25	0.04	−1.18	−1.12	−0.01
354	−1.57	2.83	2.24	1.87	1.04	1.56	0.88	−0.48
361	−0.36	0.53	2.86	1.10	2.32	−0.69	3.29	1.17
362	−1.45	1.72	0.46	0.29	−1.03	0.24	−1.70	−0.90
363	−2.84	3.08	2.68	3.24	−1.57	3.70	5.45	−0.63
364	NA	NA	2.15	1.14	−2.66	0.44	1.57	−0.54
365	NA	NA	3.37	4.34	4.79	2.67	6.78	4.27
366	NA	NA	NA	NA	NA	NA	NA	NA
367	NA	NA	0.31	2.90	1.53	0.46	3.42	−0.41
368	2.81	4.56	1.38	3.43	0.51	−1.42	2.45	2.23
369	−2.49	2.59	1.49	0.41	−3.15	−2.55	−1.54	−0.19
370	−1.13	1.88	0.81	0.76	−6.01	2.63	2.35	−2.46
380	NA	NA	1.92	−1.85	−3.84	−4.21	−1.35	−2.21
381	−1.22	2.75	1.37	−0.12	−1.50	−1.03	−0.74	1.96
382	−2.74	1.28	2.33	1.91	−2.58	−3.10	−1.35	−3.68
383	−1.13	2.30	5.25	3.33	−9.32	−1.54	4.02	3.15
384/385	−1.76	1.20	1.07	3.80	−4.29	3.47	2.49	−1.98
390	−2.52	2.84	2.51	2.72	−2.06	−3.36	−1.18	1.23
391	0.36	0.68	−0.36	0.35	−3.07	−1.19	−5.93	1.23
392	−1.88	−0.61	1.22	−2.27	−1.44	−2.47	−4.67	−1.58
393	−1.54	1.88	1.63	1.14	−8.36	−1.17	−3.24	1.54
394	−1.13	1.18	1.08	1.75	−0.33	−1.38	−0.66	0.49
395	−0.72	0.76	1.45	10.08	−4.40	−0.79	0.05	0.65
396	−2.50	0.55	0.65	−1.04	−5.53	3.16	−6.66	−1.42
399/1	−1.64	2.92	1.19	0.80	0.17	0.19	0.34	0.42
399/2/12	−1.94	2.14	2.24	−1.11	1.40	−1.87	0.20	0.08
411	−1.66	6.22	5.56	3.75	−2.78	1.28	1.17	5.06
412	1.31	2.55	−0.60	0.10	−3.13	0.43	2.18	1.36
413	1.42	1.01	−1.48	−1.01	−1.00	0.96	−0.80	2.09
414	5.78	−0.69	2.44	−5.28	7.42	−1.13	1.52	3.70
415	0.61	0.54	−4.25	0.89	−0.54	−1.21	10.44	1.07
416	1.04	−2.13	2.45	−1.05	−7.13	0.60	0.44	−0.22
417	1.24	2.52	3.23	2.19	3.62	−1.76	0.18	1.63
418	1.67	1.67	−0.34	3.38	−9.47	−6.88	0.74	−1.17
419	−1.55	0.23	−0.53	1.35	0.87	−3.42	−0.31	0.52
421	−0.67	0.72	0.12	−0.44	−2.86	0.03	−2.05	0.45
422/1	2.27	−0.32	−0.52	2.18	−3.81	−1.68	0.10	1.64
422/2	3.98	−1.57	0.56	−3.15	0.37	−2.16	2.94	−0.59
423	1.96	1.69	2.33	0.32	4.16	0.30	2.49	1.56
429	−0.14	−3.79	0.48	2.96	−1.00	−3.30	−4.27	2.27
431	3.76	−0.42	−1.28	−4.35	15.13	3.36	−4.21	−3.05
432	1.41	−0.60	0.27	0.73	0.68	−1.57	−0.36	3.23
433	−0.67	1.53	0.05	0.76	3.00	2.68	−4.10	0.17
441	0.84	2.11	1.81	2.93	1.29	0.33	−1.69	2.84
442	−1.30	2.15	1.51	2.73	−0.92	−0.08	2.64	2.72
443	−0.78	2.11	0.50	3.57	0.26	3.66	−0.61	0.41
444	−0.38	1.37	0.54	2.36	0.09	2.19	0.67	2.16
445	−0.32	1.79	1.38	3.56	2.07	1.73	−0.28	1.80
446	−4.11	0.78	0.01	0.80	1.77	−1.09	0.60	0.80

449/1	0.09	1.75	1.20	3.10	− 2.28	1.33	− 3.72	0.24
449/2	− 1.31	2.56	0.43	2.76	− 2.05	1.42	0.62	1.31
450	1.23	1.73	1.81	1.03	3.64	0.17	− 2.50	2.05
461	1.45	1.29	1.44	3.35	− 7.83	− 5.53	− 1.76	0.91
462	− 0.48	0.16	− 0.40	1.84	2.00	− 1.34	− 1.96	1.01
463	0.41	0.54	2.04	3.18	− 2.04	− 0.59	0.41	5.62
464	− 1.72	1.27	− 0.81	0.12	− 5.76	− 1.81	− 5.29	1.87
469/1	1.93	0.18	1.51	− 0.66	− 0.29	− 0.06	− 6.25	− 0.37
469/2	2.47	1.93	1.74	1.15	− 3.48	− 2.97	− 0.38	− 0.04
471	2.20	0.17	− 0.31	− 1.52	− 0.46	− 2.44	1.35	0.56
472	− 0.05	1.76	1.71	1.74	− 1.78	0.37	− 0.60	0.95
473	1.61	2.08	1.17	− 0.45	− 3.97	− 3.60	− 0.29	1.11
474	1.42	3.32	− 0.09	− 0.29	− 1.54	0.63	− 0.54	− 0.20
475	0.93	1.50	− 0.07	1.58	− 4.29	− 0.17	2.86	1.98
479	3.19	2.23	1.16	− 1.79	− 4.55	0.01	− 1.61	0.51
481	− 2.28	2.15	− 0.12	0.39	− 3.56	− 1.60	− 0.08	3.32
482/1	0.26	1.29	0.82	0.82	− 2.83	− 0.92	− 2.69	1.52
482/2	− 0.10	1.64	0.11	1.21	− 3.87	− 1.67	− 0.18	0.71
483	0.46	0.66	0.89	1.69	− 4.85	− 0.18	− 5.54	0.71
484	− 0.75	− 0.16	− 1.38	2.94	− 4.06	− 0.93	− 5.55	− 0.61
485/486	0.81	2.91	1.94	0.91	− 6.29	0.38	− 7.86	0.08
489	− 1.70	1.05	0.32	2.02	0.65	− 0.48	2.74	2.08
491	− 2.69	2.42	1.97	− 0.18	1.77	− 4.98	− 0.90	1.61
492	− 1.11	0.47	− 2.14	4.18	− 0.33	− 2.67	− 1.74	2.31
493	2.36	− 3.12	0.81	1.35	− 0.88	− 2.76	− 2.40	0.31
494/1/2	NA	NA	NA	NA	0.77	− 4.64	− 2.99	− 0.65
494/3	NA	NA	NA	NA	− 0.48	− 2.02	− 1.88	− 1.10
495	0.70	1.68	2.32	0.58	− 1.90	2.61	− 2.75	4.95
496	1.73	2.41	3.44	2.18	0.57	− 1.57	− 1.07	1.49
499	2.36	2.29	5.21	3.63	− 1.86	− 1.84	− 1.03	3.52
601	NA	NA	NA	NA	NA	NA	NA	NA
602	NA	NA	NA	NA	NA	NA	NA	NA
603	NA	NA	NA	NA	NA	NA	NA	NA

Note: Growth of MFP is growth of output *minus* growth of Törnqvist index of total in put, latter composed of Törnqvist indices of total capital input, total labour input and total intermediate input.

NOTES

1 An Overview

1 Total input growth should be a weighted sum, but not necessarily a weighted average, of individual input growth rates, because if there are increasing returns to scale the appropriate weights should sum to more than one (see chapter 2). The value shares of the inputs will of course always sum to one.

2 Calculated from table 3.1 of Jorgenson (1990). Comparable figures for his whole period 1947–85 are 0.71 per cent per annum, 22 per cent and 34 per cent respectively.

3 For a sceptical evaluation, see Crafts (1992) and (1993) and for a demonstration that there is still life in the Solow model, see Mankiw *et al.* (1992). On the other side, O'Mahony (1992b) finds evidence that part of the productivity gap between UK and German manufacturing can be explained by an externality generated by the higher proportion of skilled workers in Germany.

4 The industries covered by the study, classified by the 1968 SIC, are listed in Appendix A.

5 The Census records disposals of assets but not scrapping. So it is only insofar as assets are literally destroyed, or when a whole plant closes, that our method is in danger of overestimating the size of the capital stock, and more importantly, its growth rate.

6 Here and throughout the book, all growth rates are exponential. A variable growing at x per cent per annum will be after u years a multiple $e^{xu/100}$ of its original value.

7 The method outlined here amounts to calculating real value added by double deflation. If single deflation is employed, data on intermediate input can be dispensed with, but as chapter 2 argues this is a distinctly inferior alternative.

8 External input is *not* just the aggregate of industry-level intermediate input since the latter includes purchases by one industry from other UK manufacturing industries.

2 Theory and Methods

1 Jorgenson (1990) contains a review of the historically important contributions to productivity measurement.

2 An alternative, full-blown econometric approach has been utilised by Morrison (1990), who estimates MFP growth for seventeen sectors of US manufacturing, allowing for imperfect competition and economies of scale. The small number of time-series observations on each industry prevents this approach from being followed here. Hall (1988 and 1990) adjusts conventional

measures of MFP in US manufacturing by using cost rather than value shares, where costs include a normal profit level rather than actual profits; the resulting estimates differ little from those based on value shares. Hall's approach could have been adopted here, but the results would be sensitive to the *level* of the capital stock assumed for each industry and, as will be seen (chapter 3), far more uncertainty attaches to capital stock levels than to capital stock growth rates.

3 When calculating MFP growth, economists have of course long been accustomed to incorporate human capital in their measures of labour input (for example, Denison, 1967). But, on Lucas's view, the measures employed, such as years of schooling, are inappropriate: human capital could be rising even if the number of years of schooling (or any other similar measure) were constant, because of the cumulative nature of human knowledge, indeed, it is difficult to see how human capital in Lucas's sense *could* be measured, except by its results – a necessarily circular procedure.

4 When a new good appears, theory suggests that it should be treated as if it had always existed, but priced at a level which reduced demand to zero (Hicks, 1940). The actual appearance of a new good is then equivalent to a fall in price. Conventional price indices make no allowance for this (nor for the disappearance of old goods) and hence contain a bias of unknown size. A method of measuring this bias has been proposed by Feenstra (1991).

5 Some tests of the sensitivity of MFP growth rates in aggregate manufacturing to errors in durable goods prices will be presented in chapter 5.

6 Two further defects in producer price indices (PPIs) are often cited, usually on the authority of the influential paper by Meullbauer (1986). First, it is alleged that PPIs are list prices, not transactions prices. Second, it is claimed that the indices were systematically distorted by price controls imposed by the Price Commission during the period 1973–7. However, the official methodology (CSO, 1980b) makes clear that the *intention* is certainly to measure transactions prices and a conversation with an official of the CSO suggests that the CSO would not accept this criticism. If the indices were distorted by price controls, it would imply that the monthly returns made by firms, which require firms to notify any changes in the specification of the products reported on, had been systematically falsified. Since membership of the panel of firms supplying price data was voluntary at that time and since the information supplied is confidential (no individual price quotations are released outside the section dealing with PPIs), this seems unlikely.

7 Since so much emphasis is commonly put on R and D, it is worth pointing out that, though in total spending on R and D is quite large, the distribution of such expenditure across industries is extremely skew, so that for most industries this item is small or even negligible. Total 'intramural' R and D expenditure on manufactured products was £5,070 million in 1986 (the last year of the present study), which compares with value added in manufacturing of £80,955 million and total expenditure on fixed capital of £8,705 million (all in current prices). Employment related to R and D in 1986 was 188,000 or about 4 per cent of total manufacturing employment. However, more than half (£2,779 million) of the R and D expenditure was concen-

trated in aerospace and electronics, much of it defence-related. A further £1,038 million was in chemicals, of which half was pharmaceuticals. By contrast, the whole mechanical engineering sector spent only £268 million (Source for R and D figures: CSO, 1990).

8 The translog is an example of a 'flexible functional form'; the Törnqvist index is an example of a 'superlative' index, that is, one which is exact for some flexible functional form. Since in practice superlative indices give very similar results, it makes little difference which one of them is used (Diewert, 1980).

9 In practice, the method described in the text had to be modified somewhat. The difficulty is that (2.10) does not preclude the possibility of negative rental prices, though these are economically impossible according to the theory. It turns out that rental prices calculated to be negative do occur quite often. The remedy was primarily to use a three-year moving average of capital gains, rather than actual current capital gains. For further details, see Appendix G. These difficulties suggest that the theoretical argument of Berndt and Fuss (1986) cannot be entirely relied on.

10 Of the 147 manufacturing industries for which data are available in 1979, 35 had a ratio of sales of principal products to total sales of 95 per cent or more, 44 had a ratio between 90 per cent and 95 per cent, 28 had one between 85 per cent and 90 per cent, 24 had one between 80 per cent and 85 per cent, and sixteen had one of less than 80 per cent.

11 'Path independence' means that the value of the index at the end point depends only on the start and end points, and not on the intervening path. It is always possible to calculte a Divisia index of a set of components (or at least a Törnqvist approximation to one), but it will be meaningless unless path independence holds. Without path independence, the same set of facts, for example, growth of component A by 5 per cent and of component B by 10 per cent by the end of a five-year period, could produce different values of the index in year five, depending on the path followed by the components within the five-year period.

12 Single deflation might still be superior to double deflation in practice, because of errors in measuring Y or X (Hill, 1971), but this is not the main point at issue here, which is whether value added should be employed at all as an output measure.

13 Thus Appendix B gives references to the statistical sources consulted. Appendices D, E, F and G discuss the estimation of respectively output, price indices, labour input, and rental prices of assets. Appendix A lists the industries in the study.

14 To give an idea of how serious this loss is, note that out of 137 manufacturing industries, prices at the MLH level were available for 63 industries in 1954 and 1958, for 72 in 1963, for 83 in 1968, for 109 in 1973 and 1976, for 117 in 1979, for 118 in 1982 and for 119 in 1986.

15 The import component was calculated only back to 1968 – the domestic component alone was used prior to that date. The same methodology described above was used to estimate material and fuel prices for the food industries from 1974–9 since the official indices were only available from the latter date.

16 Matthews *et al.* (1982) estimate that for the whole economy rising educational attainments increased labour input by 0.5 per cent per annum over 1951–64 and by 0.6 per cent per annum over 1964–71 (their table 4.6, p. 111). However, since our labour input measure includes the effect of changes in the white-collar/blue-collar proportion, and since white-collar workers are likely to have higher educational attainments than blue-collar ones, some at least of the rise estimated by Matthews and his co-authors may well have been allowed for. No allowance has been made for any effect on productivity arising from the increased educational level of blue-collar workers, assuming that this did in fact occur for those employed in the sector of the economy studied here. But it is also relevant to note that, according to the same source (*op. cit.*, table 4.5), the proportion of skilled workers amongst manual workers as a whole was virtually unchanged from 1951–71 at about 37 per cent. As far as technical education and vocational training are concerned, this has traditionally been the task of the apprenticeship system. Matthews *et al.* noted (1982, p. 109) that the proportion of male school leavers entering apprenticeships has been about 35 per cent, without much trend, over the postwar period. However, since they wrote it has drastically declined. In 1981 for example 3.5 per cent of manufacturing employees were engaged in apprenticeships or on similar training schemes; by 1986, this had fallen to 1.9 per cent (Source: DE *Gazette*). The collapse of the traditional apprenticeship system in the 1980s has been palliated, to an extent difficult to assess, by the rise of the Youth Training Scheme (now called simply Youth Training). As for higher education, the numbers involved are far too small to be worth bothering about – Matthews *et al.* estimate that only 3.6 per cent of the male labour force were graduates in 1971; the graduate proportion of employment in industry was certainly lower still. For all these reasons then, it is doubtful that a more refined calculation of the educational level of the industrial labour force would change the estimates very much.

17 Needless to say, this is a highly contentious area. Nevertheless, there is some evidence that standards have fallen in mathematics, a subject arguably relevant for industrial efficiency. The National Foundation for Educational Research administered the same test to a large sample of fourteen year-olds in England and Wales in 1964 and again in 1981; the 1981 results were markedly inferior. For example, when asked to add 2/5 to 3/8, 63 per cent answered correctly in 1964, only 42 per cent in 1981 (Cresswell and Grubb, 1987).

18 The Census distinguishes between 'new buildings' and 'land and existing buildings' from 1970; these were aggregated together in the estimates of building stocks.

3 Estimating the Stock of Fixed Capital

1 Alternative methods include ones based on fire insurance records (Smith, 1986) and on balance sheets prepared in accordance with current cost accounting conventions (Wadhwani and Wall, 1986; Smith, 1987). None of these are feasible for a study, like the present one, which is at the industry level and which covers an extended period of time.

2 One of the 140 industries, MLH 104 (Petroleum and Natural Gas), is a special case since its capital stock was assumed to be zero before the 1970s. 137 industries fell within the definition of manufacturing under the 1968 SIC. In addition to MLH 104, the other non-manufacturing industries were MLH 102/103 and 109 (see Appendix A for a complete list of industries). Most of the summarised results are for 139 industries, that is, excluding MLH 104, or for the 137 manufacturing industries.

3 The CSO's current methodology is described in CSO (1985, chapter 12). The earlier methodology is in Griffin (1976). An account of the development of the CSO's approach is in Hibbert *et al.* (1977).

4 See Diewert (1980), Jorgenson (1989) and Hulten (1990) for comprehensive surveys.

5 To save notational clutter, in this section we drop the subscript or superscript i used to denote industry i. All relationships should continue to be understood as referring to industry-level variables. For the time being, for simplicity of exposition, we also ignore intermediate input and assume only one type of capital, so subscript k is also dropped; the propositions in the text can easily be restated in more general form to incorporate intermediate input and several types of capital.

6 The asset price is $P_K(t,v) = \Sigma_{s=0}^{\infty} p_K(t+s,v) d^s$, where d is the discount factor. The statement in the text follows from applying (3.6) to this formula and assuming geometric decline in the b_{t-v}.

7 The various statements in Scott (1989) and (1992), to the effect that depreciation due to obsolescence is purely a price effect and should be ignored when assessing the contribution of capital to growth, are thus seen to be incorrect; see Oulton (1992c) for a rebuttal of Scott's views. That paper also shows that the present methods of measuring depreciation are still correct in a clay–clay world, in contrast to the putty–putty world assumed by Fisher (1965).

8 Depreciation need not be geometric. Indeed, it is often argued that many types of asset need not depreciate physically at all, if properly maintained. The decision *not* to maintain an asset is an economic one, which is taken in the light of demand for the product which it produces, of the appearance of more up-to-date equipment, and so on. For other types of asset, a 'one-hoss shay' or 'light bulb' pattern of deterioration is more realistic, that is, unchanged physical efficiency up till the point of catastrophic failure, after which the asset is scrapped. But these objections do not lead to any great problem in principle. Jorgenson *et al.* (1987, chapter 2) show how the rental price can be derived from different patterns of depreciation, such as linearly declining efficiency or 'one-hoss shay'. Nevertheless, calculations are greatly simplified if depreciation is geometric so it is fortunate that the empirical evidence does support geometric depreciation as a good approximation.

9 O'Mahony and Oulton (1990a) experimented with a declining life assumption of this latter type.

10 If assets are expected to become obsolete more rapidly, it might be optimal to make them less physically durable than in earlier times. But even if older assets *are* more physically durable (which is itself debatable) this would not

save them from being scrapped before the end of their expected service lives because of more rapid obsolescence. Mendis and Muellbauer (1984) have also criticised the CSO's 'declining life' assumption. Note too that the declining lives assumption cannot be interpreted as attempting to capture the move towards the new information technology, since the CSO retains the assumption of fixed proportions of investment in plant & machinery devoted to each type of asset (including office machinery).

11 These surveys have been discussed by Bacon and Eltis (1974). They found that in both countries the service life of machine tools was about 20–25 years in 1971; the BEA assumption (Young and Musgrave, 1980, table 1) is sixteen years. See also Prais (1986), who discusses more recent versions of similar surveys.

12 The exponential and geometric rates of mortality are related as follows. If d is the rate of geometric decay, then we can find the geometric rate which corresponds to a given service life assumption from the relation $1 - d = e^{-1/T}$.

13 The use of acquisitions net of disposals by the CSO for their 'gross stock' estimates of plant and machinery leads to an inconsistency. Under the 'gross stock' convention, assets are assumed not to deteriorate with age. However, in the Census, disposals are valued at market prices, which presumably decline with an asset's age (even if the physical efficiency of the asset does not), hence assets disposed of will be undervalued, from a gross stock point of view.

14 Disposals of assets for continued use are probably also under-recorded. It is only disposals by plants which survive to fill in a Census form which feature in the statistics. When a plant has a 'closing down' sale of its assets, no record of disposals will be made.

15 Figures for net acquisition of land and existing buildings are available for 1963 and 1968 also, but a continuous series only begins in 1970, hence no attempt was made to adjust the stock estimates prior to 1970.

16 The extent to which the omission (prior to 1970) of transactions in land and existing buildings distorts the capital stock estimates for buildings depends however on a different ratio, namely *net* acquisitions of land and existing buildings as a proportion of total *net* acquisitions of land and (new and old) buildings. This ratio appears to have been small and usually negative up to 1973. But thereafter it shows a steady rise from 5.5 per cent in 1974 for total manufacturing to 16.4 per cent in 1985. Thus, during a period when manufacturing has been in decline in terms of output and employment, it has apparently been acquiring buildings from the rest of the economy.

17 A third interpretation, related to the second, is that because the quality of goods is continuously improving, older-style products can only sell for a progressively lower price; consequently equipment required to manufacture them (assumed to be specialised) declines in value relative to new equipment.

18 Consider an asset which yields a return of £1 per period for R periods and thereafter nothing (a 'one-hoss-shay' or 'light bulb' pattern of depreciation). At time $t(0 \leq t \leq R)$ the present value (PV) is

$$PV = \int_0^{R-t} e^{-ru} du = (1/r)[1 - e^{-r(R-t)}],$$

where r is the rate of discount. The proportional rate of change of present value is

$$d(\ln PV)/dt = - re^{-r(R-t)}/[1 - e^{-r(R-t)}] < 0,$$

which is declining in t, that is, $d^2 \ln(PV)/dt^2 < 0$. In other words, the present value declines at an increasing proportional rate as the end of the asset's life approaches.

19 For an early UK study of second-hand car prices, see Cramer (1958).

20 In their published work Hulten and Wykoff give the pure ageing effect only for buildings; for other assets they give what they call the 'declining balance rate' (*DBR*), defined implicitly by the relationship $d = DBR/T$, where d is the total rate of geometric decay (ageing plus retirement, or simply economic depreciation) and T is the service life. *DBR* can be deduced using figures for US service lives (T) given in Young and Musgrave (1980, table 1.1). For the UK, economic depreciation is the *American DBR*, divided by the *British* service life.

21 In addition to the conceptual differences already noted, the CSO's capital stock estimates and the present ones are also not comparable due to differences in the underlying nominal investment data. The CSO employs the Blue Book series on investment by industry groups (based on surveys of companies), while this study uses series from the Census. After allowing for differences in the assumptions, the present estimates (aggregated up to the industry group level) are somewhat lower, though mostly within a few per cent of the CSO's, except for chemicals and allied industries, where the difference is larger (particularly after the mid-1960s).

22 Financial leasing must be distinguished from operational leasing, a much older phenomenon, which is not included in our estimates. The CSO's estimates now include financial leasing but those of Allard (1982) did not.

23 Tony Smith kindly made this series available.

24 On average, the inclusion of land and existing buildings makes little difference; for example, the ratio of the stock of new buildings only to the total stock of buildings averages 103.2 per cent for manufacturing in 1985. But the effect on particular industries can be substantial: the standard deviation of the same ratio in 1985 is 8.2 per cent, the minimum value is 73.4 per cent and the maximum value is 128.7 per cent.

25 The levels of the stocks in 1980 prices by MLH for the terminal year, 1986, appear in Appendix H (table H.9). The levels of the fixed stocks in 1980 prices for earlier years (1954, 1958, 1963, 1968, 1973 and 1979), calculated under the same assumptions as here, appear in O'Mahony and Oulton (1990a, tables C12, C13 and C14).

26 Notice that this is a different point from the familiar one about premature scrapping either in the 1970s or in 1980–81; if premature scrapping occurred, it was of a one-off nature, and there is no reason to expect that as a result retirement or scrapping was higher in, say, 1986 than it had been in 1973.

27 These are exponential rates. The corresponding geometric rates are 3.92 and 13.30 for plant & machinery, and 1.66 and 3.61 for buildings, all rates being per cent per annum.

28 The average *geometric* depreciation rate for producers' durable equipment (which includes vehicles) assumed in their study was 13.3 per cent (Jorgenson *et al.*, 1987, p. 119), which corresponds to an *exponential* rate of 14.27 per cent. In fact, they distinguished twenty types of producers' durable equipment, of which sixteen could be classified as plant & machinery. For the latter, the rates ranged from 7.86 per cent per annum to 27.29 per cent per annum (see their table 4.3).

29 The terminal date is 1985 since these calculations were done at an earlier stage before the 1986 Census became available.

30 In fact, the average growth rates of investment in plant and machinery in the 139 industries were as follows:

Period	Growth rate (% p.a.)
1948–73	3.73
1963–73	4.64
1973–79	1.54
1979–85	− 2.30
1973–85	− 0.38

Thus investment did grow at a fairly steady rate up till 1973, but thereafter growth slowed considerably.

31 Chapter 2 argued that, as a basis for productivity calculations, gross output is theoretically superior to net output or value added. Capital's share in value added is, of course, higher.

32 The average age of buildings and of plant & machinery for selected years from 1954–85 is given at the industry level for the two extreme assumptions in O'Mahony and Oulton (1990a, Appendix C, tables C4–C7); the age distribution is given *ibid.* (Appendix C, tables C8–C11).

33 These results should be qualified because of the inconsistency alluded to earlier in the treatment of assets of different ages. As far as plant is concerned, investment is measured by acquisitions of assets of all ages less disposals, valued at constant market prices. From the point of view of measuring the age of the capital stock, older assets are understated both because an asset is assumed to be new when purchased and because the market prices of older assets are most probably lower than those of comparable newer ones, contrary to 'gross stock' assumptions. However, because trade in second-hand plant and machinery is small, the effect on the estimates of age is probably small too. As for buildings, investment is measured as acquisitions of *new* buildings only, that is, all trade in second-hand buildings is excluded. Hence the effect on the age estimates is likely to be more serious, since as mentioned above trade in second-hand buildings has been increasing since the earlier 1970s.

34 These papers all use indirect methods because of the absence of direct measures of scrapping. However, there is one exception to this, the steel castings industry (Baden–Fuller, 1989). Here we know that 25 per cent of the industry's capacity, measured by tonnage, was scrapped between 1979 and 1983. Nearly all this lost capacity took the form of whole plant closures. The scrap value of the plants was low and usually absorbed by clean-up costs.

35 See Oulton (1987) and the case study of the steel castings industry referred to above (Baden–Fuller, 1989). In addition, Oulton (1989) finds that the cross-industry pattern of labour productivity growth cannot be explained by assuming that the oldest, least efficient assets are scrapped first.

36 The basis for this calculation is as follows. Assume that in 1981 a quantity of capital equal to the fraction h of the 1979 stock is prematurely scrapped. The difference between the estimate of the stock in 1986 without premature scrapping, K_{86}, and the estimate with, K'_{86}, is

$$K_{86} - K'_{86} = K_{79}(1 - \delta)^7 - (1 - h(1 - \delta)^{-2})K_{79}(1 - \delta)^7 = h(1 - \delta)^5 K_{79},$$

where δ is the depreciation rate. As a proportion of the 1986 stock (without premature scrapping), this is $h(1 - \delta)^5 (K_{79}/K_{86})$.

37 These estimated premature scrapping rates are fairly robust to small changes in the sample size, for example, the rates change by less than one percentage point if the estimating time period is 1950–74. The rates for the CSO stocks are significantly above those derived for the net stocks but one should not expect scrapping rates from gross and net stocks to be equal. It was also hoped to estimate scrapping at the industry level. But it was found that the capital–output ratios were not in general trend-stationary for the disaggregated estimates. Since aggregate manufacturing capital stocks and output depend on industry magnitudes, this casts some doubt on the aggregate estimates.

38 For example, if production workers agree to do their own routine maintenance and repairs, instead of sending for a craftsman, machine down-time will be reduced, so a higher annual output can be produced from the same stock of machines.

4 Output, Input and Productivity Growth at the Industry Level

1 Persistence of MFP growth is discussed in greater detail below.

2 The five industries with significant MFP growth listed in Jorgenson *et al.* (1987, table 6.4) all conform to the above criteria.

3 This relationship, 'Fabricant's Law', is discussed below.

4 There were seventeen manufacturing Orders in the 1968 SIC; the first, Order III, is omitted and there were no observations in Order IV.

5 See chapter 7 for more extensive discussion.

6 A diametrically opposite conclusion has been reached by Darby and Wren-Lewis (1991). Basing themselves on an analysis of labour productivity growth in aggregate manufacturing 1963–87, they argue that essentially the same trend rate of growth has prevailed throughout the period. Their reasons are two-fold. First, they claim that expectations of output were over-optimistic in the 1970s, leading to firms employing more labour than they would have done if their expectations had been more realistic. This makes the productivity record of the 1970s look worse and that of the 1980s better than was really the case. Second, they claim that higher labour productivity growth in the 1980s is partly explained by substitution of capital for labour, induced by changes in relative input prices. Both these arguments are disputable. Their

evidence on output expectations is based on the CBI survey, which asks firms whether they expect output to go up, go down or stay the same. The survey yields only ordinal data, which must be cardinalised in order to be compared with the outturn to see whether expectations were optimistic or not. The method of cardinalisation is not unique and anyway relies on the estimation of a parameter whose value is uncertain (the minimum estimate of this parameter is only half the maximum estimate, according to Wren-Lewis, 1986). Darby and Wren-Lewis do not calculate MFP growth so their argument that rising capital intensity explains a substantial part of the productivity improvement is an indirect one and is indeed refuted by the evidence presented here. In any case, it seems highly implausible to say that, at a time of acknowledged weakening of trade union power, rapid growth in wages caused (*via* substitution of capital for labour) rapid productivity growth. The reverse pattern of causation – higher productivity growth (due to the elimination of restrictive practices, increased flexibility of the workforce and the like) leading to higher wage growth – is surely far more likely; evidence for this view is in Oulton (1990).

7 Note that this list is not identical to the list of industries for which MFP growth was a significant contributor to output growth (see above); high productivity growth is neither necessary nor sufficient for being an important contributor to output growth.

8 With a sample of 124 industries, a correlation coefficient must be 0.18 or more in absolute value to be significant at the 95 per cent level; at the 99 per cent level the critical value is 0.23.

9 Wragg and Robertson (1978) found a rather higher correlation (0.78) between their MFP measure and labour productivity growth for 1963–73 (compare also our table 4.13, column 1). This is not surprising since they excluded intermediate input.

10 This is usually called 'Verdoorn's Law', but as Scott (1989, chapter 13) points out, the relationship which Verdoorn studied (later) was between growth rates of output and productivity (either of manufacturing as a whole or of GDP) across *countries*, not across industries in the *same* country. A discussion in English of the original work (which was in Italian) is in Verdoorn (1980).

11 Comparisons with Salter's work must be treated with caution, since, for reasons of data availability, his sample of industries was not a random one and only covered about 30 per cent of the industrial sector (Salter, 1966, p. 104). Furthermore he estimated prices by calculating unit values of what he believed were homogeneous products, rather than using wholesale prices, which were not sufficiently plentiful in his period.

12 A constant was included. Weighting by employment produced similar results.

13 The standard error of a sample correlation coefficient is $(\mathcal{N} - 3)^{-1/2}$ where $\mathcal{N}$ is the sample size, that is, 0.09 in this case.

14 The negative correlation between $\hat{q}$ and $\hat{y}$ implies a linear relationship: $\hat{q} = a + b\hat{y} + \epsilon$, $b < 0$, where ϵ is a random error. Hence, measuring all variables as deviations from their respective means, $\text{Cov}(\hat{p}_L - \hat{y}, \hat{q}) = E(\hat{p}_L$-

$\hat{q}) - E(\hat{y}\hat{q}) = bE(\hat{p}_L\hat{y}) - E(\hat{y}\hat{q})$, assuming that $\hat{p}_L$ is independent of ϵ. Since $E(\hat{y}\hat{q}) < 0$, $\mathrm{Cov}(\hat{p}_L - \hat{y}, \hat{q}) > 0$, unless $E(\hat{p}_L\hat{y})$ is sufficiently positive.

15 The standard deviation of wage growth is about one third that of labour productivity growth in both 1954–73 and 1973–86, as can be deduced from tables 4.1 and 4.11.

16 For 1924–50, the equivalent correlation is 0.14 (calculated from data in Salter (1966, table 14, p. 107). Carruth and Oswald (1989, p. 91) cite a much higher figure from Salter (0.94) since they look at the correlation between growth of real *product* wages and growth of real labour productivity. But this relationship, whose strength is obviously influenced by the presence in both the correlated variables of the growth of output prices, is not relevant to the issue with which we, and Salter, are concerned, namely the extent to which increases in productivity are nullified by input price rises. Nor is it relevant to answering the question, do workers benefit from working in technically progressive industries, since workers have no interest in *product* wages.

5 *Output and Productivity Growth in Aggregate Manufacturing*

1 All outputs, inputs and prices are to be understood as being measured at a point in time t, but to save notational clutter the subscript t is omitted.

2 So sales of, for example, sulphuric acid by one UK chemical firm to another chemical firm would be excluded, but sales to a foreign chemical firm included. Similarly, sales of UK-produced stationery to UK non-manufacturing firms would be included, along with sales to households.

3 However, Peterson (1979) showed that Leontief's measure can be modified to meet this objection, and that the neo-classical and the input–output approaches can be made fully compatible.

4 From the point of view of a national income statistician, total final output in this economy is equal to expenditure by residents and foreigners on the single output, that is, Y_1, so he would be in agreement.

5 The discussion of value added at the industry level in chapter 2 above is also relevant here.

6 An alternative way to calculate the growth rate of aggregate value added would be to proceed as follows. First, set each V_i equal to its observed nominal value in some base year and then apply the growth rates calculated from (5.9) to compute the *level* of V_i in all other years. Second, calculate aggregate real value added V from (5.4). A drawback to this procedure is that the results of the first step will depend in general on the choice of base year. If it were true that the price of value added was the same in all industries (an assumption which is necessary for the value added approach to be correct) then the choice of base year in fact is immaterial. However, in practice this assumption could never be relied on to be exactly satisfied; the procedure in the text has the virtue of producing a unique answer.

7 Let ϵ_V, ϵ_Y and ϵ_X be the errors in measuring the growth rates of value added, output and intermediate input respectively. Then from (5.9), assuming that ϵ_Y and ϵ_X are uncorrelated and that value shares are measured without error, the variance of the measurement error in the growth rate of value added is:

$$\sigma^2(\epsilon_V) = (1/\bar{v}_V^i)^2 \sigma^2(\epsilon_Y) + (\bar{v}_X^i/\bar{v}_V^i)^2 \sigma^2(\epsilon_X) > \sigma^2(\epsilon_Y), \text{ since } 1/\bar{v}_V^i > 1.$$

8 Jorgenson *et al.* do not actually mention this qualification (though in his related work Gollop (1985) does), but it is implicit in their argument.

9 Jorgenson *et al.* refer to the right-hand side of (5.12) as Domar aggregation of industry MFP growth rates. However, this terminology is misleading: as we have just seen, the Domar weights are the ratios of nominal gross output to total nominal *final output*, not, as in (5.12), to total nominal *value added*.

10 The final output method has been advocated by Gollop (1983), who also shows its connection with Domar aggregation. He compares the value added model extensively with the final output one. The basic reasons for preferring the latter are implicit in Hulten (1978).

11 In principle, the necessary data are obtainable from the input–output tables. But in practice the tables are not available for all the years required. Also, the industry classification of the tables is more aggregated than in the present study. Finally, very few price indices are available to deflate the nominal values of imported goods, which are all that the input–output tables report.

12 Source: for 1954–79, CSO (1980, Appendix G); for later years, *Annual Abstract of Statistics*.

13 For the years 1963–85, this index is a combination, in the proportions 1/3 and 2/3, of two unit value indices, one covering sections 5 and 6 of the SITC and the other covering that part of sections 7 and 8 classified as 'intermediate' (source: *Monthly Review of External Trade Statistics: Annual Supplement*, Nos 5 and 10 (Department of Trade and Industry, 1984 and 1989). Prior to 1963, the unit value of all manufactured imports was employed (source: *Annual Abstract of Statistics*).

14 Sources: For 1968, CSO (1973), tables 3 and 7. For 1974, BSO (1981), tables C and D. For 1984, CSO (1988), tables 4 and 6.

15 It is not obvious from the methodology described in CSO (1980) that the official price index does exclude services nor that in practice it excludes imported intermediate manufactured goods such as carburettors, but correspondence with the CSO revealed that this is indeed the case.

16 Net output is used because value added is not officially available before 1973. The nominal gross and net output figures for 1954 were taken from Business Statistics Office (1978) and for 1973 from the 1973 Census of Production (Summary tables, PA1002). The 1954 net output figure was roughly adjusted for the changed definition of net output by multiplying it by the ratio of net output in 1972 under the new definition to net output in 1972 under the old definition (the latter figures being taken also from the 1973 Summary tables).

17 Given that firms pay workers for hours on the job, not for hours effectively utilised, it is not clear that one should adjust for labour utilisation when measuring productivity growth. The issue here is similar to the one involved in whether one should adjust for capital utilisation.

18 The embodiment hypothesis has been defended particularly strongly by Scott (1989 and 1992). A critique of his view is Oulton (1992c).

19 The industries considered to be producing durable goods were MLH 331–368 (except for MLH 342, 349, 362 and 364) and MLH 380 and 381.

20 Gordon's estimates have also been employed by Hulten (1992) to produce alternative MFP growth rates for the US.

21 The figures involving final output in table 5.5 differ somewhat from the corresponding ones in table 1 of Oulton (1992), due to an improved deflator for external input.

22 A simple consistency check is to compare the growth rate of the price of final output implied by these estimates (that is, $d\ln(p_z Z)/dt - d\ln Z/dt$)) with the CSO's producer price index for manufacturing output ('home sales'), which is conceptually similar. The results are quite close. For 1954–73, the implicit deflator for final output grows at 3.72 per cent per annum and the CSO's measure at 3.36 per cent p.a.; for 1973–86, the figures are respectively 11.51 per cent per annum and 11.65 per cent per annum.

23 The official index of manufacturing output, which employs single deflation, falls by 0.7 per cent per annum over 1973–9 (source: *Economic Trends, Annual Supplement, 1992 Edition*, table 15). It is widely believed that the real costs of inputs into manufacturing rose sharply in the 1970s, as a result of the oil shock, and if so one would expect a single deflation measure of output (such as the CSO's) to show a larger fall than a double deflation one (such as the one in the text). The fact that the opposite appears to be the case seems to require an explanation. Two points can be made. First, it is not clear that input prices *did* rise relative to output prices in the period 1973–9. Our measure of the price of external input (which is *not* involved in the measurement of real value added) rises at 15.57 per cent per annum, while the CSO producer price index for manufacturing as a whole ('home sales') rose at 15.79 per cent per annum (Source: CSO, 1980, Appendix G). It is true that the 'home sales' index rises more rapidly than the 'materials and fuel' index, but as we have seen, the latter is only one component of the price of external input. Second, the CSO's estimates of manufacturing output do not rely for nominal data on the Census of Production, but use instead company sources.

24 In chapter 6 production functions at the Order level of the 1968 SIC will be estimated and it will be shown that technical progress is biased towards the use of intermediate input in all thirteen Orders studied.

25 For example, Crafts (1992, table 1) gives growth rates of labour productivity and of MFP for the business sector in nineteen OECD countries for the periods 1960–73, 1973–9, and 1979–88, based on estimates by Kendrick. The cross-country correlation between the two growth rates is 0.96 for 1960–73, 0.95 for 1973–9, and 0.93 for 1979–88. Input growth accounts on average for 33 per cent of labour productivity growth in 1960–73, but 80 per cent in 1973–9 when labour productivity growth was less than half what it had been in the earlier period.

26 At the industry level, the share of profits in gross output is even smaller – varying between 13 and 17 per cent over 1954–86 when averaged across industries (table 4.2).

6 Raw Material Prices and the Post-1973 Productivity Slowdown

1 Maddison (1987) and Englander and Mittelstädt (1988) both employ a two-factor (labour and capital) approach to measuring MFP growth. As

pointed out in chapter 5, when measured in this way MFP growth rates are systematically biased by the omission of inputs purchased outside the country under study, so that inter-country comparisons are invalid (Gollop, 1983); MFP growth rates of small countries which purchase more inputs from the rest of the world than large countries will be overestimated. However, inter-temporal comparisons may be less affected by this criticism.

2 As is clear from the charts in Englander and Mittelstädt (1988), MFP growth tends to follow the same cyclical path as labour productivity growth; probably the reason is the same in both cases, namely variation in capital and labour utilisation.

3 Kilpatrick and Naisbitt (1988) have found some evidence for a direct connection between the slowdown in MFP growth and energy intensity in the UK, though without providing a theoretical mechanism. In a cross-section regression of the MFP growth slowdown (1973–9 over 1969–73) on the output slowdown, the concentration ratio, capital intensity, import penetration, export propensity and energy intensity, they find that the latter variable is negative. However, it is only significant at the 10 per cent level. Moreover, their MFP measure is based on capital and labour only. But as was argued in chapter 2, this measure is systematically biased in a cross-section context, since it is approximately equal to the true measure divided by the ratio of value added to gross output, and this latter ratio varies across industries. The basic point here, which as noted in an earlier footnote causes analogous difficulties in cross-country comparisons, goes back to Domar (1961); see also JGF (1987, chapter 2) on the pitfalls of a value-added-based measure of MFP growth.

4 In this chapter, it is convenient, for reasons of symmetry, to use the symbol v_t^i to stand for MFP growth, instead of μ as elsewhere.

5 The translog production function was introduced by Christensen, Jorgenson and Lau (1973). Jorgenson et al. (1987), chapter 7, discuss its properties and ways of overcoming the econometric problems which its estimation presents. Jorgenson (1986) contains a parallel discussion of the translog price function.

6 Here we have assumed that $x_i'(t - u) = x_i(t - u)$ and $k_i'(t - u) = k_i(t - u)$, that is, that input prices and hence input intensities are the same at the beginning of the period in both situations.

7 The parameter estimates come from Jorgenson et al. (1987, table 7.3) and the prices and quantities in 1973 and 1979 from their Appendices B–D. In solving equations (6.4) and (6.5), the right-hand sides of equations (6.1) were used to calculate v_X^i, v_K^i and v_L^i, rather than the observed shares in 1973, since empirically we must allow for the presence of a random error in equations (6.1).

8 In two sectors, Petroleum & coal products and Primary metal industries, the method failed since one or more of the estimated value shares was negative.

9 Aside from being more aggregative, the later production function estimates used different data; for one thing the estimation period was longer (1954–79, compared with 1958–79). Quite apart from these differences, one should not necessarily expect identical results from the two separate exercises, since a translog price function is not the dual of a translog production function. Nevertheless, as we have seen, a similar picture with respect to effect on MFP growth of intermediate input prices does emerge.

10 According to the maintained hypothesis, real input prices are exogenous at the level of the firm; they are not necessarily exogenous at the level of the industry. However, in the UK case, output and intermediate input prices are heavily influenced by foreign competition, while labour costs may well be mainly determined by economy-wide, rather than industry-specific factors. These points gain force since our estimates will be for a large number of industries (119 – see below) within manufacturing, itself only a fraction of the economy. Lagged values of the right-hand side variables might also be candidate instruments, but in our case the paucity of time-series observation would make their use very expensive.

11 This can be shown as follows. Since $\bar{\epsilon}^i_X(T) = (1/2)[\epsilon^i_X(T) + \epsilon^i_X(T-u)]$, then $\mathrm{Var}(\bar{\epsilon}^i_X) = (1/4)E[\epsilon^i_X(T) + \epsilon^i_X(T-u)]^2 = (1/4)[\mathrm{Var}(\epsilon^i_X(T)) + \mathrm{Var}(\epsilon^i_X(T-u))] = (1/2)\sigma^2_X$. Similarly, $\mathrm{Cov}(\bar{\epsilon}^i_X(T), \bar{\epsilon}^i_X(T-u)) = (1/4)E[\epsilon^i_X(T) + \epsilon^i_X(T-u)][\epsilon^i_X(T-u) + \epsilon^i_X(T-2u)] = (1/4)\sigma^2_X$.

12 This use of industry dummies is exactly analogous to the use of country dummies within a translog production function by Jorgenson and Nishimizu (1978) in their comparison of US and Japanese productivity growth.

13 The nature of panel data, by contrast with pure time series, dictated a slight difference in procedure. In our data, a panel consists of eight observations on industry 1, followed by eight observations on industry 2, . . ., followed by eight observations on industry M, where M is the number of industries in the panel. The same transforming matrix R, of order 8×8, was applied in turn to each set of eight observations in the panel.

14 The superscript i is now dropped from the β coefficients since these are now assumed constant across the industries in each panel.

15 Over all industries for which estimates could be made, the change in MFP growth averaged -2.47 per cent (chapter 4, table 4.1).

16 The two will differ if returns to scale are not constant. The evidence for and against the presence of non-constant returns will be reviewed in chapter 7.

17 The estimates will not however be correct if there are several quasi-fixed inputs, for each of which capacity utilisation may be different. This in effect was Baily's (1981) hypothesis: he argued that the utilisation of energy-intensive capital equipment fell particularly heavily, leading to an overestimate of capital stock growth and consequently an underestimate of MFP growth. Hulten *et al.* (1989) however conclude that such an effect must be small in the US; amongst other evidence, they cite the failure of second-hand prices of energy-intensive equipment to show any marked decline after the oil shock.

7 Investment, Increasing Returns, and the Pattern of Productivity Growth

1 In 1973 GDP at factor cost (average estimate) rose at the temporarily tigerish rate of 7.4 per cent. (Source: *Economic Trends Annual Supplement: 1992* Edition, table 1).

2 More precisely, a Törnqvist (chain) index is employed which uses the average of the shares at the beginning and end of each time period (see chapter 2).

3 Scott's views have been rebutted by Denison (1991), from a mainly empirical point of view; see also Scott's reply, Scott (1991). Oulton (1992c) is a critique of Scott from a theoretical point of view.

4 The most pronounced divergence from the null hypothesis occurs in 1973–6. A possible explanation is errors in measuring the prices of intermediate inputs. As pointed out in chapter 3, this kind of error is likely to be larger in the 1973–6 period, which saw particularly rapid inflation, than at other times. The estimates of $\Delta \ln X$ may be biased upwards in 1973–6, leading to a downward bias in the estimates of $\Delta \ln MFP$; indeed, many of the latter are negative.

5 Whatever the merits of a catch-up variable in a cross-country study, it clearly has no place in a *cross-industry* study: there is no reason to expect convergence over time in gross output per unit of labour in different industries.

6 Romer (1987) claims that time-series evidence at the whole economy level supports his view that capital generates externalities (although Romer (1990) takes a different view). As the results in table 7.2 also have a time-series basis but do *not* support the view that capital generates externalities, there is an apparent conflict with Romer. However, Benhabib and Jovanovic (1991) have disputed Romer's conclusions, arguing that the coefficient on capital in Romer's regressions is biased upwards because at the macro level saving generates a positive correlation between output and the capital stock. But there is no reason to expect saving to generate such a correlation at the *industry* level. Hence there is no contradiction between the present (negative) results and the positive ones of Romer, when the latter are properly interpreted.

7 Identical regressions to the ones in tables 7.2 and 7.3 using disaggregated capital were also run with the growth rates of the two kinds of inventory included as well – 'materials, stores and fuel', and 'work in progress and goods on hand for sale', both measured per unit of labour. These two inventory stocks, together with the three types of fixed capital, make up total capital (see chapter 2). The results were very similar to the ones reported in the text.

8 A more likely, common-across-industries error in measuring capital stock growth rates arises from the fact that the estimates neglect the possibility, some would say probability, of premature scrapping in the 1980–81 recession; premature scrapping may also have occurred in the 1974–9 period, though this is less likely. This issue was extensively discussed in chapter 3 without however being resolved, the difficulty being the absence of independent data on scrapping. To the extent that premature scrapping occurred, the capital stock growth rates will be overestimated.

9 Britton (1991, table 18.5) has considered year-to-year growth rates for a sample of 94 industries and notes that the relationship between labour productivity and output has remained very similar over 1971–86.

10 Including the growth rates of plant & machinery and of buildings was also tried. The coefficients were usually negative and insignificant, results which are consistent with the earlier discussion.

11 In the short periods, the same battery of controls is employed in every period.

The nineteen basic IC variables are all entered as beginning-of-period levels; no change of level terms are included. For the long periods, some change of level terms are included also. Because of data availability, the numbers of these latter variables differ between 1954–73 and 1973–86. For 1954–73, seven such change variables were included; for 1973–86, thirteen.

12 For example, we know from elementary trade theory that a change in the pattern of demand and output causes a change in relative goods prices and raises the price of the factor used intensively by the good whose production has risen.

13 See for example, Chatterji and Wickens (1982), though they considered the relationship between labour productivity and employment. They looked at aggregate UK manufacturing in the 1960s and 1970s, although they actually rejected an explanation based on externalities or increasing returns, preferring one based on varying rates of labour utilisation. Matthews *et al.* (1982, chapter 9) find the evidence for a relationship between MFP and output or input growth in UK manufacturing over long periods rather unconvincing.

14 In table 7.7, the period effects come from column 3 of table 7.2 (the estimates without fixed effects, as the fixed effects turned out not to be significant) – more precisely, they are the coefficients on the seven time-periods dummies to which has been added the estimated constant.

15 Here we assume for simplicity that for each industry the growth rate of gross output is equal to the growth rate of final output; a sufficient condition is that external input is growing at the same rate as gross output.

16 In 1986, the 100 largest private sector businesses (defined by size of total employment) accounted for 38 per cent of total gross value added and 33 per cent of total employment in manufacturing (Source: 1986 Census of Production, Summary Volume, table 15 (PA 1002)).

17 This kind of increasing return is consistent with competition if the source is external to the firm (learning from others). This matters since the estimates of MFP growth assume competitive conditions.

18 Because of the smaller sample size, these regressions included fewer IC variables than those of table 7.5: the Order dummies and the change variables were omitted, so that only nineteen IC variables were included.

19 If the nineteen variables are omitted, the degree of significance of LOWGDY is little changed.

20 Blue-collar workers are identified with those termed 'operatives' by the Census. The complementary category is 'administrative, technical and clerical' employees. There is also a third category, 'working proprietors', but this latter group is very small.

21 The tests on industry data are concerned with the question of whether investment in a particular industry generates higher than expected productivity growth *in that industry*. The possibility remains that investment, particularly in plant & machinery, creates general benefits which diffuse somehow throughout the whole economy. The latter was the type of effect which DeLong and Summers (1991) purported to demonstrate. Oulton (1992b) examines their cross-country results and gives reasons for thinking them less robust than they claimed.

Appendix B Data Sources

1 Again thanks are owed to R.J. Allard for providing us with the unpublished CSO series.
2 These variables are calculated as simple differences over (respectively) a nineteen and a thirteen-year period. Since the units of the original variables are percentage points, so are those of the differenced variables.

Appendix C The Reclassification of the Standard Industrial Classification from the 1980 to the 1968 Basis

1 In producing table C.3, there were a couple of cases in which an AH was excluded from the list of AH corresponding to a given MLH. This was done both when it was judged that the excluded AH made a negligible contribution to the MLH in question and when inclusion of the AH would have made the system mathematically insoluble (see the next section). Both conditions had to be satisfied for an AH to be excluded.
2 The reclassification program checks whether this condition is satisfied; see next section.
3 Listings of the three programs, written in Basic, are available on request.

Appendix D The Estimation of Gross Output

1 The lbs of tobacco products for which duty was paid from the 1958 Census was multiplied by the excise duty rate per lb, derived from the annual report of the Customs and Excise – the resulting estimate was consistent with that for 1963, about 75 per cent of gross output in both years.

Appendix E Construction of Price Indices

1 The regression equation for MLH 221 was unsatisfactory, so for this industry an index for 1973 only was generated.

Appendix F Labour Input

1 An alternative to the 'Annual Inquiry' would have been the *New Earnings Survey* (NES). However this survey has a much smaller sample size than the one used and hence often shows less detail at the industry level, particularly in earlier years. Moreover the NES began only in 1968.

Appendix G Rental Prices of Capital Services

1 Due to the lack of reasonable price data in the 1950s we did not attempt the 3-year moving average for the years 1954 and 1958 but instead used the single period changes in prices.

REFERENCES

Abramovitz, M. (1956), 'Resource and output trends in the United States since 1870', *American Economic Review*, vol. 46, pp. 5–23.

Allard, R.J. (1982), 'Estimates of capital stock for manufacturing industry by MLH', Study prepared for the Office of Fair Trading, mimeo.

Arrow, K.J. (1962), 'The Economic implications of learning by doing', *Review of Economic Studies*, vol. 80, pp. 155–73.

Armstrong, A.G. (1974), *Structural Change in the British Economy, 1948–68*, (No. 12 of *A Programme for growth*), London, Chapman and Hall.

Bacon, R.W. and Eltis, W.A. (1974), 'The age of US and UK machinery', NEDO Monograph 3, London.

Baden-Fuller, C.W.F. (1989), 'Exit from declining industries and the case of steel castings', *Economic Journal*, vol. 99, pp. 949–61.

Baily, M.N. (1981), 'Productivity and the services of capital and labour', *Brookings Papers on Economic Activity*, 1, pp. 1–50.

Barna, T. (1961), 'On measuring capital', Chapter 5 of *The Theory of Capital* by F.A. Lutz, edited by D.C. Hague, London, Macmillan and Co.

Baumol, W.J. and Wolff, E.N. (1984), 'On interindustry differences in absolute productivity', *Journal of Political Economy*, vol. 92, pp. 1017–34.

Belsley, D.A., Kuh, E. and Welsch, R.E. (1980), *Regression Diagnostics: Identifying Influential Data and Sources of Collinearity*, New York, J. Wiley.

Bernanke, B.S. and Parkinson, M.L. (1991), 'Procyclical labor productivity and competing theories of the business cycle: some evidence from interwar U.S. manufacturing industries', *Journal of Political Economy*, vol. 99, pp. 439–59.

Berndt, E.R. and Fuss, M.A. (1986), 'Productivity measurement with adjustments for variations in capacity utilisation and other forms of temporary equilibrium', *Journal of Econometrics*, vol. 33, pp. 7–29.

Berndt, E.R. and Wood, D.A. (1986), 'Energy price shocks and productivity growth in US and UK manufacturing', *Oxford Review of Economic Policy*, vol. 2 (Autumn), pp. 1–31.

Benhabib, J. and Jovanovic, B. (1991), 'Externalities and growth accounting', *American Economic Review*, vol. 81, pp. 82–113.

Blades, D. (1983), 'Service lives of fixed assets', OECD Working Paper no. 4, mimeo.

Britton, A.J.C. (1991), *Macroeconomic Policy in Britain 1974–87*, Cambridge, Cambridge University Press.

Bruno, M. (1978), 'Duality, intermediate inputs and value-added', in Fuss, M. and McFadden, D. (eds), *Production Economics: A Dual Approach to Theory and Applications*, Amsterdam, North-Holland.

Bruno, M. and Sachs, J. (1985), *The Economics of World-wide Stagflation*, Oxford, Basil Blackwell.

Business Statistics Office (1978), *Historical Record of the Census of Production 1907–1970*, London, HMSO.

Business Statistics Office (1981), *Input–output Tables for the United Kingdom 1974* (PA1004), London, HMSO.

Business Statistics Office (1982), *Report on the Census of Production 1979: Summary Tables (PA 1002 1979)*, London, HMSO.

Business Statistics Office (1983), *Census of Production and Purchases Inquiry: Analysis of Production Industries by Standard Industrial Classification Revised 1980 (PA 1002.1 1979)*, London, HMSO.

Caballero, R.J. and Lyons, R.K. (1989), 'The role of external economies in U.S. manufacturing', NBER Working Paper no. 3033, Cambridge, MA.

Caballero, R.J. and Lyons, R.K. (1990), 'Internal versus external economies in European industry', *European Economic Review*, vol. 34, pp. 805–30.

Caballero, R.J. and Lyons, R.K. (1991), 'Short and long run externalities', NBER Working Paper no. 3810, Cambridge, MA.

Carruth, A.A. and Oswald, A.J. (1989), *Pay Determination and Industrial Prosperity*, Oxford, Clarendon Press.

Caves, R.E. and Barton, D.R. (1990), *Efficiency in U.S. Manufacturing Industries*, Cambridge, M.A., The MIT Press.

Central Statistical Office (1968), *Standard Industrial Classification Revised 1968*, London, HMSO.

Central Statistical Office (1973), *Input–output Tables for The United Kingdom 1968*, London, HMSO.

Central Statistical Office (1979), *Standard Industrial Classification Revised 1980*, London, HMSO.

Central Statistical Office (1980a), *Standard Industrial Classification Revised 1980: Reconciliation with Standard Industrial Classification 1968*, London, HMSO.

Central Statistical Office (1980b), *Wholesale Price Index: Principles and Procedures*, Studies in Official Statistics no. 32, London, HMSO.

Central Statistical Office (1983), *United Kingdom National Accounts: Sources and Methods, Third Edition*, Studies in Official Statistics no. 37, London, HMSO.

Central Statistical Office (1988), *Input–output Tables for the United Kingdom 1984*, London, HMSO.

Central Statistical Office (1990), *Industrial Research and Development Expenditure: 1988*, Business Bulletin no. 12, London.

Chatterji, M. and Wickens, M.R. (1982), 'Productivity, factor transfers and economic growth in the UK', *Economica*, vol. 49, February, pp. 21–38.

Christensen, L.R. and Jorgenson, D.W. (1969), 'The measurement of U.S. real capital input, 1919–67', *Review of Income and Wealth*, Series 15, no. 4, pp. 293–320.

Christensen, L.R., Cummings, D. and Jorgenson, D.W. (1980), 'Economic growth 1947–73: an international comparison', in Kendrick, J.W. and Vaccara, B. (eds), *New Developments in Productivity Measurement*, Chicago, University of Chicago Press.

Christensen, L.R., Jorgenson, D.W. and Lau, L.J. (1973), 'Transcendental logarithmic production frontiers', *Review of Economics and Statistics*, vol. 55, pp. 28–46.

Cole, R., Chen, Y.C., Barquin-Stolleman, J.A., Dullberger, E., Helvecian, N. and Hodge, J.H. (1986), 'Quality-adjusted price indexes for computer processors and selected peripheral equipment', *Survey of Current Business*, vol. 66, pp. 41–50.

Crafts, N. (1992), 'Productivity growth reconsidered', *Economic Policy*, no. 15, October, pp. 387–414.

Crafts, N.F.R. (1993), 'Can de-industrialisation seriously damage your wealth?', Hobart Paper no. 120, London, Institute for Economic Affairs.

Cramer, J.S. (1958), 'The depreciation and mortality of motor cars', *Journal of the Royal Statistical Society*, Series A, vol. 121, part I, pp. 18–59.

Cresswell, M. and Grubb, J. (1987), *The Second International Mathematics Study in England and Wales*, London, NFER-Nelson.

Darby, J. and Wren-Lewis, S. (1991), 'Trends in labour productivity in UK manufacturing', *Oxford Economics Papers*, vol. 43, pp. 424–42.

Davies, S.W. and Caves, R.E. (1987), *Britain's Productivity Gap*, Cambridge, Cambridge University Press.

Dean, G. (1964), 'The stock of fixed assets in the United Kingdom in 1961', *Journal of the Royal Statistical Society*, series A, vol. 127, pp. 327–52.

DeLong, J.B., and Summers, L.H. (1991), 'Equipment investment and economic growth', *Quarterly Journal of Economics*, vol. CVI, pp. 445–502.

Denison, E.F. (1967), *Why Growth Rates Differ*, Washington, DC, Brookings Institution.

Denison, E.F. (1991), 'Scott's *A New View of Economic Growth*: a review article', *Oxford Economic Papers*, vol. 43, pp. 224–36.

Department of Employment and Productivity (1971), *British Labour Statistics: Historical Abstract 1886–1968*, London, HMSO.

Dickey, W.A. (1976), *Introduction to Statistical Time Series*, New York, John Wiley and Sons.

Diewert, W.E. (1976), 'Exact and Superlative Index Numbers', *Journal of Econometrics*, vol. 4, pp. 115–46.

Diewert, W.E. (1978), 'Hicks' aggregation theorem and the existence of a real value-added function', in Fuss, M. and McFadden, D. *op. cit.*

Diewert, W.E. (1980), 'Aggregation problems in the measurement of capital', in Usher, D. (ed.), *The Measurement of Capital*, Studies in income and wealth, vol. 45, Chicago, University of Chicago Press.

Domar, E.D. (1961), 'On the measurement of technological change', *Economic Journal*, vol. LXXI, pp. 709–29.

Driffill, J., Mizon, G.E. and Ulph, A. (1990), 'Costs of inflation', in Friedman, B.M. and Hahn, F.H. (eds), *Handbook of monetary economics*, Vol. 2, Amsterdam, North-Holland.

Englander, S. and Mittelstädt, A. (1988), 'Total factor productivity: macroeconomic and structural aspects of the slowdown', *OECD Economic Studies*, no. 10, Spring, pp. 7–56.

Fabricant, S. (1942), *Employment in Manufacturing, 1899–1939: An Analysis of Its Relation to the Volume of Production*, New York, National Bureau of Economic Research.

Feenstra, R.C. (1991), 'New goods and index numbers: US import prices', NBER Working Paper no. 3610, Cambridge, MA.

Feinstein, C.H. (1965), *Domestic Capital Formation in the U.K. 1920–1938*, Cambridge, Cambridge University Press.

Fisher, F.M. (1965), 'Embodied technical change and the existence of an aggregate capital stock', *Review of Economic Studies*, vol. 32, pp. 263–88.

Gollop, F.M. (1983), 'Growth accounting in an open economy', in Dogramaci, A. (ed.), *Developments in Econometric Analyses of Productivity*, Boston, Klumer Nijhoff.

Gollop, F.M. (1985), 'Analysis of the productivity slowdown: evidence for a sector-biased or sector-neutral industrial policy', in Baumol, W.J. and McLennan, K. (eds), *Productivity Growth and US Competitiveness*, New York, Oxford University Press.

Gordon, R.J. (1990), *The Measurement of Durable Goods Prices*, Chicago and London, University of Chicago Press.

Granger, C.W. (1986), 'Developments in the study of cointegrated economic variables', *Oxford Bulletin of Economics and Statistics*, vol. 48, pp. 213–28.

Griffin, T. (1976), 'The stock of fixed assets in the United Kingdom: how to make best use of the statistics', *Economic Trends*, no. 276, October, pp. 130–43.

Griliches, Z. (1991), 'The search for R and D spillovers', NBER Discussion Paper no. 3768, Cambridge, MA.

Hall, R.E. (1988), 'The relation between price and marginal cost in US industry', *Journal of Political Economy*, vol. 96, pp. 921–47.

Hall, R.E. (1990), 'Invariance properties of Solow's productivity residual', in Diamond, P. (ed.), *Growth/productivity/unemployment: essays to celebrate Bob Solow's birthday*, Cambridge, MA, The MIT Press.

Hall, R.E. and Jorgenson, D.W. (1967), 'Tax policy and investment behaviour', *American Economic Review*, vol. 57, pp. 391–414.

Harper, M.J., Berndt, E.R. and Wood, D.A. (1989), 'Rates of return and capital aggregation using alternative rental prices', Chapter 8 in Jorgenson, D.W. and Landau, R. (eds), *Technology and Capital Formation*, Cambridge, MA, MIT Press.

Hibbert, J., Griffin, T.J. and Walker, R.L. (1977), 'Development of estimates of the stock of fixed capital in the United Kingdom', *Review of Income and Wealth*, series 23, pp. 117–35.

Hicks, J.R. (1940), 'The valuation of the social income', *Economica*, vol. VII, pp. 105–24.

Hill, T.P. (1971), *The Measurement of Real Product: A Theoretical and Empirical Analysis of the Growth Rates, for Different Industries and Countries*, Paris, OECD.

Hulten, C.R. (1973), 'Divisia index numbers', *Econometrica*, vol. 41, pp. 1017–25.

Hulten, C.R. (1978), 'Growth accounting with intermediate inputs', *Review of Economic Studies*, vol. 45, pp. 511–18.

Hulten, C.R. (1990), 'The measurement of capital', in Berndt, E.R. and Triplett, J.E. (eds), *Fifty Years of Economic Measurement*, Chicago and London, Chicago University Press.

Hulten, C.R. (1992), 'Growth accounting when technical change is embodied in capital', NBER Working Paper no. 3971, Cambridge, MA.

Hulten, C.R. and Wykoff, F.C. (1981a), 'The estimation of economic depreciation using vintage asset prices: an application of the box-cox transformation', *Journal of Econometrics*, vol. 15, pp. 367–96.

Hulten, C.R. and Wykoff, F.C. (1981b), 'The measurement of economic depreciation', in Hulten, C.R. (ed.), *Depreciation, Inflation and the Taxation of Income from Capital*, Washington, D.C., Urban Institute Press.

Hulten, C.R., Robertson, J.W. and Wykoff, F.C. (1989), 'Energy, obsolescence and the productivity slowdown', in Jorgenson, D.W. and Landau, R. (eds), *Technology and Capital Formation*, Cambridge, MA, MIT Press.

Inland revenue (1953), *Wear and Tear Allowances for Machinery or Plant: List of Percentage Rates*, London, HMSO.

Jorgenson, D.W. (1966), 'The embodiment hypothesis', *Journal of Political Economy*, vol. 74, pp. 1–17.

Jorgenson, D.W. (1984a), 'The role of energy in productivity growth', *American Economic Review* (Papers and Proceedings), vol. 74, pp. 26–30.

Jorgenson, D.W. (1984b), 'The role of energy in productivity growth', (expanded version of Jorgenson, 1984a), Chapter 7 in Kendrick, J.W. (ed.), *International Comparisons of Productivity and Causes of the Slowdown*, Cambridge, MA, American Enterprise Institute and Ballinger.

Jorgenson, D.W. (1986), 'Econometric methods for modeling producer behavior', in Griliches, Z. and Intriligator, M.D. (eds.), *Handbook of Econometrics*, vol. III. Amsterdam, North-Holland.

Jorgenson, D.W. (1988), 'Productivity and postwar US economic growth', *Journal of Economic Perspectives*, vol. 2, Fall, pp. 23–42.

Jorgenson, D.W. (1989), 'Capital as a factor of production', in Jorgenson, D.W. and Landau, R. (eds), *Technology and Capital Formation*, Cambridge, MA, MIT Press.

Jorgenson, D.W. (1990), 'Productivity and economic growth', in Berndt, E.R. and Triplett, J.E. (eds), *Fifty Years of Economic Measurement: the Jubilee of the Conference on Income and Wealth*, edited by Chicago, University of Chicago Press.

Jorgenson, D.W. and Griliches, Z. (1967), 'The explanation of productivity change', *Review of Economic Studies*, vol. 34, pp. 249–83.

Jorgenson, D.W., Gollop, F.M. and Fraumeni, B.M. (1986), 'Productivity and sectoral output growth in the United States', in Kendrick, J.W. and Vaccara, B.N. (eds), *New Developments in Productivity Measurement and Analysis*, Chicago, University of Chicago Press.

Jorgenson, D.W., Gollop, F.M. and Fraumeni, B.M. (1987), *Productivity and US economic growth*, Cambridge, MA, Harvard University Press.

Jorgenson, D.W. and Nishimizu, M. (1978), 'US and Japanese economic growth, 1952–74: an international comparison', *Economic Journal*, vol. 88, pp. 707–26.

Kay, J.A. and King, M. (1986), *The British Tax System*, 3rd edition, Oxford, Oxford University Press.

Kelly, C. and Owen, D. (1985), 'Factor prices in the Treasury model', Government Economic Service Working Paper, no. 83, London.

Kilpatrick, A. and Naisbitt, B. (1988), 'Energy intensity, industrial structure and the 1970s productivity slowdown', *Oxford Bulletin of Economic Statistics*, vol. 50, pp. 229–41.

Leontief, W. *et al.* (1953), *Studies in the Structure of the American Economy*, New York, Oxford University Press.

Leslie, D. (1985), 'Productivity growth in UK manufacturing industries, 1948–68', *Applied economics*, vol. 17, p. 1–16.

Lindbeck, A. (1983), 'The recent slowdown of productivity growth', *Economic Journal*, vol. 93, pp. 13–34.

Lucas, R.E. (1988), 'On the mechanics of economic development', *Journal of Monetary Economics*, vol. 22, pp. 3–42.

McCormick, B. (1988), 'Quit rates over time in a job-rationed labour market: the British manufacturing sector, 1971–83', *Economica*, vol. 55, pp. 81–94.

Maddison, A. (1987), 'Growth and slowdown in advanced capitalist economies: techniques of quantitative assessment', *Journal of Economic Literature*, vol. 25, pp. 649–98.

Mankiw, N.G., Romer, D. and Weil, D.N. (1992), 'A contribution to the empirics of economic growth', *Quarterly Journal of Economics*, vol. CVII, May, pp. 407–37.

Marston, A., Winfrey, R. and Hampstead, J.C. (1953), *Engineering Valuation and Depreciation*, Ames, Iowa, Iowa State University Press.

Matthews, R.C.O. (1988), 'Research on productivity and the productivity gap', *National Institute Economic Review*, no. 124, May, pp. 66–72.

Matthews, R.C.O., Feinstein, C.H. and Odling-Smee, J.C. (1982), *British Economic Growth 1856–1973*, Oxford, Clarendon Press.

Melliss, C.L. and Richardson, P.W. (1975), 'Value of investment incentives for manufacturing industry 1946–1974', in Whiting, A. (ed.), *The Economics of Industrial Subsidies*, London, Department of Industry.

Mendis, L. and Muellbauer, J. (1984), 'British manufacturing productivity 1955–83: measurement problems, oil shocks and Thatcher effects', CEPR Discussion Paper no. 32, November, London.

Minford, M., Wall, M. and Wren-Lewis, S. (1988), 'Manufacturing capacity: A measure derived from survey data using the Kalman filter', NIESR Discussion Paper (Old Series), no. 146, London.

Morrison, C.J. (1990), 'Market power, economic profitbility and productivity growth measurement: an integrated structural approach', NBER Working Paper no. 3355, May, Cambridge, MA.

Muellbauer, J. (1986), 'The assessment: productivity and competitiveness in British manufacturing', *Oxford Review of Economic Policy*, vol. 2, pp. i–xxv.

Nelson, C.R. and Kang, H. (1984), 'Pitfalls in the use of time as an explanatory variable in regression', *Journal of Business and Economic Statistics*, vol. 2, pp. 73–82.

Nelson, C.R. and Plosser, C.I. (1982), 'Trends and random walks in macroeconomic time series: some evidence and implications', *Journal of Monetary Economics*, vol. 10, pp. 139–62.

O'Mahony, M. (1992a), 'Productivity levels in British and German manufacturing industry', *National Institute Economic Review*, no. 139, February, pp. 46–63.

O'Mahony, M. (1992b), 'Productivity and human capital formation in UK and German manufacturing', NIESR Discussion Paper (New Series), no. 28, London.

O'Mahony, M. and Oulton, N. (1990a), 'Industry-level estimates of the capital stock in UK manufacturing, 1948–1986', NIESR Discussion Paper (Old Series), no. 172, London.

O'Mahony, M. and Oulton, N. (1990b), 'Growth of multi-factor productivity in British industry, 1954–86' (Part I: Text and Tables; Part II: Appendices), NIESR Discussion Paper (Old Series), no. 182, London.

Oulton, N. (1987), 'Plant closures and the productivity "miracle" in manufacturing', *National Institute Economic Review*, no. 121, August, pp. 53–9.

Oulton, N. (1988), 'Productivity, investment and scrapping in UK manufacturing: a vintage capital approach', NIESR Discussion Paper (Old Series), no. 148, London.

Oulton, N. (1989), 'Productivity growth in manufacturing, 1963–85: the roles of new investment and scrapping', *National Institute Economic Review*, no. 127, February, pp. 64–75.

Oulton, N. (1990), 'Labour productivity in UK manufacturing in the 1970s and in the 1980s', *National Institute Economic Review*, no. 132, May, pp. 71–91.

Oulton, N. (1991), 'Did raw material prices cause the productivity slowdown? Evidence from the US and the UK', NIESR Discussion Paper (Old Series), no. 198, London.

Oulton, N. (1992a), 'Investment, increasing returns and the pattern of productivity growth in UK manufacturing, 1954–86', NIESR Discussion Paper (New Series), no. 5, London.

Oulton, N. (1992b), 'Investment and productivity growth', in Britton, A. (ed.), *Industrial Investment as a Policy Objective*, NIESR Report Series, no. 3, London.

Oulton, N. (1992c), 'Depreciation, obsolescence, and the role of capital in growth accounting: a comment on Scott's "Policy implications of 'A new view of Economic Growth'"', NIESR Discussion Paper (New Series), no. 17, London.

Paige, D. and Bombach, G. (1959), *A Comparison of National Output and Productivity of the United Kingdom and the United States*, Paris, OEEC.

Penneck, S. and Woods, R. (1982), 'Effects of leasing on statistics of manufacturing capital expenditure', *Economic Trends*, February, pp. 97–104.

Peterson, W. (1979), 'Total factor productivity in the UK: a disaggregated analysis', in Patterson, K. and Schott, K. (eds), *The Measurement of Capital*, London, Macmillan.

Prais, S.J. (1981), *Productivity and Industrial Structure: A Statistical Study of Manufacturing Industry in Britain, Germany and the United States*, Cambridge, Cambridge University Press.

Prais, S.J. (1986), 'Some international comparisons of the age of the machine stock', *Journal of Industrial Economics*, vol. 34, pp. 261–77.

Prescott, E.C. (1986), 'Theory ahead of business cycle measurement', *Federal Reserve Bank of Minneapolis Quarterly Review*, vol. 10 (Fall), pp. 9–22.

Redfern, P. (1955), 'Net investment in fixed assets in the United Kingdom, 1938–1953', *Journal of the Royal Statistical Society*, Series A, vol. 118, pp. 141–82.

Robinson, B. (1985), 'How to create new jobs', *Economic Outlook*, vol. 9, April, pp. 1–4.

Robinson, B. and Wade, K. (1985), 'Unemployment, scrapping and factor prices', *Economic Outlook*, vol. 9, July, pp. 1–4.

Romer, P. (1987), 'Crazy explanations for the productivity slowdown', *NBER Macroeconomics Annual*, 1987, vol. 1, pp. 163–201.

Romer, P. (1986), 'Increasing returns and long-run growth', *Journal of Political Economy*, vol. 94, pp. 1002–37.

Romer, P. (1990), 'Capital, labor, and productivity', *Brookings Papers on Microeconomics 1990*, pp. 337–420.

Rotemberg, J.J. and Summers, L.H. (1990), 'Inflexible prices and procyclical productivity', *Quarterly Journal of Economics*, vol. CV, pp. 851–75.

Salter, W.E.G. (1966), *Productivity and Technical Change*, 2nd edition, London, Cambridge University Press.

Scott, M.Fg. (1989), *A New View of Economic Growth*, Oxford, Clarendon Press.

Scott, M.Fg. (1991), 'A reply to Denison', *Oxford Economic Papers*, vol. 43, pp. 237–44.

Scott, M.Fg. (1992), 'Policy implications of "A new view of economic growth"', *Economic Journal*, vol. 102, pp. 622–32.

Smith, A.D. (1986), 'The feasibility of fire insurance measures of capital stock', NIESR Discussion Paper (Old Series), no. 116, London, mimeo.

Smith, A.D. (1986), 'A current cost accounting measure of Britain's stock of equipment', *National Institute Economic Review*, no. 120, May, pp. 42–57.

Smith, A.D. (1988), 'Changes in output, employment and the stock of equipment during the 1980s: the experience of fifty companies', NIESR Discussion Paper (Old Series), no. 144, London.

Smith, A.D., Hitchens, D.M.W.N. and Davies, S.W. (1982), *International Industrial Productivity: A Comparison of Britain, America and Germany*, Cambridge, Cambridge University Press.

Solow, R.M. (1957), 'Technical change and the aggregate production function', *Review of Economics and Statistics*, vol. 39, pp. 312–20.

Solow, R.M. (1960), 'Investment and technical progress', in Arrow, K.J., Karlin, S. and Suppes, P. (eds), *Mathematical methods in the social sciences*, Stanford, CA, Stanford University Press.

Steedman, H. and Wagner, K. (1987), 'A second look at productivity, machinery and skills in Britain and Germany', *National Institute Economic Review*, no. 122, November, pp. 84–95.

Steedman, H. and Wagner, K. (1989), 'Productivity, machinery and skills: clothing manufacturing in Britain and Germany', *National Institute Economic Review*, no. 128, May, pp. 40–57.

Sterlacchini, A. (1989), 'R and D, innovations, and total factor productivity growth in British manufacturing', *Applied Economics*, vol. 21, pp. 1549–62.

Stone, R. and Brown, J.A.C. (1962), *A Computable Model of Economic Growth (A Programme for Growth 1)*, London, Chapman and Hall.

Summers, L.H. (1986), 'Some skeptical observations on real business cycle theory', *Federal Reserve Bank of Minneapolis Quarterly Review*, vol. 10 (Fall), pp. 23–7.

Verdoorn, P.J. (1980), 'Verdoorn's Law in retrospect: a comment', *Economic Journal*, vol. 90, pp. 382–5.

Vining, D.R. and Elwertowski, T.C. (1976), 'The relationship between relative prices and the general price level', *American Economic Review*, vol. 66, pp. 699–708.

Wadhwani, S. and Wall, M. (1986), 'The UK capital stock – new estimates of premature scrapping', *Oxford Review of Economic Policy*, vol. 2 (Autumn), pp. 44–55.

Winfrey, R. (1935), 'Statistical analyses of industrial property retirements', Iowa State College, Engineering Experiment Station, Bulletin 125.

Wolff, E.N. (1985), 'Industrial composition, interindustry effects and the US productivity slowdown', *Review of Economics and Statistics*, vol. LXVII, pp. 268–77.

Wolff, E.N. (1991), 'Capital formation and productivity convergence over the long term', *American Economic Review*, vol. 81, pp. 565–79.

Wragg, R. and Robertson, J. (1978), 'Post-war trends in employment, productivity, output, labour costs and prices by industry in the United Kingdom', Department of Employment, Research Paper no. 3, London.

Wren-Lewis, S. (1986), 'An econometric model of U.K. manufacturing employment using survey data on expected output', *Journal of Applied Econometrics*, vol. 1, pp. 297–316.

Young, A.H. and Musgrave, J.C. (1980), 'Estimation of capital stock in the United States', in Usher, D. (ed.), *The Measurement of Capital*, Chicago and London, University of Chicago Press.

INDEX

THE NATIONAL INSTITUTE OF
ECONOMIC AND SOCIAL RESEARCH
PUBLICATIONS IN PRINT

published by
THE CAMBRIDGE UNIVERSITY PRESS
(available from booksellers, or in case of difficulty from the publishers)

XLV   *International Financial Markets. The performance of Britain and its rivals*
      By ANTHONY D. SMITH. 1992. pp. 206. £24.95 net.

NIESR STUDENTS' EDITION
   4. *British Economic Policy, 1960–74: Demand Management* (an abridged version of *British Economic Policy, 1960–74*)
       Edited by F.T. BLACKABY. 1979. pp. 472. £10.95 net.

THE NATIONAL INSTITUTE OF
ECONOMIC AND SOCIAL RESEARCH

publishes regularly

THE NATIONAL INSTITUTE ECONOMIC REVIEW

A quarterly analysis of the general economic situation in the United Kingdom and overseas with forecasts eighteen months ahead. The last issue each year usually contains an assessment of medium-term prospects. There are also in most issues special articles on subjects of interest to academic and business economists.

Annual subscriptions, £80.00 (UK and EC) and £100 (rest of world), also single issues for the current year, £25.00, are available direct from NIESR, 2 Dean Trench Street, Smith Square, London, SW1P 3HE.

Subscriptions at a special reduced price are available to students and teachers in the United Kingdom on application to the Secretary of the Institute.

Back numbers and reprints of issues which have gone out of stock are distributed by Wm. Dawson and Sons Ltd., Cannon House, Park Farm Road, Folkestone. Microfiche copies for the years 1961–89 are available from EP Microform Ltd., Bradford Road, East Ardsley, Wakefield, Yorks.

Published by
HEINEMANN EDUCATIONAL BOOKS
(distributed by Gower Publishing Company and available from booksellers)

THE FUTURE OF PAY BARGAINING
Edited by FRANK BLACKABY. 1980. pp. 256. £32.00 (hardback),
£10.50 (paperback) net.

INDUSTRIAL POLICY AND INNOVATION
Edited by CHARLES CARTER. 1981. pp. 250. £32.50 (hardback),
£9.95 (paperback) net.

SLOWER GROWTH IN THE WESTERN WORLD
Edited by R.C.O. MATTHEWS. 1982. pp. 182. £10.95 (paperback) net.

NATIONAL INTERESTS AND LOCAL GOVERNMENT
Edited by KEN YOUNG. 1983. pp. 180. £30.00 (hardback), £10.95 (paperback) net.

EMPLOYMENT, OUTPUT AND INFLATION
Edited by A.J.C. BRITTON. 1983. pp. 208. £37.50 net.

THE TROUBLED ALLIANCE, ATLANTIC RELATIONS IN THE 1980s
Edited by LAWRENCE FREEDMAN. 1983. pp. 176. £32.50 (hardback),
£8.95 (paperback) net.

(Available from Heinemann and from booksellers)
THE UK ECONOMY
By the NIESR. 1993. pp. 96. £4.50 net.

Published by
GOWER PUBLISHING COMPANY
(Available from Gower Publishing Company and from booksellers)

ENERGY SELF-SUFFICIENCY FOR THE UK
Edited by ROBERT BELGRAVE and MARGARET CORNELL. 1985. pp. 224.
£35.00 net.

THE FUTURE OF BRITISH DEFENCE POLICY
Edited by JOHN ROPER. 1985. pp. 214. £32.50 net.

ENERGY MANAGEMENT: CAN WE LEARN FROM OTHERS?
By GEORGE F. RAY. 1985. pp. 131. £30.00 net.

UNEMPLOYMENT AND LABOUR MARKET POLICIES
Edited by P.E. HART. 1986. pp. 230. £34.00 net.

NEW PRIORITIES IN PUBLIC SPENDING
Edited by M.S. LEVITT. 1987. pp. 136. £29.50 net.

POLICYMAKING WITH MACROECONOMIC MODELS
Edited by A.J.C. BRITTON. 1989. pp. 285. £37.00 net.

HOUSING AND THE NATIONAL ECONOMY
Edited by JOHN ERMISCH. 1990. pp. 158. £35.00 net.

Published by
SAGE PUBLICATIONS LTD
(Available from Sage and from booksellers)

*ECONOMIC CONVERGENCE AND MONETARY UNION
IN EUROPE*
Edited by RAY BARRELL. 1992. pp. 288. £35.00 (hardback,
£12.95 (paperback) net.

ACHIEVING MONETARY UNION IN EUROPE
By ANDREW BRITTON AND DAVID MAYES. 1992. pp. 160.
£25.00 net (hardback), £9.95 (paperback) net.

*MACROECONOMIC POLICY COORDINATION
IN EUROPE: THE ERM AND MONETARY UNION*
Edited by RAY BARRELL and JOHN D. WHITLEY. 1993. pp. 294.
£35.00 (hardback), £12.95 (paperback).